T0139326

Multiple-valued logic design: an introduction

Multiple-valued logic design: an introduction

George Epstein

Department of Computer Science
University of North Carolina, Charlotte

Institute of Physics Publishing

Bristol and Philadelphia

British Library Cataloguing in Publication Data
A catalogue record for this book is available from the British Library

ISBN 0-7503-0210-0

Library of Congress Cataloging-in-Publication Data are available

Published by IOP Publishing Ltd, a company wholly owned by the Institute of Physics, London
Techno House, Redcliffe Way, Bristol BS1 6NX, England
US Editorial Office: IOP Publishing Inc., The Public Ledger Building, Suite 1035, Philadelphia, PA 19106

Typeset by P&R Typesetters Ltd, Salisbury, Wiltshire, UK
Printed in Great Britain by J W Arrowsmith Ltd, Bristol

Contents

Preface

The subject of multiple-valued logic and logic design was largely developed during the twentieth century. In the first half of this century, an algebra was presented by P C Rosenbloom based on earlier work by E L Post. This algebra is now called Post algebra. There were subsequent developments during the period 1960–75, including work by C C Chang, G Epstein, A Horn, G Rousseau, and T Traczyk. In the second half of this century, various aspects of multiple-valued logic design were presented in many different papers. A number of these results were motivated by results in the field of two-valued logic design.

The algebra for two-valued logic comes from work in the nineteenth century by G Boole. This algebra is now called Boolean algebra. There were a number of subsequent developments, including work by E V Huntington and M H Stone.

Two-valued logic design has origins in the first half of the twentieth century. A number of books on two-valued logic design appeared during the period 1955–90. Four such books are by S H Caldwell (1958), F J Hill and G R Peterson (1981), E J McCluskey (1986), and D Green (1986). There is some discussion of multiple-valued logic design in the books by E J McCluskey and D Green.

It should be noted that multiple-valued logic and logic design as presented in this book include the two-valued case. Throughout this book, the n-valued presentation allows n to be an integer greater than or equal to 2. Thus, for example, Post algebras of order n allow n to be a fixed integer greater than or equal to 2. In particular, Post algebras of order 2 coincide with Boolean algebras. With respect to logic design, binary designs are applications which correspond to the n-valued case where $n = 2$, ternary designs are applications which correspond to the case where $n = 3$, and quaternary designs are applications which correspond to the case where $n = 4$.

Chapter 1 provides the motivation for and background to the book. Examples are presented and an historical perspective is given which covers the period 1910–90.

Chapter 2 uses tables to introduce basic operations. The implementation of these operations is discussed. Basic circuit considerations such as fan-in, fan-out, and gate delays are also discussed. There are treatments of implicational calculi, and of fixed radix number systems, such as the binary, ternary, and balanced ternary number systems.

Chapter 3 extends the tabular approach in Chapter 2 to multiple-valued Venn diagrams and Karnaugh maps, along with Hasse diagrams and certain algebras, such as Stone algebras and Heyting algebras. The last section of this chapter introduces ideals and prime ideals.

Chapters 4 and 5 present Post algebras and sub-Post algebras respectively. Representation theory is discussed in terms of finite-valued functions, and also in terms of prime ideals.

Chapter 6 considers basic arithmetic operations—namely, addition, subtraction and multiplication. Ripple adder circuits are given for the binary, ternary, and quaternary cases. There is also a discussion of the mixed radix case using the factorial number system. A ripple adder circuit is given for this mixed radix case.

Chapter 7 examines finite state diagrams and the design of logic circuits. Binary and ternary examples are given.

Chapter 8 presents multiple-valued propositional calculi. There is a development which uses networks composed of just three basic logic circuits.

Chapter 9 talks about special functions—namely, symmetric, positive, negative, unate, and threshold functions. These special functions are currently used in numerous applications.

Chapter 10 discusses special applications, including programmable logic arrays, linear feedback shift registers, parity checkers, built-in self-test, pseudo-random generators, and data compaction.

This book is suitable as a text for graduate or senior undergraduate students. A graduate course in computer science based upon this book was used during 1980–5 at Indiana University, Bloomington, and an undergraduate course based on this book was used during 1985–90 at the University of North Carolina, Charlotte. Students and colleagues at these universities made many valuable suggestions concerning the book. The names of these students and colleagues as well as other names mentioned later in the preface should be taken as representative, rather than exhaustive.

A course based on this book might follow a course on logic, algorithms, or discrete mathematics. The use of this book as a text for such a purpose would depend upon the background and needs of the students.

The core of the book for all students is represented by Chapters 1–4. This can be covered within the first half of a one-semester course. There are various possibilities for the remainder of the course.

For students who have no previous background in finite state diagrams or propositional calculi, the material in Chapter 7, Sections 8.1–8.3 and 9.1 may be covered. For students who wish to concentrate on applications, one possibility is to read Section 6.1, Chapter 7, Sections 9.1–9.4, and Chapter 10. For those wishing to study sub-Post algebras a possibility is to read Chapters 5, 6, and 8.

Assistance with the preparation of the manuscript came from my colleagues D M Miller, J C Muzio, M Serra, H Rasiowa, and H M Razavi; and from my students M Bahraini, H M Bakkour, T Corwin, E A Crocker, S A Hatley, R S Jones, and L T Sigmon at the University of North Carolina, Charlotte. The book was prepared with the help of M Clarke, Commissioning Editor, N Scriven, Copy Editor, and A Tovey, Studio Artist, at IOP Publishing Ltd, While citations in the references indicate some of the help contributed by others, mention is made below of the insight and support received from my colleagues J T Butler, S S Chen, G Frieder, the late F E Hohn, A Horn, R Lejk, C Moraga, and Z Ras; and from my students R Bechtel, D Feaster, J Lee, L Lin, Y W Liu, R R Loka, P O Mandayam, and S Rajamani at Indiana University, Bloomington.

The help and encouragement received from my wife, Laurie, was generous and supportive. It was a pleasure to receive valuable suggestions from my two sons and fellow computer scientists, David and Mark.

1 The Digital Theme

1.1 A framework for the discussion of digital characteristics

This book presents an introduction to the theory and logic design of multiple-valued subsystems. The digital subsystems under consideration are understood to contain internal signals which have been quantized to take a finite number of values. If n is a positive integer denoting the number of discrete values which can be assumed by such signals, then the subsystem is said to be n-valued, where $n \geq 2$. The case $n = 2$ corresponds with binary subsystems and computers, in wide use over the last 50 years.

There are a number of reasons for considering n-valued subsystems where $n \geq 2$, rather than $n = 2$ alone. First, creative logic designs do not spring from a mechanistic understanding of binary procedures alone. The main educative purpose of this book is to stimulate the inquisitive reader who wants to broaden his or her background beyond binary considerations. Second, the n-valued approach of this book includes the important binary case. Hence the presentation puts the binary case into a multiple-valued perspective which sheds new light on the case $n = 2$. Third, there are existing applications where $n > 2$. These include 3-valued pseudo-random generators (Serra 1987) and 4-valued read-only memories (Rich *et al* 1985). A goal of this book is to lay a foundation for the understanding of such multiple-valued applications. Fourth, it is clear from an implementation standpoint that primary interest is concerned with low values of n, such as $n = 2$, $n = 3$, or $n = 4$. Further, since such low values of n are helpful in understanding multiple-valued results for general n, examples throughout the book tend to use these low values of n.

An illustrative application follows. This application provides a self-contained example which introduces some basic ideas. In this example, binary and ternary solutions are given for the problem of telling the digitized position of a rotating shaft.

1.2 Digital characteristics, an example

Consider the problem of converting an angular position p_m of a shaft, where p_m is in the range $0° \leq p_m < 360°$, into an n-valued word measurement of m digits, where $n \geq 2$ and $m \geq 1$. Here each digit of the m-digit word takes values $0, 1, 2, \ldots, n - 1$. The quantization size Q in degrees for this analog-to-digital conversion is given by $Q = 360°/n^m$. In this section, only binary and ternary solutions are given. Hence, for the binary case $Q = 360°/2^m$ and for the ternary case $Q = 360°/3^m$. The shaft's full 360° is partitioned into angular sectors, where the size of each sector is equal to the quantization size.

To illustrate for the binary case using a 3-digit word measurement, there are $2^3 = 8$ sectors each of size $360°/8 = 45°$; for the ternary case using a 2-digit word measurement, there are $3^2 = 9$ sectors each of size $360°/9 = 40°$.

The quantization position p_q for each sector is taken to be the midpoint of that sector. If 0° is selected as a quantization position, then the 2^m quantization positions for the binary case are given by $i360°/2^m$, $i = 0, 1, 2, \ldots, 2^m - 1$, and the 3^m quantization positions for the ternary case are given by $j360°/3^m$, $j = 0, 1, 2, \ldots, 3^m - 1$. To continue the above illustration for the binary case using $m = 3$, the eight quantization positions are 0°, 45°, 90°, 135°, 180°, 225°, 270°, and 315°; for the ternary case using $m = 2$, the nine quantization positions are 0°, 40°, 80°, 120°, 160°, 200°, 240°, 280°, and 320°.

There is a one-to-one correspondence between each quantization position p_q and each digital measurement word. The actual position p_m of the shaft is converted to the digital measurement word corresponding to the quantization position whose sector contains the shaft position p_m. The error caused by quantizing is $p_q - p_m$. Suppose, for example, that $p_m = 83°$. In the binary case with $m = 3$, p_m lies within the 45° sector containing the quantization position 90°. Hence the corresponding measurement word of three binary digits is too high by $90° - 83° = 7°$. In the ternary case with $m = 2$, $p_m = 83°$ lies within the 40° sector containing the quantization position 80°. Hence the corresponding measurement of two ternary digits is too low by 3°, that is $80° - 83° = -3°$. It follows that the maximum magnitude of error is limited by $Q/2$. For the binary case with $m = 3$, $Q/2 = 22.5°$; for the ternary case with $m = 2$, $Q/2 = 20.0°$. In the binary case with $m = 3$, either $p_m = 22.6°$ or $p_m = 67.4°$ lie in the sector containing the quantization position $p_q = 45°$, with magnitude of error equal to 22.4°. In the ternary case with $m = 2$, either $p_m = 20.1°$ or $p_m = 59.9°$ lie in the sector containing the quantization position $p_q = 40°$, with magnitude of error equal to 19.9°.

It remains to accomplish the analog-to-digital conversion at the shaft. What kind of analog-to-digital equipment will be required and what are the mounting requirements for this equipment in the vicinity of the shaft?

The solution below uses a photoelectric shaft encoder. A coder disk with m circular tracks is fixed to the shaft so that the disk rotates as the shaft rotates. Examples are shown in figure 1.1 for $n = 2$, $m = 3$ and in figure 1.2 for $n = 3$, $m = 2$. For the binary case, each circular track is composed of two kinds of arc: opaque (marked 'B' for black and cross-hatched) and transparent (marked 'W' for white and unhatched). For the ternary case,

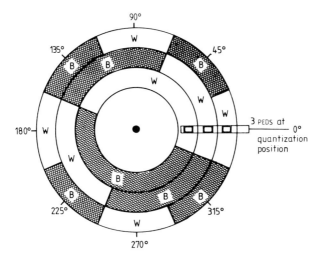

Figure 1.1   Three-track binary encoder.

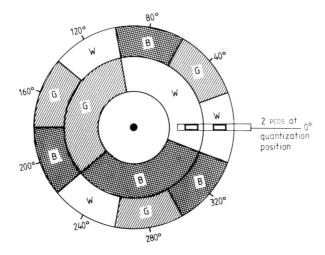

Figure 1.2   Two-track ternary encoder.

each circular track is composed of three kinds of arc: opaque (B), partially opaque (marked 'G' for gray and half-hatched), and transparent or white (W).

A light source is positioned on one side of the coder disk and photoelectric devices (PED) are positioned on the other side, so that each track is sensed. The binary and ternary solutions which follow are based on the following design table for the required PED.

Table 1   On–off characteristics of required PED.

PED_B: this device fires only if sensed arc is black (light is blocked)

PED_W: this device fires only if sensed arc is white (light passes fully)

PED_G: this device fires only if sensed arc is gray (light passes partially)

For the binary solution, the first two of the three PED above are used. These two (PED_B and PED_W) are positioned behind each track of the 3-track coder disk shown in figure 1.1. The maximum magnitude of error for this solution is 22.5°. In the solution of figure 1.1, each track has alternating white and black arcs. The frequency of alternation doubles with each track, from the innermost track to the outermost track. There is 180° black and 180° white on the innermost track, black–white–black–white on the next-to-innermost track, etc. Any position of the shaft can be sensed through the PED_B and PED_W which are behind each track, as both PED are binary devices which either fire or do not fire. In particular, if the sensed arc is black, the PED_B fires and the PED_W does not fire. On the other hand, if the sensed arc is white, the PED_W fires but the PED_B does not fire. Hence any arc which is black or white can be detected. In this binary case, only one of these two PEDs are needed at each track, as the state of one determines the state of the other. The resulting sequence of sensed 'B's and 'W's has length 3. There are $2^3 = 8$ such sequences, corresponding to the 8 quantization positions. In figure 1.1, the shaft is shown in 0° position, corresponding to the sensed sequence WWW at the PED, where the entry at the left of this word corresponds to the innermost track and the entry at the right corresponds to the outermost track. Writing 0 for W and 1 for B, WWW becomes the binary word 000 for 0°. If the shaft of figure 1.1 were to rotate clockwise by $45° \pm 22.4°$, then the sensed word would be WWB, corresponding with the binary word 001 and quantization position 45°.

For the ternary solution, all three of the above PED are positioned behind each track of the 2-track encoder shown in figure 1.2. The maximum magnitude of error for this solution is 20.0°. In the solution of figure 1.2, each track has alternating white, gray, and black arcs. The frequency of alternation triples with each track, from the innermost track to the outermost track. There is 120° black, 120° gray, and 120° white on the innermost track, black–gray–white–black–gray–white–black–gray–white on the next track, etc. Any position of the shaft can be sensed through PED_B, PED_G, and PED_W which are behind each track. If the sensed arc is black, PED_B fires but the other two PED do not. If the sensed arc is gray, PED_G fires but the other two PED do not. If the sensed arc is white, PED_W fires but the other two do not. In this ternary case, only two of these three PED are actually needed at each track—for example, PED_G can be eliminated, since a gray arc occurs if and only if both PED_B and PED_W do not fire. The resulting sequence of sensed Bs and Ws has length 2. There are $3^2 = 9$ such sequences, corresponding to the 9 quantization positions. In figure 1.2, the shaft is shown in $0°$ position, corresponding to the sensed sequence WW, where the entry at the left corresponds to the innermost track and the entry at the right corresponds to the outermost track. Writing 0 for W, 1 for G, and 2 for B, this becomes the ternary word 00. If the shaft of figure 1.2 were to rotate clockwise by $40° \pm 19.9°$, then the sensed word at the PED would be WG, corresponding to the ternary word 01 and quantization position $40°$.

The contrast between the binary and ternary approaches in figures 1.1 and 1.2 is clear. The binary approach requires 3 tracks, but the ternary approach requires only 2 tracks. The maximum magnitude of error in the binary approach is $22.5°$, but the maximum magnitude of error in the ternary approach is only $20.0°$. On the other hand, the shaft encoder for the binary approach requires the sensing of only two distinct conditions (black, white) while the shaft encoder for the ternary approach requires the sensing of three distinct conditions (black, gray, white). Finally, the reliable operation of the PEDs may depend on the environment being relatively free of electrical and optical fluctuations. In a noisy environment, the binary approach is preferable—it is easier to distinguish between black and white than between black, white, and gray.

Further examples may be found in the exercises at the end of this chapter. These examples include the following cases: $n = 4$, $m = 2$; $n = 3$, $m = 5$; $n = 2$, $m = 8$. A representative high-accuracy example using current technology is $n = 2$, $m = 16$. Such a binary shaft encoder with 16 tracks on the coder disk yields a maximum magnitude of error of about $0.003°$. There is a discussion of binary shaft encoders on pages 434–6 of Bartee (1981).

1.3 Digital characteristics: hard and soft

The application in the previous section dealt with interface equipment. In the block diagram of a digital computer shown in figure 1.3 such equipment would occur within the INPUT block. Other possible inputs include card readers, remote terminals, and radar receiver signals. There is also a wide variety of outputs, including printers and robot arms. The intermediate equipment between INPUT and OUTPUT in the block diagram of figure 1.3 is the main computer, consisting of CONTROL, LOGICO-ARITHMETIC, and MEMORY blocks.

Computer processing occurs with the logico-arithmetic block under command of the control block. The logico-arithmetic block typically contains a number of registers for the performance of arithmetic operations such as addition and subtraction, or digit-by-digit logical operations such as disjunction and conjunction. These are implemented through switching

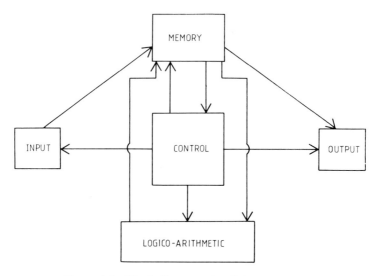

Figure 1.3   Block diagram of a digital computer.

devices such as high-speed transistors embedded in a compact integrated circuit. The main register which holds the answers for most operations is often called the accumulator register. A register of m binary digits can hold 2^m different binary words. A register of m ternary digits can hold 3^m different ternary words. Thus a ternary register requires fewer digits to produce the same number of different words as a binary register. In general, an n-valued register of m digits can represent n^m different n-valued words of length m.

The control block contains switching devices of the kind mentioned above. The exact sequence of control commands usually stems from a program stored in the memory block. This program resides in the memory block as a result of input by some programmer, or as a result of internal activity in the main computer. Each location in memory is called an *address* and is said to contain a *memory word*.

The main hardware interest in this book is concerned with the control and logico-arithmetic blocks. There is a peripheral interest in other blocks. For example, Section 1.2 was concerned with input equipment.

There is an interest in the aspects of programs stored within memory—many programs exhibit multiple-valued switching. A program may contain multiple-valued switches which cause n-way branches within the program. High-level programming languages such as PASCAL can mirror the logic operations which occur in switching circuitry such as OR-gates and AND-gates by providing the logic operations OR and AND, respectively. Recent research in the logic of programs extends these operations to the global level, where individual variables are extended to whole programs, and modal logics are used to treat the universe of all programs. Finally, programs can simulate the operation of switching equipment. The appearance of logic operations within a program can make a simulation or emulation program quite similar to the actual hardware.

Consider a simulation of the shaft encoder of figure 1.2. Starting at quantization position 0° as shown in figure 1.2, let the shaft rotate clockwise for 320°. This rotation touches all nine 40° sectors. The nine resulting sensed sequences and corresponding ternary words are shown below.

WW	00
WG	01
WB	02
GW	10
GG	11
GB	12
BW	20
BG	21
BB	22.

The consecutive rows of ternary words shown in the right hand column are simulated by the PASCAL program given in figure 1.4. The program is so easy to understand, it is possible to inspect the program without realizing any connection to ternary logic design. It is shown in Section 2.6 of the next chapter that these ternary words are nine counts of a ternary counter, corresponding to decimal counts 0, 1, 2, 3, 4, 5, 6, 7, 8.

```
PROGRAM ENCODER (INPUT, OUTPUT);
   VAR
      TRACK1, TRACK2: INTEGER;

   BEGIN
      FOR TRACK1:=0 TO 2 DO
         FOR TRACK2:=0 TO 2 DO
            WRITELN (TRACK1, TRACK2)
   END.
```

Figure 1.4 PASCAL simulator of two-track ternary shaft encoder, clockwise-rotating shaft

1.4 History of theory and applications in the twentieth century

There is a well established connection between 2-valued logic and computer structures. The connection of 2-valued logic and Boolean algebra to computer science was observed in Japan (Nakasima and Hanzawa 1938), in the United States (Shannon 1938), in Austria (Piesch 1939) and in Russia (Shestakov

1941). It had already been noted in a review (Ehrenfest 1910). This connection became well established as a result of the subsequent construction of actual computers, together with an increasing number of comparisons of logical, computing, and biological systems by engineers and scientists from a wide range of disciplines.

The development of multiple-valued logic in its modern form began with work in Poland (Łukasiewicz 1920) and in the USA (Post 1921). This development was affected over ensuing years by relationships with the development of intuitionist logic (Brouwer 1908) and modal logic (Lewis 1918). The first algebra corresponding to the work of Post was formulated in Rosenbloom (1942). This algebra was called Post algebra of order n, where n is an integer ≥ 2.

Motivated toward disjunctive normal forms which correspond in a transparent way with logic truth tables and associated minimization techniques, some computer scientists in the period 1955–60 described the normal form theorem for n-valued functions using disjoint operators. An algebraic development of Post algebras using these operators is given in Epstein (1960). Subsequent algebraic developments in the period 1960–70 include Traczyk (1963 and 1964), Rousseau (1969) and Rasiowa (1969). A consequence was the identification of certain operations occurring in other nonclassical logics which are of interest in computer science. In particular, operations having properties of Brouwer's intuitionist negation, Lewis' strict implication, and Łukasiewicz's negation were identified. The identification of an operation having properties of intuitionist implication was first reported in 1966 by Rousseau at the Polish Academy of Sciences Institute of Mathematics in Warsaw. Another consequence was various generalizations of Post algebras. Generalizations which appeared in the period 1960–70 include Chang and Horn (1961), Traczyk (1967) and Dwinger (1968). Generalizations of Post algebras in the period 1970–90 include: pseudo-Post algebras in Rousseau (1970); Post algebras of order ω^+ in Rasiowa (1973); P-algebras in Epstein and Horn (1974a); P_0-lattices, P_1-lattices, and P_2-lattices in Epstein and Horn (1974b); semi-Post algebras in Cat Ho and Rasiowa (1987); plain semi-Post algebras in Cat Ho and Rasiowa (1989); and Post algebras of order $\omega + \omega^*$ in Epstein and Rasiowa (1990 and 1991). In this book P_2-lattices of order n are called sub-Post algebras of order n.

Early contributions were made in Moisil (1941) and Shestakov (1953) which built upon work in Łukasiewicz (1920) and Bochvar (1939), respectively. A focus of interest was the change of state of relays within relay circuits. The use of 4-valued logic for the analysis of transients was discussed in Metze (1955), and the use of 3-valued logic for this purpose was examined in Eichelberger (1965). Subsequent uses of n-valued logic in fault diagnosis and fault tolerance are discussed in Breuer and Epstein (1973), Mor (1976), Chiang and Vranesic (1982), Knudsen (1982), Hławiczka and Badura (1982), Leonetti and Butler (1985), Huang and Chen (1985), Butler (1986),

Andrew (1986), and Katter and Razavi (1990). While the $n = 3$ case is used frequently in these papers, other values of n also occur. Five of the papers just listed use values $n = 4, 6, 8, 9$, or 16.

Different kinds of number systems have been used since ancient times. The Babylonians used a sexagesimal system. Ternary systems for computation were discussed in Lalanne (1840). By the middle of the present century there were ternary devices widely enough known to be included in a survey book (Engineering Research Associates 1950); ternary computers were proposed in Grosch (1952). However, it was not until 1958 that the first full-scale ternary computer was completed at Moscow University, as reported in Again (1960) and Brusentsov (1960). While this development encouraged work on ternary subsystems, such as work on arithmetic units in Canada (Hamacher and Vranesic 1971), Japan (Mine *et al* 1971), Switzerland (Haberlin and Muller 1970) and Israel (Halpern and Yoeli 1968), the low-level programming language devised for the Russian computer was so difficult to use that little insight was provided into the ternary approach.

The first appearance of a high-level programming language with n-valued branching was IBM's FORTRAN I (Programming Research Group 1954). This language contained an instruction called the 'computed GO TO' which allowed branching to any one of n program statements depending on the value of a positive integer argument. There were subsequent improvements in the structuring of programs. The GO TO concept was replaced with the idea of the CASE clause by the Algol 68 international committee and in the language ALGOL 68 (Wijngaarden 1969). This was repeated later with the language PASCAL (Wirth 1971). The consequence of using these n-valued branching statements is a significant reduction in program complexity.

It has been suggested (Goto 1985) that the relationships between logic programming and multiple-valued logic should be investigated. Programming languages such as PROLOG use what is termed rule-based logic, and mappings of such logic into multiple-valued logic are investigated in Rine (1987). Some foundations for these investigations may be found in Rine (1974) and McAllester (1980).

An emulation of a full-scale ternary computer was completed in 1973 at SUNY, Buffalo, as reported in Frieder *et al* (1973). This emulation proved that both the speed and price of a full ternary computer are of the order of magnitude of the speed and price of a computationally equivalent binary computer.

Connections between logic, computer science, and neural science were established in McCulloch and Pitts (1943) and Kleene (1956). Some connections of multiple-valued logic with neural science and neural nets may be found in Pao (1988), Yamamoto and Mukaidono (1989), Watanabe *et al* (1990), and Hsu *et al* (1990). For a connection of multiple-valued logic with molecular computing, see Kameyama and Higuchi (1988).

Interest in optical computing and multiple-valued logic has led to discussions in Hurst (1980), Arrathoon (1986), Arrathoon and Kozaitis (1986), Mirsalehi and Gaylord (1986), and Hurst (1986). For work on uncertainty in computer vision, including edge detection and shape representation, see Huntsberger *et al* (1986). Finite-valued orthogonal functions and transforms are discussed in Chrestsenson (1955), Liebler and Roesser (1971), Zhang (1984), and Epstein and Loka (1985a and b). There are many applications for such functions, including image processing and logic design (Moraga 1984).

1.5   Overview

Books relating to multiple-valued logic since 1950 include: Rosser and Turquette (1952), Zinov'ev (1963), Rescher (1969), Rasiowa (1974), Balbes and Dwinger (1974), Dunn and Epstein (1977), Rine (1977), Muzio and Wesselkamper (1986), and Butler (1991).

There were 20 annual International Symposia on multiple-valued logic during the period 1971–90. There are over 850 papers in all the proceedings of these symposia.

Special issues devoted to multiple-valued logic during the period 1974–89 include the following: two issues of *Computer* (September 1974 and April 1988), two issues of the *IEEE Transactions on Computers* (September 1981 and February 1986), and two issues of the *International Journal of Electronics* (August 1987 and November 1989). Survey papers during this period include Epstein *et al* (1974), Smith (1981), and Hurst (1984).

There are professional groups on multiple-valued logic in both Japan and the United States. The *Bulletin of the Multiple-valued Logic Technical Committee* of the IEEE Computer Society has been published three times a year since the early 1980s.

Exercises

E1.1   For a photoelectric shaft encoder, contrast the case $n = 2, m = 8$ with the case $n = 3, m = 5$. For each case, give: (a) the quantization size; (b) the quantization positions; and (c) the maximum magnitude of error.

E1.2   For (a) $n = 2$ and (b) $n = 3$, what is the minimum number of tracks needed to ensure a maximum magnitude of error of $0.01°$ or less?

E1.3   Contrast the case $n = 2, m = 4$ with the case $n = 4, m = 2$. Show the coder disk for each case, using for $n = 4$ dark gray (D) and light gray (L) in addition to black (B) and white (W). Prove that the quantization sizes, quantization positions, and maximum magnitudes of error are the same for both cases. Discuss the advantages and disadvantages of building a photoelectric shaft encoder for each case. Write a PASCAL simulation program for each case, where the shaft rotates clockwise and touches each angular sector exactly once. Which program do you find preferable and why?

E1.4   Consider a usual traffic light which shows red at the top, yellow in the middle, and green at the bottom. Under normal traffic operation, is this traffic light a 2-valued device, a 3-valued device, or some other kind of device? Explain your answer.

E1.5   For any value of $n \geq 2$, give a formula for m which determines the minimum number of tracks needed to ensure a maximum magnitude of error of e or less.

2 Logic Tables and Switching Functions

2.1 Switching functions and their description by tables

Engineers, scientists, and philosophers use various kinds of tables and maps in order to pictorially describe functions and basic connectives. This chapter is concerned primarily with the description of logic or switching functions through the use of tables which are commonly called truth tables. In Chapter 3 there will be a discussion of some pictorial variants, such as Venn diagrams and Karnaugh maps.

Truth tables have been used to describe 2-valued logic functions for many years. Some tables are not restricted to 2-valued functions, nor to logic functions, and may be used to describe a variety of functions in other fields. Consider the function in m variables whose output value is 1 when the total number of odd-valued inputs is odd, and whose output value is 0 when the total number of odd-valued inputs is even. The table in figure 2.1(a) illustrates the function $g(X, Y, Z)$ for the case of $m = 3$ binary inputs X, Y, Z. The table in figure 2.1(b) illustrates the function $h(V, W)$ for the case of $m = 2$ ternary inputs V, W.

Throughout this book, functions whose table entries are all numbers are usually called *switching functions*. On the other hand, functions whose table entries are logic values are usually called *logic functions*. For fixed $n \geq 2$ logic values are denoted by $F = E_0, E_1, \ldots, E_{n-2}, E_{n-1} = T$, where F stands for FALSE, T stands for TRUE, and the other logic values stand for the $n - 2$ intermediate logic values. A standard rule of correspondence for switching functions and logic functions is that T be assigned to the maximum of the possible integer inputs, that F be assigned to the minimum of the possible integer inputs, and that E_j be assigned to the intermediate integers, with E_j for increasing subscript j corresponding to the increasing intermediate integer values. In some hardware applications, the E_j stands for voltages satisfying $E_0 \leq E_1 \leq \cdots \leq E_{n-1}$.

The switching functions of figure 2.1 are shown as logic functions in figure 2.2. For the 2-valued example, 0, 1 of figure 2.1(a) appear in figure 2.2(a) as F, T respectively. For the 3-valued example, 0, 1, 2 of figure 2.1(b) appear in figure 2.2(b) as F, E_1, T, respectively.

A logic table gives a vertical picture of a logic function in the sense that the output function appears as a column. It is helpful to picture a switching

(a)

	X	Y	Z	g
Row 0	0	0	0	0
1	0	0	1	1
2	0	1	0	1
3	0	1	1	0
4	1	0	0	1
5	1	0	1	0
6	1	1	0	0
7	1	1	1	1

(b)

	V	W	h
Row 0	0	0	0
1	0	1	1
2	0	2	0
3	1	0	1
4	1	1	0
5	1	2	1
6	2	0	0
7	2	1	1
8	2	2	0

Figure 2.1 Switching functions g, h are each 1 if the total number of odd-valued inputs is odd, and 0 if the total number of odd-valued inputs is even.

(a)

X	Y	Z	g
F	F	F	F
F	F	T	T
F	T	F	T
F	T	T	F
T	F	F	T
T	F	T	F
T	T	F	F
T	T	T	T

(b)

V	W	h
F	F	F
F	E_1	E_1
F	T	F
E_1	F	E_1
E_1	E_1	F
E_1	T	E_1
T	F	F
T	E_1	E_1
T	T	F

Figure 2.2 Logic functions g, h.

function horizontally as an n-valued function defined on an x-axis whose domain is the row numbers. This is illustrated in figure 2.3(a) for the table of figure 2.1(a) and in figure 2.3(b) for the table of figure 2.1(b). For example, row 5 of figure 2.1(a) with value $g = 0$ is shown in figure 2.3(a) as $g(5) = 0$.

Definition 2.1. If f, g are n-valued switching functions having the same domain D, then

(i) $f \leq g$ denotes that $f(x) \leq g(x)$ for each x in D, and
(ii) $f = g$ if and only if $f(x) \leq g(x)$ and $g(x) \leq f(x)$ for each x in D; i.e. $f(x) = g(x)$ for each x in D.

A system example is given below for the 3-valued case. This is followed by discussions for the 4-valued and 2-valued case.

Consider a defensive site, such as a military installation, and the problem of determining which defensive action to take based on aircraft attacking in a group or raid. Let V represent the size of a raid by high-speed aircraft: the

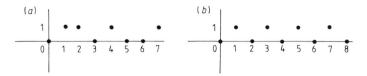

Figure 2.3 Horizontal pictures of the switching functions g, shown in (a), and h, shown in (b).

value of V will be 2 if it has been determined that the raid size is 16 aircraft or more, the value of V will be 1 if it has been determined that the raid size is between 5 and 15 aircraft, and the value of V will be 0 if it has been determined that the raid size is 4 aircraft or less. Let W represent the size of a raid by medium-speed aircraft: the value of W will be 2 if it has been determined that the raid size is 21 aircraft or more, the value of W will be 1 if it has been determined that the raid size is between 10 and 20 aircraft, and the value of W will be 0 if it has been determined that the raid size is 9 aircraft or less. This takes into account the fact that high-speed aircraft are more of a threat to the defensive site than medium-speed aircraft.

The defensive ACTION function A_1 shown in the table of figure 2.4 is designed to illustrate a possible system response to the various situations which might arise. The three values of A_1 are: 2, corresponding to "red-alert"; 1, corresponding to "yellow-alert"; and 0, corresponding to "green-and-quiet". Red alerts indicate a need for immediate action; yellow alerts indicate a need for preparatory action; green-and-quiet indicates a continuation of monitoring action.

Of course there are other ACTION functions which could be construed as possible system responses. The table in figure 2.4 is one example for the purpose of illustration. The ACTION function A_1 is a unate function and a positive function. These special functions are discussed in Chapter 9.

This system example for A_1 in terms of V and W illustrates a number of points. First, each of the entries in the table of figure 2.4 are precisely defined. Second, the assignment of an integer value to a variable does not depend on fixed interpretations—other interpretations are possible. Third, this example could occur within a software system, within a hardware system, or within a man–machine system. Finally, the choice of $n = 3$ in this example is clearly a system parameter—this example could be approached as a 2-valued or as a 4-valued example. It is worthwhile to explore this, for in the framework of possible n-valued approaches, it is important that the value of n be considered carefully.

Consider a 4-valued approach. Here, any raid of size 5 to 15 by high-speed aircraft or raid of size 10 to 20 by medium-speed aircraft is split into upper and lower halves. For V and W the value 1 is taken for the lower half and the value 2 is taken for the upper half. The value 0 is taken for the lowest

V	W	A_1
0	0	0
0	1	0
0	2	1
1	0	0
1	1	1
1	2	2
2	0	1
2	1	2
2	2	2

Figure 2.4   3-valued ACTION function A_1.

V	W	A_2
0	0	0
0	1	0
0	2	1
0	3	2
1	0	0
1	1	1
1	2	2
1	3	3
2	0	1
2	1	2
2	2	2
2	3	3
3	0	2
3	1	3
3	2	3
3	3	3

Figure 2.5   4-valued ACTION function A_2.

raid sizes and the value 3 is taken for the highest raid sizes. A possible choice for the ACTION function A_2 in this case is shown in figure 2.5; this shows a higher resolution for raid sizes in the intermediate range, but otherwise preserves the approach in figure 2.4.

Consider a 2-valued approach as shown for the ACTION function A_3 in figure 2.6. In this table, there is no intermediate range. For V and W, the value 0 is taken for raid sizes of 10 or less, and the value 1 is taken for raid sizes of 11 or more. The intermediate range is dropped.

V	W	A_3
0	0	0
0	1	0
1	0	0
1	1	1

Figure 2.6   2-valued ACTION function A_3.

2.2   Basic structural properties of multiple-valued logic tables

Hereafter, for given n, the n logic values will be represented by $F = E_0, E_1, \ldots, E_{n-2}, E_{n-1} = T$ and the corresponding n integer values will be represented by $0, 1, \ldots, n - 1$. When $n = 2$, there are no intermediate values—this is the 2-valued case. Examples in the book may allow other values, such as WHITE, GRAY, BLACK for the 3-valued case—see Section 1.2.

It should be mentioned that there are systems which use other values. In the fractional system, each of the above n integers is divided by $n - 1$. To illustrate the case for $n = 4$, the four values in the fractional system are scaled between 0 and 1 as follows: 0, 1/3, 2/3, 1.

In the examples of Section 2.1, system problems were construed in 2-, 3-, and 4-valued terms. The final choice of interpretation and approach is made by a system or logic designer. Primary considerations include cost and efficiency. Does the introduction of more than 2 values lead to high efficiency in a cost-effective way? If so, is this efficiency a real and practical advantage within the system as a whole? The system examples of Section 2.1 illustrate some of these considerations.

If inputs take the values $0, 1, \ldots, n - 1$, for fixed $n \geq 2$, functions described by tables with these inputs are called *n-valued Postian functions*. Figure 2.7 shows a table for a 3-valued Postian function. This table shows ternary inputs X, Y. The output is the magnitude of the arithmetic difference of the two inputs.

There are cases where some of the inputs are 2-valued, some are 3-valued, etc. If the maximum of such values assumed by all the inputs is n, the functions are called *n-valued sub-Postian functions*. Figure 2.8 shows a 3-valued sub-Postian function of two inputs, W, Y. The input variable W is binary while the input variable Y is ternary. The resulting table has 6 rows. The output is the magnitude of the difference of the two inputs.

By definition, any n-valued Postian function is an n-valued sub-Postian function. Figure 2.7 shows a 3-valued function which is both Postian and sub-Postian. Figure 2.8 shows a 3-valued function which is sub-Postian but is not Postian. For $n = 2$,   2-valued Postian functions are called Boolean functions.

X	Y	$\|X - Y\|$
0	0	0
0	1	1
0	2	2
1	0	1
1	1	0
1	2	1
2	0	2
2	1	1
2	2	0

Figure 2.7 A 3-valued Postian function.

W	Y	$\|W - Y\|$
0	0	0
0	1	1
0	2	2
1	0	1
1	1	0
1	2	1

Figure 2.8 A 3-valued sub-Postian function.

It is instructive to give a PASCAL function MAGDIF for the function of figure 2.8 using WHITE, GRAY, BLACK for 0, 1, 2, respectively. Types and variables are created in PASCAL as shown below.

```
TYPE
   SHADE = (WHITE, GRAY, BLACK);
   LIGHT = WHITE .. GRAY;
VAR
   Y: SHADE;
   W: LIGHT;
FUNCTION MAGDIF(W:LIGHT; Y:SHADE): SHADE;
 BEGIN
   CASE ABS(ORD(W) - ORD(Y)) OF
     0 : MAGDIF:= WHITE;
     1 : MAGDIF:= GRAY;
     2 : MAGDIF:= BLACK
   END
 END
```

In the PASCAL program above ORD(WHITE) = 0, ORD(GRAY) = 1, and ORD(BLACK) = 2. The expression ABS(ORD(W) − ORD(Y)) uses arithmetic subtraction and absolute value. Note that for the 2-valued case, for binary inputs U, V, the expression ABS(ORD(U) − ORD(V)) is equivalent to the logic expression (U AND (NOT V)) OR ((NOT U) AND V). Subsequent work will develop similar equivalences for the n-valued case, where $n \geq 2$.

The logic table for an output function in which exactly two different values F, T appear is called a *2-cisive table* and the output function is called a *2-cisive function*. If exactly m different values appear in the logic table for an output function, where these m values include F and T with $m \leq n$, then the table is called an *m-cisive table* and the output function is called an *m-cisive function*. Following Rescher (1969), 2-cisive logic tables including tautology and contradiction are called *decisive tables*.

In Bochvar (1939) there are two different logic systems, called the "internal" and "external" systems. In the internal system, the number of different intermediate output values is limited to a single intermediate value, so that the only other output values are F and T. In the external system this single intermediate entry is resolved to either F or T so that there are no intermediate output values in the resulting table. Hence Bochvar's internal system is based on 3-cisive tables and his external system is based on 2-cisive tables. The example in figure 2.9 shows that Bochvar's 5-valued internal conjunction is 3-cisive and that Bochvar's 5-valued external conjunction is 2-cisive. 2-valued conjunction may be obtained from the tables of figure 2.9 by focusing on input values which are F or T alone—the corresponding output values in figure 2.9 are shown in highlight boxes. While the output values for 2-valued conjunction are well known, the remaining entries in the tables of figure 2.9 simply reflect Bochvar's orientation.

The logic table for a multiple-valued function which has only F or T values when the input values are F or T alone, is called a *categorical table*. Every categorical table preserves some reduced 2-valued table, and in a sense is a generalization of that 2-valued table. This was illustrated for conjunction using the categorical tables in figure 2.9.

(a)

X \ Y	F	E_1	E_2	E_3	T
F	F	E_2	E_2	E_2	F
E_1	E_2	E_2	E_2	E_2	E_2
E_2	E_2	E_2	E_2	E_2	E_2
E_3	E_2	E_2	E_2	E_2	E_2
T	F	E_2	E_2	E_2	T

(b)

X \ Y	F	E_1	E_2	E_3	T
F	F	F	F	F	F
E_1	F	F	F	F	F
E_2	F	F	F	F	F
E_3	F	F	F	F	F
T	F	F	F	F	T

Figure 2.9 Bochvar's (a) internal and (b) external conjunctions.

Example 2.1. For $n = 5$ there are 2^{21} decisive tables which are categorical for conjunction.

The details are as follows. It may be seen from the 5×5 table in figure 2.9(b) that 4 boxed values determine 2-valued conjunction, leaving $5^2 - 4 = 21$ entries, each of which may be F or T. Thus, there are 2^{21} such tables. One of these is shown in figure 2.9(b).

Example 2.2. For $n = 5$ there are $3(3^{21} - 2^{21})$ 3-cisive tables which are categorical for conjunction.

The details are as follows. Consider first F, E_2, T entries for the unboxed positions in figure 2.9(a). There are 3^{21} such tables, of which 2^{21} are decisive by Example 2.1. It follows that there are $3^{21} - 2^{21}$ 3-cisive tables using the three entries F, E_2, T. One of these is shown in figure 2.9(a). Likewise there are $3^{21} - 2^{21}$ 3-cisive tables using the three entries F, E_1, T and $3^{21} - 2^{21}$ 3-cisive tables using the three entries F, E_3, T. It follows that there are $3(3^{21} - 2^{21})$ 3-cisive tables which are categorical for conjunction.

2.3 Basic logic connectives and their physical realizations: single input

There are a number of basic connectives with the property that the table for each connective has one input column. The discussion of connectives in Sections 2.3–2.4 lays the groundwork for the remainder of this book.

There are n different *constant functions*, each of which has a constant output value. Each of these is called a *nullary operation*—the output value is independent of the input value. To illustrate for $n = 4$, there are four constant functions, denoted by E_0, E_1, E_2, and E_3, where each function E_i assumes the constant value i for each $i = 0, 1, 2, 3$. The constant function $F = E_0$ is equal to all 0s and is called *contradiction*; the constant function $T = E_3$ is equal to all 3s and is called *tautology*. These four functions are shown in figure 2.10. It should be noted that for general $n \geq 2$, tautology is E_{n-1} (all $(n-1)$s).

In figure 2.10 the tables for contradiction and tautology are categorical. There are many other tables which are categorical for given $n \geq 2$. Since there are $n - 2$ other possible input values and n possible output values

(a)	X	E_0	(b)	X	E_1	(c)	X	E_2	(d)	X	E_3
	0	0		0	1		0	2		0	3
	1	0		1	1		1	2		1	3
	2	0		2	1		2	2		2	3
	3	0		3	1		3	2		3	3

Figure 2.10 The four-valued constant functions E_i, $i = 0, 1, 2, 3$.

X	$C_0(X)$	$C_1(X)$	$C_2(X)$	$C_3(X)$	$C_4(X)$	$C_5(X)$
0	5	0	0	0	0	0
1	0	5	0	0	0	0
2	0	0	5	0	0	0
3	0	0	0	5	0	0
4	0	0	0	0	5	0
5	0	0	0	0	0	5

Figure 2.11 $C_i(X)$ for $n = 6$, $i = 0, 1, 2, 3, 4, 5$.

(a)

X	$C_0(X)$
0	2
1	0
2	0

(b)

X	$N(X)$
0	2
1	1
2	0

(c)

X	$C_0(C_2(X))$
0	2
1	2
2	0

Figure 2.12   The three 3-valued tables for which the 0, 2 entries at the top and bottom rows are interchanged.

which can be assumed for each of these input values, the total number of categorical tables where the 2-valued outputs for 2-valued inputs is fixed, is n^{n-2}. Since there are a total of four possible categorical outputs for the two 2-valued inputs, the total number of categorical tables having a single input column is $4n^{n-2}$. Of these, exactly 2^n are decisive. For example, for $n = 5$ there are a total of 500 different categorical tables which have a single input column, and 32 of these are decisive.

Of the decisive n-valued functions, there are exactly n functions which have the property that the output column has exactly one T value and $n - 1$ F values. These n functions have the algebraic names $C_0, C_1, \ldots, C_{n-1}$, where $C_i(X) = n - 1$ for $i = X$ and $C_i(X) = 0$ otherwise. An illustration of these functions for $n = 6$ is given in figure 2.11.

Next consider the case where F, T inputs have the outputs T, F respectively. In the 2-valued case, this inversion of the extremal logic values is termed *negation* or *inversion*. Let X denote the input variable. In PASCAL this 2-valued negation is denoted by NOT X, and within a propositional calculus by $\sim X$. For $n = 2$, $\bar{X} = C_0(X)$ may be used.

Using the same argument as above, there are n^{n-2} n-valued tables which preserve this inversion of 2-valued input values. In particular, for $n = 3$ there are exactly 3 such tables. These 3 tables are shown in figure 2.12.

The function in figure 2.12(a) for $n = 3$ is $C_0(X)$. For general n, the operation C_0 is n-valued intuitionist negation, and appears algebraically as $\neg X$. For $n = 2$, $\bar{X} = \neg X$. The function in figure 2.12(b) for $n = 3$ shows n-valued inversion $N(X)$. For general n, this function simply turns the input column upside-down. It is the only one of the three functions in figure 2.12

(a)	X	$C_2(X)$
	0	0
	1	0
	2	2

(b)	X	$\text{Id}(X)$
	0	0
	1	1
	2	2

(c)	X	$C_0(C_0(X))$
	0	0
	1	2
	2	2

Figure 2.13 The three 3-valued tables for which the 0, 2 entries at the top and bottom rows remain the same.

X	$C_0(X)$	$C_1(X)$	$C_2(X)$	$C_3(X)$	$D_1(X)$	$D_2(X)$	$D_3(X)$	$N(X)$	$\text{Id}(X)$	X'
0	3	0	0	0	0	0	0	3	0	1
1	0	3	0	0	3	0	0	2	1	2
2	0	0	3	0	3	3	0	1	2	3
3	0	0	0	3	3	3	3	0	3	0

Figure 2.14 Basic 4-valued unary operations.

which is not decisive. For $n = 2$, $\bar{X} = N(X)$. The function in figure 2.12(c) for $n = 3$ is $C_0(C_2(X)) = N(C_2(X))$.

It remains to discuss the case where F, T inputs have the outputs F, T, respectively. In the 2-valued case this is just the identity function $\text{Id}(X)$. There are n^{n-2} tables which preserve this function when the input values are F, T. In particular, for $n = 3$, there are three such tables, shown in figure 2.13.

The function in figure 2.13(a) is $C_2(X)$. For general n, this function is $C_{n-1}(X)$. Of the three functions shown in figure 2.13, only the identity function in figure 2.13(b) is not decisive. The function in figure 2.13(c) is $C_0(C_0(X)) = N(C_0(X))$.

$C_{n-1}(X)$ is denoted logically by $\square X$ and algebraically by $!X$.

There are $n - 1$ D_j functions, $j = 1, 2, \ldots, n - 1$, where $D_j(X) = n - 1$ for $X \geq j$, and $D_j(X) = 0$ otherwise. It can be seen that the function in figure 2.13(c) for $n = 3$ is $D_1(X)$. For general n, $D_1(X) = C_0(C_0(X))$. It can be seen that the function in figure 2.13(a) for $n = 3$ is $D_2(X)$. For general n, $D_{n-1}(X) = C_{n-1}(X)$.

The C_i are called *disjoint operators* because $C_i(X) \& C_j(X) = E_0$ (all 0s) for $i \neq j$. The D_j are called *monotonic operators* because $D_i(X) \leq D_j(X)$ for each X when $j \leq i$.

These single input connectives are all shown in figure 2.14 for the case $n = 4$. For the sake of completeness, this table also shows Post's prime operation X'. For this operation, if the input value X is less than $n - 1$, the output X' is $X + 1$; if the input value X is equal to $n - 1$, the output X' is 0.

Lemma 2.2. Some basic relations involving unary operations are given below.

(i) $X \leq C_0(C_0(X))$.

This follows by inspection of the table below.

X	$C_0(X)$	$C_0(C_0(X))$	$C_0(C_0(C_0(X)))$
0	$n-1$	0	$n-1$
1	0	$n-1$	0
2	0	$n-1$	0
$\vdots$	$\vdots$	$\vdots$	$\vdots$
$n-1$	0	$n-1$	0

The result follows because at each row the entry for X is less than or equal to the entry for $C_0(C_0(X))$.

(ii) $C_0(X) = C_0(C_0(C_0(X)))$.

The result follows by inspection of the above table. The column for $C_0(X)$ is identical with the column for $C_0(C_0(C_0(X)))$.

(iii) $C_{n-1}(X) \leq X$.

This follows easily from the columns for X and $C_{n-1}(X)$ in the table below.

X	$C_{n-1}(X)$	$C_{n-1}(C_{n-1}(X))$
0	0	0
$\vdots$	$\vdots$	$\vdots$
$n-2$	0	0
$n-1$	$n-1$	$n-1$

(iv) $C_{n-1}(X) = C_{n-1}(C_{n-1}(X))$.

This follows by inspection of the table in (iii).

(v) $N(N(X)) = X$.

This follows by inspection of the table below.

X	$N(X)$	$N(N(X))$
0	$n-1$	0
1	$n-2$	1
$\vdots$	$\vdots$	$\vdots$
$n-2$	1	$n-2$
$n-1$	0	$n-1$

(vi) $X \leq D_1(X)$.

This follows by inspection of the table below.

X	$D_1(X)$
0	0
1	$n-1$
$\vdots$	$\vdots$
$n-2$	$n-1$
$n-1$	$n-1$

(vii) $D_i(D_j(X)) = D_j(X)$, $1 \leq i, j \leq n-1$.

If f is any column whose entries are 0, $n-1$ alone, then $D_i(f) = f$. Since the column for $D_j(X)$ consists solely of 0, $n-1$ entries, the result follows.

(viii) $\mathbf{E}_i \leq \mathbf{E}_j$, $0 \leq i \leq j \leq n-1$.

At any row of the table, the entry for $\mathbf{E}_i$ is i and the entry for $\mathbf{E}_j$ is j. The result follows because $i \leq j$ at each row of the table. For example, if $n = 7$, $i = 3$, and $j = 5$, the table is

X	$\mathbf{E}_3$	$\mathbf{E}_5$
0	3	5
1	3	5
$\vdots$	$\vdots$	$\vdots$
6	3	5

(ix) $C_{n-1}(X) = D_{n-1}(X)$.

This is immediate from the definitions of $C_{n-1}(X)$ and $D_{n-1}(X)$.

(x) $D_1(X) = C_0(C_0(X))$; $C_0(X) = C_0(D_1(X))$.

These two results are established by the table below.

X	$D_1(X)$	$C_0(X)$	$C_0(C_0(X))$	$C_0(D_1(X))$
0	0	$n-1$	0	$n-1$
1	$n-1$	0	$n-1$	0
$\vdots$	$\vdots$	$\vdots$	$\vdots$	$\vdots$
$n-1$	$n-1$	0	$n-1$	0

$$(\text{xi}) \quad C_i(\mathbf{E}_j) = \begin{cases} \mathbf{E}_0 & \text{for } i \neq j \\ \mathbf{E}_{n-1} & \text{for } i = j. \end{cases}$$

$$(\text{xii}) \quad D_k(\mathbf{E}_j) = \begin{cases} \mathbf{E}_0 & \text{for } k > j \\ \mathbf{E}_{n-1} & \text{for } k \leq j. \end{cases}$$

In (xi) and (xii) the subscripts i, j, k may take all possible values allowed by the definitions of the disjoint operators C_i, the monotonic operators D_k, and the constant functions $\mathbf{E}_j$. (xi) and (xii) follow directly from these definitions.

Intuitively, $C_i(X)$ corresponds with a kind of pulse device whose output is T if $X = i$, and whose output is F otherwise. Also, $D_i(X)$ corresponds with a kind of threshold device whose output is T if $X \geq i$, and whose output is F otherwise.

It is instructive to view $D_j(X)$ and $C_i(X)$ as functions in the programming language PASCAL using logico-arithmetic expressions. For $D_j(X)$ consider the following.

```
FUNCTION D(J:DINDEX; X:VALUE): VALUE;
  BEGIN
    D := ORD(J<=X) * (N-1)
  END
```

Here DINDEX has the range $1, 2, \ldots, N - 1$ and VALUE has the n-valued range $0, 1, 2, \ldots, N - 1$. Note that ORD(J<=X) has the value 0 or 1, depending whether the Boolean logico-arithmetic expression (J<=X) is FALSE or TRUE. The multiplication by $(N - 1)$ performs the scaling which is needed to satisfy the definition of $D_j(X)$. The multiplication at this line can be avoided by using the following instead:

```
IF (J<=X) THEN D := N-1 ELSE D := 0.
```

In similar fashion, consider for $C_i(X)$ the following PASCAL function.

```
FUNCTION C(I:CINDEX; X:VALUE): VALUE;
  BEGIN
    C := ORD(I = X) * (N-1)
  END
```

Here CINDEX has the range $0, 1, 2, \ldots, N - 1$. The resulting PASCAL function corresponds to $C_i(X)$.

There are a variety of applications. Consider, for example, an input X which can be at any one of nine levels: 0, 1, 2, 3, 4, 5, 6, 7, 8. A statement that a device activates fully for input 6 but does not activate for any other input level, has a switching table corresponding to $C_6(X)$, with $n = 9$. For a second example, a statement that another device activates fully for inputs which are greater than 5 but does not activate at all for inputs which are less than or equal to 5, has a switching table corresponding to $D_6(X)$. There are many applications which utilize these devices. Such binary triggering may be found in firing circuits within electrical networks, and in electrochemical firing of neurons within neural networks.

The switching table for inversion corresponds with the output of an electrical circuit called the *inverter*. In the 2-valued case, the *inverter* inverts a high input voltage at logic 1 to a low output voltage at logic 0. Conversely a low input voltage at logic 0 is inverted to a high output voltage at logic 1. The actual voltages may be scaled—for example, logic 0 may be represented by -6 volts and logic 1 by $+3$ volts.

In the 2-valued case, nonbinary voltages occur whenever there is a transition between a voltage at logic 0 and a voltage at logic 1, as shown in figure 2.15. This illustrates noise margins about logic 0 and logic 1. Any voltage signal within the noise margins about logic 0 is regarded as logic 0; any voltage signal within the noise margins about logic 1 is regarded as logic 1.

A signal during transition which has a target binary value b, but assumes the value $\bar{b}$ during the transition, is called a *hazard*. In figure 2.15, during the transition from logic 0 to logic 1 the downward spike at 0 is a hazard. In practice, the value of n for the analysis of hazards is low, such as $n = 3$ (Eichelberger 1965). There are approaches in the literature where the value of n for such analyses is in the range $3 \leq n \leq 16$, as mentioned in Section 1.4.

A modern electrical version of the inverter may use an NPN transistor, as shown in figure 2.16. The transistors here are high-speed switches which change in nanoseconds, while neurons, for example, change in milliseconds.

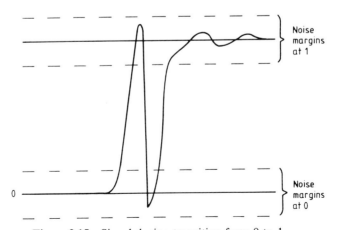

Figure 2.15 Signal during transition from 0 to 1.

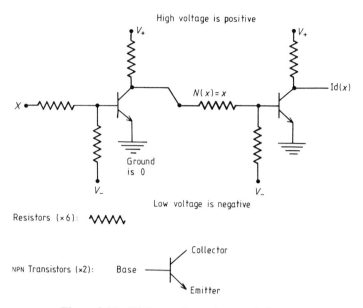

Figure 2.16   High-speed transistor switches.

The resistor–transistor logic (RTL) circuitry in figure 2.16 has an easy explanation in terms of switches which open or close. If the base input goes negative with respect to the emitter voltage, the NPN transistor switch opens. As a result, the collector output voltage moves toward the collector supply voltage V_+. Thus, input $X = 0$ results in output $N(X) = \bar{X} = 1$. On the other hand, if the base input goes positive with respect to the emitter voltage, the NPN transistor switch closes. As a result, the output collector voltage is brought toward the emitter voltage 0. Thus, input $X = 1$ results in output $N(X) = \bar{X} = 0$.

It should be mentioned that the amplified identity output $\mathrm{Id}(X)$ is clearly marked as a point in the circuitry which is different from the point X at the input. While the logic values of X and $\mathrm{Id}(X)$ are identical, X and $\mathrm{Id}(X)$ have distinguishing circuit characteristics, as explained below.

In electrical circuits there is usually a maximum number of points to which a signal may be connected. This is called the *maximum fan-out*. To give an example, while an input signal such as X in figure 2.16 might have a maximum fan-out of only 3, the output of a transistor might have a maximum fan-out of 7. Thus, continuing this example, X would have a remaining fan-out of 2, while $\mathrm{Id}(X)$ would have a fan-out of 7. Logic diagram symbols for 2-valued operations $N(X) = \bar{X}$ and $\mathrm{Id}(X)$ are shown in figure 2.17. In control applications, the circuitry of figure 2.16 may be used as a starting point to provide, through the use of buffer amplifiers, large amounts of fan-out. Concluding the example just given, figure 2.18 shows X amplified to provide

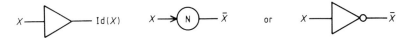

Figure 2.17 Some 2-valued operations.

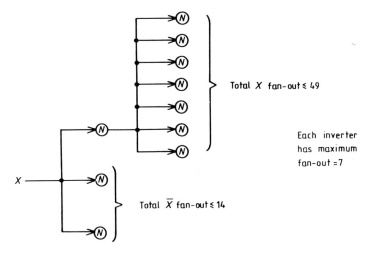

Figure 2.18 Buffer fan-out.

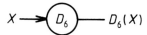

Figure 2.19 The 9-valued operation $D_6(x)$.

a fan-out which is ≤ 49. In the configuration of figure 2.18, the fan-out for $\bar{X}$ is ≤ 14.

As shown in figure 2.17, the conventional triangle symbol may be used for identity amplification when $n = 2$. See also the two alternate forms for $N(x)$ in figure 2.17 when $n = 2$.

For the n-valued case, a single input function may be shown diagrammatically by a single circle with a single input and a single output. The name of the function appears within the circle. Figure 2.19 shows the monotonic operation D_6 with $n = 9$.

For $n = 9$, the D_6 function is a designating or threshold kind of function. Any input which is 6 or greater is designated to have output T (i.e. 8). Any input below 6 has output F (i.e. 0). In other words, 6 is a threshold for which this device activates. An electronic example is the Schmitt trigger, which fires only if the input voltage is sufficiently high. An electrochemical example is the neuron, which fires at its axon if the total dendritic input is sufficiently strong.

Finally, innovative design approaches might entail the coding of different values into a small number of wires or values. To illustrate, a 4-valued signal could be constructed by coding each value onto 2 wires, so that 0 becomes 00, 1 becomes 01, 2 becomes 10, and 3 becomes 11. A different coding converts 0 into 11, 1 into 10, 2 into 00, and 3 into 01. The first coding simply converts a value into its binary equivalent. This coding is used in the quaternary adder of Chapter 6. The second coding has the feature that 0, 1, 2, 3, 0, 1, 2, ... codes into 11, 10, 00, 01, 11, 10, 00, ..., and in any two consecutive binary pairs of this sequence one digit at most changes. This latter coding is called a Gray coding. For Gray code applications relating to shaft encoders, see pp 435–6 in Bartee (1981). It is clear that the number of different codings for the 4 values 0, 1, 2, 3 into binary pairs is $4! = 24$. Certain of these codings are used within the framework of programmable logic arrays in Sasao (1988).

2.4   Basic logic connectives and their physical realizations: two or more inputs

The approach taken in the previous section for one input can be extended to the case for two inputs. In the binary case for one input, there are $2^2 = 4$ possible 2-valued tables. In the binary case for two inputs there are $2^4 = 16$ possible 2-valued tables. Following the argument of the previous section for the n-valued case, for each of these 16 tables there are n^{n^2-4} corresponding categorical tables, hence a total of $16(n^{n^2-4})$ categorical tables.

The 16 different 2-valued functions of two inputs are shown in figure 2.20, labeled from $t_0(X, Y)$ to $t_{15}(X, Y)$. In this section, emphasis is placed on categorical tables which preserve t_8, t_{11}, and t_{14}.

The function t_8 is a 2-valued conjunction, denoted logically by $X \& Y$, algebraically by $X \wedge Y$, and briefly by XY. It is read in English as X and Y, and written in PASCAL as X AND Y. Of the n^{n^2-4} categorical tables which preserve t_8, two have been discussed, namely Bochvar's two conjunctions in Section 2.2. Of all possible conjunctions, however, there is one which is used in many applications. This will be given after the following remarks on t_{14}.

While t_8 represents 2-valued conjunction, t_{14} represents 2-valued

X	Y	t_0	t_1	t_2	t_3	t_4	t_5	t_6	t_7	t_8	t_9	t_{10}	t_{11}	t_{12}	t_{13}	t_{14}	t_{15}
0	0	0	1	0	1	0	1	0	1	0	1	0	1	0	1	0	1
0	1	0	0	1	1	0	0	1	1	0	0	1	1	0	0	1	1
1	0	0	0	0	0	1	1	1	1	0	0	0	0	1	1	1	1
1	1	0	0	0	0	0	0	0	0	1	1	1	1	1	1	1	1

Figure 2.20   The 16 2-valued two-input operations.

(a) $X \& Y$

X \ Y	0	1	2	3
0	0	0	0	0
1	0	1	1	1
2	0	1	2	2
3	0	1	2	3

(b) $X \sqcup Y$

X \ Y	0	1	2	3
0	0	1	2	3
1	1	1	2	3
2	2	2	2	3
3	3	3	3	3

Figure 2.21 4-valued (*a*) conjunction and (*b*) disjunction.

disjunction. This is denoted logically by $X \sqcup Y$, algebraically by $X \vee Y$. It is read in English as X inclusive or Y, and is written in PASCAL as `X OR Y`.

For the n-valued case, $X \& Y$ is taken to be the greatest lower bound of X, Y and $X \sqcup Y$ is taken to be the least upper bound of X, Y. Thus, in this chapter $X \& Y$ is $\text{MIN}(X, Y)$ and $X \sqcup Y$ is $\text{MAX}(X, Y)$. These minimum and maximum values for conjunction and disjunction are illustrated in figure 2.21 for the case $n = 4$. It can be observed from this figure that these tables are indeed categorical generalizations which preserve 2-valued conjunction and disjunction. Physical realizations for these operations are given later.

These definitions for conjunction and disjunction are easily extended to three or more inputs. The conjunction of m input values yields the minimum of the m input values, where $m \geq 2$. The disjunction of m input values yields the maximum of the m input values, where $m \geq 2$. Since $X \& (Y \& Z) = (X \& Y) \& Z$, parentheses are usually dropped, and this is written $X \& Y \& Z$. Similarly, $X \sqcup (Y \sqcup Z) = (X \sqcup Y) \sqcup Z = X \sqcup Y \sqcup Z$.

Lemma 2.3. Some basic relations involving conjunction and disjunction are given below.

(i) $X \& C_0(X) = \mathbf{E}_0$.

This follows by inspection of the table below.

X	$C_0(X)$	$X \& C_0(X)$	$\mathbf{E}_0$
0	$n-1$	0	0
1	0	0	0
⋮			
$n-1$	0	0	0

(ii) $C_0(X \sqcup Y) = C_0(X) \& C_0(Y).$

It is straightforward to verify that both the left and right hand sides of (ii have the table shown below.

X \ Y	0	1	$\cdots$	$n-1$
0	$n-1$	0		0
1	0	0		0
$\vdots$				
$n-1$	0	0		0

(iii) $C_0(X \& Y) = C_0(X) \sqcup C_0(Y).$

Again, it is easy to verify that both the left and right hand sides of (iii) hav the table shown below.

X \ Y	0	1	$\cdots$	$n-1$
0	$n-1$	$n-1$		$n-1$
1	$n-1$	0		0
$\vdots$				
$n-1$	$n-1$	0		0

(iv) $C_{n-1}(X \sqcup Y) = C_{n-1}(X) \sqcup C_{n-1}(Y).$

It is evident that both the left and right hand sides of (iv) have the tab shown below.

X \ Y	0	1	$\cdots$	$n-2$	$n-1$
0	0	0		0	$n-1$
1	0	0		0	$n-1$
$\vdots$					
$n-2$	0	0		0	$n-1$
$n-1$	$n-1$	$n-1$		$n-1$	$n-1$

(v) $C_{n-1}(X \& Y) = C_{n-1}(X) \& C_{n-1}(Y).$

Both the left and right hand sides of (v) have the table shown below.

X \ Y	0	1	$\cdots$	$n-2$	$n-1$
0	0	0		0	0
1	0	0		0	0
$\vdots$					
$n-2$	0	0		0	0
$n-1$	0	0		0	$n-1$

(vi) $N(X \sqcup Y) = N(X) \& N(Y)$.

Both the left and right hand sides of (vi) have the table shown below.

X \ Y	0	1	2	$\cdots$	$n-2$	$n-1$
0	$n-1$	$n-2$	$n-3$		1	0
1	$n-2$	$n-2$	$n-3$		1	0
2	$n-3$	$n-3$	$n-3$		1	0
$\vdots$						
$n-2$	1	1	1		1	0
$n-1$	0	0	0		0	0

(vii) $N(X \& Y) = N(X) \sqcup N(Y)$.

Both the left and right hand sides of (vii) have the table shown below.

X \ Y	0	1	2	$\cdots$	$n-2$	$n-1$
0	$n-1$	$n-1$	$n-1$		$n-1$	$n-1$
1	$n-1$	$n-2$	$n-2$		$n-2$	$n-2$
2	$n-1$	$n-2$	$n-3$		$n-3$	$n-3$
$\vdots$						
$n-2$	$n-1$	$n-2$	$n-3$		1	1
$n-1$	$n-1$	$n-2$	$n-3$		1	0

Relations (ii) and (iii) of this lemma are De Morgan's laws for the operation C_0, while (vi) and (vii) are De Morgan's laws for the operation N.

(viii) $D_i(X \& Y) = D_i(X) \& D_i(Y)$, $i = 1, 2, \ldots, n-1$.

$D_i(X \& Y)$ is T if and only if $X \geq i$ and $Y \geq i$. Obviously $D_i(X) \& D_i(Y)$ is T if and only if $X \geq i$ and $Y \geq i$. Hence the table for $D_i(X \& Y)$ is identical with that for $D_i(X) \& D_i(Y)$ for each $i = 1, 2, \ldots, n-1$.

(ix) $D_i(X \sqcup Y) = D_i(X) \sqcup D_i(Y)$, $i = 1, 2, \ldots, n-1$.

$D_i(X \sqcup Y)$ is T if and only if $X \geq i$ or $Y \geq i$. The table for $D_i(X) \sqcup D_i(Y)$ is T if and only if $X \geq i$ or $Y \geq i$. Hence the table for $D_i(X \sqcup Y)$ is identical with the table for $D_i(X) \sqcup D_i(Y)$ for each $i = 1, 2, \ldots, n-1$.

(x) $X = (E_1 \& C_1(X)) \sqcup (E_2 \& C_2(X)) \sqcup \cdots \sqcup (E_{n-1} \& C_{n-1}(X))$.

This follows from the table overleaf.

X	$\mathbf{E}_1$	$\mathbf{E}_2$ $\cdots$ $\mathbf{E}_{n-1}$		$C_1(X)$	$C_2(X)$ $\cdots$ $C_{n-2}(X)$		$C_{n-1}(X)$	$\mathbf{E}_1\&C_1(X)$	$\mathbf{E}_2\&C_2(X)$ $\cdots$ $\mathbf{E}_{n-2}\&C_{n-2}(X)$		$\mathbf{E}_{n-1}\&C_{n-1}(X)$
0	1	2	$n-1$	0	0	0	0	0	0	0	0
1	1	2	$n-1$	$n-1$	0	0	0	1	0	0	0
2	1	2	$n-1$	0	$n-1$	0	0	0	2	0	0
$\cdots$											
$n-2$	1	2	$n-1$	0	0	$n-1$	0	0	0	$n-2$	0
$n-1$	1	2	$n-1$	0	0	0	$n-1$	0	0	0	$n-1$

(xi) $C_i(X) \& C_j(X) = \mathbf{E}_0$ for $i \neq j, 0 \leq i, j \leq n - 1$.

(xii) $C_0(X) \sqcup C_1(X) \sqcup \cdots \sqcup C_{n-2}(X) \sqcup C_{n-1}(X) = \mathbf{E}_{n-1}$.

Relations (xi) and (xii) follow by inspection of the tables for $C_0(X), C_1(X)$, $C_2(X), \ldots, C_{n-2}(X), C_{n-1}(X)$. For $n = 2$, (xi) becomes $C_1(X) \& C_0(X) = X \& \bar{X} = \mathbf{F}$. This is known as the law of contradiction for the 2-valued case. Thus (xi) may be viewed as an n-valued generalization of the law of contradiction. For $n = 2$, (xii) becomes $C_1(X) \sqcup C_0(X) = X \sqcup \bar{X} = \mathbf{T}$. This is known as the law of excluded middle for the 2-valued case. Thus, (xii) may be viewed as an n-valued law of included middle, with middle part

$$C_1(X) \sqcup C_2(X) \sqcup \cdots \sqcup C_{n-2}(X).$$

(xiii) $D_i(X) = C_i(X) \sqcup C_{i+1}(X) \sqcup \cdots \sqcup C_{n-1}(X), \quad i = 1, 2, \ldots, n - 1$.

For each i, the table for the right hand side coincides with the table which defines the monotonic operation on the left hand side.

(xiv) $C_i(X) = D_i(X) \& C_0(D_{i+1}(X)), \quad i = 1, 2, \ldots, n - 1$.

$D_i(X)$ is T if $X \geq i$ and is F otherwise. $C_0(D_{i+1}(X))$ is T if $X < i + 1$ and is F otherwise. Thus $D_i(X) \& C_0(D_{i+1}(X))$ is T if $X = i$ and is F otherwise. This is the definition of the disjoint operation on the left hand side of (xiv).

The function t_{11} is called *2-valued implication*. The table in figure 2.22 for $n = 3$ is decisive, and the function shown in this table is called *3-valued decisive implication*. This is written logically as $X \supset Y$, using a horseshoe symbol, and algebraically as $X \Rightarrow Y$, using a double arrow. As can be seen in figure 2.22 $X \supset Y$ is T whenever $X \leq Y$, and is F otherwise.

The number of categorical tables which generalize 2-valued implication t_{11} and for which each entry is T if and only if $X \leq Y$, is $(n - 1)^{[(n-2)(n+1)/2]}$. This follows from the fact that there are $(n - 1)n/2$ entries below the main diagonal each of which can assume $n - 1$ values which are not equal to T excepting the lower left box which must be F. Thus for $n = 3$, there are 4 such tables, one of which has already been given in figure 2.22. Of the remaining three, two are of importance both historically and in the theory of multiple-valued logic. One of these is *Łukasiewicz's 3-valued implication*; the other is *3-valued intuitionist implication*. All four 3-valued tables for implication may be found in figures 2.22 and 2.23.

X \ Y	0	1	2
0	2	2	2
1	0	2	2
2	0	0	2

Figure 2.22   3-valued decisive implication.

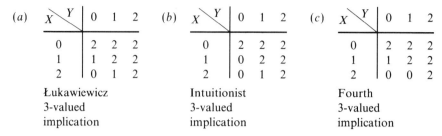

(a)

X \ Y	0	1	2
0	2	2	2
1	1	2	2
2	0	1	2

Łukawiewicz
3-valued
implication

(b)

X \ Y	0	1	2
0	2	2	2
1	0	2	2
2	0	1	2

Intuitionist
3-valued
implication

(c)

X \ Y	0	1	2
0	2	2	2
1	1	2	2
2	0	0	2

Fourth
3-valued
implication

Figure 2.23   Three 3-valued implications.

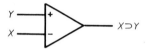

Figure 2.24   Implementation for 3-valued decisive implication.

A feature of 3-valued decisive implication is that it is readily implemented with a binary differential amplifier whose diagram is shown in figure 2.24. For inputs X, Y, the output of this differential amplifier is T if $X \leq Y$ and is F if $X > Y$.

Diode logic circuits for two- and three-input conjunction (AND-gate) and disjunction (OR-gate) are shown in figure 2.25. A diode is a two-terminal nonlinear element, as shown below. The diode symbol and voltage current characteristics of a diode are shown. A diode is said to be forward-biased if its anode voltage is greater than the cathode voltage. In this case the diode will allow current to flow easily from anode to cathode—the diode acts as a closed switch. However, if the cathode has a greater voltage than the anode voltage, the diode is said to be reverse-biased and the diode will act as an open switch. In the circuits shown for AND in figure 2.25, if any of the inputs

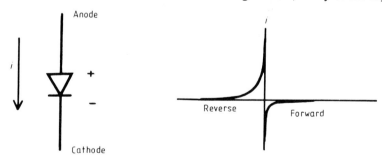

is low, the corresponding diode would be conducting and the output would be equal to the low minimum input voltage. In the circuits shown for OR in figure 2.25, since the cathodes of all diodes are tied together to a negative voltage, the diode with the highest anode voltage would be conducting and

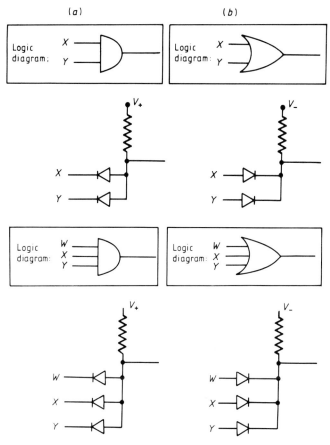

Figure 2.25 (*a*) AND-gates and (*b*) OR-gates.

the output equal to the high maximum input voltage. Thus in the circuits shown for AND-gates, the output is the minimum of the inputs as a result of the current flow from highest to lowest voltage. In the circuits shown for OR-gates, the output is the maximum of the inputs. The fan-out of such a gate might be low, so buffers of inverter amplifiers may be used to increase the fan-out. Resulting diode–transistor logic (DTL) circuits are shown in figure 2.26. In the DTL circuits of figure 2.26, both the inverted signal and the amplified signal are provided. The inverted AND-gate is called a NAND-gate. The inverted OR-gate is called a NOR-gate. Logic diagram symbols for these gates are shown in figure 2.27.

There is a practical limit as to how many input signals can be accepted by such gates. This limit is called the *maximum fan-in*. The circuits of figure 2.25 show AND-gates and OR-gates having fan-in = 2 and fan-in = 3. Fan-in can be increased in a straightforward way. Figure 2.28 shows how

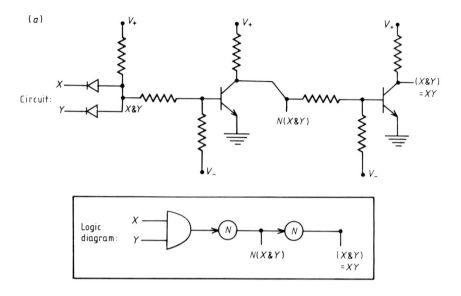

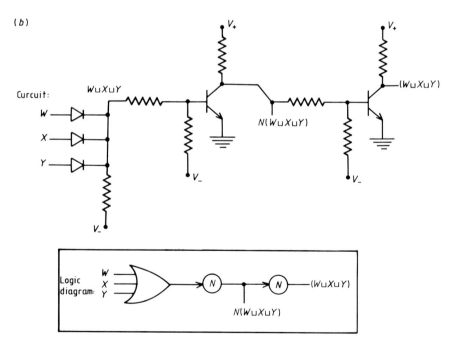

Figure 2.26 (*a*) 2-input AND-gate with amplification and (*b*) 3-input OR-gate with amplification.

(a)

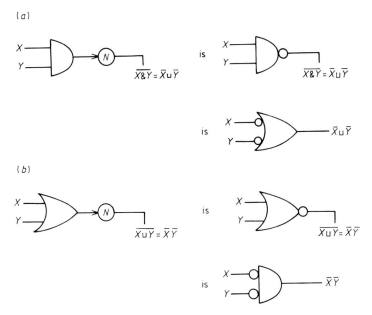

(b)

Figure 2.27 Logic diagram symbols for (a) binary NAND-gate and (b) binary NOR-gate.

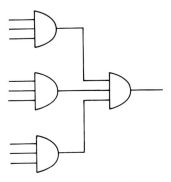

Figure 2.28 AND-gates with maximum fan-in = 3 configured to perform AND with an effective fan-in = 9.

AND-gates with maximum fan-in = 3 can be configured to perform AND with an effective fan-in of 9.

While current flow considerations are a main cause for such limitations, there may be other considerations as well. There may be pin limitations that physically do not allow the number of input or output wires to exceed certain bounds. Further, high speed requirements might not allow certain signal paths to exceed certain lengths.

Because of speed requirements, there is a limit on the number of gates which can be connected serially. This limit is called the *maximum gate depth*. For example, the circuit in figure 2.28 has a maximum of two serially connected gates. It is understood that there is a certain delay associated with each gate, say on the order of 25 nanoseconds. Thus, the circuit of figure 2.28 might involve a delay of 50 nanoseconds.

To conclude this section it should be mentioned that RTL and DTL are just two examples of bipolar logic families. Other examples include transistor–transistor logic (TTL) and integrated-injection logic (I^2L). Unipolar examples within the metal-oxide semiconductor (MOS) logic families include NMOS logic and CMOS logic. Details may be found in Maly (1987) and Chapter 4 of McCluskey (1986).

2.5   Axiomatic implicational calculi

An axiomatic *propositional calculus* is a system for generating new logical formulas from given ones. These formulas involve *propositional letters* $A_1, A_2, \ldots$ and *logical connectives* such as $\supset$ (implication), & (conjunction), and $\sim$ (negation). In this section, $\supset$ is the only logical connective used, so the propositional calculi in this section are called *implicational calculi*. For propositional calculi which involve additional logical connectives, see Chapter 8.

Three implicational calculi are given below: an implicational calculus for 2-valued implication; an implicational calculus for intuitionist implication; and the implicational calculus C5 (see p 295 of Hughes and Cresswell 1968). The development in Chapter 8 builds upon C5.

In what follows, some connections are made between these three calculi and certain implications discussed earlier in this chapter—namely, 2-valued implication given by t_{11} in figure 2.20, 3-valued intuitionist implication given in figure 2.23(b), and 3-valued decisive implication given in figure 2.22.

A *formula* is a finite expression built from propositional letters and allowed logical connectives. An *I formula* is built from propositional letters and connectives $\supset$. Examples are $(A_1 \supset A_1) \supset A_1, (A_1 \supset A_1) \supset (A_2 \supset A_2)$, and $((A_1 \supset A_2) \supset (A_2 \supset A_3)) \supset (A_1 \supset (A_2 \supset A_3))$. An axiomatic implicational calculus consists of a set of *axioms* and a set of *rules of inference*. Each axiom is an I formula.

A formula F is *provable* or a *provable formula* if there exists a finite sequence of formulas $F_1, F_2, \ldots, F_P$ such that each F_i is either an axiom or is generated from preceding formulas in the sequence by one of the rules of inference, and F_P is the resulting formula F. Such a sequence is a *proof of F*. In particular, each axiom is a provable formula, as there is a one-step proof of it.

The propositional calculi in this book use exactly two rules of inference. Provable formulas are generated by these two rules, given below.

(Ri) Rule of substitution.
Any formula α may be substituted for a propositional letter A_j in a formula F_i, provided that all occurrences of A_j in F_i are replaced by α.

(Rii) Rule of detachment (*modus ponens*).
If F_j is a provable formula and $F_j \supset F_k$ is a provable formula, then F_k is a provable formula.

If I is an implicational calculus each of whose provable formulas is a provable formula of some propositional calculus P with additional logical connectives, then I is an *implicational fragment* of P means that the provable formulas of P which involve $\supset$ alone coincide with the provable formulas of I.

There is a distinction in the following between I formulas which are tautologies using certain defining tables for $\supset$, and I formulas which are provable in some axiomatic implicational calculus. Tables which are tautologies have been looked at in previous sections. In this section, axiomatic implicational calculi generate provable formulas whose relation to those I formulas which are tautologies may be difficult to determine.

Some specifics are given below.

Axioms for the 2-valued implicational calculus (implicational fragment of the 2-valued propositional calculus):
(M1) $(A_1 \supset (A_2 \supset A_3)) \supset ((A_1 \supset A_2) \supset (A_1 \supset A_3))$
(M2) $A_1 \supset (A_2 \supset A_1)$
(M3) $((A_1 \supset A_2) \supset A_1) \supset A_1.$

Axioms for the intuitionist implicational calculus (implicational fragment of the intuitionist propositional calculus):
(M1) $(A_1 \supset (A_2 \supset A_3)) \supset ((A_1 \supset A_2) \supset (A_1 \supset A_3))$
(M2) $A_1 \supset (A_2 \supset A_1).$

Axioms for C5 (implicational fragment of the modal logic S5):

(C1) $A_1 \supset A_1$
(C2) $(A_1 \supset (A_2 \supset A_3)) \supset ((A_1 \supset A_2) \supset (A_1 \supset A_3))$
(C3) $(A_2 \supset A_3) \supset (A_1 \supset (A_2 \supset A_3))$
(C4) $(((A_1 \supset A_2) \supset A_3) \supset (A_1 \supset A_2)) \supset (A_1 \supset A_2).$

First, consider the 2-valued implicational calculus. It is a straightforward exercise to verify that each of the three formulas (M1), (M2), (M3) is a tautology using t_{11} as defined in figure 2.20 for $\supset$. Consequently each axiom is a tautology and the two rules of inference, substitution and detachment, have the property that they generate only provable formulas which are tautologies. Hence, every provable formula in the 2-valued implicational calculus is a tautology using t_{11} for $\supset$. Further, there is the following *completeness* result. If G is any I formula which is a tautology using t_{11} for $\supset$, then G is a provable formula of the 2-valued implicational calculus.

Second, the intuitionist implicational calculus may be obtained from the 2-valued implicational calculus by simply dropping axiom (M3). It is easy to verify that both (M1) and (M2) are tautologies using 3-valued intuitionist implication as defined in figure 2.23(b) for $\supset$. It follows that each provable formula is a tautology using 3-valued implication for $\supset$. However, there are I formulas using 3-valued intuitionist implication for $\supset$ which are tautologies but are not provable in the intuitionist implicational calculus. An example is given at the end of this section. This implicational fragment and axioms for the intuitionist propositional calculus may be found in Horn (1962). The following theorem shows a proof of $A_1 \supset A_1$ in this calculus.

THEOREM 2.4. $A_1 \supset A_1$ is a provable formula in the intuitionist implicational calculus.

Proof. Substitute A_1 for A_3 in (M1). The result is $(A_1 \supset (A_2 \supset A_1)) \supset ((A_1 \supset A_2) \supset (A_1 \supset A_1))$. This secures the desired formula, $A_1 \supset A_1$ at the far right. Also (M2) may be recognized at the far left. By detachment, $(A_1 \supset A_2) \supset (A_1 \supset A_1)$. It remains to find a successful substitution for A_2. One such substitution is $A_2 \supset A_1$ for A_2. The result is $(A_1 \supset (A_2 \supset A_1)) \supset (A_1 \supset A_1)$. Once again (M2) may be recognized at the far left. By detachment, $A_1 \supset A_1$ is a provable formula.

Third, each of the formulas (C1)–(C4) in the implicational calculus C5 is a tautology using 3-valued decisive implication as defined in figure 2.22 for $\supset$. However, there are I formulas using 3-valued decisive implication for $\supset$ which are tautologies but are not provable in C5. An example is given at the end of this section. Propositional calculi and implicational fragments for modal logics may be found in Hacking (1963) and Hughes and Cresswell (1968) ∎

Definition 2.5. n-valued intuitionist implication, denoted by $J \rightarrow K$, using n linearly ordered values $0 \leq 1 \leq 2 \leq \cdots \leq n - 1$ is defined to be the value T (that is, $n - 1$) for $J \leq K$, and the value K for $J > K$.

An example is given for $n = 3$ in figure 2.23(b).

Definition 2.6. n-valued decisive implication, denoted by $J \Rightarrow K$, using n linearly ordered values $0 \leq 1 \leq 2 \leq \cdots \leq n - 1$ is defined to be the value T (that is, $n - 1$) for $J \leq K$, and the value F (that is, 0) for $J > K$.

An example is given for $n = 3$ in figure 2.22. The implementation in figure 2.24 applies for $n \geq 2$.

Corollary 2.7. For the case $n = 2$, t_{11} coincides with both 2-valued intuitionist implication and 2-valued decisive implication, as $\mathbf{F} \supset \mathbf{F} = \mathbf{T}$, $\mathbf{F} \supset \mathbf{T} = \mathbf{T}$, $\mathbf{T} \supset \mathbf{F} = \mathbf{F}$, *and* $\mathbf{T} \supset \mathbf{T} = \mathbf{T}$ for each of these.

Lemma 2.8. Some basic relations involving these two n-valued implications are given below.

(i) $X \Rightarrow Y = C_{n-1}(X \to Y)$.

The tables for $X \to Y$ and $C_{n-1}(X \to Y)$ are shown below.

$$X \to Y$$

X \ Y	0	1	2	$\cdots$	$n-2$	$n-1$
0	$n-1$	$n-1$	$n-1$		$n-1$	$n-1$
1	0	$n-1$	$n-1$		$n-1$	$n-1$
2	0	1	$n-1$		$n-1$	$n-1$
3	0	1	2		$n-1$	$n-1$
$\vdots$						
$n-2$	0	1	2		$n-1$	$n-1$
$n-1$	0	1	2		$n-2$	$n-1$

$$C_{n-1}(X \to Y)$$

X \ Y	0	1	2	$\cdots$	$n-2$	$n-1$
0	$n-1$	$n-1$	$n-1$		$n-1$	$n-1$
1	0	$n-1$	$n-1$		$n-1$	$n-1$
2	0	0	$n-1$		$n-1$	$n-1$
3	0	0	0		$n-1$	$n-1$
$\vdots$						
$n-2$	0	0	0		$n-1$	$n-1$
$n-1$	0	0	0		0	$n-1$

The table for $C_{n-1}(X \to Y)$ is identical with the defining table for $X \Rightarrow Y$.

(ii) $X \to Y = (X \Rightarrow Y) \sqcup Y$.

The tables for $X \Rightarrow Y$ and Y are shown below.

$$X \Rightarrow Y$$

X \ Y	0	1	2	$\cdots$	$n-2$	$n-1$
0	$n-1$	$n-1$	$n-1$		$n-1$	$n-1$
1	0	$n-1$	$n-1$		$n-1$	$n-1$
2	0	0	$n-1$		$n-1$	$n-1$
3	0	0	0		$n-1$	$n-1$
$\vdots$						
$n-2$	0	0	0		$n-1$	$n-1$
$n-1$	0	0	0		0	$n-1$

Y

X \ Y	0	1	2	$\cdots$	$n-1$	$n-1$
0	0	1	2		$n-2$	$n-1$
1	0	1	2		$n-2$	$n-1$
2						
$\vdots$						
$n-2$	0	1	2		$n-2$	$n-1$
$n-1$	0	1	2		$n-2$	$n-1$

The disjunction of these two tables yields a table which is identical with the defining table for $X \to Y$ on the left hand side.

(iii) $(X \Rightarrow Y) \sqcup (Y \Rightarrow X) = \mathbf{T}$.

It can be seen from the table for $X \Rightarrow Y$ in (ii) above that there are entries which are all $n - 1$ on the main diagonal and above this diagonal. The table for $Y \Rightarrow X$ has entries which are all $n - 1$ on the main diagonal and below this diagonal. Hence, the disjunction of these two tables has entries which are $n - 1$ in each position of the table.

(iv) $(X \to Y) \sqcup (Y \to X) = \mathbf{T}$

This follows from (ii) and (iii) above.

THEOREM 2.9. The I formula $((X \supset Y) \supset Z) \supset ([(Y \supset X) \supset Z] \supset Z)$ is a tautology using either n-valued intuitionist implication for $\supset$ or n-valued decisive implication for $\sqsupset$, for any fixed $n \geq 2$.

Proof. The proof for n-valued intuitionist implication is in (i) below. The proof for n-valued decisive implication is in (ii) below. It is helpful to recall that $F \supset K$ is T and $K \supset T$ is T for all K by Definitions 2.6 and 2.7. The two results depend on the fact that the values are linearly ordered.

(i)   *Using n-valued intuitionist implication for $\supset$.*
Consider substitution of linearly ordered values for X, Y, and Z in three cases, as follows: (1) $X = Y$, (2) $X < Y$, and (3) $Y < X$.
Case 1. $X = Y$.
The formula becomes $[T \supset Z] \supset ([T \supset Z] \supset Z)$. If $Z < T$, then using n-valued intuitionist implication this becomes $Z \supset (Z \supset Z)$ which is T. If $Z = T$ this becomes $T \supset (T \supset T)$ which is T.
Case 2. $X < Y$.
The formula becomes $[T \supset Z] \supset ([X \supset Z] \supset Z)$. Then $Z < T$ leads to $Z \supset ([X \supset Z] \supset Z)$ which is T and $Z = T$ leads to $(T \supset T) \supset ([X \supset T] \supset T)$ which is T.

Case 3. $Y < X$.
The formula becomes $(Y \supset Z) \supset ([T \supset Z] \supset Z)$. This is T for either $Z < T$ or $Z = T$.

(ii) *Using n-valued decisive implication for* $\supset$.
Case 1. $X = Y$.
The formula becomes $[T \supset Z] \supset ([T \supset Z] \supset Z)$. Using *n*-valued decisive implication for $\supset$, $Z < T$ leads to $F \supset (F \supset Z)$ which is T, while $Z = T$ leads to $T \supset (T \supset T)$ which is T.
Case 2. $X < Y$.
Using *n*-valued decisive implication for $\supset$, the formula becomes $[T \supset Z] \supset ([F \supset Z] \supset Z)$. Then $Z < T$ leads to $F \supset ([F \supset Z] \supset Z)$ which is T and $Z = T$ leads to $T \supset (T \supset T)$ which is T.
Case 3. $Y < X$.
The formula becomes $(F \supset Z) \supset ([T \supset Z] \supset Z)$. This becomes $T \supset ([T \supset Z] \supset Z)$ which is T for either $Z < T$ or $Z = T$ ∎

Corollary 2.10. The *I* formula of Theorem 2.9 is a provable formula in the 2-valued implicational calculus.

Proof. The proof of Theorem 2.9 for $n = 2$ shows that this *I* formula is a tautology using t_{11} for $\supset$, by Corollary 2.7. Hence this formula is provable in the 2-valued implicational calculus by the completeness result mentioned above ∎

The linearity formula of Theorem 2.9 is an example of an *I* formula which is a tautology using either *n*-valued intuitionist implication for $\supset$ or *n*-valued decisive implication for $\supset$, but is *not* a provable formula in either the intuitionist implicational calculus or in C5.

2.6 Number systems

A familiar fixed radix positional number system is the decimal number system. Consider decimal integers ≥ 0. Any decimal number consists of digits 0, 1, 2, 3, 4, 5, 6, 7, 8, 9 placed in marker positions which give from right to left the number of units, tens, hundreds, etc.

Definition 2.11. For fixed *radix* or *base* n, where n is an integer ≥ 2, an r digit number may be represented in the form

$$\sum_{i=0}^{r-1} (d_i n^i) = d_{r-1} n^{r-1} + \cdots + d_1 n + d_0,$$

written $d_{r-1} \ldots d_1 d_0$ where the allowed digits for the d_i are selected from $0, 1, 2, \ldots, n-1$.

The *r* digit number is said to be of *length r*. The base in the decimal number system mentioned above is 10, the base in the binary number system is 2, the base in the ternary number system is 3, and the base in the quaternary number system is 4.

There are other fixed radix number systems which depart from the above formulation. For example, in certain number systems digits may be negative. (See the balanced number systems described below, and Examples 2.10–2.12.) In other fixed radix number systems, the base can be negative or even a complex number.

The first eight 3-digit binary numbers are 000, 001, 010, 011, 100, 101, 110, 111, corresponding to decimal 0, 1, 2, 3, 4, 5, 6, 7. The first nine 2-digit ternary numbers are 00, 01, 02, 10, 11, 12, 20, 21, 22, corresponding to decimal 0, 1, 2, 3, 4, 5, 6, 7, 8. The first sixteen 2-digit quaternary numbers are 00, 01, 02, 03, 10, 11, 12, 13, 20, 21, 22, 23, 30, 31, 32, 33, corresponding to decimal 0, 1, 2, 3, 4, 5, 6, 7, 8, 9, 10, 11, 12, 13, 14, 15.

Example 2.3. Decimal $48 = 1(3^3) + 2(3^2) + 1(3^1) + 0(3^0)$ is ternary 1210.

Example 2.4. Decimal $48 = 1(2^5) + 1(2^4) + 0(2^3) + 0(2^2) + 0(2^1) + 0(2^0)$ is binary 110000.

Example 2.5. Quaternary $223 = 2(4^2) + 2(4^1) + 3(4^0)$ is decimal $32 + 8 + 3 = 43$.

Some eight digit-length additions are shown below, using $n = 10$, $n = 2$, and $n = 3$. For each addition, four rows are shown. The carries are at the top row, the augend and addend are at the two middle rows, and the sum is at the bottom row.

Example 2.6. $n = 10$.

carries:	00111100
augend:	24391387
addend:	32409822
sum:	56801209

Example 2.7. $n = 2$.

carries:	00011100
augend:	10000111
addend:	00101010
sum:	10110001

Example 2.8. $n = 3$.

carries:	00010010
augend:	10112002
addend:	12002101
sum:	22121110

Example 2.9. $n = 4$.

carries:	00011000
augend:	10201322
addend:	22003110
sum:	32211032

Next consider balanced number systems. The fixed radix balanced positional number system requires the base n to be odd, with $n = 1 - 2s$ and s an integer <0, where any r digit number has the form given in Definition 2.8 and the digits d_i are selected from $s, s + 1, \ldots, s + n - 1$. For example, the base in the balanced ternary number system is 3, with $s = -1$ and allowed digits -1, 0, 1. With respect to fixed radix balanced positional number systems, the balanced ternary number system has received the most attention, see Lalanne (1840), pp 173–5 in Knuth (1969), and Frieder *et al* (1973). As another example, consider the balanced quinary number system, in which the base is 5, with $s = -2$ and allowed digits -2, -1, 0, 1, 2. Since $s = -2$, $n = 1 - 2s = 1 - 2(-2) = 5$ and the digits d_i are selected from $s = -2$, $s + 1 = -1$, $s + 2 = 0$, $s + 3 = 1$, $s + 4 = 2$.

There are some computational advantages to such balanced number systems. One advantage is that the negative of a number is obtained simply by replacing each nonzero digit d_i of the number with the digit $-d_i$. Another advantage is that the sign of the number may be determined by inspecting the number's most significant nonzero digit—hence an extra sign digit is not required.

To illustrate the representation of a number in the balanced ternary number system, decimal -23 is $(-1)(0)(1)(1)$ in balanced ternary. Specifically, $(-1)(3^3) + (0)(3^2) + (1)(3^1) + (1)(3^0) = (-27) + 0 + 3 + 1 = -23$.

In a similar manner, decimal 13 in the balanced quinary number system is $(1)(-2)(-2)$. This follows from $(1)(5^2) + (-2)(5^1) + (-2)(5^0) = 25 + (-10) + (-2) = 13$.

The ease with which additions and subtractions can be performed in these balanced number systems is indicated below.

Example 2.10. $n = 3$ (a 4-digit addition in balanced ternary).

carries:	0	0	-1	0
augend:	(1)	(1)	0	(-1)
addend:	(-1)	0	(1)	(-1)
sum:	0	(1)	0	(1)

Example 2.11. $n = 3$ (a 4-digit subtraction in balanced ternary).

minuend:	(1)	(1)	0	(-1)
subtrahend:	(1)	0	(-1)	(1)

Since the negative of the subtrahend is $(-1)0(1)(-1)$, the difference for this subtraction is given by the answer in Example 2.10 above: $0(1)0(1)$.

Example 2.12. $n = 5$ (a 4-digit addition in balanced quinary).

carries:	1	0	0	0
augend:	(2)	(2)	0	(−1)
addend:	(−1)	(1)	(−2)	(1)
sum:	2	(−2)	(−2)	0

There are mixed radix positional number systems in which the marker positions do *not* represent consecutive powers of a fixed base. A well-known example is the factorial number system discussed in Chapter 6. Mixed radix systems are used in the measuring of length, time, mass and various other quantities. (See pp 175–6 in Knuth (1969) and pp 173–4 in Scott (1985).)

2.7   Congruence modulo n

The concept of congruence modulo n is important in mathematics and computer science. There are connections with the previous section, as shown below.

Definition 2.12.   Let n be a fixed integer ≥ 2. Integers b, c are said to be congruent modulo n, written $b \equiv c \pmod{n}$, provided that $b - c$ is divisible by n—in other words, n divides $b - c$ with 0 remainder. It is said that b is congruent to c modulo n. When n, the modulus of the congruence, is understood, b, c are called congruent numbers.

Some basic properties follow from Definition 2.12.

Lemma 2.13.
   (i)   For any fixed integer s and each integer b, there is exactly one integer c in the integer set $\{s, s + 1, \ldots, s + n - 1\}$ such that $b \equiv c \pmod{n}$.
   (ii)   For each integer b, $b \equiv b \pmod{n}$.
   (iii) $b \equiv c \pmod{n}$ implies $c \equiv b \pmod{n}$.
   (iv) $b \equiv c \pmod{n}$ and $c \equiv d \pmod{n}$ implies $b \equiv d \pmod{n}$.
   (v)   If $b \equiv c \pmod{n}$ and $d \equiv e \pmod{n}$, then $b + d \equiv c + e \pmod{n}$.
   (vi)   If $b \equiv c \pmod{n}$ and $d \equiv e \pmod{n}$, then $bd \equiv ce \pmod{n}$.
Some proofs of these properties are left for exercises at the end of this chapter.

Example 2.13.   In Lemma 2.13(i) let $n = 3$ and $s = -1$. The integer set is $\{-1, 0, 1\}$. It is clear that each member of this set is in exactly one of the three rows below.

$$\ldots, -6, -3, \quad 0, 3, 6, \ldots$$
$$\ldots, -7, -4, \quad -1, 2, 5, \ldots$$
$$\ldots, -5, -2, \quad 1, 4, 7, \ldots$$

Each integer b is in exactly one of these rows. But each number in the first row is congruent to $c = 0$, each number in the second row is congruent to $c = -1$, and each number in the third row is congruent to $c = 1$.

Example 2.14. In Lemma 2.13(i) let $n = 2$, $s = 0$. The integer set is $\{0, 1\}$. If b is even, then b is congruent to $c = 0$. If b is odd, then b is congruent to $c = 1$.

Example 2.15. To illustrate Lemma 2.13(iv),
$-14 \equiv 56 \pmod{10}$ and $56 \equiv 26 \pmod{10}$ imply $-14 \equiv 26 \pmod{10}$.

Example 2.16. To illustrate Lemma 2.13(v),
$-1 \equiv 27 \pmod 4$ and $-3 \equiv 5 \pmod 4$ imply $-4 \equiv 32 \pmod 4$.

Example 2.17. To illustrate Lemma 2.13(vi),
$-1 \equiv 5 \pmod 3$ and $-5 \equiv 7 \pmod 3$ imply $5 \equiv 35 \pmod 3$.

Given n and an integer set determined by s as occurs in Lemma 2.13(i), the following definitions determine certain sums and products which are members of this set.

Definition 2.14. Let d, e be integers in the integer set $\{s, s + 1, \ldots, s + n - 1\}$. Then $d \oplus e$, the circle-sum of d, e, is the integer in this set which is congruent to the sum $d + e$ modulo n.

Definition 2.15. Let d, e be integers in the integer set $\{s, s + 1, \ldots, s + n - 1\}$. Then $d \otimes e$, the circle-product of d, e, is the integer in this set which is congruent to the product $(d)(e)$ modulo n.

Example 2.18. Consider $n = 10$ and $s = 0$. By Definition 2.14, $7 \oplus 9$ is 6, as $7 + 9 = 16$ and $6 \equiv 16 \pmod{10}$. By Definition 2.15, $7 \otimes 9$ is 3, as $7 \times 9 = 63$ and $3 \equiv 63 \pmod{10}$.

Example 2.19. Consider $n = 4$ and $s = 0$. By Definition 2.14, $2 \oplus 3$ is 1, as $2 + 3 = 5$ and $1 \equiv 5 \pmod 4$. By Definition 2.15, $2 \otimes 3$ is 2, as $2 \times 3 = 6$ and $2 \equiv 6 \pmod 4$.

Example 2.20. Consider $n = 5$ and $s = -2$, so that the integer set in Definitions 2.14 and 2.15 is $\{-2, -1, 0, 1, 2\}$. By Definition 2.14, $2 \oplus (-2)$ is 0 as $2 + (-2) = 0$. By Definition 2.15, $2 \otimes (-2)$ is 1, as $2 \times (-2) = -4$ and $1 \equiv -4 \pmod 5$.

It is possible to construct exhaustive tables which include Examples 2.18–2.20 above. Corresponding to the presentation in the previous section, tables are given for the following cases.

n	Integer set	s
10	$\{0, 1, 2, 3, 4, 5, 6, 7, 8, 9\}$	0
2	$\{0, 1\}$	0
3	$\{0, 1, 2\}$	0
3	$\{-1, 0, 1\}$	-1
4	$\{0, 1, 2, 3\}$	0
5	$\{-2, -1, 0, 1, 2\}$	-2

$$d \oplus e$$

d \ e	0	1	2	3	4	5	6	7	8	9
0	0	1	2	3	4	5	6	7	8	9
1	1	2	3	4	5	6	7	8	9	0
2	2	3	4	5	6	7	8	9	0	1
3	3	4	5	6	7	8	9	0	1	2
4	4	5	6	7	8	9	0	1	2	3
5	5	6	7	8	9	0	1	2	3	4
6	6	7	8	9	0	1	2	3	4	5
7	7	8	9	0	1	2	3	4	5	6
8	8	9	0	1	2	3	4	5	6	7
9	9	0	1	2	3	4	5	6	7	8

$$d \otimes e$$

d \ e	0	1	2	3	4	5	6	7	8	9
0	0	0	0	0	0	0	0	0	0	0
1	0	1	2	3	4	5	6	7	8	9
2	0	2	4	6	8	0	2	4	6	8
3	0	3	6	9	2	5	8	1	4	7
4	0	4	8	2	6	0	4	8	2	6
5	0	5	0	5	0	5	0	5	0	5
6	0	6	2	8	4	0	6	2	8	4
7	0	7	4	1	8	5	2	9	6	3
8	0	8	6	4	2	0	8	6	4	2
9	0	9	8	7	6	5	4	3	2	1

Figure 2.29 $\oplus$, $\otimes$ tables ($n = 10$, $s = 0$).

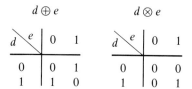

$$d \oplus e \qquad\qquad d \otimes e$$

d \ e	0	1
0	0	1
1	1	0

d \ e	0	1
0	0	0
1	0	1

Figure 2.30 $\oplus$, $\otimes$ tables ($n = 2$, $s = 0$).

Circle-sum and circle-product tables for each of these six cases may be found in figures 2.29–2.34, respectively. With respect to the circle-sum tables for these cases, the following observations may be made. Consider the additions given in the previous section. If a carry digit in column i is 0, then the sum digit in column i is the circle-sum of the augend digit a_i and the

$d \oplus e$

d \ e	0	1	2
0	0	1	2
1	1	2	0
2	2	0	1

$d \otimes e$

d \ e	0	1	2
0	0	0	0
1	0	1	2
2	0	2	1

Figure 2.31 $\oplus$, $\otimes$ tables ($n = 3$, $s = 0$).

$d \oplus e$

d \ e	−1	0	1
−1	1	−1	0
0	−1	0	1
1	0	1	−1

$d \otimes e$

d \ e	−1	0	1
−1	1	0	−1
0	0	0	0
1	−1	0	1

Figure 2.32 $\oplus$, $\otimes$ tables ($n = 3$, $s = -1$).

$d \oplus e$

d \ e	0	1	2	3
0	0	1	2	3
1	1	2	3	0
2	2	3	0	1
3	3	0	1	2

$d \otimes e$

d \ e	0	1	2	3
0	0	0	0	0
1	0	1	2	3
2	0	2	0	2
3	0	3	2	1

Figure 2.33 $\oplus$, $\otimes$ tables ($n = 4$, $s = 0$).

$d \oplus e$

d \ e	−2	−1	0	1	2
−2	1	2	−2	−1	0
−1	2	−2	−1	0	1
0	−2	−1	0	1	2
1	−1	0	1	2	−2
2	0	1	2	−2	−1

$d \otimes e$

d \ e	−2	−1	0	1	2
−2	−1	2	0	−2	1
−1	2	1	0	−1	−2
0	0	0	0	0	0
1	−2	−1	0	1	2
2	1	−2	0	2	−1

Figure 2.34 $\oplus$, $\otimes$ tables ($n = 5$, $s = -2$).

addend digit b_i. If a carry digit c_i in column i is 1, then the sum digit in column i is $(a_i \oplus b_i) \oplus 1$.

THEOREM 2.16. Every r digit number ≥ 0 is congruent modulo $n - 1$ to the sum of its digits d_i, where $0 \leq d_i \leq n - 1$, $i = 0, 1, \ldots, r - 1$, using the number representation in Definition 2.11. This may be written as follows.

$$\sum_{i=0}^{r-1} d_i n^i \equiv \sum_{i=0}^{r-1} d_i \quad (\mathrm{mod}\,(n - 1)).$$

Proof. It is obvious that $n \equiv 1 \pmod{(n - 1)}$. Hence $n^i \equiv 1 \pmod{(n - 1)}$ for all i by Lemma 2.13(vi). It follows that $d_i n^i \equiv d_i \pmod{(n - 1)}$ by Lemma 2.13(ii) and (vi) for each i. The result follows by Lemma 2.13(v) ∎

Example 2.21. To prove that decimal 38497266 is divisible by decimal 9, $r = 8$, $n = 10$, and $n - 1 = 9$ in Theorem 2.16. Note that $3 + 8 + 4 + 9 + 7 + 2 + 6 + 6 = 45$ and $45 \equiv 0 \pmod 9$. By Theorem 2.16, $38497266 \equiv 45 \pmod 9$. Hence $38497266 \equiv 0 \pmod 9$ by Lemma 2.13(iv). By Definition 2.12, decimal 38497266 is divisible by 9.

2.8   Overview

There is an intensive focus on logic tables in Rescher (1969). For a focus on switching tables see, for example, Epstein *et al* (1974). The bibliography by R G Wolf in Dunn and Epstein (1977), has over 300 entries on multiple-valued switching theory alone. Additional results on multiple-valued switching theory may be found in Muzio and Wesselkamper (1986).

Propositional calculi have been developed by various authors since the late nineteenth century. Notable references include Frege (1879) and Hilbert and Ackermann (1959). Theorem 2.4 in Section 2.5 indicates that there may be some difficulty in constructing proofs within such calculi. Alternative proof approaches may be found in Chapter 15 of Kleene (1952) and in Section 1.3 of Anderson and Belnap (1975). A multiple-valued propositional calculus is presented in Chapter 8 of this book.

Many switching applications use tables whose entries are integers. Typical number system applications use binary, ternary, balanced ternary, or quaternary number systems. Arithmetic units for such applications may include adders, subtractors, multipliers, or dividers. Further details are given in Chapter 6. Valuable historical remarks may be found in Chapter 4 of Knuth (1969).

There are a number of books which have been written on the subject of 2-valued logic design and switching theory. Of many excellent books on this subject, Lewin (1974) is written in an attractive tutorial style for students.

Winkel and Prosser (1980) and McCluskey (1986) emphasize that logic design is an art.

Exercises

E2.1 For each of the four different implications shown in figures 2.22 and 2.23, give the 27-row table for

$$(B \supset G) \supset [(A \supset B) \supset (A \supset G)].$$

Which of these four 27-row tables are tautologies?

E2.2 Prove that $D_i(N(X)) = N(D_{n-1}(X))$. Use tables for this proof, where $n \geq 2$.

E2.3 Prove that $C_i(N(X)) = C_{n-i-1}(X)$. Use tables for this proof, where $n \geq 2$.

E2.4 For $n \geq 2$, use tables to prove that

$$(X \& N(X)) \leq (Y \sqcup N(Y)).$$

E2.5 For $n \geq 2$, use tables to prove that

$$X = N(E_1 \& C_{n-2}(X)) \& N(E_2 \& C_{n-3}(X)) \& \cdots \& N(E_{n-2} \& C_1(X))$$
$$\& N(E_{n-1} \& C_0(X)).$$

E2.6 For $n \geq 2$, prove that

$$N(X) = (E_1 \& C_{n-2}(X)) \sqcup (E_2 \& C_{n-3}(X)) \sqcup \cdots \sqcup (E_{n-1} \& C_0(X)).$$

E2.7 For $n \geq 2$, use tables to prove each of the following, where $i = 0, 1, \ldots, n-1$.
(a) $C_i(X \sqcup Y) = (C_i(X) \& C_0(D_{i+1}(Y))) \sqcup (C_i(Y) \& C_0(D_{i+1}(X)))$
(b) $C_i(X \& Y) = (C_i(X) \& D_i(Y)) \sqcup (C_i(Y) \& D_i(X))$.

E2.8 Demonstrate in the intuitionist implicational calculus that $B \supset (A \supset A)$ is a provable formula.

E2.9 Demonstrate in the intuitionist implicational calculus that $(B \supset G) \supset ((A \supset B) \supset (A \supset G))$ is a provable formula.

E2.10 Using n-valued intuitionist implication for $\supset$, prove that each of the two formulas (M1), (M2) in Section 2.5 is a tautology, for any fixed $n \geq 2$.

E2.11 Using n-valued decisive implication for $\supset$, prove that each of the four formulas (C1), (C2), (C3), (C4) in Section 2.5 is a tautology, for any fixed $n \geq 2$.

E2.12   In the balanced ternary number system, is the sum of

$$(1)(-1)(-1)$$

and $$(-1)(-1)\quad(0)$$

positive or negative? Show the carries at the top as well as the sum at the bottom line. To double-check your answer, express each of $(1)(-1)(-1)$, $(-1)(-1)(0)$, and the balanced ternary sum in decimal.

E2.13   Consider the decimal addition of 419 to 382:

$$
\begin{array}{r}
110 \\
\hline
382 \\
+419 \\
\hline
801
\end{array}
$$

Here the carries are at the top line and the sum is at the bottom line.
   Repeat this example in (a) binary; (b) ternary; and (c) balanced ternary.

E2.14
(a) What is quaternary 3102 in ternary?
(b) What is ternary 1202 in binary?
(c) State an easy rule for converting between binary and quaternary numbers.

E2.15   In the ternary number system, subtract 210112 from 22001. Show the borrows at the top line and the difference at the bottom line.

E2.16   Prove property (v) of Lemma 2.13: if $b \equiv c \pmod{n}$ and $d \equiv e \pmod{n}$, then $b + d \equiv c + e \pmod{n}$.

E2.17   Prove property (vi) of Lemma 2.13: if $b \equiv c \pmod{n}$ and $d \equiv e \pmod{n}$, then $bd \equiv ce \pmod{n}$.

E2.18   Prove the following modified cancellation law: if c and n are relatively prime (i.e. c and n have no common divisors other than ± 1), then $ca \equiv cb \pmod{n}$ implies $a \equiv b \pmod{n}$.

E2.19   For every r digit number ≥ 0 as represented in Definition 2.11, where n is a fixed integer ≥ 2, using digits d_i where $0 \leq d_i \leq n - 1$, $i = 0, 1, \ldots, r - 1$, prove that

$$\sum_{i=0}^{r-1} (d_i n^i) \equiv \sum_{i=0}^{r-1} ((-1)^i d_i) \qquad (\bmod\,(n + 1)).$$

E2.20   Use the result of E2.19 to show that decimal 93514223 is divisible by decimal 11.

3 Visualizations: Venn Diagrams, Karnaugh Maps, Hasse Diagrams; from Logic Tables to Lattices

This chapter gives visualizations and corresponding basic ideas. In addition to exhibiting multiple-valued Karnaugh or *K-maps*, this chapter gives a method using these maps for simplifying n-valued functions. There is a discussion of basic concepts in partially ordered sets, lattices, and special lattices such as Heyting algebras and Kleene algebras.

This chapter begins with a discussion of certain special functions, called *fundaments*. These fundaments are basic building blocks from which any logic or switching function can be constructed. Next, visualizations are given for these fundaments through multiple-valued Venn diagrams and K-maps. For the cases where the number of variables is at most 3 or 4, these visualizations allow a convenient picturing of a function through a visual display of the fundaments. Lastly, there is a discussion of Hasse diagrams, partially ordered sets, lattices, and special lattices. While Venn diagrams and K-maps display the fundaments, Hasse diagrams display all the functions for a given number of variables. In Hasse diagrams, the fundaments occur as foundational elements. The Hasse diagram is a full picture of all the functions, but if the number of variables is large, this diagram may have so many elements that it cannot, as a practical matter, be drawn in full. Nevertheless, Hasse diagrams can be sketched very often to good advantage, and allow valuable illustrations for basic concepts in partially ordered sets and lattices. These concepts are essential for understanding Chapter 4.

3.1 The fundaments

Consider any n-valued Postian function. If there are m input columns in the corresponding logic table, there are n^m distinct rows and the output column for the function can have n different entries at each row. Hence there are n^{n^m} different possible functions. For the first example of this section, consider the 4-valued function g of 2 variables X, Y shown in figure 3.1. Here $n = 4$

X	Y	g
F	F	F
F	E_1	F
F	E_2	F
F	T	E_1
E_1	F	F
E_1	E_1	F
E_1	E_2	E_1
E_1	T	F
E_2	F	T
E_2	E_1	E_2
E_2	E_2	F
E_2	T	E_1
T	F	F
T	E_1	T
T	E_2	F
T	T	F

Figure 3.1 A 4-valued function $g(X, Y)$ and its table of 16 rows.

and $m = 2$. Note that in this example there are $4^2 = 16$ rows, so that the function g is one of 4^{16} or over 4 billion possible output functions. In particular, g has the output value E_1 three times, the value E_2 once, and the value T twice. Consequently there are $16 - 3 - 1 - 2 = 10$ rows with the output value F.

This example leads to the definition of the *fundaments* for an n-valued function of m input variables.

Definition 3.1. For an n-valued Postian function of m input variables X_1, $X_2, \ldots, X_m$, there are n^m different decisive fundaments, each being a conjunction of m terms where each term is of the form $C_i(X_j)$, where the unary operators C_i are defined in the previous chapter, $0 \leq i \leq n - 1$ and $j = 1, \ldots, m$.

Referring to the table in figure 3.1, there are 16 fundaments:

$$C_0(X) \,\&\, C_0(Y), \; C_0(X) \,\&\, C_1(Y), \; C_0(X) \,\&\, C_2(Y), \; C_0(X) \,\&\, C_3(Y),$$

$$C_1(X) \,\&\, C_0(Y), \; C_1(X) \,\&\, C_1(Y), \; C_1(X) \,\&\, C_2(Y), \; C_1(X) \,\&\, C_3(Y),$$

$$C_2(X) \,\&\, C_0(Y), \; C_2(X) \,\&\, C_1(Y), \; C_2(X) \,\&\, C_2(Y), \; C_2(X) \,\&\, C_3(Y),$$

$$C_3(X) \,\&\, C_0(Y), \; C_3(X) \,\&\, C_1(Y), \; C_3(X) \,\&\, C_2(Y), \; \text{and } C_3(X) \,\&\, C_3(Y).$$

Each of these fundaments is of the form $C_i(X) \,\&\, C_j(Y)$ where $0 \leq i, j \leq 3$. Each fundament has the property that its table shows a single T in the output column with all other entries in the output column for that fundament being F. Hence each fundament is decisive. These remarks follow from the definitions for C_i and conjunction given in the preceding chapter.

To illustrate, in the logic table of figure 3.1 there is only one row which has E_2 in the output column. The decisive fundament $C_2(X) \& C_1(Y)$ corresponds to this row in the sense that the table for this fundament has a T at this row and has F at all the other 15 rows. These decisive fundaments may be used to help construct the function g.

Consider the conjunction of the last-mentioned decisive fundament with E_2. This new conjunction $E_2 \& C_2(X) \& C_1(Y)$ is no longer a decisive function, for the entry for this new conjunction at the row in question is E_2. The entry at each of the other 15 rows for this new function is F.

A similar construction can be made for each row which has entry E_j, for each $j \geq 1$. For example, in the table of figure 3.1 there are three rows which have an E_1 output value. This yields three new conjunctions. The disjunction of these three conjunctions is

$$E_1 \& C_0(X) \& C_3(Y) \sqcup E_1 \& C_1(X) \& C_2(Y) \sqcup E_1 \& C_2(X) \& C_3(Y).$$

It is easy to verify that the logic table for this disjunction has the value E_1 at the three rows in question and the value F at each of the other 13 rows.

Continuing, there are two rows having a T output. These lead to two corresponding decisive fundaments, and their disjunction is $C_2(X) \& C_0(Y) \sqcup C_3(X) \& C_1(Y)$. This last disjunction has a logic table with T as output at the two rows in question and the output value F at the other 14 rows.

The disjunction of the three results just obtained yields the switching function g shown in the logic table of figure 3.1. This final result for g is

$$g(X, Y) = E_1 \& C_0(X) \& C_3(Y) \sqcup E_1 \& C_1(X) \& C_2(Y)$$

$$\sqcup E_1 \& C_2(X) \& C_3(Y) \sqcup E_2 \& C_2(X) \& C_1(Y)$$

$$\sqcup C_2(X) \& C_0(Y) \sqcup C_3(X) \& C_1(Y).$$

For the second example of this section, consider the 3-valued decisive function $h(X, Y)$ shown in figure 3.2. Here $n = 3$ and the number of variables

X	Y	h
F	F	F
F	E_1	F
F	T	T
E_1	F	F
E_1	E_1	F
E_1	T	F
T	F	T
T	E_1	T
T	T	T

Figure 3.2 A 3-valued decisive function $h(X, Y)$ and its table of 9 rows.

$m = 2$. For this example there are $3^2 = 9$ rows and all the 9 output values take the two values F, T. In particular, h takes the value T four times and the value F five times. Following the lines of the previous example, h may be expressed as a disjunction of four conjunctions

$$h(X, Y) = C_2(X) \& C_0(Y) \sqcup C_2(X) \& C_1(Y)$$

$$\sqcup C_2(X) \& C_2(Y) \sqcup C_0(X) \& C_2(Y).$$

While the above two examples were for a 4-valued function $g(X, Y)$ and a 3-valued function $h(X, Y)$, the same development may be followed for any n-valued Postian function of m variables. This is summarized below.   Every n-valued Postian function of m variables $X_1, X_2, \dots, X_m$ may be expressed in terms of E_k, $k = 1, \dots, n - 1$, $C_{i_j}(X_j)$, $j = 1, \dots, m$, $0 \leq i_j \leq n - 1$, as a disjunction of conjunctions, where each conjunction consists of $m + 1$ terms:

$$E_k \& C_{i_1}(X_1) \& \dots \& C_{i_m}(X_m).$$

For the case $k = n - 1$, since $E_{n-1} = \mathbf{T}$, any conjunction

$$E_{n-1} \& C_{i_1}(X_1) \& \dots \& C_{i_m}(X_m)$$

simplifies to a conjunction of m terms:

$$C_{i_1}(X_1) \& \dots \& C_{i_m}(X_m).$$

Any disjunction of conjunctions for a Postian function where each conjunction uses E_k, $C_{i_j}(X_j)$ is called a *disjunctive normal form* (dnf). In each of the two examples above, the disjunction of conjunctions in these primitive terms for g is called a *full disjunctive normal form* (fdnf) because each of the m variables occurs in each of the conjunctions. To give an example of a 3-valued function f in three variables which is in dnf but not in fdnf, consider

$$f(X_1, X_2, X_3) = (E_1 \& C_1(X_1) \& C_1(X_3)) \sqcup (C_2(X_2)).$$

Note that the variable X_2 is missing from the first conjunction. Both variables X_1, X_3 are missing from the second conjunction. The above expression for the function f is called a simplified dnf.

3.2   Venn diagrams

Venn diagrams, originated in Venn (1894) for the case $n = 2$, show the fundaments by means of regions on a two-dimensional diagram. For the case $n = 2$ using one, two, or three variables, these regions are intersections and complements of circular disks. It is not possible, however, for $n = 2$ to draw the required number of regions for four or more ·variables using circular disks alone. If m is the number of variables, then such diagrams for $n = 2$ must show 2^m different regions corresponding to 2^m different fundaments. These

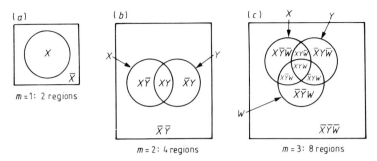

Figure 3.3 Venn diagrams for (*a*) 1, (*b*) 2, and (*c*) 3 variables (the & symbols are dropped for brevity).

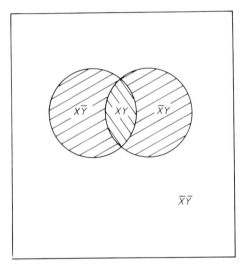

Figure 3.4 A 2-variable example for $n = 2$, where shading is used to indicate the example function.

well known diagrams for the cases $n = 2$ and $m = 1, 2, 3$ are shown in figure 3.3.

For $n = 2$ and $m = 4, 5, \ldots$ figures may be given using noncircular shapes. As m increases, these figures become increasingly complex—see Venn (1894) and Bechtel (1976). For ease of visualization in this section, the emphasis is on $m \le 3$, as shown for $n = 2$ in figure 3.3 and for $n = 3$ in figures 3.6(*a*), 3.8(*a*), and 3.11. For $n = 4$, $m \le 2$ see figures 3.6(*b*) and 3.8(*b*).

For $n = 2$ consider the function shown in figure 3.4. Three of the four regions are shaded and the fourth region is unshaded. An advantage of this diagram is its pictorial display—the three shaded regions together form a picture of the function. Observe that the four regions in this diagram each

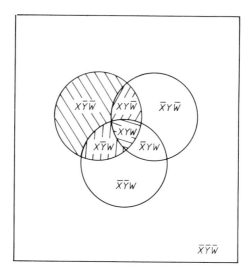

Figure 3.5   A 3-variable example for $n = 2$.

bear the name of the corresponding fundament. Note that the fourth unshaded region is $\bar{X} \,\&\, \bar{Y}$. Clearly $\bar{X} \,\&\, \bar{Y} = X \sqcup Y = X \,\&\, \bar{Y} \sqcup X \,\&\, Y \sqcup \bar{X} \,\&\, Y$.

With some practice it may be possible to recognize simplified expressions such as $X \sqcup Y$ in the above example. Unfortunately Venn diagrams have a great variety of shapes even when the number of variables is small. For three variables there are three-quarter moon shapes, full moon shapes, etc.

Consider next the case $n = 2$ for 3 variables W, X, Y. In the Venn diagram of figure 3.5 exactly 4 of the 8 regions are shaded. The pictured 2-valued function has 4 conjuncts, namely

$$X \,\&\, \bar{Y} \,\&\, \bar{W} \sqcup X \,\&\, Y \,\&\, \bar{W} \sqcup X \,\&\, \bar{Y} \,\&\, W \sqcup X \,\&\, Y \,\&\, W.$$

However, it is clear by inspection of this diagram that all four shaded regions constitute the circular disk X. This expression simplifies to the single variable X alone

$$X = X \,\&\, \bar{Y} \,\&\, \bar{W} \sqcup X \,\&\, Y \,\&\, \bar{W} \sqcup X \,\&\, \bar{Y} \,\&\, W \sqcup X \,\&\, Y \,\&\, W.$$

This simplification is made possible using a Venn diagram because of the easily recognizable full moon shape.

For $n > 2$, it is easy to depict the situation for $m = 1$, a single variable X. To motivate this situation, suppose that certain points are so close to the circle boundary in figure 3.3(a) for $m = 1$ that it is not possible to say whether such points are in the interior of the circle or in the exterior of the circle. So, for $n = 3$, an annule is introduced at the circle boundary which constitutes a third region. For $n = 4$, $m = 1$ this annule is subdivided into two contiguous regions. Thus for $n = 4$, $m = 1$ such indeterminate points fall either within

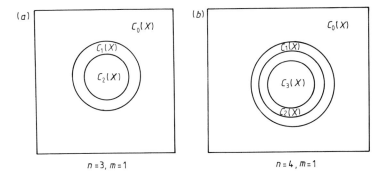

Figure 3.6 The cases (*a*) $n = 3$, $m = 1$ and (*b*) $n = 4$, $m = 1$.

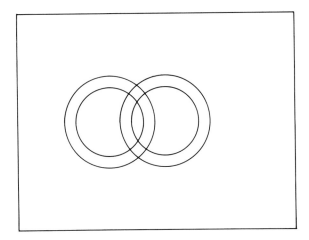

Figure 3.7 A diagram with 10 regions.

the inner annule close to the interior of the circle, or within the outer annule close to the exterior of the circle. Successive subdivisions of this kind correspond to successively higher values of *n*. The diagrams for $n = 3$, $m = 1$ and $n = 4$, $m = 1$ are shown in figure 3.6.

For the case $n = 3$, $m = 2$, nine regions are required, corresponding to the nine decisive fundaments. It turns out that the apparently reasonable diagram in figure 3.7 is not correct because it has 10 rather than the desired 9 regions.

The diagram of figure 3.7 can be modified to show exactly 9 regions. Each annule is replaced with a scythe-like annule as shown in figure 3.8. This figure illustrates the two cases $n = 3$, $m = 2$ and $n = 4$, $m = 2$. Extensions are obvious for $n \geq 4$, $m = 2$.

For $n = 3$, $m = 2$ consider the decisive function displayed by the shaded regions in figure 3.9. The four shaded regions in this figure indicate that this

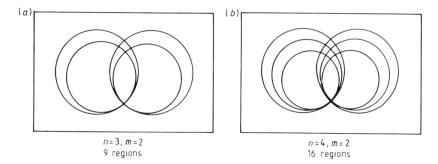

$n = 3, m = 2$
9 regions

$n = 4, m = 2$
16 regions

Figure 3.8   The cases (*a*) $n = 3$, $m = 2$ and (*b*) $n = 4$, $m = 2$.

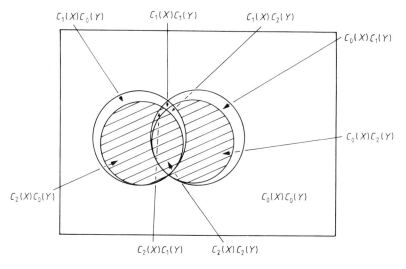

Figure 3.9   An example for $n = 3$, $m = 2$.

decisive function in fdnf is

$$C_2(X) \& C_0(Y) \sqcup C_2(X) \& C_1(Y) \sqcup C_2(X) \& C_2(Y) \sqcup C_0(X) \& C_2(Y).$$

This function corresponds with $h(X, Y)$ appearing as the second example in the previous section. That is, the Venn diagram in figure 3.9 is a pictorial representation of h. Of the four shaded regions in figure 3.9 there are three shaded regions (at the left) which constitute the interior of the disk at the left. Recall that the interior of the disk at the left is known as $C_2(X)$. Thus

$$h(X, Y) = C_2(X) \sqcup C_0(X) \& C_2(Y).$$

This dnf for h is substantially simpler than the fdnf for h given before.

The situation is more complicated for $n = 3$, $m = 3$, where 27 regions are required corresponding to the 27 decisive fundaments. Now the apparently

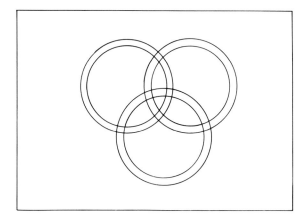

Figure 3.10 A diagram with 26 regions.

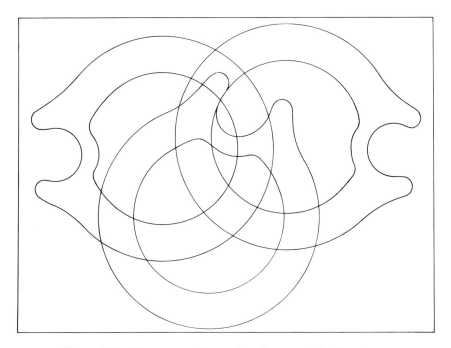

Figure 3.11 The case $n = 3$, $m = 3$; a diagram with 27 regions.

reasonable diagram in figure 3.10 is not correct because it has 26 regions rather than 27 regions; however, it can be modified to show exactly 27 regions. To accomplish this, each annule is redrawn in the shape of identical collar-bones. The exact positioning of the three collar-bones, as devised in 1980 by L Lin, is shown in figure 3.11.

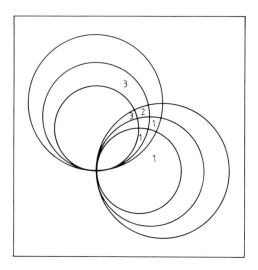

Figure 3.12 A diagram for the 4-valued function $g(X, Y)$ of Section 3.1.

For general n, m, a table has n^m rows and the corresponding Venn diagram has n^m regions, one region for each decisive fundament. Each entry of the output column in the table is selected from $0, 1, 2, \ldots, n - 1$. There are corresponding labels for each region of the Venn diagram. By convention each region in the Venn diagram which corresponds to a row with a 0 entry in the output column of the logic table is usually unmarked; that is, the 0 label in the Venn diagram is dropped. An illustration is given by the Venn diagram of figure 3.12 for the 4-valued function $g(X, Y)$ of the previous section whose table is shown in figure 3.1.

The shapes of regions in these Venn diagrams become increasingly complicated as n, m increase. Sections 3.3 and 3.4 present an n-valued map procedure based on work by Bahraini and Epstein (1988) for $n = 3$ which extends work in Veitch (1952) and Karnaugh (1953) for the case $n = 2$.

3.3   K-maps

The K-map and procedure for the simplification of n-valued functions consist of:

(i) a redrawing of Venn diagrams which uses regular square-shaped cells throughout and allows a picturing of any number of variables up to $m = 4$;

(ii) a procedure for systematically simplifying functions shown on these maps using certain player shapes.

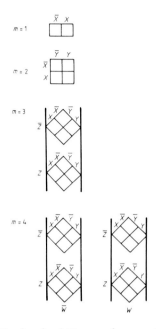

Figure 3.13   2-valued K-maps for $m = 1, 2, 3, 4$.

This section treats (i) above, giving n-valued maps for 1 to 4 variables, $1 \leq m \leq 4$, where $n = 2, 3, \ldots$. Section 3.4 gives the procedure mentioned in (ii) above, with various examples.

2-valued, 3-valued, and 4-valued K-maps for 1 to 4 variables are shown in figures 3.13–3.15, respectively. Given m variables, the extension of these figures for the n-valued case where $n \geq 4$ is obvious—the K-maps for n-valued functions are just n^m hypercubes. Readers with previous experience in 2-valued Karnaugh maps will note that the 2-valued three-dimensional map of $2 \times 2 \times 2 = 8$ cells for $m = 3$ of figure 3.13 is commonly used in a variant two-dimensional form of $2 \times 4 = 8$ cells, and the 2-valued four-dimensional map of $2 \times 2 \times 2 \times 2 = 16$ cells for $m = 4$ used in figure 3.13 is commonly used in a variant two-dimensional form of $4 \times 4 = 16$ cells.

While the picturing of an n-valued function on a Karnaugh map is just a redrawing of the corresponding table or Venn diagram having n^m rows or regions, respectively, it is worthwhile to give another example. Figure 3.16 gives a 4×4 K-map for a 4-valued function $f(X, Y)$. As usual, 0 entries are omitted from the ten unmarked cells; there are four cells marked with 2 entries; there is one cell marked with a 3 entry; there is one cell marked with a 1 entry. A k entry at the intersection of row $C_i(X)$ and column $C_j(Y)$ corresponds with the conjunction $E_k \, \& \, C_i(X) \, \& \, C_j(Y)$ in the fdnf of the

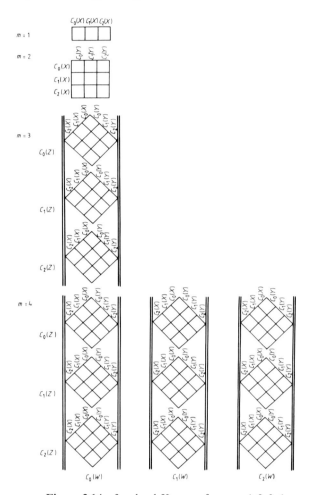

Figure 3.14   3-valued K-maps for $m = 1, 2, 3, 4$.

function at hand. Accordingly the fdnf for the function in figure 3.16 is

$$f(X, Y) = E_2 \& C_1(X) \& C_0(Y) \sqcup E_2 \& C_1(X) \& C_1(Y) \sqcup E_2 \& C_1(X) \& C_2(Y)$$

$$\sqcup E_2 \& C_1(X) \& C_3(Y) \sqcup E_1 \& C_3(X) \& C_0(Y) \sqcup C_3(X) \& C_2(Y).$$

It is instructive to display this function as a corresponding Venn diagram of 16 regions. The result is figure 3.17. It is clear from this figure that the four regions marked with a 2-entry constitute the entire inner scythe-like annule known as $C_1(X)$. Hence it becomes clear that the 4-valued function under discussion has the simplified dnf

$$f(X, Y) = E_2 \& C_1(X) \sqcup E_1 \& C_3(X) \& C_0(Y) \sqcup C_3(X) \& C_2(Y).$$

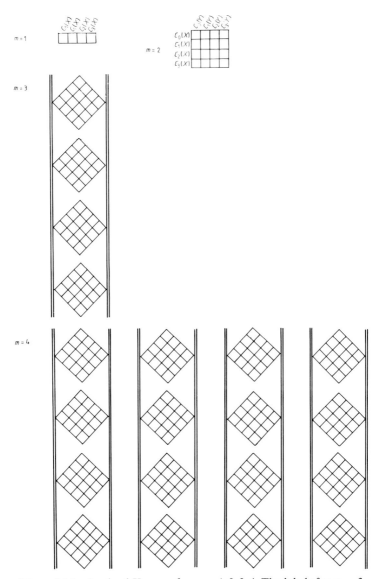

Figure 3.15 4-valued K-maps for $m = 1, 2, 3, 4$. The labels for $m = 3$ and $m = 4$ (omitted here for simplicity) proceed in a way analogous to the labels for $m = 3$ and $m = 4$ in figure 3.14 ($n = 3$, the 3-valued case).

The next section gives a systematic procedure for obtaining simplified dnf's pictorially through the use of K-maps. For brevity, the operation & is dropped, with A&B written as AB. It is understood that a disjunction of conjunctions is implemented by 2-level AND–OR gating. The conjunctions are

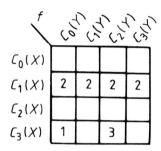

Figure 3.16   A 4-valued K-map for $f(X, Y)$.

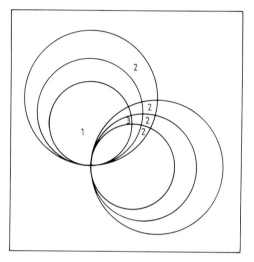

Figure 3.17   The 4-valued function of figure 3.16 shown on a Venn diagram.

performed first and provide AND-gate inputs to an OR-gate. The implementation of the dnf for $f(X, Y)$ above is:

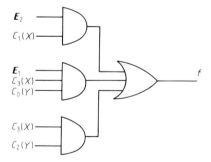

3.4 Karnaugh simplification

This section presents a procedure for simplifying n-valued functions of m variables. In the discussion which follows, $n \leq 4$ and $m \leq 3$. The K-maps used for the method of this section were introduced in Section 3.3.

The simplification procedure
The format for the procedure given below consists of: INPUT, CONSTANTS, OUTPUT, and METHOD.

INPUT. The input is an n-valued function f of m variables in fdnf represented on an n^m K-map each of whose n^m cells is marked with an entry selected from $0, 1, 2, \ldots, n - 1$. For convenience, each 0 entry is dropped.

CONSTANTS. There are two kinds of constants used in this procedure.

(1) *Primitive terms.* The primitive terms are the terms from which a function can be built using the operations of conjunction and disjunction. That is, each conjunction of a dnf is a conjunction of one or more primitive terms. While different sets of primitive terms may be used for different applications, the discussion in subsections 3.4.1–3.4.3 uses the primitive terms $C_i(X_j)$, E_i, X_j, and $N(X_j)$, where $i = 0, 1, \ldots, n - 1$ and $j = 1, \ldots, m$. This set of primitive terms is larger than the set of primitive terms used in Section 3.3 but is ideally suited with respect to geometric properties. The primitive set of Section 3.1, $C_i(X_j)$, E_i where $i = 0, 1, \ldots, n - 1$ and $j = 1, \ldots, m$, is contained in every set of primitive terms considered in this section.

(2) *Conjunctive-i-players.* A conjunctive-i-player is a shape (like a transparent paper-thin 2×1 domino or 3×1 triomino) which may be placed on a K-map, and whose placement corresponds to a name which is a conjunction (or conjunct) of i different primitive terms, for fixed $i \geq 1$. By definition, each conjunctive-1-player may be placed on a K-map with its name corresponding to some primitive term. Different placements of a conjunctive-i-player on a K-map generate different names, each of which is a conjunct of i different primitive terms. Finally, each conjunctive-i-player which is placed on a K-map can be represented mathematically as an array P.

OUTPUT. The output is a set of simplified dnf's, each of which has a minimum number of conjuncts (corresponding to different conjunctive-i-players placed upon the K-map) and each of which has a minimum number of total primitive terms over all the conjuncts of the dnf.

METHOD.

(1) *Preliminaries.* Let an n-valued function f of m variables be represented on an n^m K-map and corresponding n^m array M. For a conjunctive-i-player to be placed on such a K-map, it is required that $P \leq M$—that is,

the entry at each cell of P must be less than or equal to the entry at each corresponding cell of M. Let a conjunctive-i-player be placed on the K-map. If at one nonzero cell of M the entry at that cell is equal to the entry of the corresponding cell of P, then the conjunctive-i-player is said to *touch* f at that cell. Whenever a conjunctive-i-player is placed on a K-map, a check ($\checkmark$) is entered at each touched cell which does not already have a check. All nonzero cells on the K-map which are not checked are called *untouched cells*. Consider a K-map of f with a certain number of untouched cells. For fixed i, let a conjunctive-i-player be placed on this K-map such that the number of untouched cells which are touched by the placement of this conjunctive-i-player is a maximum over all possible placements of conjunctive-i-players on this map. Such a conjunctive-i-player and its placement on the K-map is said to *maximally touch* the function f.

Lastly, suppose that a subset of conjunctive-i-players has been placed upon a K-map, touching a certain number of cells. If one of these players can be removed such that the remaining players touch the same number of cells, then the removed conjunctive-i-player is called a *redundant* conjunctive-i-player.

(2) *Part I of the K method.* For a given function pictured on a K-map, initially all nonzero cells of the map are untouched.
  (i)   Using conjunctive-1-players, make all possible placements on the K-map using all possible maximally touching players. At each placement check the touched cells. Repeat until done.
  (ii) Using conjunctive-2-players, make all possible placements on the K-map using all possible maximally touching players. At each placement check the touched cells. Repeat until done.
  (iii) Continue the above steps for conjunctive-3-players, conjunctive-4-players, etc, until all nonzero cells are touched.

(3) *Part II of the K method.*
  (i)   Part I of this method generates various sets of conjunctive players. Each set of conjunctive players touches all the nonzero cells of the function shown on the K-map. However, these sets do not have to be distinct. It is an easy matter to reduce these sets to distinct sets. Each of these distinct sets yields a dnf which is equal to the given function f displayed on the K-map.
  (ii) Remove all redundant players from each of these distinct sets.
  (iii) Find the simplified dnf's which result after applying the above step.
  (iv) If there are cost preferences, select those dnf's from the above step which satisfy these cost preferences.

3.4.1 The case $n = 3$, $m = 2$

The conjunctive-i-players for this case are given in table 3.1 below. The player

1	1	1
1	1	1
1	1	1

called E_1, has one and only one position on the 3×3 K-map. Further, the player which contains 2s only, called E_2, is used solely for tautology, and the player which contains 0s only, called E_0, is used solely for contradiction. Each of these has only one position on the 3×3 K-map, but are not shown in table 3.1.

Conjunctive-i-players consist of conjunctions of i terms. In the case $n = 3$, $m = 2$, any conjunction of 4 or more terms reduces to a conjunction of 3 terms at most. For example, $E_1 X Y N(X)$ is a conjunction of 4 terms which reduces to $E_1 C_1(X) Y$. The examples below demonstrate the K method for $n = 3$, $m = 2$.

Example 3.1. Beginning with Part I of the K method, the K-map for $h_1(X, Y)$ is

h_1	$C_0(Y)$	$C_1(Y)$	$C_2(Y)$
$C_0(X)$	1	2	
$C_1(X)$	1	1	
$C_2(X)$	2		

I(i) No conjunctive-1-players touch the function on this K-map.
I(ii) The conjunctive-2-player

0	1	2
0	1	1
0	0	0

maximally touches the function on this K-map at 4 cells, as shown below.

$1^{\vee}$	$2^{\vee}$	
$1^{\vee}$	$1^{\vee}$	
2		

The name for this placement is $N(X)Y$.

There are two different conjunctive-2-players which touch the remaining

Table 3.1 Conjunctive-i-players for $n = 3$, $m = 2$.

Player	Number of positions and names	Example of K-map

Conjunctive-1-players

1	1	1
1	1	1
1	1	1

1 possible position:
E_1

	$C_0(Y)$	$C_1(Y)$	$C_2(Y)$
$C_0(X)$	1	1	1
$C_1(X)$	1	1	1
$C_2(X)$	1	1	1

E_1

0	0	0
1	1	1
2	2	2

4 possible positions:
$X, Y, N(X), N(Y)$

	$C_0(Y)$	$C_1(Y)$	$C_2(Y)$
$C_0(X)$	0	0	0
$C_1(X)$	1	1	1
$C_2(X)$	2	2	2

X

2	2	2

6 possible positions:
$C_i(X), C_j(Y)$
$(i, j = 0, 1, 2)$

	$C_0(Y)$	$C_1(Y)$	$C_2(Y)$
$C_0(X)$	0	0	0
$C_1(X)$	2	2	2
$C_2(X)$	0	0	0

$C_1(X)$

Conjunctive-2-players

0	0	0
1	1	1
1	1	1

4 possible positions:
$E_1 X, E_1 Y, E_1 N(X), E_1 N(Y)$

	$C_0(Y)$	$C_1(Y)$	$C_2(Y)$
$C_0(X)$	0	0	0
$C_1(X)$	1	1	1
$C_2(X)$	1	1	1

$E_1(X)$

1	1	1

6 possible positions:
$E_1 C_i(X), E_1 C_j(Y)$
$(i, j = 0, 1, 2)$

	$C_0(Y)$	$C_1(Y)$	$C_2(Y)$
$C_0(X)$	0	0	0
$C_1(X)$	0	0	0
$C_2(X)$	1	1	1

$E_1 C_2(X)$

0	0	0
0	1	1
0	1	2

4 possible positions:
$XY, XN(X), N(X)Y, N(X)N(Y)$

	$C_0(Y)$	$C_1(Y)$	$C_2(Y)$
$C_0(X)$	0	0	0
$C_1(X)$	0	1	1
$C_2(X)$	0	1	2

XY

continued

Table 3.1 *Continued.*

Player	Number of positions and names	Example of K-map

| 0 1 2 | 12 possible positions:
$C_i(X)N(Y)$, $XC_i(Y)$, $C_i(X)Y$,
$N(X)C_i(Y)$ $(i, j = 0, 1, 2)$ | $XC_1(Y)$ |

K-map for row 1:

X \ Y	$C_0(Y)$	$C_1(Y)$	$C_2(Y)$
$C_0(X)$	0	0	0
$C_1(X)$	0	1	0
$C_2(X)$	0	2	0

| 2 | 9 possible positions:
$C_i(X)C_j(Y)$
$(i, j = 0, 1, 2)$ | $C_1(X)C_2(Y)$ |

X \ Y	$C_0(Y)$	$C_1(Y)$	$C_2(Y)$
$C_0(X)$	0	0	0
$C_1(X)$	0	0	2
$C_2(X)$	0	0	0

Conjunctive-3-players

| 0 0 0 / 0 1 1 / 0 1 1 | 4 possible positions:
E_1XY, $E_1XN(Y)$, $E_1N(X)Y$,
$E_1N(X)N(Y)$ | E_1XY |

X \ Y	$C_0(Y)$	$C_1(Y)$	$C_2(Y)$
$C_0(X)$	0	0	0
$C_1(X)$	0	1	1
$C_2(X)$	0	1	1

| 0 1 1 | 12 possible positions:
$E_1C_i(Y)$, $E_1C_i(X)Y$,
$E_1N(X)C_i(Y)$, $E_1C_i(X)N(Y)$
$(i, j = 0, 1, 2)$ | $E_1XC_2(Y)$ |

X \ Y	$C_0(Y)$	$C_1(Y)$	$C_2(Y)$
$C_0(X)$	0	0	0
$C_1(X)$	0	0	1
$C_2(X)$	0	0	1

| 1 | 9 possible positions:
$E_1C_i(X)C_j(Y)$
$(i, j = 0, 1, 2)$ | $E_1C_2(X)C_1(Y)$ |

X \ Y	$C_0(Y)$	$C_1(Y)$	$C_2(Y)$
$C_0(X)$	0	0	0
$C_1(X)$	0	0	0
$C_2(X)$	0	1	0

untouched cell. The first is the shape

0
1
2

with name $XC_1(Y)$; the second is

2

with name $C_2(X)C_1(Y)$. Part I is now complete, as all nonzero cells are touched.

Part II now follows.

II(i)   The distinct sets are $\{N(X)Y, XC_1(Y)\}$ and $\{N(X)Y, C_2(X)C_1(Y)\}$.

II(ii)   There are no redundant players.

II(iii) There are two distinct answers: $h_1 = N(X)Y \sqcup XC_1(Y)$ and $h_1 = N(X)Y \sqcup C_2(X)C_1(Y)$.

II(iv) If X is preferred with respect to cost over $C_2(X)$ (as the latter requires the cost of a unary operation but the former does not), then the preferred cost answer is $h_1 = N(X)Y \sqcup XC_1(Y)$.

Example 3.2.   The K-map for $h_2(X, Y)$ is

	$C_0(Y)$	$C_1(Y)$	$C_2(Y)$
$C_0(X)$	2	1	
$C_1(X)$		1	2
$C_2(X)$	2	1	

I(i) No conjunctive-1-players touch the function on this K-map.

I(ii) The conjunctive-2-player

1
1
1

maximally touches the function on this K-map at three cells, as shown below.

2	$1^\vee$	
	$1^\vee$	2
2	$1^\vee$	

The name for this placement is $E_1C_1(Y)$.

The three remaining untouched cells may be treated in any order. There are two possibilities for each of these cells, namely

| 0 | 1 | 2 | or | 2 |

The names for the placements will be given in Part II below.

This completes Part I as all nonzero cells are now touched.

II(i) The 8 distinct sets are:

$$\{E_1C_1(Y), C_0(X)N(Y), C_1(X)Y, C_2(X)N(Y)\}$$
$$\{E_1C_1(Y), C_0(X)N(Y), C_1(X)Y, C_2(X)C_0(Y)\}$$
$$\{E_1C_1(Y), C_0(X)N(Y), C_1(X)C_2(Y), C_2(X)N(Y)\}$$
$$\{E_1C_1(Y), C_0(X)N(Y), C_1(X)C_2(Y), C_2(X)C_0(Y)\}$$
$$\{E_1C_1(Y), C_0(X)C_0(Y), C_1(X)Y, C_2(X)N(Y)\}$$
$$\{E_1C_1(Y), C_0(X)C_0(Y), C_1(X)Y, C_2(X)C_0(Y)\}$$
$$\{E_1C_1(Y), C_0(X)C_0(Y), C_1(X)C_2(Y), C_2(X)N(Y)\}$$
$$\{E_1C_1(Y), C_0(X)C_0(Y), C_1(X)C_2(Y), C_2(X)C_0(Y)\}.$$

II(ii) There are no redundant players in seven of these eight sets. However, $E_1C_1(Y)$ is a redundant player in the first of these eight sets, and the removal of this redundant player from the first set above yields

$$\{C_0(X)N(Y), C_1(X)Y, C_2(X)N(Y)\}.$$

II(iii) The single answer is

$$h_2 = C_0(X)N(Y) \sqcup C_1(X)Y \sqcup C_2(X)N(Y).$$

3.4.2 The case $n = 3$, $m = 3$

The conjunctive-i-players for this case are given in table 3.2 below. As can be seen, E_1 is obtained by placing the player shown on the $3 \times 3 \times 3$ K-map in its one position. (The $3 \times 3 \times 3$ K-map is shown in Section 3.3.) Note again that the player which contains only 2s, called E_2, is used only for tautology, and the player containing only 0s, called E_0, is used only for contradiction.

Recall that a conjunctive-i-player represents a conjunct of i terms. In this case any conjunction of five or more terms is reducible to a conjunction of four terms at most.

The K method is applied below to a 3-valued function of 3 variables.

Table 3.2   Conjunctive-i-players for $n = 3$, $m = 3$.

Player	Number of positions and names

Conjunctive-1-players

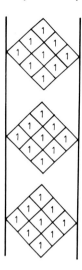

1 possible position:
E_1

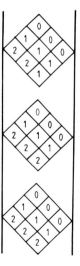

6 possible positions:
$X, Y, Z, N(X), N(Y), N(Z)$

9 possible positions:
$C_i(X), C_j(Y), C_k(Z)$
$(i, j, k = 0, 1, 2)$

continued

Table 3.2 *Continued.*

Player	Number of positions and names
Conjunctive-2-players	

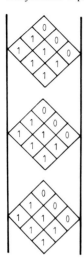

6 possible positions:
$E_1X, E_1Y, E_1Z, E_1N(X), E_1N(Y), E_1N(Z)$

9 possible positions:
$E_1C_i(X), E_1C_j(Y), E_1C_k(Z)$

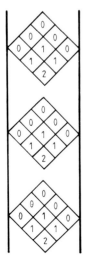

12 possible positions:
$XY, XZ, YZ, XN(Y), XN(Z), N(X)Y, N(X)Z, YN(Z),$
$N(Y)Z, N(X)N(Y), N(X)N(Z), N(Y)N(Z)$

continued

Table 3.2 *Continued.*

Player	Number of positions and names
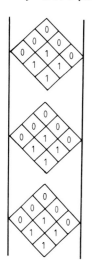	36 possible positions: $XC_i(Y)$, $XC_i(Z)$, $C_i(X)Y$, $YC_i(Z)$, $C_i(X)Z$, $C_i(Y)Z$, $C_i(X)N(Y)$, $C_i(X)N(Z)$, $N(X)C_i(Y)$, $C_i(Y)N(Z)$, $N(X)C_i(Z)$, $N(Y)C_i(Z)$ $(i = 0, 1, 2)$
	27 possible positions: $C_i(X)C_j(Y)$, $C_i(X)C_j(Z)$, $C_i(Y)C_j(Z)$ $(i, j = 0, 1, 2)$

Conjunctive-3-players

	12 possible positions: E_1XY, E_1XZ, E_1YZ, $E_1XN(Y)$, $E_1XN(Z)$, $E_1N(X)Y$, $E_1YN(Z)$, $E_1N(X)Z$, $E_1N(Y)Z$, $E_1N(X)N(Y)$, $E_1N(X)N(Z)$, $E_1N(Y)N(Z)$

| | 36 possible positions:
$E_1XC_i(Y)$, $E_1XC_i(Z)$, $E_1C_i(X)Y$, $E_1YC_i(Z)$, $E_1C_i(X)Z$,
$E_1C_i(Y)Z$, $E_1C_i(X)N(Y)$, $E_1C_i(X)N(Z)$, $E_1C_i(Y)N(Z)$,
$E_1N(X)C_i(Z)$, $E_1N(Y)C_i(Z)$, $E_1N(X)C_i(Y)$ $(i = 0, 1, 2)$ |

| | 27 possible positions:
$E_1C_i(X)C_j(Y)$, $E_1C_i(X)C_j(Z)$, $E_1C_i(Y)C_j(Z)$
$(i, j = 0, 1, 2)$ |

continued

Table 3.2 *Continued.*

Player	Number of positions and names

8 possible positions:
XYZ, $XYN(Z)$, $XN(Y)N(Z)$, $XN(Y)Z$, $N(X)YZ$,
$N(X)YN(Z)$, $N(X)N(Y)Z$, $N(X)N(Y)N(Z)$

36 possible positions:
$XYC_i(Z)$, $XC_i(Y)Z$, $C_i(X)YZ$, $XN(Y)C_i(Z)$,
$XC_i(Y)N(Z)$, $N(X)YC_i(Z)$, $C_i(X)YN(Z)$,
$N(X)C_i(Y)Z$, $C_i(X)N(Y)Z$, $N(X)N(Y)C_i(Z)$,
$N(X)C_i(Y)N(Z)$, $C_i(X)N(Y)N(Z)$ ($i = 0, 1, 2$)

54 possible positions:
$C_i(X)C_j(Y)Z$, $XC_i(Y)C_j(Z)$, $C_i(X)YC_j(Z)$,
$N(X)C_i(Y)C_j(Z)$, $C_i(X)N(Y)C_j(Z)$,
$C_i(X)C_j(Y)N(Z)$ ($i, j = 0, 1, 2$)

27 possible positions:
$C_i(X)C_j(Y)C_k(Z)$ ($i, j, k = 0, 1, 2$)

continued

Table 3.2   *Continued.*

Player	Number of positions and names

Conjunctive-4-players

8 possible positions:
E_1XYZ, $E_1XYN(Z)$, $E_1XN(Y)Z$, $E_1XN(Y)N(Z)$,
$E_1N(X)YZ$, $E_1N(X)YN(Z)$, $E_1N(X)N(Y)Z$,
$E_1N(X)N(Y)N(Z)$

36 possible positions:
$E_1XYC_i(Z)$, $E_1XC_i(Y)Z$, $E_1C_i(X)YZ$,
$E_1XN(Y)C_i(Z)$, $E_1XC_i(Y)N(Z)$, $E_1N(X)YC_i(Z)$,
$E_1C_i(X)YN(Z)$, $E_1N(X)C_i(Y)Z$, $E_1C_i(X)N(Y)Z$,
$E_1N(X)N(Y)C_i(Z)$, $E_1N(X)C_i(Y)N(Z)$,
$E_1C_i(X)N(Y)N(Z)$ $(i = 0, 1, 2)$

54 possible positions:
$E_1C_i(X)C_j(Y)Z$, $E_1C_i(X)C_j(Y)N(Z)$,
$E_1C_i(X)YC_j(Z)$, $E_1C_i(X)N(Y)C_j(Z)$,
$E_1N(X)C_i(Y)C_j(Z)$, $E_1XC_i(Y)C_j(Z)$ $(i, j = 0, 1, 2)$

27 possible positions:
$E_1C_i(X)C_j(Y)C_k(Z)$
$(i, j, k = 0, 1, 2)$

Example 3.3. The $3 \times 3 \times 3$ K-map for $r(X, Y, Z)$ is given below.

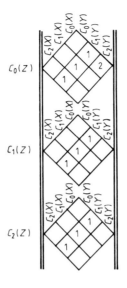

I(i) No conjunctive-1-player touches the function on this K-map.
I(ii) The conjunctive-2-player

1	1	1
1	1	1
1	1	1

maximally touches the function on this K-map, as shown below.

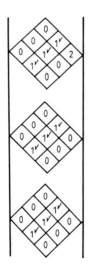

The name for this placement is $E_1 C_1(Y)$. No other conjunctive-2-player touches this function.

I(iii) There are two different conjunctive-3-players which touch the remaining untouched cell. The player

0	1	2

having the name $C_0(X) Y C_0(Z)$ accomplishes this, as does the player

2

having the name $C_0(X) C_2(Y) C_0(Z)$.

This completes Part I, as all nonzero cells are now touched.

II(i) The two distinct sets are

$$\{E_1 C_0(X) C_1(Y), C_0(X) Y C_0(Z)\} \text{ and } \{E_1 C_0(X) C_1(Y), C_0(X) C_2(Y) C_0(Z)\}.$$

II(ii) There are no redundant players in either of these sets.

II(iii) There are two answers:

$$r = E_1 C_0(X) C_1(Y) \sqcup C_0(X) Y C_0(Z)$$

and

$$r = E_1 C_0(X) C_1(Y) \sqcup C_0(X) C_2(Y) C_0(Z).$$

II(iv) If Y is preferred in cost over $C_2(Y)$, then the first of these two expressions is the preferred answer with respect to cost. In the absence of cost preferences, there are two different answers for $r(X, Y, Z)$.

3.4.3   The case $n = 4$, $m = 2$

The conjunctive-i-players for this case are given in table 3.3 below. As can be seen, E_1 is obtained by placing the player shown on the 4×4 K-map in its one position. E_2 is obtained also by placing the player on the K-map in its one position. The player which contains only 3s, called E_3, is used solely for tautology, and the player which contains only 0s, called E_0, is used solely for contradiction.

Any conjunction of primitive terms in this case $n = 4$, $m = 2$ reduces to one of the conjuncts in table 3.3.

Table 3.3 Conjunctive-*i*-players for $n = 4$, $m = 2$.

Player	Number of positions and names

Conjunctive-1-players

1	1	1	1
1	1	1	1
1	1	1	1
1	1	1	1

1 possible position:
E_1

2	2	2	2
2	2	2	2
2	2	2	2
2	2	2	2

1 possible position:
E_2

0	0	0	0
1	1	1	1
2	2	2	2
3	3	3	3

4 possible positions:
$X, Y, N(X), N(Y)$

Conjunctive-2-players

0	0	0	0
1	1	1	1
2	2	2	2
2	2	2	2

4 possible positions:
$E_2 X, E_2 Y, E_2 N(X), E_2 N(Y)$

0	0	0	0
1	1	1	1
1	1	1	1
1	1	1	1

4 possible positions:
$E_1 X, E_1 Y, E_1 N(X), E_1 N(Y)$

2	2	2	2

8 possible positions:
$E_2 C_i(X), E_2 C_j(Y)$
$(i, j = 0, 1, 2, 3)$

1	1	1	1

8 possible positions:
$E_1 C_i(X), E_1 C_i(Y)$
$(i, j = 0, 1, 2, 3)$

continued

Table 3.3 *Continued.*

Player	Number of positions and names
0 0 0 0 / 0 1 1 1 / 0 1 2 2 / 0 1 2 3	4 possible positions: $XY, XN(Y), N(X)Y, N(X)N(Y)$
0 1 2 3	16 possible positions: $C_i(X)Y, XC_j(Y), C_i(X)N(Y), N(X)C_j(Y)$ $(i, j = 0, 1, 2, 3)$
3	16 possible positions: $C_i(X)C_j(X)$ $(i, j = 0, 1, 2, 3)$
0 0 0 0 / 1 1 1 1 / 1 1 1 1 / 0 0 0 0	2 possible positions: $XN(X), YN(Y)$

Conjunctive-3-players

Player	Number of positions and names
0 0 0 0 / 0 1 1 1 / 0 1 2 2 / 0 1 2 2	4 possible positions: $E_2XY, E_2XN(Y), E_2N(X)Y,$ $E_2N(X)N(Y)$
0 0 0 0 / 0 1 1 1 / 0 1 1 1 / 0 1 1 1	4 possible positions: $E_1XY, E_1XN(Y), E_1N(X)Y,$ $E_1N(X)N(Y)$
0 1 2 2	16 possible positions: $E_2C_i(X)Y, E_2XC_j(Y), E_2N(X)C_j(Y),$ $E_2C_i(X)N(Y)$ $(i, j = 0, 1, 2, 3)$
0 1 1 1	16 possible positions: $E_1C_i(X)Y, E_1XC_j(Y), E_1N(X)C_j(Y),$ $E_1C_i(X)N(Y)$ $(i, j = 0, 1, 2, 3)$

continued

Table 3.3 *Continued.*

Player	Number of positions and names
2 (boxed)	16 possible positions: $E_2 C_i(X) C_j(Y)$ $(i, j = 0, 1, 2, 3)$
1 (boxed)	16 possible positions: $E_1 C_i(X) C_j(Y)$ $(i, j = 0, 1, 2, 3)$

0	0	0	0
0	1	1	1
0	1	1	1
0	0	0	0

4 possible positions:
$XN(X)Y, XN(X)N(Y), XYN(Y), N(X)YN(Y)$

0	0	0	0
0	1	0	0
0	1	0	0
0	0	0	0

8 possible positions:
$XN(X)C_j(Y), C_i(X)N(Y)$
$(i, j = 0, 1, 2, 3)$

Conjunctive-4-players

0	0	0	0
0	1	1	0
0	1	1	0
0	0	0	0

1 possible position:
$XN(X)YN(Y)$

Example 3.4.   The 4×4 K-map for $t(X, Y)$ is given below.

t	$C_0(Y)$	$C_1(Y)$	$C_2(Y)$	$C_3(Y)$
$C_0(X)$	3	2	1	1
$C_1(X)$	2	2	1	1
$C_2(X)$	2	2	1	1
$C_3(X)$	2	2	1	1

The K method yields the following.

I(i) The conjunctive-1-player E_1 maximally touches this function on the K-map at 8 cells, as shown below.

	$C_0(Y)$	$C_1(Y)$	$C_2(Y)$	$C_3(Y)$
$C_0(X)$	3	2	1√	1√
$C_1(X)$	2	2	1√	1√
$C_2(X)$	2	2	1√	1√
$C_3(X)$	2	2	1√	1√

No further conjunctive-1-players may be placed.
I(ii) The conjunctive-2-player $E_2 N(Y)$ maximally touches this function on the K-map at 7 additional cells, as shown below.

	$C_0(Y)$	$C_1(Y)$	$C_2(Y)$	$C_3(Y)$
$C_0(X)$	3	2√	1√	1√
$C_1(X)$	2√	2√	1√	1√
$C_2(X)$	2√	2√	1√	1√
$C_3(X)$	2√	2√	1√	1√

This leaves three alternate conjunctive-2-players each of which touches the remaining untouched cell at the upper left of the K-map: $N(X)N(Y)$, $C_0(X)N(Y)$, and $N(X)C_0(Y)$.

Part I is now complete, as all nonzero cells are touched.
II(i) The distinct sets are

$$\{E_1, E_2 N(Y), N(X)N(Y)\}$$
$$\{E_1, E_2 N(Y), C_0(X)N(Y)\}$$
$$\{E_1, E_2 N(Y), N(X)C_0(Y)\}.$$

II(ii) There are no redundant players.
II(iii) There are 3 distinct answers for $t(X, Y)$:

$$E_1 \sqcup E_2 N(Y) \sqcup N(X)N(Y)$$
$$E_1 \sqcup E_2 N(Y) \sqcup C_0(X)N(Y)$$
$$E_1 \sqcup E_2 N(Y) \sqcup N(X)C_0(Y).$$

3.4.4   Alternate sets of primitive terms

The development in subsections 3.4.1–3.4.3 uses the primitive terms $C_i(X_j)$, E_i, X_j, and $N(X_j)$, where $i = 0, 1, \ldots, n-1$ and $j = 1, \ldots, m$. These terms are well suited for the simplification procedure presented in this section.

However, other sets of primitive terms may be used, and three of these sets are described below. It will be sufficient in what follows to discuss the case $n = 3$, $m = 2$. For the purpose of contrast, the one example function throughout will be the 3-valued function $h_1(X, Y)$ of subsection 3.4.1, repeated below.

h_1	$C_0(Y)$	$C_1(Y)$	$C_2(Y)$
$C_0(X)$	1	2	
$C_1(X)$	1	1	
$C_2(X)$	2		

This function was shown in subsection 3.4.1 to have two distinct simplified dnf's

$$h_1 = N(X)Y \sqcup XC_1(Y)$$

and

$$h_1 = N(X)Y \sqcup C_2(X)C_1(Y).$$

3.4.4(a) Disallowing the operation N

If the operation N is dropped from the primitive terms used in the K method of the previous subsections, the resulting set of primitive terms is $C_i(X)$, E_i, X_j, where $i = 0, 1, \ldots, n - 1$ and $j = 1, \ldots, m$. This is the set of primitive terms discussed in Section 4 of Epstein (1960). For this set of terms, all the conjunctive-i-players of subsection 3.4.1 remain the same—it is only necessary to disallow the rotation of players so that the operation N does not appear in the simplified dnf's. The result upon application of the K method to $h_1(X, Y)$ is one simplified dnf

$$h_1 = XC_1(Y) \sqcup C_0(X)Y \sqcup E_1C_1(X)C_2(Y).$$

While this answer does not involve the operation N, it requires three conjuncts whereas each of the two previous answers for h_1 requires only two conjuncts.

3.4.4(b) A minimal set of primitive terms

If the primitive terms X_j as well as $N(X_j)$, $j = 1, \ldots, m$, are dropped from those primitive terms used in the K method of the previous subsections, the resulting set of primitive terms is $C_i(X_j)$, E_i, where $i = 0, 1, \ldots, n - 1$ and $j = 1, \ldots, m$. This is the set of primitive terms used in Section 3.1, and is commonly used in various applications. It is clear from the discussion in Section 3.1 that this set cannot be minimized further.

For this minimal set of primitive terms, all the conjunctive players in subsection 3.4.1 involving primitive terms $X, Y, N(X), N(Y)$ must be dropped. Accordingly, the conjunctive-1-player

0	0	0
1	1	1
2	2	2

is dropped, the three conjunctive-2-players

0	0	0
1	1	1
1	1	1

0	0	0
0	1	1
0	1	2

0	1	2

are dropped, and the two conjunctive-3-players

0	0	0
0	1	1
0	1	1

0	1	1

are dropped.

The result upon application of the K method to $h_1(X, Y)$ using this reduced set of conjunctive-i-players is the simplified dnf

$$h_1 = E_1 C_1(Y) \sqcup C_2(X)C_1(Y) \sqcup C_0(X)C_2(Y) \sqcup E_1 C_1(X)C_2(Y).$$

While this answer does not use $X, Y, N(X), N(Y)$ as primitive terms within any conjunct, the total number of conjuncts has increased to four.

3.4.4(c)   Adding the Allen and Givone primitive terms to the minimal set
The notation in Allen and Givone (1977) is altered somewhat to the case $n = 3$ of this subsection. The two new primitive terms are denoted here by $D_1(X) = C_1(X) \sqcup C_2(X)$ and $A_1(X) = C_0(X) \sqcup C_1(X)$. The corresponding tables are

X	$D_1(X)$	$A_1(X)$
0	0	2
1	2	2
2	2	0

The resulting set of primitive terms is $C_0(X)$, $C_1(X)$, $C_2(X)$, $C_0(Y)$, $C_1(Y)$, $C_2(Y)$, E_0, E_1, E_2, $D_1(X)$, $A_1(X)$, $D_1(Y)$, $A_1(Y)$.

The new conjunctive-1-player. $A_1(X)$, $A_1(Y)$, $D_1(X)$, $D_1(Y)$ are obtained by placing the player

2	2	2
2	2	2
0	0	0

on the K-map in 4 different positions.

The three new conjunctive-2-players. Three new conjunctive-2-players are added to those in subsection 3.4.4(b): $E_1A_1(X)$, $E_1A_1(Y)$, $E_1D_1(X)$, $E_1D_1(Y)$ are obtained by placing the player

1	1	1
1	1	1
0	0	0

on the K-map in 8 different positions.

$$A_1(X)C_i(Y), D_1(X)C_i(Y), C_i(X)A_1(Y), C_i(X)D_1(Y)\ (i = 0, 1, 2)$$

are obtained by placing the player

0	2	2

on the K-map in 12 different positions.

$$A_1(X)A_1(Y), A_1(X)D_1(Y), D_1(X)A_1(Y), D_1(X)D_1(Y)$$

are obtained by placing the player

0	0	0
0	2	2
0	2	2

on the K-map in 4 different positions.

The conjunctive-3-players coincide with the three conjunctive-3-players in subsection 3.4.1 but with changes in names using the 8 identities below.

$$E_1A_1(X)A_1(Y) = E_1N(X)N(Y)$$

$$E_1A_1(X)D_1(Y) = E_1N(X)Y$$

$$E_1 D_1(X) A_1(Y) = E_1 X N(Y)$$

$$E_1 D_1(X) D_1(Y) = E_1 X Y$$

$$E_1 D_1(X) C_i(Y) = E_1 X C_i(Y)$$

$$E_1 C_i(X) D_1(Y) = E_1 C_i(X) Y$$

$$E_1 A_1(X) C_i(Y) = E_1 N(X) C_i(Y)$$

$$E_1 C_i(X) A_1(Y) = E_1 C_i(X) N(Y).$$

Application of the K method to $h_1(X, Y)$ using this resulting set of conjunctive-i-players yields 3 simplified dnf's

$$h_1 = E_1 C_1(Y) \sqcup C_0(X) C_2(Y) \sqcup C_2(X) C_1(Y) \sqcup E_1 C_1(X) C_2(Y)$$

$$= E_1 C_1(Y) \sqcup C_0(X) C_2(Y) \sqcup C_2(X) C_1(Y) \sqcup E_1 A_1(X) D_1(Y)$$

$$= E_1 C_1(Y) \sqcup C_0(X) C_2(Y) \sqcup C_2(X) C_1(Y) \sqcup E_1 C_1(X) D_1(Y).$$

Each of these dnf's requires 4 conjunctions.

3.4.5 "Don't-cares"

In a table, Venn diagram or K-map, a "don't-care" (DC) designates an entry which can be any value chosen from $0, 1, \ldots, n - 1$. If the simplification procedure of this section is being used, the DC entries are located at certain cells of a K-map. To obtain simplified dnf's by the K method, DC entries are chosen so that the K method is optimized, with the resulting answers simplified as much as possible.

Example 3.5.　Consider the 3-valued function $p(X, Y)$ shown on the 3×3 K-map below.

p	$C_0(Y)$	$C_1(Y)$	$C_2(Y)$
$C_0(X)$	DC	2	DC
$C_1(X)$		DC	
$C_2(X)$	DC	2	DC

Here there are five don't-cares. Each of these is signified by an entry DC and each can be a value chosen from 0, 1, or 2. If the DC at the center is chosen to be 2 and the four DCs at the corners are each chosen to be 0, the map becomes

	$C_0(Y)$	$C_1(Y)$	$C_2(Y)$
$C_0(X)$		2	
$C_1(X)$		2	
$C_2(X)$		2	

The K method places one conjunctive-1-player on this K-map, then terminates. The resulting answer is $p = C_1(Y)$.

Notice that other choices for the five DCs lead to answers which are less simple than the one above. To illustrate, if the DC at the center is chosen to be 0 and the 4 DCs at the corners are each chosen to be 2, the K-map for p becomes

	$C_0(Y)$	$C_1(Y)$	$C_2(Y)$
$C_0(X)$	2	2	2
$C_1(X)$			
$C_2(X)$	2	2	2

The K method places two conjunctive-1-players on this K-map, then terminates. The resulting answer is $p = C_0(X) \sqcup C_2(X)$. For another illustration, if the five DCs are each chosen to be 0, the K-map for p becomes

	$C_0(Y)$	$C_1(Y)$	$C_2(Y)$
$C_0(X)$		2	
$C_1(X)$			
$C_2(X)$		2	

No conjunctive-1-player can be placed on this K-map. The K method places two conjunctive-2-players on this K-map, then terminates. The resulting answer is $p = C_0(X)C_1(Y) \sqcup C_2(X)C_1(Y)$.

3.5 Hasse diagrams and partially ordered sets

Definition 3.2. Consider an arbitrary collection of elements P in which there is defined an equivalence relation ($=$) and a binary relation ($\leq$). The nature of the binary relation depends on the set P and the purposes at hand. For all a, b, c in P:

(i) $a \leq a$, i.e. the relation $\leq$ is *reflexive*.
(ii) If $a \leq b$ and $b \leq a$, then $a = b$, i.e. the relation $\leq$ is *antisymmetric*.
(iii) If $a \leq b$ and $b \leq c$, then $a \leq c$, i.e. the relation $\leq$ is *transitive*.

A set P satisfying Definition 3.2 is a *partially ordered set* (poset) with respect to the binary relation $\leq$, written $(P, \leq)$, where the underlying nonempty set is P. The poset may be denoted by $\underline{P}$, or when possible by P. In a partially ordered set it is not required that $a \leq b$ or $b \leq a$ must hold for every pair of elements a, b in P. If neither $a \leq b$ nor $b \leq a$, the elements a, b are said to be *incomparable*.

As an example, consider a set of positive integers and let $a \leq b$ mean 'a is a divisor of b'. Then, (i)–(iii) of Definition 3.2 are satisfied. That is, every set of positive integers is a poset with respect to the relation 'is a divisor of'.

It is also easy to give an example of a set which is not a poset. Consider the set of all complex numbers $Z = X + iY$ where X, Y are real, and $i^2 = -1$. Then $|Z| = \sqrt{X^2 + Y^2}$. Let the relation $W \leq Z$ mean $|W| \leq |Z|$, where $\leq$ has its usual meaning of "less than or equal to". Then, Definition 3.2(i) and (iii) are each satisfied. However, from $W \leq Z$ and $Z \leq W$ it cannot be concluded that $Z = W$. For example, $|2 - i| = |1 + 2i|$ but $2 - i \neq 1 + 2i$.

In a poset P it may be the case that $a \leq b$ but $a \neq b$. In this case it is written that $a < b$. If $a < b$ and there exists no x in P such that $a < x$ and $x < b$, then it is said that b *covers* a, or a *is covered by* b.

When, along with (i)–(iii) of Definition 3.2, there is the additional property

(iv) For every pair a, b in P, $a < b$, $a = b$, or $b < a$,

then P is called a *linearly ordered set* or *chain*. Using the "less than or equal to" meaning of $\leq$, the real numbers are a familiar example of a linearly ordered set. Note that a chain has no incomparable elements.

When a finite poset P contains a reasonable number of elements, it can be represented conveniently by a Hasse diagram. The elements of P are represented as points in this diagram. If b covers a, b is drawn at a higher level than a and a is connected to b by a line. For example, consider the poset consisting of the integers 1, 2, 3, 5, 6, 10, 15, 30, which are all the positive integer divisors of 30, and let $\leq$ mean "is a divisor of". The Hasse diagram for this poset is shown in figure 3.18.

The word *under* will be used for the relation $\leq$, so that if $a \leq b$, then a is under b. The word *over* will be used for the relation $\geq$, so that if $a \geq b$, then a is over b.

A *maximal element* of a poset is an element which is under no other element of P and a *minimal element* is an element which is over no other element of P. The poset in the Hasse diagram of figure 3.19 has 2 minimal elements and 3 maximal elements.

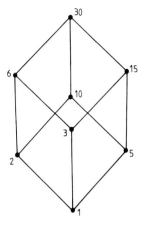

Figure 3.18   A Hasse diagram for the positive integer divisors of 30.

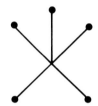

Figure 3.19   A Hasse diagram with two minimal elements and three maximal elements.

THEOREM 3.3.   A nonempty, finite poset P contains at least one maximal element and at least one minimal element.

Proof.   Let a be any element in P. If a is not a maximal element, there exists b in P such that $a < b$. If b is not a maximal element, there exists c such that $a < b$ and $b < c$. Since P is finite, this chain must eventually terminate. The last element of the chain is a maximal element since it is under no other element. A similar proof establishes the existence of at least one minimal element   ∎

Definition 3.4.   If a poset contains an element ∧ which is under every element of P, then ∧ is called the *zero element* of P, satisfying:

   (i) For all a in P, $∧ \le a.\}$ 　　　　　　　　　　　　　　　　**∧**-*property*
If a poset contains an element ∨ which is over every element of P, then ∨ is called the *unit element* of P, satisfying:
   (ii) For all a in P, $a \le ∨.\}$ 　　　　　　　　　　　　　　　　**∨**-*property*

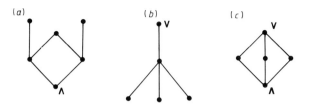

Figure 3.20   Posets with **∧** or **∨**.

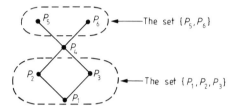

Figure 3.21 P_4 is the lub of $\{P_1, P_2, P_3\}$ and the glb of $\{P_5, P_6\}$.

THEOREM 3.5.   A poset has at most one zero element and at most one unit element.

Proof.   If z_1 and z_2 are both zero elements, then $z_1 \leq z_2$ and also $z_2 \leq z_1$. Hence, $z_1 = z_2$ by antisymmetry. Similarly if u_1 and u_2 are both unit elements, then $u_1 \leq u_2$ and also $u_2 \leq u_1$. Hence $u_1 = u_2$ by antisymmetry ■

A poset may have a zero element but no unit element as in figure 3.20(a), a unit element but no zero element as in figure 3.20(b), or both a zero element and unit element as in figure 3.20(c). In a poset with a zero element, each element which covers **∧** is called an *atom*. In a poset with a unit element, each element covered by **∨** is called an *antiatom*.

Consider a subset Q of a poset P. There may exist an element a in P such that for all b in $Q, b \leq a$. Such an element, a, is called an *upper bound* of Q.

For example, in figure 3.21 let $Q = \{P_1, P_2, P_3\}$. Then P_4, P_5, P_6 are all upper bounds of Q. The upper bound P_4 obviously has a minimal property with respect to the other upper bounds. This leads to the following definition.

Definition 3.6.   If a is an upper bound of a subset Q of a poset P and if a is under every upper bound of Q, then a is called a *least upper bound* (lub) of Q. In the example of figure 3.21 P_4 is the lub of $\{P_1, P_2, P_3\}$.

A *lower bound* of a subset Q of a poset P is defined to be an element b in P with $b \leq a$ for all a in Q. If $Q = \{P_5, P_6\}$ in figure 3.21, then P_1, P_2, P_3, P_4 are all lower bounds for this subset Q. In this example P_4 has an obvious maximal property with respect to the other lower bounds. This leads to the following definition.

Definition 3.7.   If b is a lower bound of a subset Q of a poset P and if b is over every lower bound of Q, then b is the *greatest lower bound* (glb) of Q.

Referring again to figure 3.21, the subset $\{P_1, P_2, P_3, P_4\}$ has the glb P_1 and the lub P_4. The set $\{P_4, P_5, P_6\}$ has glb P_4 but no upper bound. Note that a glb or lub of a subset Q of a poset may or may not belong to the subset.

THEOREM 3.8.   The lub or glb of a subset Q of a poset P is unique if it exists.

Proof.   If a_1 and a_2 are both lub's, then $a_1 \leq a_2$ and $a_2 \leq a_1$. Hence $a_1 = a_2$ by antisymmetry. There is a similar proof for the glb   ■

Definition 3.9.   In a poset $\underline{P}$ partially ordered by $\leq$, define the *dual* partial ordering as follows: $a \geq b$ if and only if $b \leq a$. It is easy to verify that (i)–(iii) of Definition 3.5 hold for $\geq$. The *dual* of $(P, \leq)$ is $(P, \geq)$, denoted by $\underline{P}^{\ddagger}$.

Since any theorem which is true for every partial ordering $\leq$ is true for the partial ordering $\geq$, there is the following principle of duality for posets.

THEOREM 3.10.   In every theorem about posets expressed in terms of the relation $\leq$, this relation may be replaced by $\geq$ throughout, resulting in another theorem which holds.

For example, in any poset $a \leq b$, $b \leq c$, and $c \leq a$ imply $b = c$, because $b \leq a$ and $a \leq c$ by transitivity, so $b = a$ and $a = c$ by antisymmetry. Dually by Theorem 3.10, $a \geq b$, $b \geq c$, and $c \geq a$ imply $b = c$.

3.6   Lattices and Hasse diagrams

Definition 3.11.   A *lattice* is defined to be a poset in which every pair of elements has an lub and a glb.

Example 3.6.   The 10-element poset shown below is a lattice. The pair of elements a, b in this lattice have glb (a, b) and lub (a, b) as shown below.

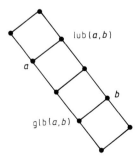

THEOREM 3.12.   In a lattice L, every finite nonempty subset has an lub and a glb.

Proof.   The theorem is true if the subset has 1 element, the element being its own glb and lub. It is also true if the subset has 2 elements, by Definition 3.11.

Suppose the theorem holds for all subsets containing $1, 2, \ldots, k$ elements, so that a subset $a_1, a_2, \ldots, a_k$ of L has a glb and an lub. If L contains more than k elements, consider the subset $\{a_1, a_2, \ldots, a_{k+1}\}$ of L. Let $w = \text{lub}\,(a_1, a_2, \ldots, a_k)$. Let $t = \text{lub}\,(w, a_{k+1})$. If s is any upper bound of $a_1, a_2, \ldots, a_{k+1}$, then s is $\geq$ each of $a_1, a_2, \ldots, a_k$ and therefore $s \geq w$. Also, $s \geq a_{k+1}$ and therefore s is an upper bound of w and a_{k+1}. Hence $s \geq t$. That is, since $t \geq$ each a_j, t is the lub of $a_1, a_2, \ldots, a_{k+1}$. The theorem follows for the lub by finite induction. If L is finite and contains m elements, the induction process stops when $k + 1 = m$.

A dual proof yields the result for the glb ∎

Definition 3.13.   In a lattice, if every nonempty subset of L has an lub and a glb then the lattice is a *complete* lattice.

The following theorem is an obvious consequence.

THEOREM 3.14.   Every finite lattice is complete.

Definition 3.15.   The symbol $\vee$, called the *join*, is defined to be $a \vee b = \text{lub}\,(a, b)$ and the symbol $\wedge$, called the *meet*, is defined to be $a \wedge b = \text{glb}\,(a, b)$. In general

$$\text{lub}\,(a_1, a_2, \ldots, a_k) = a_1 \vee a_2 \vee \cdots \vee a_k = \bigvee_{i=1}^{k} a_i$$

and

$$\text{glb}\,[a_1, a_2, \ldots, a_k] = a_1 \wedge a_2 \wedge \cdots \wedge a_k = \bigwedge_{i=1}^{k} a_i.$$

If L is finite and equal to $\{a_1, a_2, \ldots, a_m\}$, then the following two elements exist

$$\text{glb}\,(a_1, a_2, \ldots, a_m) = \wedge$$

and

$$\text{lub}\,(a_1, a_2, \ldots, a_m) = \vee.$$

The following theorem is an immediate consequence.

THEOREM 3.16. Every finite lattice $\{a_1, \ldots, a_m\}$ contains Λ and V, where

$$\Lambda = \bigwedge_{i=1}^{m} a_i \quad \text{and} \quad V = \bigvee_{i=1}^{m} a_i.$$

Some important properties of join and meet are given in the next theorem.

THEOREM 3.17. In every lattice the following identities hold.

(i) $a \vee b = b \vee a$ $\left.\right\}$ *commutativity* properties
(ii) $a \wedge b = b \wedge a$

(iii) $(a \vee b) \vee c = a \vee (b \vee c)$ $\left.\right\}$ *associativity* properties
(iv) $(a \wedge b) \wedge c = a \wedge (b \wedge c)$

(v) $a \vee a = a$ $\left.\right\}$ *idempotence* properties
(vi) $a \wedge a = a$

(vii) $(a \wedge b) \vee a = a$ $\left.\right\}$ *absorption* properties.
(viii) $(a \vee b) \wedge a = a$

Proof of (i) and (ii). These identities follow from the symmetrical nature of the definitions of $a \vee b$ and $a \wedge b$ in Definition 3.15.

Proof of (iii) and (iv). To prove (iii), let $w = \text{lub}\,((a \vee b),\, c)$ and let $s = \text{lub}\,(a, b, c)$. Then $a \vee b \leq w$ and $c \leq w$, that is $a \leq w$, $b \leq w$, $c \leq w$. Hence $s \leq w$ since s is the lub. On the other hand, $a \leq s$, $b \leq s$ and $c \leq s$. Therefore $a \vee b \leq s$, $c \leq s$. Hence $w \leq s$ since $w = \text{lub}\,(a \vee b, c)$. Thus $s = w$ by antisymmetry. Similarly, $\text{lub}\,(a, (b \vee c)) = s$, and (iii) follows. There is a dual proof for (iv).

Proof of (v) and (vi). From Definition 3.15, $a \vee a = a$ and $a \wedge a = a$.

Proof of (vii) and (viii). To prove (vii), $a \wedge b \leq a$ by Definition 3.15. Then $\text{lub}\,((a \wedge b), a) = a$ since $a \wedge b$ is under a—that is, $(a \wedge b) \vee a = a$. There is a dual proof for (viii) ∎

THEOREM 3.18. If the algebra $(L, \wedge, \vee)$, denoted by $\underline{L}$, where L is the underlying nonempty set of elements and $\vee$, $\wedge$ are binary operations, satisfies identities (i)–(viii) of Theorem 3.17 above, then $\underline{L}$ is a lattice.

Proof. It has to be shown that there is a relation $\leq$ satisfying Definition 3.2(i)–(iii), and with respect to this relation, $a \wedge b = \text{glb}\,(a, b)$ and $a \vee b = \text{lub}\,(a, b)$.

To prove the theorem,

(i) define $a \leq b$ to mean $a \vee b = b$.

Definition 3.2(i) follows because $a \vee a = a$ by idempotence.

Definition 3.2(ii) follows because $a \leq b$ and $b \leq a$ imply $a \vee b = b$ and $b \vee a = a$, so that $a = b$ by commutativity.

Definition 3.2(iii) follows because $a \leq b$ and $b \leq c$ imply $a \vee b = b$ and $b \vee c = c$. Consequently $a \vee c = a \vee (b \vee c) = (a \vee b) \vee c = b \vee c = c$ by associativity. By (i), $a \leq c$.

It remains to prove that $a \vee b = \text{lub} \ (a, b)$ and $a \wedge b = \text{glb} \ (a, b)$ with respect to $\leq$ as defined in (i) of this theorem. Note that $a \vee (a \vee b) = (a \vee a) \vee b = a \vee b$ by associativity and idempotence. Hence $a \leq a \vee b$ by (i). Similarly, $b \leq a \vee b$. Hence $a \vee b$ is an upper bound for a, b. Let c be any upper bound for a, b. Then $a \leq c$ and $b \leq c$—that is, $a \vee c = c$ and $b \vee c = c$. Hence $(a \vee b) \vee c = a \vee (b \vee c) = a \vee c = c$ by associativity, so that $a \vee b \leq c$ by (i). This completes the proof that $a \vee b$ is the lub of a, b.

At this point, it is convenient to introduce the following companion to (i) of this theorem

(ii) $a \leq b$ if and only if $a = a \wedge b$.

First, if $a = a \wedge b$, then $a \vee b = (a \wedge b) \vee b = b$ by absorption. Hence $a \leq b$ by (i).

Second, if $a \leq b$, then $a \vee b = b$ by (i), so $a \wedge b = a \wedge (a \vee b) = a$ by commutativity and absorption.

To complete the proof of Theorem 3.18, the proof of $a \wedge b = \text{glb} \ (a, b)$ is dual to the proof of $a \vee b = \text{lub} \ (a, b)$, using (ii)   ∎

Definition 3.19.   A lattice L with $\wedge$ and $\vee$ is said to be *atomic* if for each $x \neq \wedge$ in L there is some atom a_0 in L such that $a_0 \leq x$. Dually, a lattice is said to be *antiatomic* if for each $x \neq \vee$ in L there is some antiatom a_1 in L such that $x \leq a_1$.

Example 3.7.   The 6-element lattice shown below is atomic and antiatomic, with two atoms y, z and two antiatoms x, w.

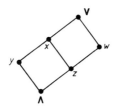

THEOREM 3.20.   Every finite lattice L is both atomic and antiatomic.

Proof.   By Theorem 3.16, L contains $\wedge$ and $\vee$. Assume that there is no atom $a_0 \leq x$. In other words, there is no element under x which covers $\wedge$. Hence x cannot be an atom, and there is some $d_1 \neq \wedge$ such that $d_1 < x$. Now d_1 cannot be an atom, so there is some $d_2 \neq \wedge$ such that $d_2 < d_1$.

Continuing, this leads to an infinite sequence of distinct elements $x, d_1, d_2, d_3, \ldots$, where $d_1 < x$ and $d_{i+1} < d_i$ for $i \geq 1$. This contradicts the fact that there are only a finite number of elements in L. By a dual argument, a contradiction would be obtained if it were assumed that there were no antiatom a_1 satisfying $x \leq a_1$ ∎

Some remarks follow on algebras, lattices, mappings, *subalgebras* and *sublattices*. A subset A_1 of an algebra A is said to be a subalgebra of A if A_1 is closed under all operations of A. Hence L_1 is a *sublattice* of a lattice L if it satisfies the following conditions

(i) L_1 is a subset of L, (ii) a, b in L_1 implies that $a \wedge b$ in L is in L_1 and $a \vee b$ in L is in L_1.

Let S be any nonempty subset of L. Then the set theoretic intersection of sublattices of L which contain S, is the least sublattice of L which contains S, called the *sublattice of L generated by S*.

If a, b are in the lattice L and $a \leq b$, then the set of elements q satisfying $a \leq q \leq b$, written $\{q: a \leq q \leq b\}$, is a sublattice of L called the *interval* $[a, b]$.

Example 3.8. Consider the 6 element lattice L shown below. The subset $\{\wedge, y, z, x\}$ yields a sublattice of L—it is the interval $[\wedge, x]$. However, the subset $\{\wedge, y, z, \vee\}$ does *not* yield a sublattice of L, for $y \vee z = x$ in L is *not* in this subset. Finally, $L_1 = \{\wedge, y, z, x, \vee\}$ *is* a sublattice of L.

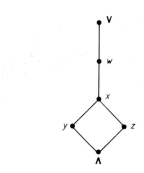

A mapping m of an algebra A_1 into a similar algebra A_2 is called a *homomorphism* provided it preserves all operations. Let A_1 and A_2 be algebras whose operations include join and meet. A mapping m from A_1 into A_2 which preserves joins and meets is called a *lattice homomorphism*. That is, a lattice homomorphism from an algebra A_1 into an algebra A_2 maps each element x in A_1 to an element $m(x)$ in A_2, such that

$$m(a \wedge b) = m(a) \wedge m(b) \text{ and } m(a \vee b) = m(a) \vee m(b) \text{ for } a, b \text{ in } A_1.$$

A homomorphism is said to be a many-to-one mapping, as different elements in A_1 may map to the same element in A_2. If a homomorphism is a one-to-one mapping from an algebra A onto a similar algebra A_0, then the mapping is called an *isomorphism*, and the algebras A, A_0 are *isomorphic*.

3.6.1   Bounded lattices

Note that a lattice with an infinite number of elements need not have a $\wedge$ or a $\vee$.

Definition 3.21.   Any lattice which has a $\wedge$ and a $\vee$ is called a *bounded lattice*.

THEOREM 3.22.   In a bounded lattice $(L, \wedge, \vee, \wedge, \vee)$ the following identities hold.

(i) $a \vee \wedge = a$ $\left.\right\}$ $\wedge$-*properties*

(ii) $a \wedge \wedge = \wedge$

(iii) $a \vee \vee = \vee$ $\left.\right\}$ $\vee$-*properties.*

(iv) $a \wedge \vee = a$

Either (i) or (ii) may be used to define the zero element, and either (iii) or (iv) may be used to define the unit element, by Theorem 3.18(i), (ii).

Proof.   This follows directly from Definition 3.4(i) and Theorem 3.18(i), (ii) on the one hand, and Definition 3.4(ii) and Theorem 3.18(i), (ii) on the other hand ∎

By Theorem 3.16 every finite lattice is a bounded lattice. The closed real interval $[0, 1]$ with the usual ordering over the reals is an example of a bounded lattice with an infinite number of elements having no atoms or antiatoms. The open real interval $(0, 1)$ with the usual ordering over the reals is an example of a lattice which is not a bounded lattice. If L is a bounded lattice, then a sublattice of L containing the $\wedge$ and $\vee$ of L is called a $\{\wedge, \vee\}$-*sublattice*.

Definition 3.23.   In a bounded lattice, if $x \wedge y = \wedge$, then x, y are called *disjoint*.

3.6.2   Distributive lattices

THEOREM 3.24.   In a lattice L the following two conditions are equivalent.

(i) $a \wedge (b \vee c) = (a \wedge b) \vee (a \wedge c)$ $\left.\right\}$ *distributivity* properties.

(ii) $a \vee (b \wedge c) = (a \vee b) \wedge (a \vee c)$

Proof. To prove that (i) implies (ii), suppose that (i) holds. Then

$$a \vee (b \wedge c) = [a \vee (a \wedge c)] \vee (b \wedge c) \qquad \text{by absorption and commutativity}$$

$$= a \vee [(a \wedge c) \vee (b \wedge c)] \qquad \text{by associativity}$$

$$= a \vee [c \wedge (a \vee b)] \qquad \text{by commutativity and the hypothesis}$$

$$= [(a \vee b) \wedge a] \vee [(a \vee b) \wedge c] \qquad \text{by absorption and commutativity}$$

$$= (a \vee b) \wedge (a \vee c) \qquad \text{by the hypothesis.}$$

There is a dual proof that (ii) implies (i) ■

Definition 3.25. A *distributive lattice* is a lattice satisfying the distributivity conditions (i) or (ii) of Theorem 3.24.

Some experience is needed to distinguish between Hasse diagrams of partially ordered sets which are not lattices and partially ordered sets which are lattices. A number of Hasse diagrams are shown in Section 3.5 which are not lattices. Each of these have two points within the diagram which either do not have an lub or do not have a glb.

Figure 3.22 shows fifteen Hasse diagrams of posets which are lattices. The first two of these fifteen lattices are key examples of two different kinds of nondistributive lattices; in each of these two examples, elements *a*, *b*, *c* are identified, with the property that the distributivity condition Theorem 3.24(i) is *not* satisfied. It can be shown that a lattice is not a distributive lattice if and only if it contains one of these two examples as a sublattice (Birkhoff 1934). Of the remaining thirteen lattices, all except the last two are distributive. Each of the last two diagrams shows one of the two example nondistributive sublattices by identifying elements *a*, *b*, *c* with the property that Theorem 3.24(i) is *not* satisfied.

3.6.3 Complemented lattices

Definition 3.26. A *complemented lattice* L is a bounded distributive lattice in which for every *a* in *L* there exists $\bar{a}$ in *L* such that

$$\left. \begin{array}{l} \text{(i)} \quad a \vee \bar{a} = \mathbf{V} \\ \text{(ii)} \quad a \wedge \bar{a} = \mathbf{\Lambda} \end{array} \right\} \quad \textit{complementarity} \text{ properties.}$$

A simple example of a complemented lattice is the lattice of all subsets of a set, partially ordered by set inclusion. A Hasse diagram of the subsets of the 3-element set $\{a, b, c\}$ is shown in figure 3.23(*a*).

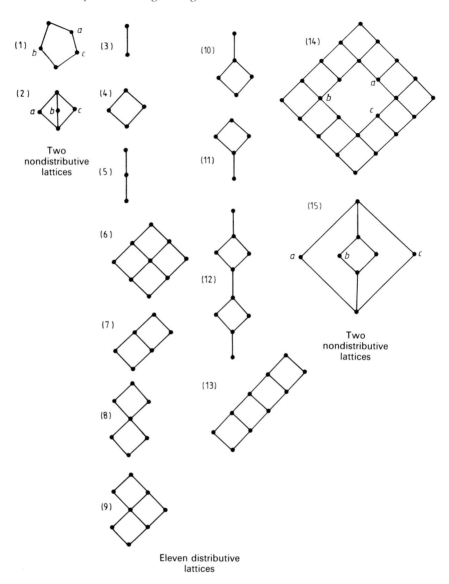

Figure 3.22   Distributive and nondistributive lattices.

Definition 3.27. In a bounded distributive lattice let a, $\bar{a}$ be elements satisfying Definition 3.26(i), (ii). The element $\bar{a}$ is called the complement of a, and each of the elements a, $\bar{a}$ is called a complemented element.

THEOREM 3.28.   In a bounded distributive lattice, let a be a complemented element. Then the complement of a is unique.

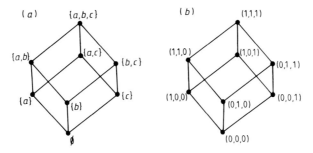

Figure 3.23 (*a*) The eight subsets of a 3-element set and (*b*) the eight 2-valued functions over a 3-point set.

Proof. Suppose there were two complements of *a*, called $\bar{a}$ and *b*. Then $a \vee \bar{a} = \mathbf{V}$ and $a \wedge \bar{a} = \mathbf{\Lambda}$; also $a \vee b = \mathbf{V}$ and $a \wedge b = \mathbf{\Lambda}$. Consequently $\bar{a} = \bar{a} \wedge \mathbf{V} = \bar{a} \wedge (a \vee b) = (\bar{a} \wedge a) \vee (\bar{a} \wedge b) = \mathbf{\Lambda} \vee (\bar{a} \wedge b) = \bar{a} \wedge b$. By a similar computation, $b = (b \wedge \bar{a})$. Thus $b = \bar{a}$ by commutativity, and the complement is unique ∎

THEOREM 3.29. In a bounded distributive lattice let *a*, *b* each be a complemented element. Then $a \vee b$ is a complemented element and $a \wedge b$ is a complemented element.

Proof. The complement of $a \vee b$ is $\bar{a} \wedge \bar{b}$, for

$$(a \vee b) \vee (\bar{a} \wedge \bar{b}) = a \vee (b \vee (\bar{a} \wedge \bar{b})) = a \vee ((b \vee \bar{a}) \wedge (b \vee \bar{b}))$$

$$= a \vee (b \vee \bar{a}) = a \vee (\bar{a} \vee b) = (a \vee \bar{a}) \vee b = \mathbf{V} \vee b = \mathbf{V}$$

and

$$(a \vee b) \wedge (\bar{a} \wedge \bar{b}) = (a \wedge \bar{a} \wedge \bar{b}) \vee (b \wedge \bar{a} \wedge \bar{b}) = \mathbf{\Lambda} \vee \mathbf{\Lambda} = \mathbf{\Lambda}.$$

A similar computation shows that the complement of $a \wedge b$ is $\bar{a} \vee \bar{b}$ ∎

The set of complemented elements of a bounded distributive lattice *L* is a sublattice of *L*, called the *center* of *L*.

An alternative naming of the eight points in the Hasse diagram of the complemented lattice in figure 3.23(*a*) should be noted. Place *a*, *b*, *c* as names of distinct consecutive points on an *x*-axis. For each subset of figure 3.23(i) there corresponds in figure 3.23(*b*) a two-valued function over these three points which takes the values 0, 1. If a point is in the given subset, then the function takes the value 1 at that point; if the point is not in the given subset, then the function takes the value 0 at that point. For example, the subset $\{a, c\}$ corresponds to the function $(1, 0, 1)$. Also, the empty set corresponds to the function $(0, 0, 0)$ and the universal set $\{a, b, c\}$ corresponds to the function $(1, 1, 1)$. These last two functions for any number of points are called the constant function of all 0s and the constant function of all 1s, respectively.

3.6.4   Lattices for *n*-valued functions

3.6.4(a)   Lattices for 2-valued functions—Boolean lattices

Definition 3.30. A *Boolean lattice* is a complemented distributive lattice. Accordingly, a Boolean lattice satisfies postulates consisting of identities as follows: Theorem 3.17(i)–(viii), Theorem 3.22(ii)–(iii), Theorem 3.24(i), and Definition 3.26(i)–(ii). If L is a bounded distributive lattice, then the center of L is a Boolean lattice denoted by B.

In subsection 3.6.3 it was shown that the 2-valued functions over 3 points form a Boolean lattice of eight elements. It is easy to extend this and show that the 2-valued functions over c points, for finite $c \geq 1$, form a Boolean lattice of 2^c elements. Hasse diagrams for 2-valued functions over 1, 2, 3, 4 points are shown in figure 3.24. In these diagrams **V** corresponds with the constant function which is all 1s and **Λ** corresponds with the constant function which is all 0s.

Figure 3.25 shows three Hasse diagrams of bounded distributive lattices which are *not* complemented lattices, hence are not Boolean lattices. In each of these three Hasse diagrams the complemented elements are circled, and the elements which are not complemented are not circled. In figures 3.25(a) and (b) each of the 5-element lattices has only two complemented elements, while the 6-element lattice in figure 3.25(c) has four complemented elements.

If the interval $[x, y]$ of a lattice is a Boolean lattice, then $[x, y]$ is called a *Boolean interval*.

3.6.4(b)   Lattices for 3-valued functions—Post lattices of order 3

A Post lattice of order 3 is a bounded distributive lattice which satisfies certain additional conditions. A discussion of these additional conditions may be found in Chapter 4. It suffices to mention here that the 3-valued function over c points, for finite $c \geq 1$, are such a lattice consisting of 3^c elements. In this case there are three constant functions: all 0s; all 1s; and all 2s.

The **Λ** of the lattice is the constant function which is all 0s. The **V** of the lattice is the constant function which is all 2s. For this 3-valued case, the complemented elements of the lattice are all those functions whose values are 0 or 2 alone. In figure 3.26, three Hasse diagrams for Post algebras of order 3 are shown using 3-valued functions over 1, 2, and 3 points. The three diagrams show lattices of 3, 9, and 27 elements, respectively.

It will be a result of Chapter 4 that any Post algebra of order n with a finite number of elements is isomorphic to the n-valued functions over c points, where $c \geq 0$, and hence must possess exactly n^c elements. The case

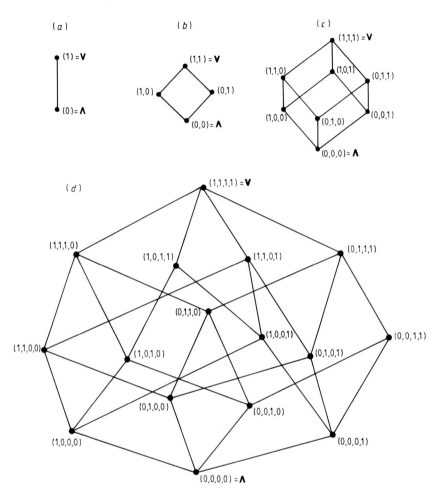

Figure 3.24 The first four nondegenerate Boolean algebras, consisting of (*a*) 2, (*b*) 4, (*c*) 8, and (*d*) 16 elements.

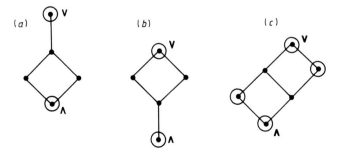

Figure 3.25 Some lattices which are not Boolean algebras. The complemented elements are circled.

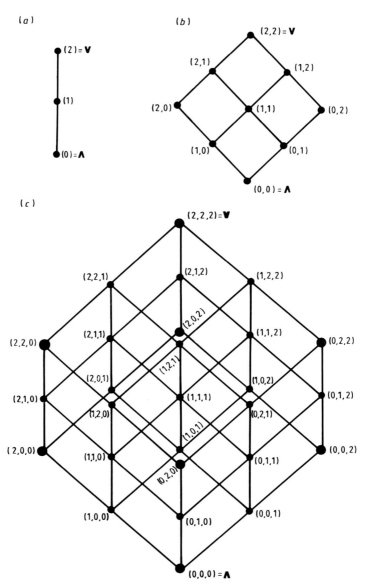

Figure 3.26   The first three nondegenerate Post algebras of order 3, consisting of 3, 9, and 27 elements.

$c = 0$ corresponds to a *degenerate Post algebra* consisting of one element in which $\Lambda = V$. In *nondegenerate Post algebras,* $\Lambda \neq V$.

The following subsections introduce a number of special lattices. These special lattices are important because they provide basic concepts and background for the development in Chapters 4 and 5.

3.6.5 Pseudo-complemented lattices

Definition 3.31. An element x of a bounded distributive lattice is said to be pseudo-complemented if there is a greatest element q satisfying $x \wedge q = \bigwedge$. This greatest such element q is denoted by $\neg x$, and is called the pseudo-complement of x. That is,

(i) $x \wedge \neg x = \bigwedge$ and
(ii) $x \wedge y = \bigwedge$ implies $y \leq \neg x$.

Definition 3.32. A bounded distributive lattice is called pseudo-complemented if every element of the lattice is pseudo-complemented.

Any distributive lattice with a finite number of elements is a pseudo-complemented lattice. Figure 3.27 shows a 5-element pseudo-complemented lattice, with some identities in this lattice.

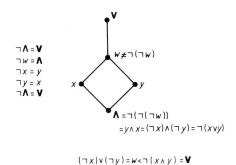

$\neg\bigwedge = \bigvee$
$\neg w = \bigwedge$
$\neg x = y$
$\neg y = x$
$\neg\bigwedge = \bigvee$

$w \neq \neg(\neg w)$

$\bigwedge = \neg(\neg(\neg w))$
$= y \wedge x = (\neg x) \wedge (\neg y) = \neg(x \vee y)$

$(\neg x) \vee (\neg y) = w < \neg(x \wedge y) = \bigvee$

Figure 3.27 A pseudo-complemented lattice of five elements.

THEOREM 3.33. In any bounded distributive lattice, if x is a complemented element, then x is pseudo-complemented with $\neg x = \bar{x}$.

Proof. First, x satisfies $x \wedge \bar{x} = \bigwedge$ by complementarity. Second, if $x \wedge q = \bigwedge$, it follows that $q \leq \bar{x}$. This is because $x \wedge q = \bigwedge$ leads to $\bar{x} \vee (x \wedge q) = \bar{x} \vee \bigwedge = \bar{x}$. But $\bar{x} \vee (x \wedge q) = (\bar{x} \vee x) \wedge (\bar{x} \vee q) = \bigvee \wedge (\bar{x} \vee q) = \bar{x} \vee q$. Thus $q \leq \bar{x}$ by Theorem 3.18(i). This completes the proof ∎

THEOREM 3.34. Some basic properties are given below.

(i) $y \leq \neg x$ implies $x \wedge y = \bigwedge$
(ii) $\neg \bigvee = \bigwedge$
(iii) $\neg \bigwedge = \bigvee$
(iv) $\neg x \wedge \neg\neg x = \bigwedge$, where $\neg\neg x$ denotes $\neg(\neg x)$
(v) $x \leq \neg\neg x$
(vi) $x \leq y$ implies $\neg y \leq \neg x$
(vii) $\neg\neg\neg y = \neg y$
(viii) $\neg x \vee \neg y \leq \neg(x \wedge y)$. *continued overleaf*

(ix) $\neg(x \vee y) = \neg x \wedge \neg y$
(x) $\neg(x \vee \neg x) = \Lambda$.

Proof of (i). $x \wedge \neg x \wedge y = \Lambda$ by Definition 3.31(i) and Λ-property, so $x \wedge y = \Lambda$ by the hypothesis and Theorem 3.18(ii).

Proof of (ii). This follows from Definition 3.31(i).

Proof of (iii). Since $\Lambda \wedge x = \Lambda$ by Λ-property, $x \leq \neg\Lambda$ by Definition 3.31(ii). That is, $\neg\Lambda = V$.

Proof of (iv). This follows by substituting $\neg y$ for x in Definition 3.31(i).

Proof of (v). This follows from Definition 3.31.

Proof of (vi). From $x \leq y$, $x = x \wedge y$ by Theorem 3.18(ii). So $x \wedge \neg y = (x \wedge y) \wedge \neg y = x \wedge \Lambda = \Lambda$ by associativity, Definition 3.31(i), and Λ-property. Hence $\neg y \leq \neg x$ by Definition 3.31(ii).

Proof of (vii). First, $\neg y \leq \neg\neg\neg y$, substituting $\neg y$ for x in (v). Second, $\neg\neg\neg y \leq \neg y$ by (v) and (vi). Hence $\neg\neg\neg y = \neg y$.

Proof of (viii). From $x \wedge y \leq x$ and $x \wedge y \leq y$, $\neg x \leq \neg(x \wedge y)$ and $\neg y \leq \neg(x \wedge y)$ by (vi). Thus $\neg(x \wedge y)$ is an upper bound of $\neg x, \neg y$, and $\neg x \vee \neg y \leq \neg(x \wedge y)$.

Proof of (ix). First,

$$(x \vee y) \wedge (\neg x \wedge \neg y) = (x \wedge \neg x \wedge \neg y) \vee (y \wedge \neg x \wedge \neg y) = \Lambda \vee \Lambda = \Lambda.$$

Second, if $(x \vee y) \wedge w = \Lambda$, then $(x \wedge w) \vee (y \wedge w) = \Lambda$, so $x \wedge w = \Lambda$ and $y \wedge w = \Lambda$. Hence $w \leq \neg x$ and $w \leq \neg y$. Thus w is a lower bound of $\neg x, \neg y$, and $w \leq \neg x \wedge \neg y$.

Proof of (x). This follows by substituting $\neg x$ for y in (ix) and using (iv) ∎

To conclude this subsection, if $\neg x = \Lambda$, then x is called a *dense element*, or *dense*.

3.6.6 Stone algebras

It may be seen from figure 3.27 that the operation of pseudo-complement in a pseudo-complemented lattice need not obey both of De Morgan's identities (i.e., both identities $\neg(x \vee y) = \neg x \wedge \neg y$ and $\neg(x \wedge y) = \neg x \vee \neg y$). In Stone algebras the operation of pseudo-complement satisfies both of De Morgan's identities.

THEOREM 3.35. In a pseudo-complemented lattice the following two conditions are equivalent.

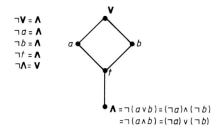

Figure 3.28 A Stone algebra of five elements.

(i) $\neg x \vee \neg y = \neg(x \wedge y)$
(ii) $\neg x \vee \neg\neg x = \mathbf{V}$.

Proof. First, suppose that $\neg x \vee \neg y = \neg(x \wedge y)$. Then $\neg x \vee \neg\neg x = \neg(x \wedge \neg x) = \neg\mathbf{\Lambda} = \mathbf{V}$ by Definition 3.31(i) and Theorem 3.34(iii).

Second, suppose that $\neg x \vee \neg\neg x = \mathbf{V}$. It will be shown that $\neg x \vee \neg y$ is the pseudo-complement of $x \wedge y$. It is clear that $(x \wedge y) \wedge (\neg x \vee \neg y) = \mathbf{\Lambda}$ by distributivity, commutativity, Definition 3.31(i), and $\mathbf{\Lambda}$-property. Suppose that $(x \wedge y) \wedge w = \mathbf{\Lambda}$. Then $(y \wedge w) \leq \neg x$ by associativity and Definition 3.31(ii). Consequently $(y \wedge w) \wedge \neg\neg x \leq \neg x \wedge \neg\neg x = \mathbf{\Lambda}$ by Theorem 3.34(iv). Hence $w \wedge \neg\neg x \leq \neg y$ by associativity and Definition 3.31(ii).

Finally, $w = w \wedge \mathbf{V} = w \wedge (\neg x \vee \neg\neg x) = (w \wedge \neg x) \vee (w \wedge \neg\neg x) \leq \neg x \vee \neg y$ by $\mathbf{V}$-property and distributivity ∎

Definition 3.36. A pseudo-complemented lattice which satisfies Theorem 3.35(i) or Theorem 3.35(ii) is called a Stone algebra.

Figure 3.28 shows a 5-element lattice which is a Stone algebra, with some identities for this lattice.

3.6.7 Kleene algebras

Definition 3.37. A bounded distributive lattice with an operation $\sim$ satisfying the three conditions (i)–(iii) below is called a Kleene algebra.

(i) $\sim\sim x = x$, where $\sim\sim x$ denotes $\sim(\sim x)$
(ii) $\sim(x \wedge y) = \sim x \vee \sim y$
(iii) $x \wedge \sim x \leq y \vee \sim y$.

THEOREM 3.38. In a Kleene algebra, L, the following conditions hold.

(i) $\sim(x \vee y) = \sim x \wedge \sim y$
(ii) $\sim\mathbf{\Lambda} = \mathbf{V}$
(iii) $\sim\mathbf{V} = \mathbf{\Lambda}$
(iv) If x has a complement $\bar{x}$ in L, then $\sim x = \bar{x}$.

Proof of (i).

$$\sim(\sim x \wedge \sim y) = \sim\sim x \vee \sim\sim y \qquad \text{by Definition 3.37(ii)}$$
$$\sim(\sim x \wedge \sim y) = x \vee y \qquad \text{by Definition 3.37(i)}$$
$$(\sim x \wedge \sim y) = \sim(x \vee y) \qquad \text{by Definition 3.37(i)}$$

Proof of (ii) and (iii). From $\wedge \wedge \sim x = \wedge$, $\sim\wedge \vee x = \sim\wedge$ by Definition 3.37(ii), (i), so $x \le \sim\wedge$ and $\sim\wedge = \vee$.

Similarly $\sim\vee = \wedge$

Proof of (iv).

$$x \wedge \sim x \le \bar{x} \vee \sim\bar{x} \qquad \text{by substituting } \bar{x} \text{ for } y \text{ in Definition 3.37(iii). Hence}$$

$$x \wedge \sim x = (x \wedge \sim x) \wedge (\bar{x} \vee \sim\bar{x}) \qquad \text{by Theorem 3.18(ii)}$$

$$= \wedge \vee (x \wedge \sim x \wedge \sim\bar{x}) \qquad \begin{array}{l}\text{by distributivity, complementarity,}\\ \text{and } \wedge\text{-property}\end{array}$$

$$= x \wedge \sim x \wedge \sim\bar{x} \qquad \text{by } \wedge\text{-property}$$

$$= x \wedge \sim(x \vee \bar{x}) = x \wedge \sim\vee = x \wedge \wedge = \wedge$$

by (i), complementarity, (iii), and $\wedge$-property. From $(x \wedge \sim x) = \wedge$, $\sim(x \wedge \sim x) = \sim\wedge$, $\sim x \vee x = \vee$ by Definition 3.37(ii), Definition 3.37(i), and (ii). The result follows by Theorem 3.28   ∎

Note that Definition 3.37(ii) and Theorem 3.38(i) are De Morgan's identities. It is interesting to contrast Stone algebras with Kleene algebras. First, in Stone algebras $x \wedge \neg x = \wedge$ but in Kleene algebras it is only the case that $x \wedge \sim x \le y \vee \sim y$. Second, in Kleene algebras $\sim\sim x = x$ but in Stone algebras it is only the case that $\neg\neg\neg x = \neg x$. A 6-element Kleene algebra is shown in figure 3.29, and it is easy to verify that conditions (i)–(iii) of Definition 3.37 are satisfied.

3.6.8 Supplemented lattices

Definition 3.39. An element x of a bounded distributive lattice is said to be supplemented if there is a greatest complemented element which is $\le x$. The greatest such complemented element is denoted by $!x$ and is called the

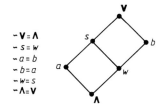

Figure 3.29 A Kleene algebra of six elements.

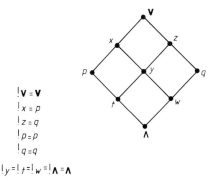

$$!\mathbf{V} = \mathbf{V}$$
$$!x = p$$
$$!z = q$$
$$!p = p$$
$$!q = q$$

$$!y = !t = !w = !\wedge = \wedge$$

Figure 3.30 A supplemented lattice of nine elements.

supplement of x. That is,

(i) $!x$ is a complemented element satisfying $!x \leq x$ and
(ii) if y is a complemented element satisfying $y \leq x$, then $y \leq !x$.

Definition 3.40. A bounded distributive lattice is called a supplemented lattice if every element of the lattice is supplemented.

Figure 3.30 shows a 9-element supplemented lattice. The operation $!$ is given for each of the 9 elements in this figure. It is evident that a Boolean algebra is a supplemented lattice, as every element x of the Boolean algebra is supplemented with $!x = x$.

THEOREM 3.41. Some basic properties in supplemented lattices are given below.

(i)   If b is a complemented element, then $!b = b$
(ii) $!\wedge = \wedge$
(iii) $!\mathbf{V} = \mathbf{V}$
(iv) $!!x = !x$, where $!!x$ denotes $!(!x)$
(v) $!x \wedge !y = !(x \wedge y)$
(vi) if $y \leq x$, then $!y \leq !x$
(vii) $!x \vee !y \leq !(x \vee y)$.

Proof of (i). This is obvious from Definition 3.39.

Proof of (ii)–(iv). These are immediate from (i).

Proof of (v). First, $!x \wedge !y$ is a complemented element by Theorem 3.29, and $!x \wedge !y \leq x \wedge y$ by Definition 3.39(i). Second, suppose that w is a complemented element and $w \leq x \wedge y$. Since $x \wedge y \leq x$ and $x \wedge y \leq y$, $w \leq x$ and $w \leq y$ by transitivity. Hence $w \leq !x$ and $w \leq !y$ by Definition 3.39(ii). Thus $w \leq (!x \wedge !y)$.

Proof of (vi). Using Theorem 3.18(ii), $y = y \wedge x$, so $!y = !(y \wedge x) = (!y \wedge !x)$ by (v)—that is, $!y \leq !x$.

Proof of (vii). From $x \leq x \vee y$ and $y \leq x \vee y$, $!x \leq !(x \vee y)$ and $!y \leq !(x \vee y)$ by (vi). Hence $!x \vee !y \leq !(x \vee y)$ ■

3.6.9   Kleene–Stone algebras

Definition 3.42.   A bounded distributive lattice L having operations $\neg$ and $\sim$ such that L is a Stone algebra and a Kleene algebra, respectively, is called a Kleene–Stone algebra.

It is interesting to note some relations holding in Kleene–Stone algebras.

THEOREM 3.43.
(i) $\sim \neg x = \neg \neg x$
(ii) $\neg x \leq \sim x$
(iii) $!x = \neg \sim x$
(iv) $!(x \vee y) = !x \vee !y$.

Proofs and other properties may be found in Epstein and Mukaidono (1987). Owing to Theorem 3.43(iii), (iv), a Kleene–Stone algebra is a supplemented lattice in which $!(x \vee y) = !x \vee !y$.

3.6.10   Heyting algebras

Definition 3.44.   A single arrow is used to denote the implicative operation of a Heyting algebra. For any pair of elements x, y in a bounded lattice L, $x \rightarrow y$ denotes the greatest element q in L satisfying $x \wedge q \leq y$, whenever such an element exists. That is,

(i) $x \wedge (x \rightarrow y) \leq y$ and
(ii) $x \wedge w \leq y$ implies $w \leq x \rightarrow y$.

Definition 3.45.   A bounded lattice L in which $x \rightarrow y$ exists for every pair of elements x, y in L is a Heyting algebra.

THEOREM 3.46.   A Heyting algebra is a distributive lattice.

Proof.   From

$$w \wedge x \leq (w \wedge x) \vee (w \wedge y)$$

and

$$w \wedge y \leq (w \wedge x) \vee (w \wedge y), \quad x \leq w \rightarrow ((w \wedge x) \vee (w \wedge y))$$

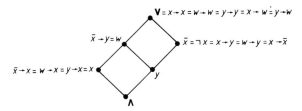

Figure 3.31   A Heyting algebra of six elements.

and

$$y \leq w \rightarrow ((w \wedge x) \vee (w \wedge y))$$

by Definition 3.44(ii). Hence

$$x \vee y \leq w \rightarrow ((w \wedge x) \vee (w \wedge y))$$

and

$$w \wedge (x \vee y) \leq ((w \wedge x) \vee (w \wedge y))$$

by Definition 3.44. But

$$w \wedge x \leq w \wedge (x \vee y)$$

and

$$w \wedge y \leq w \wedge (x \vee y)$$

so that

$$((w \wedge x) \vee (w \wedge y)) \leq w \wedge (x \vee y).$$

Thus

$$w \wedge (x \vee y) = (w \wedge x) \vee (w \wedge y) \qquad \blacksquare$$

Any finite distributive lattice is a Heyting algebra. The example in figure 3.31 shows a 6-element Heyting algebra, with some identities in this lattice. If L is a Heyting algebra, then L is a pseudo-complemented lattice, because $\neg x = x \rightarrow \wedge$.

THEOREM 3.47.   Some basic properties in Heyting algebras are given below.

(i)   If $w \leq x \rightarrow y$, then $(x \wedge w) \leq y$
(ii) $x \rightarrow y = \vee$ if and only if $x \leq y$
(iii) $\vee \rightarrow y = y$
(iv)   If $x_1 \leq x_2$, then $x_2 \rightarrow y \leq x_1 \rightarrow y$
(v)   If $y_1 \leq y_2$, then $x \rightarrow y_1 \leq x \rightarrow y_2$
(vi) $y \leq x \rightarrow y$

(vii) $x \wedge (x \rightarrow y) = x \wedge y$
(viii) $w \rightarrow (x \wedge y) = (w \rightarrow x) \wedge (w \rightarrow y)$
(ix) $(x \vee y) \rightarrow w = (x \rightarrow w) \wedge (y \rightarrow w)$
(x) $\neg x = x \rightarrow \bigwedge$
(xi) $\neg x \vee y \leq x \rightarrow y$
(xii) $x \rightarrow \neg x = \neg x$
(xiii) $\neg x \rightarrow x = \neg \neg x.$

Proof of (i).   By Definition 3.44(i)

$$x \wedge (x \rightarrow y) \leq y$$

and by the hypothesis

$$(x \rightarrow y) \wedge w = w.$$

Hence

$$x \wedge w = x \wedge ((x \rightarrow y) \wedge w) = (x \wedge (x \rightarrow y)) \wedge w \leq y \wedge w \leq y.$$

Proof of (ii).   If $x \rightarrow y = \mathbf{V}$, then $x = x \wedge \mathbf{V} \leq y$ by Definition 3.44(i) and $\mathbf{V}$-property. If $x \leq y$, then $x \wedge \mathbf{V} \leq y$ by $\mathbf{V}$-property, and $x \rightarrow y = \mathbf{V}$ by $\mathbf{V}$-property.

Proof of (iii). $q = \mathbf{V} \wedge q$ by $\mathbf{V}$-property. The greatest element q satisfying $q = \mathbf{V} \wedge q \leq y$ is y.

Proof of (iv). $x_2 \wedge (x_2 \rightarrow y) \leq y$ by Definition 3.44(i). Since $x_1 \leq x_2$, $x_1 \wedge (x_2 \rightarrow y) \leq y$. Thus $x_2 \rightarrow y \leq x_1 \rightarrow y$ by Definition 3.44(ii).

Proof of (v). $x \wedge (x \rightarrow y_1) \leq y_1$ by Definition 3.44(i). Since $y_1 \leq y_2$, $x \wedge (x \rightarrow y_1) \leq y_2$. Thus $x \rightarrow y_1 \leq x \rightarrow y_2$ by Definition 3.44(ii).

Proof of (vi).   From $x \wedge y \leq y$, it follows that $y \leq x \rightarrow y$, using Definition 3.44(ii).

Proof of (vii). $x \wedge (x \rightarrow y) \leq y$ by Definition 3.44(i), so $x \wedge (x \rightarrow y) \leq x \wedge y$. But $y \leq x \rightarrow y$ by (vi), so $x \wedge y \leq x \wedge (x \rightarrow y)$. Thus $x \wedge (x \rightarrow y) = x \wedge y$.

Proof of (viii).   The proof determines $w \rightarrow (x \wedge y)$ through Definition 3.44(i), (ii).
   First, $w \wedge (w \rightarrow x) \wedge (w \rightarrow y) \leq (x \wedge y)$ by idempotence, associativity, and Definition 3.44(i).
   Second, suppose q in L satisfies $w \wedge q \leq x \wedge y$. Then $w \wedge q \leq x \wedge y \leq x$ and $w \wedge q \leq x \wedge y \leq y$, so that $q \leq (w \rightarrow x)$ and $q \leq (w \rightarrow y)$ by Definition 3.44(ii). Thus $q \leq (w \rightarrow x) \wedge (w \rightarrow y)$.

Proof of (ix).   The proof determines $(x \vee y) \rightarrow w$ through Definition 3.44(i), (ii).
   First

$$(x \vee y) \wedge (x \rightarrow w) \wedge (y \rightarrow w)$$

$$= (x \wedge (x \rightarrow w) \wedge (y \rightarrow w)) \vee (y \wedge (x \rightarrow w) \wedge (y \rightarrow w))$$

by distributivity

$$\leq (w \wedge (y \to w)) \vee (w \wedge (x \to w)) \leq w \vee w = w$$

by associativity and Definition 3.44(i).

Second, suppose q in L satisfies

$$(x \vee y) \wedge q \leq w.$$

Then

$$((x \wedge q) \vee (y \wedge q)) = (x \vee y) \wedge q \leq w$$

by distributivity. Hence

$$x \wedge q \leq (x \wedge q) \vee (y \wedge q) \leq w$$

and

$$y \wedge q \leq (x \wedge q) \vee (y \wedge q) \leq w$$

so that

$$x \wedge q \leq w$$

and

$$y \wedge q \leq w.$$

Thus

$$q \leq (x \to w) \text{ and } q \leq (y \to w)$$

by Definition 3.44(ii), and $q \leq (x \to w) \wedge (y \to w)$.

Proof of (x). This follows by definition.

Proof of (xi).

$$x \wedge (\neg x \vee y) = (x \wedge \neg x) \vee (x \wedge y) = \boldsymbol{\wedge} \vee (x \wedge y) = x \wedge y \leq y$$

by distributivity, complementarity, and $\boldsymbol{\wedge}$-property. The result follows from Definition 3.44(ii).

Proof of (xii). This proof determines $x \to \neg x$ through Definition 3.44(i), (ii). First, $x \wedge \neg x \leq \neg x$. Second, if $x \wedge w \leq \neg x$, then $x \wedge (x \wedge w) = \boldsymbol{\wedge}$ by Theorem 3.34(i). So $x \wedge w = \boldsymbol{\wedge}$ by associativity and idempotence, and $w \leq \neg x$ by Definition 3.31(ii).

Proof of (xiii). First, $\neg x \wedge \neg\neg x \leq \neg\neg\neg x$. Second, if $\neg x \wedge w \leq \neg\neg\neg x$, then $\neg\neg x \wedge \neg x \wedge w = \neg x \wedge w$ using Theorem 3.18(ii). Consequently, $\neg x \wedge w = \boldsymbol{\wedge}$ by Theorem 3.34(iv) and $\boldsymbol{\wedge}$-property. Thus, $w \leq \neg\neg\neg x$ by Definition 3.31(ii) ∎

To conclude this subsection, if the dual of L is a Heyting algebra, then $x \leftarrow y$ is used to denote the least element r in L satisfying $x \vee r \geq y$.

3.6.11   *L*-algebras

Definition 3.48.   An *L*-algebra is a Heyting algebra in which the condition

(i) $$(w \rightarrow y) \vee (y \rightarrow w) = \mathbf{V}$$

is satisfied for all w, y.

THEOREM 3.49.   An *L*-algebra is a Stone algebra.

Proof.   To prove condition (ii) of Theorem 3.35,

$$(x \rightarrow \neg x) \vee (\neg x \rightarrow x) = \mathbf{V}$$

by setting

$$w = x \text{ and } y = \neg x \text{ in (i).}$$

But

$$x \rightarrow \neg x = \neg x$$

by Theorem 3.47(xii), and

$$\neg x \rightarrow x = \neg \neg x$$

by Theorem 3.47(xiii). Thus $\neg x \vee \neg \neg x = \mathbf{V}$.

Figure 3.32 shows two 5-element Heyting algebras, one of which is an *L*-algebra and one of which is not an *L*-algebra.

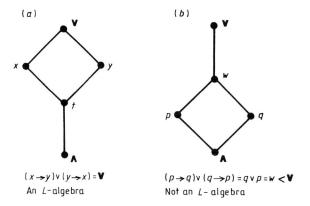

Figure 3.32   Two 5-element Heyting algebras: (*a*) is an *L*-algebra and (*b*) is *not* an *L*-algebra.

3.6.12   *B*-algebras

Definition 3.50.   A double arrow is used to denote the implicative operation of a *B*-algebra. For any pair of elements x, y in a bounded distributive lattice L, $x \Rightarrow y$ denotes the greatest complemented element b in L satisfying

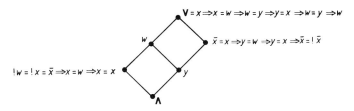

$V = x \Rightarrow x = w \Rightarrow w = y \Rightarrow y = x \Rightarrow w = y \Rightarrow w$

$\bar{x} = x \Rightarrow y = w \Rightarrow y = x \Rightarrow \bar{x} = ! \, \bar{x}$

$! w = ! x = \bar{x} \Rightarrow x = w \Rightarrow x = x$

Figure 3.33   A *B*-algebra of six elements.

$x \wedge b \leq y$, whenever such an element exists. That is,

(i) $x \Rightarrow y$ is a complemented element satisfying $x \wedge (x \Rightarrow y) \leq y$
and
(ii) if b is a complemented element and $x \wedge b \leq y$, then $b \leq (x \Rightarrow y)$.

Definition 3.51.   A bounded distributive lattice L in which $x \Rightarrow y$ exists for all x, y in L is called a *B*-algebra. Any finite distributive lattice is a *B*-algebra. An example is shown in figure 3.33, with some identities in this lattice. If L is a *B*-algebra, then L is a supplemented lattice, because $! y = \mathbf{V} \Rightarrow y$.

THEOREM 3.52.   Some relations in *B*-algebras are given below.

(i)   If $w \leq x \Rightarrow y$, then $x \wedge w \leq y$
(ii) $x \Rightarrow y = \mathbf{V}$ if and only if $x \leq y$
(iii) $\mathbf{V} \Rightarrow y = ! y$
(iv) $! y \leq x \Rightarrow y$
(v)   If $x_1 \leq x_2$, then $x_2 \Rightarrow y \leq x_1 \Rightarrow y$
(vi)   If $y_1 \leq y_2$, then $x \Rightarrow y_1 \leq x \Rightarrow y_2$
(vii) $w \Rightarrow (x \wedge y) = (w \Rightarrow x) \wedge (w \Rightarrow y)$
(viii) $(x \vee y) \Rightarrow w = (x \Rightarrow w) \wedge (y \Rightarrow w)$
(ix)   The dual of a *B*-algebra is a *B*-algebra.

Proof of (i).   From $(x \Rightarrow y) \wedge w = w$ and $x \wedge (x \Rightarrow y) \leq y$,

$$x \wedge w = x \wedge (x \Rightarrow y) \wedge w \leq y \wedge w \leq y.$$

Proof of (ii).   If $x \Rightarrow y = \mathbf{V}$, a complemented element, then $x = x \wedge \mathbf{V} \leq y$ by Definition 3.50(i) and **V**-property. If $x \leq y$, then **V** is a complemented element satisfying $x \wedge \mathbf{V} \leq y$, by **V**-property. Thus $x \Rightarrow y = \mathbf{V}$ by **V**-property and Definition 3.50.

Proof of (iii).   The greatest complemented element b satisfying $b = \mathbf{V} \wedge b \leq y$ is $! y$, by **V**-property and Definition 3.39.

Proof of (iv). $x \wedge ! y \leq x \wedge y \leq y$, so $! y \leq x \Rightarrow y$ using Definition 3.39 and Definition 3.50(ii).

Proof of (v). $x_2 \wedge (x_2 \Rightarrow y) \leq y$ by Definition 3.50(i). Since $x_1 \leq x_2$, $x_1 \wedge (x_2 \Rightarrow y) \leq y$. Thus $(x_2 \Rightarrow y) \leq (x_1 \Rightarrow y)$ by Definition 3.50(ii).

Proof of (vi). $x \wedge (x \Rightarrow y_1) \leq y_1$ by Definition 3.50(i). Since $y_1 \leq y_2$, $x \wedge (x \Rightarrow y_1) \leq y_2$. Thus $x \Rightarrow y_1 \leq x \Rightarrow y_2$.

Proof of (vii).   First, $(w \Rightarrow x) \wedge (w \Rightarrow y)$ is a complemented element by Theorem 3.29, and $w \wedge (w \Rightarrow x) \wedge (w \Rightarrow y) \leq x \wedge y$ by idempotence, associativity, and Definition 3.50(i). Second, suppose b is a complemented element in L satisfying $w \wedge b \leq (x \wedge y)$. Consequently $w \wedge b \leq (x \wedge y) \leq x$ and $w \wedge b \leq (x \wedge y) \leq y$, so that $b \leq (w \Rightarrow x)$ and $b \leq (w \Rightarrow y)$ by Definition 3.50(ii). Thus $b \leq (w \Rightarrow x) \wedge (w \Rightarrow y)$.

Proof of (viii).   First

$$(x \Rightarrow w) \wedge (y \Rightarrow w)$$

is a complemented element by Theorem 3.29, and

$$(x \vee y) \wedge (x \Rightarrow w) \wedge (y \Rightarrow w)$$
$$= (x \wedge (x \Rightarrow w) \wedge (y \Rightarrow w)) \vee (y \wedge (x \Rightarrow w) \wedge (y \Rightarrow w))$$
$$\leq (w \wedge (y \Rightarrow w)) \vee (w \wedge (x \Rightarrow w)) \leq w \vee w$$
$$= w$$

by distributivity, associativity, and Definition 3.50(i).
   Second, suppose b is a complemented element satisfying

$$(x \vee y) \wedge b \leq w.$$

Then

$$((x \wedge b) \vee (y \wedge b)) = (x \vee y) \wedge b \leq w$$

by distributivity, so

$$x \wedge b \leq w \qquad \text{and} \qquad y \wedge b \leq w.$$

Hence

$$b \leq x \Rightarrow w \qquad \text{and} \qquad b \leq y \Rightarrow w$$

by Definition 3.50(ii). Thus

$$b \leq (x \Rightarrow w) \wedge (y \Rightarrow w).$$

Proof of (ix).   It must be shown that there is a least complemented element b satisfying $y \leq x \vee b$. Indeed this element b is $\overline{y \Rightarrow x}$. To show this, for any complemented element c, note that $y \leq x \vee c$ if and only if $y \wedge \bar{c} \leq x$. The result follows   ∎

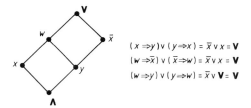

Figure 3.34 A *P*-algebra of six elements.

3.6.13   *P*-algebras

Definition 3.53.   A *P*-algebra is a *B*-algebra in which the condition

(i) $(x \Rightarrow y) \vee (y \Rightarrow x) = \mathbf{V}$

is satisfied for all x, y.

Figure 3.34 shows a 6-element *P*-algebra, with some identities in this lattice.

THEOREM 3.54.   Some relations in *P*-algebras are given below.

(i) $x \rightarrow y = (x \Rightarrow y) \vee y$
(ii) $(x \rightarrow y) \vee (y \rightarrow x) = \mathbf{V}$
(iii) $\neg x = (x \rightarrow \mathbf{\Lambda}) = (x \Rightarrow \mathbf{\Lambda}) = !\neg x$
(iv) $(x \Rightarrow y) = !(x \rightarrow y)$
(v) $!x = \neg\neg !x$
(vi) $\neg(x \wedge y) = \neg x \vee \neg y$
(vii) $!(x \vee y) = !x \vee !y$
(viii) $w \Rightarrow (x \vee y) = (w \Rightarrow x) \vee (w \Rightarrow y)$
(ix)   The dual of a *P*-algebra is a *P*-algebra.

Proofs and other properties may be found in Epstein and Horn (1974a). A *P*-algebra is a Heyting algebra through Theorem 3.54(i) and an *L*-algebra through Theorem 3.54(ii).

3.7   Lattice ideals in Hasse diagrams

The previous section dealt with properties of elements in a lattice. This section deals with sets of elements in a lattice. Lattice ideals are discussed in subsection 3.7.1. Lattice prime ideals are discussed in subsection 3.7.2. Ideals and prime ideals are shown as sets of elements in Hasse diagrams.

3.7.1   Lattice ideals

Definition 3.55.   An *ideal* of a lattice L is a nonempty subset of elements in L satisfying the following two conditions.

(i) If x is in the ideal and $y \leq x$, then y is in the ideal.
(ii) If x, y are in the ideal, then $x \vee y$ is in the ideal.

If there is an element w such that every element x in an ideal satisfies $x \leq w$, then the ideal is called the *principal ideal generated by w*. If L has a finite number of elements, then every ideal is a principal ideal generated by some element of L, and there is an ideal generated by each element of the lattice. Any ideal which is not all of L is called a *proper ideal*. A proper ideal does not contain $\mathbf{V}$. An illustration of a 5-element lattice and its proper ideals may be found in figure 3.35. While the set intersection of any two ideals must be an ideal, the set union of two ideals need not be an ideal. The intersection of two ideals is never the null set, as the element $\mathbf{\Lambda}$ is contained in each ideal.

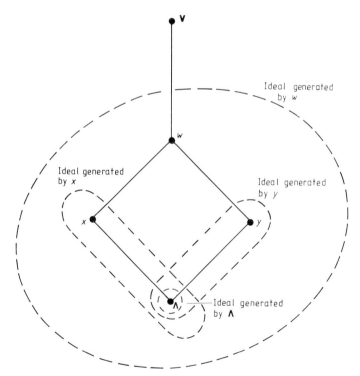

Figure 3.35   Proper ideals of a 5-element lattice.

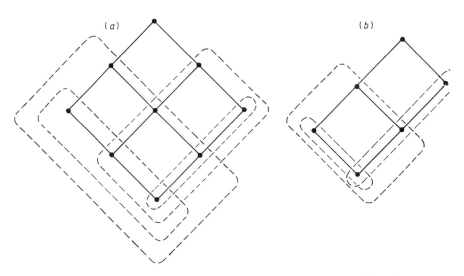

Figure 3.36 (*a*) A 9-element lattice with four prime ideals and (*b*) a 6-element lattice with three prime ideals.

3.7.2 Lattice prime ideals

A proper ideal is a *prime ideal* if for all x, y in L, whenever $x \wedge y$ is in the ideal, then x or y must be in the ideal.

Two illustrations are given in figure 3.36. In the 9-element lattice of figure 3.36(*a*), there are 4 different prime ideals. In the 6-element lattice of figure 3.36(*b*), there are 3 different prime ideals.

Some observations may be made concerning the prime ideals of a Boolean algebra and the prime ideals of a Post algebra of order 3. First, observe from the Hasse diagrams given for Boolean algebras in figure 3.24 that any prime ideal has the property that there is no other prime ideal in the Boolean algebra which properly contains it or is properly contained within it. Second, observe from the Hasse diagrams given for Post algebras of order 3 in figure 3.26 that any prime ideal has the property that there is exactly one other prime ideal which either properly contains it or is properly contained within it. This is shown explicitly in figure 3.36(*a*) for the 9-element Post algebra of order 3. It is a consequence of the next chapter that the prime ideals of a Post algebra of order n lie in disjoint chains each of length $n - 1$.

3.8 Overview

The work of G Boole and J Venn occurred around the second half of the nineteenth century. Venn diagrams for decisive functions are called decisive Venn diagrams in Epstein (1976). Applications of the K simplification in this chapter start with the case $n = 3$, $m = 2$. For the case $n = 3$, $m = 1$, the 27 3-valued functions of one variable may be found in Bahraini and Epstein (1987). The K simplification as presented here is flexible with respect to primitive operations, but the procedure is restricted to a small number of variables. There are various minimization approaches in the literature which are not so restricted. See Smith (1977), Miller and Muzio (1979), and Dueck and Miller (1990).

For first concepts on partially ordered sets and lattices, see Grätzer (1971). Alternative postulates for lattices may be found in Padmanabhan (1969), and for distributive lattices in Sholander (1951). In each of these, the postulates consist of just two identities. Special lattices are discussed in Balbes and Dwinger (1974). For lecture notes on Boolean algebra, see Halmos (1963). Many books on 2-valued logic design or switching theory contain introductions to Boolean algebra. For discussions relating to applied Boolean algebra, see Harrison (1965) and Hohn (1966).

There are alternative postulates for Boolean algebras in Huntington (1904), Byrne (1946), and Sioson (1964).

Exercises

E3.1   Consider the 3-valued function g of 3 variables X_1, X_2, X_3 given in dnf below.

$$g(X_1, X_2, X_3) = E_1 C_1(X_1) C_1(X_3) \sqcup C_2(X_2).$$

(a) Give a logic table of 27 rows for g.
(b) Give a Venn diagram of 27 regions for g.
(c) From (a) or (b), give the fdnf for g.

E3.2   Consider the 3-valued dnf of 2-variable X, Y:

$$E_1 C_0(X) C_1(Y) \sqcup E_1 C_1(X) C_1(Y) \sqcup E_1 C_2(X) C_1(Y) \sqcup C_1(X) C_0(Y).$$

(a) Give a Venn diagram of 9 regions for this function.
(b) From (a), give a simplified dnf for this function.

E3.3   In figure 3.8 Venn diagrams are shown for $n = 3$, $m = 2$ and $n = 4$, $m = 2$ using scythe-like annules. These diagrams are easily extended for general n, $m = 2$. Prove that the number of regions in such diagrams is exactly n^2.

E3.4   For 4 variables, draw a Venn diagram using 4 ellipses which yields exactly 16 different regions corresponding to the $2^4 = 16$ different 2-valued fundaments.

E3.5   For general m, given m variables, is there a method for finding and placing m shapes on a Venn diagram to yield exactly 2^m different regions corresponding to the 2^m different 2-valued fundaments?

E3.6
(a) Display the function of **E3.2** on a 3×3 K-map.
(b) Show that the K method of Section 3.4 applied to this function yields 2 distinct simplified dnf's.

E3.7   Use the K method to obtain all the simplified dnf's for the 3-valued function of two variables X, Y shown below.

	$C_0(Y)$	$C_1(Y)$	$C_2(Y)$
$C_0(X)$	1	0	0
$C_1(X)$	2	2	2
$C_2(X)$	1	2	2

E3.8   Use the K method to obtain all the simplified dnf's for the 3-valued function of two variables X, Y shown below.

	$C_0(Y)$	$C_1(Y)$	$C_2(Y)$
$C_0(X)$	1	2	1
$C_1(X)$	2	2	2
$C_2(X)$	1	2	1

E3.9   Use the K method to obtain all the simplified dnf's for the 3-valued function of three variables X, Y, Z shown below.

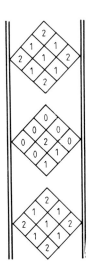

E3.10 Use the K method to obtain all the simplified dnf's for the 4-valued function of two variables X, Y shown below.

	$C_0(Y)$	$C_1(Y)$	$C_2(Y)$	$C_3(Y)$
$C_0(X)$	0	1	2	3
$C_1(X)$	1	1	1	1
$C_2(X)$	2	1	2	2
$C_3(X)$	3	1	2	3

E3.11 Consider the K-map of **E3.7**. Apply the K method using the primitive terms of: (a) subsection 3.4.4(a); (b) subsection 3.4.4(b); (c) subsection 3.4.4(c).

E3.12 Is the 7-element partially ordered set shown below a lattice? If your answer is "No", identify 2 elements in this partially ordered set which do not have an lub, or do not have a glb.

E3.13 Is the 7-element lattice shown below a distributive lattice? If your answer is "No", identify 3 elements a, b, c which violate Theorem 3.24(i) or Theorem 3.24(ii).

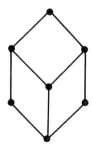

E3.14 Give all the nonisomorphic lattices of 5 elements.

E3.15 Give all the nonisomorphic distributive lattices of 6 elements.

E3.16 Prove that $(x \wedge y) \vee (x \wedge z) \le x \wedge (y \vee z)$ in any lattice.

E3.17 Let L be a lattice satisfying the identity

$$(x \wedge y) \vee (y \wedge z) \vee (z \wedge x) = (x \vee y) \wedge (y \vee z) \wedge (z \vee x).$$

Prove that L is a distributive lattice.

E3.18 Identify all the complemented elements in the 12-element distributive lattice shown below.

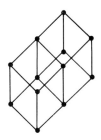

E3.19 Identify the 6-element distributive lattices in **E3.15** which are:

(a) Stone algebras
(b) L-algebras
(c) P-algebras
(d) Kleene–Stone algebras.

E3.20 Give a finite distributive lattice in which

$$x \to y \neq (x \Rightarrow y) \vee y$$

for some pair of elements x, y. By Theorem 3.54(i) the answer cannot be a P-algebra.

E3.21 For each of the 6-element distributive lattices in **E3.15**, give all the different prime ideals.

4 Post Algebras

The following definition of Post algebras of order n, for fixed $n \geq 2$, is a modification of the definition in Epstein (1973). The two definitions use the same operations, and postulates consisting solely of identities. It is immediate from the postulates below that a Post algebra of order n is a bounded distributive lattice with additional properties involving operations $C_0, \ldots, C_{n-1}$ and $e_0, \ldots, e_{n-1}$. For $n = 2$, these become postulates for Boolean algebras. Chapter 2 uses values $E_0, E_1, \ldots, E_{n-1}$ which are related to linearly ordered Post algebras of order n. A linearly ordered Post algebra of order n is a simple example of a Post algebra of order n which contains exactly n elements—namely, the elements $e_0, \ldots, e_{n-1}$.

4.1 Postulates for the disjoint system of Post algebras of order n

Definition 4.1. An algebra $(A, \vee, \wedge, C_0, C_1, \ldots, C_{n-1}, e_0, e_1, \ldots, e_{n-1})$, $n \geq 2$, where $\vee$ and $\wedge$ are binary operations, $C_0, \ldots, C_{n-1}$ are n unary operations, and $e_0, \ldots, e_{n-1}$ are n nullary operations, is said to be a Post algebra of order n if for all x, y, z in A the following postulates are satisfied.

$P1$ (i) $x \vee y = y \vee x$
      (ii) $x \wedge y = y \wedge x$
      (iii) $(x \vee y) \vee z = x \vee (y \vee z)$
      (iv) $(x \wedge y) \wedge z = x \wedge (y \wedge z)$
      (v) $x \vee x = x$
      (vi) $x \wedge x = x$
      (vii) $(x \wedge y) \vee x = x$
      (viii) $(x \vee y) \wedge x = x$
      (ix) $x \wedge (y \vee z) = (x \wedge y) \vee (x \wedge z)$.

$P2$ (i) $e_0 \vee x = x$
      (ii) $e_{i+1} \wedge e_i = e_i$ for $0 < i < n - 2$
      (iii) $x \wedge e_{n-1} = x$.

$P3$ (i) $C_i(x) \wedge C_j(x) = e_0$ for $i \neq j$, $0 \leq i, j \leq n - 1$
      (ii) $C_0(x) \vee C_1(x) \vee \cdots \vee C_{n-2}(x) \vee C_{n-1}(x) = e_{n-1}$.

P4 (i) $C_i(x \wedge y)$
$$= \{C_i(x) \wedge [C_i(y) \vee C_{i+1}(y) \vee \cdots \vee C_{n-1}(y)]\}$$
$$\vee \{C_i(y) \wedge [C_i(x) \vee C_{i+1}(x) \vee \cdots \vee C_{n-1}(x)]\}$$
for $i = 0, 1, \ldots, n-1$

(ii) $C_{n-1}(x \vee y) = C_{n-1}(x) \vee C_{n-1}(y)$.

P5 (i) $C_i(e_j) = e_0$ for $i \neq j$, $0 \leq i < n-1$, $0 \leq j \leq n-1$

(ii) $C_{n-1}(e_0) = e_0$

(iii) $C_{n-1}(e_{n-2}) = e_0$.

P6 $x = [e_1 \wedge C_1(x)] \vee [e_2 \wedge C_2(x)] \vee \cdots \vee [e_{n-1} \wedge C_{n-1}(x)]$.

Note that *P2* is the same as $\wedge = e_0 \leq e_1 \leq e_2 \leq \cdots \leq e_{n-2} \leq e_{n-1} = \vee$ by Theorem 3.18(i), (ii). Hence, because of *P1*, *P2*(i), and *P2*(iii), a Post algebra of order n is a bounded distributive lattice by Theorem 3.18 and Definition 3.25. The unary operations $C_i(x)$ are called disjoint operations and the system is called a disjoint system because of *P3*(i) and Definition 3.23. While the postulates allow the degenerate Post algebra consisting of one element, the focus in the remainder of this chapter is on nondegenerate Post algebras of order n.

In figure 4.1 Hasse diagrams of nondegenerate Post algebras of order n, $n = 2, 3, \ldots$ consisting of n^c elements, $c = 1, 2, \ldots$ are shown. In this figure Post algebras of order 2, called Boolean algebras, are shown at row 1, Post algebras of order 3 are shown at row 2, etc. Chains consisting of n elements ($c = 1$) are shown at column 1, direct products of two n-element chains consisting of n^2 elements ($c = 2$) are shown at column 2, etc.

Two important cases for the above postulates are $n = 2$ and $n = 3$. The case $n = 2$ is in subsection 4.1.1. The case $n = 3$ is in subsection 4.1.2. Linearly ordered Post algebras of order n are in subsection 4.1.3. Some further remarks are in subsection 4.1.4.

4.1.1 Post algebras of order 2 are Boolean algebras

In the case $n = 2$: *P1* and *P2* yield a bounded distributive lattice with $e_0 = \wedge$ and $e_1 = \vee$; *P3* yields $C_0(x) \wedge C_1(x) = \wedge$ and $C_0(x) \vee C_1(x) = \vee$; *P4*(i) yields $C_0(x \wedge y) = C_0(x) \vee C_0(y)$ and $C_1(x \wedge y) = C_1(x) \wedge C_1(y)$; *P4*(ii) yields $C_1(x \vee y) = C_1(x) \vee C_1(y)$; *P5* yields $C_0(\vee) = \wedge$ and $C_1(\wedge) = \wedge$; *P6* yields $x = \vee \wedge C_1(x)$, so $x = C_1(x)$ by $\vee$-property. Also $\bar{x} = C_0(x)$ by *P3* and Theorem 3.28. (For $n = 2$, circuit diagrams for $C_0(x)$ and $C_1(x)$ may be found in Section 2.3.} Thus Post algebras of order 2 yield Boolean algebras. Postulates *P1*–*P6* generate other identities for $n = 2$ which are basic identities in Boolean algebras.

Lemma 4.2. Certain identities in Boolean algebras are so basic that it is worthwhile to collect some of them here.

(i) $\overline{\vee} = \wedge$

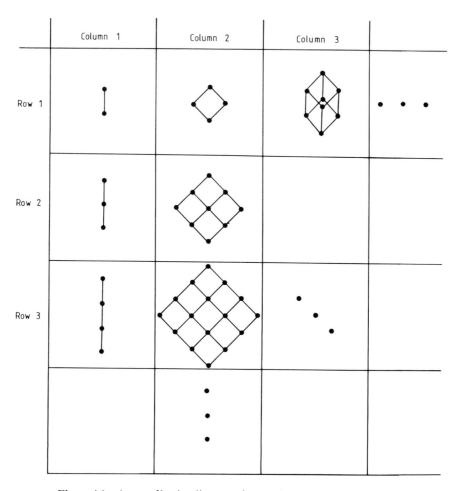

Figure 4.1   Array of lattice diagrams for nondegenerate Post algebras.

(ii) $\overline{\wedge} = \mathbf{V}$
(iii) $x \to y = x \Rightarrow y = \bar{x} \vee y$
(iv) $\bar{x} = \neg x = \sim x$
(v) $!x = x$
(vi) $x \vee \bar{x} = \mathbf{V}$
(vii) $x \wedge \bar{x} = \mathbf{\Lambda}$
(viii) $\overline{x \vee y} = \bar{x} \wedge \bar{y}$
(ix) $\overline{x \wedge y} = \bar{x} \vee \bar{y}$
(x) $(\bar{\bar{x}}) = x$
(xi) $x \vee (x \to y) = (x \to y) \vee \bar{y} = \mathbf{V}$
(xii) $x \wedge \bar{y} \wedge (x \to y) = \mathbf{\Lambda}$

(xiii) $\overline{x \to y} = x \wedge \bar{y}$

(xiv) $x \leq y$ if and only if $\bar{y} \leq \bar{x}$.

4.1.2   Post algebras of order 3

In the case $n = 3$: $P1$ and $P2$ yield a bounded distributive lattice with an intermediate constant: $e_0 = \wedge \leq e_1 \leq e_2 = \vee$; $P3$ yields $C_0(x) \wedge C_0(x) = C_0(x) \wedge C_2(x) = C_1(x) \wedge C_2(x) = \wedge$ and $C_0(x) \vee C_1(x) \vee C_2(x) = \vee$; $P4$(i) yields $C_0(x \wedge y) = C_0(x) \vee C_0(y)$, $C_1(x \wedge y) = [C_1(x) \wedge C_1(y)] \vee [C_1(x) \wedge C_2(y)] \vee [C_2(x) \wedge C_1(y)]$, $C_2(x \wedge y) = C_2(x) \wedge C_2(y)$;   and $P4$(ii) yields $C_2(x \vee y) = C_2(x) \vee C_2(y)$; $P5$ yields $C_0(e_1) = C_0(e_2) = C_1(e_0) = C_1(e_2) = C_2(e_0) = C_2(e_1) = \wedge$; $P6$ yields $x = [e_1 \wedge C_1(x)] \vee C_2(x)$.

Further simplifications can be made. For example, for $n = 3$ the unary operation C_1 can be dropped from the postulates by setting $C_1(x) = C_0(C_0(x)) \wedge C_0(C_2(x))$ throughout.

4.1.3   Linearly ordered Post algebras of order n

The set of elements $\{e_0, e_1, \ldots, e_{n-1}\}$ yields a *linearly ordered Post algebra* or *Post chain of order* n consisting of n elements with $\wedge = e_0 \leq e_1 \leq \cdots \leq e_{n-1} = \vee$. The following hold:

$e_i \wedge e_j = e_{\min(i,j)}$

$e_i \vee e_j = e_{\max(i,j)}$

and

$C_i(e_j) = \wedge$ for $i \neq j$

$\qquad\quad = \vee$ for $i = j$.

Consequently, for any e_k in P, $k = 0, 1, \ldots, n-1$, $P6$ is satisfied: $e_k = [e_1 \wedge C_1(e_k)] \vee \cdots \vee [e_{n-1} \wedge C_{n-1}(e_k)]$. Applications may be found in Chapter 2. Relevant tables are in Lemmas 2.2 and 2.3.

4.1.4   Some further remarks

It can be proved that the $C_i(x)$ and e_i, $i = 0, 1, 2, \ldots, n-1$, given by the postulates are unique, and in the nondegenerate case the e_i are distinct. Specifically, (1) if the n element sequence $C_0(x), C_1(x), \ldots, C_{n-1}(x)$ and the n element sequence $C'_0(x), C'_1(x), \ldots, C^1_{n-1}(x)$ each satisfy postulates $P3$ and $P6$, then $C_i(x) = C'_i(x)$ for each $i = 0, 1, \ldots, n-1$; and (2) if the n element sequence $e_0, e_1, \ldots, e_{n-1}$ and the n element sequence $e'_0, e'_1, \ldots, e^1_{n-1}$ each satisfy postulates $P2$, $P5$, and $P6$, then $e_1 = e'_i$ for each $i = 0, 1, \ldots, n-1$ and in the nondegenerate case these elements are distinct. A proof for $n = 2$ is in Chapter 3. For $n > 2$, see Section 3 of Epstein (1960) or Chapter 10 of Balbes and Dwinger (1974).

Hereafter, as a notational convenience, $x \wedge y$ will be written xy.

4.2   Basic properties in the disjoint system of Post algebras of order n

This section gives certain basic properties involving the disjoint operations C_i and the constants e_i, $i = 0, 1, \ldots, n - 1$.

THEOREM 4.3.   If $x \vee e_{n-2} = \mathbf{V}$, then $x = \mathbf{V}$.

Proof.   Since $x \vee e_{n-2} = \mathbf{V}$, $C_{n-1}(x \vee e_{n-2}) = C_{n-1}(\mathbf{V})$. Hence $C_{n-1}(x) \vee C_{n-1}(e_{n-2}) = C_{n-1}(\mathbf{V})$ by $P4$(ii), and $C_{n-1}(x) \vee \mathbf{\Lambda} = \mathbf{V}$ by $P5$, $P2$(i), and $P3$(ii). Thus $C_{n-1}(x) = \mathbf{V}$ and $x = \mathbf{V}$ by $P6$, using $\mathbf{\Lambda}$, $\mathbf{V}$-properties ∎

THEOREM 4.4
(i) $C_i(y)$ is a complemented element.
(ii)   If x is a complemented element then $x = C_{n-1}(x)$.

Proof.   Part (i) follows from $P3$. To prove part (ii), $x \leq e_{n-2} \vee C_{n-1}(x)$ follows from $P6$, so $e_{n-2} \vee C_{n-1}(x) \vee \bar{x} = \mathbf{V}$ by complementarity and $\mathbf{V}$-property. Hence $C_{n-1}(x) \vee \bar{x} = \mathbf{V}$ by Theorem 4.3. Thus $x \wedge (C_{n-1}(x) \vee \bar{x}) = x \wedge \mathbf{V}$ and $x \wedge C_{n-1}(x) = x$ by distributivity, complementarity, and $\mathbf{\Lambda}$, $\mathbf{V}$-properties. Consequently, $x \leq C_{n-1}(x)$ by Theorem 3.18(ii). But $C_{n-1}(x) \leq x$ by $P6$, so $x = C_{n-1}(x)$ ∎

THEOREM 4.5.   For each i in the range $0 \leq i \leq n - 1$

(i) $$C_{n-1}(C_i(x)) = C_i(x)$$

(ii) $$C_j(C_i(x)) = \mathbf{\Lambda} \qquad \text{for } 0 < j < n - 1$$

and

(iii) $$C_0(C_i(x)) = \bigvee_{k \neq i} C_k(x)$$
$$= \overline{C_i(x)}.$$

Proof.   For given i, the n element sequence $\bigvee_{k \neq i} C_k(x), \mathbf{\Lambda}, \mathbf{\Lambda}, \ldots, \mathbf{\Lambda}, C_i(x)$ satisfies $P3$ and $P6$. The result follows from the uniqueness of the disjoint operations ∎

THEOREM 4.6.   If b is a complemented element, then $C_0(b) = \bar{b}$, $C_j(b) = \mathbf{\Lambda}$ for $0 < j < n - 1$, and $C_{n-1}(b) = b$.

Proof.   This follows from Theorems 4.4(ii) and 4.5 ∎

THEOREM 4.7.   If $i \neq j$, then $C_i(e_j) = \mathbf{\Lambda}$ and $C_i(e_i) = \mathbf{V}$.

Proof. This is an easy consequence of the uniqueness of the disjoint operations. It is straightforward to verify that *P3* and *P6* are satisfied ∎

THEOREM 4.8. If b_i are complemented elements $i = 1, \ldots, n - 1$, and

$$x = \bigvee_{i=1}^{n-1} e_i b_i$$

then

(i)
$$x = \bigvee_{i=1}^{n-1} e_i \left(\bigvee_{j=i}^{n-1} b_j \right)$$

and

(ii)
$$C_0(x) = \bigwedge_{j=1}^{n-1} \overline{b_j}$$

$$C_i(x) = b_i \bigwedge_{j=i+1}^{n-1} \overline{b_j} \qquad \text{for } i = 1, 2, \ldots, n - 2$$

$$C_{n-1}(x) = b_{n-1}.$$

Proof of (i). This follows by distributivity, absorption, and $e_1 \leq e_2 \leq \cdots \leq e_{n-1}$.

Proof of (ii). Using distributivity and complementarity, it is straightforward to establish that

$$\bigvee_{i=k}^{n-2} b_i \left(\bigwedge_{j=i+1}^{n-1} \overline{b_j} \right) \vee b_{n-1} = \bigvee_{i=k}^{n-1} b_i$$

for $0 < k < n - 1$. Let

$$c_{n-1} = b_{n-1} \qquad \text{and} \qquad c_0 = \bigwedge_{i=1}^{n-1} \overline{b_i}.$$

Let

$$c_i = b_i \left(\bigwedge_{j=i+1}^{n-1} b_j \right) \qquad \text{for } 0 < i < n - 1.$$

It follows that

$$x = \bigvee_{i=1}^{n-1} e_i \left(\bigvee_{j=i}^{n-1} b_j \right) = \bigvee_{i=1}^{n-1} e_i \left(\bigvee_{j=i}^{n-1} c_j \right) = \bigvee_{j=1}^{n-1} e_j c_j.$$

Since $c_0, c_1, \ldots, c_{n-2}, c_{n-1}$ is a sequence of n elements satisfying *P3* and *P6*, the result follows by the uniqueness of the disjoint operations ∎

4.3   Monotonic operations

In this section the monotonic operations D_j are developed as follows.

Definition 4.9.

(i) $D_j(x) = C_j(x) \vee C_{j+1}(x) \vee \cdots \vee C_{n-1}(x)$ for $j = 1, \ldots, n-1$.

As a notational convenience, $D_0(x)$ stands for $C_0(x) \vee C_1(x) \vee \cdots \vee C_{n-1}(x) = \mathbf{V}$. Also, setting $j = n-1$ in (i) yields $D_{n-1}(x) = C_{n-1}(x)$. Note that $D_j(x)$ for each j is a complemented element by Theorem 4.4(i) and Theorem 3.29.

THEOREM 4.10. $C_i(x) = D_i(x)\overline{D_{i+1}(x)}$ for $i = 0, 1, \ldots, n-2$ and $C_{n-1}(x) = D_{n-1}(x)$.

Proof.   This follows from Definition 4.9 and *P3*(i)   ∎

THEOREM 4.11. $D_i(e_j) = \mathbf{V}$ for $i \le j$ and $D_i(e_j) = \mathbf{\Lambda}$ for $i > j$.

Proof.   This follows from Definition 4.9 and Theorem 4.7   ∎

THEOREM 4.12. $D_i(D_j(x)) = D_j(x)$ for $1 \le i, j \le n-1$.

Proof.   This follows from Definition 4.9 and Theorem 4.6   ∎

THEOREM 4.13.   The following hold for all i, j satisfying $1 \le i \le j \le n-1$.

(i) $D_j(x) \le D_i(x)$

(ii) $x = \displaystyle\bigvee_{k=1}^{n-1} e_k D_k(x)$

(iii) If $b_j \le b_i$ are complemented elements satisfying

$$x = \bigvee_{i=1}^{n-1} e_i b_i$$

then $b_i = D_i(x)$ for each i.

Proof.   These follow from Definition 4.9, Theorem 4.8, and *P6*   ∎

THEOREM 4.14   For each $i = 1, 2, \ldots, n-1$, $D_i(x \vee y) = D_i(x) \vee D_i(y)$.

Proof.   Since $D_j(x) \le D_i(x)$ and $D_j(y) \le D_i(y)$ for $1 \le i \le j \le n-1$ by Theorem 4.13(i), $D_j(x) \vee D_j(y) \le D_i(x) \vee D_i(y)$. Also

$$x \vee y = \bigvee_{i=1}^{n-1} e_i D_i(x) \vee \bigvee_{i=1}^{n-1} e_i D_i(y)$$

$$= \bigvee_{i=1}^{n-1} e_i (D_i(x) \vee D_i(y))$$

by Theorem 4.13(ii) and distributivity. The result follows by Theorem 4.13(iii).

The monotonic operations are helpful in obtaining certain results. The following is a companion to *P4*(i) ∎

THEOREM 4.15. For each $i = 0, 1, \ldots, n - 1$

$$C_i(x \vee y) = C_i(x) \bigvee_{j=0}^{i} C_j(y) \vee C_i(y) \bigvee_{j=0}^{i} C_j(x).$$

Proof. For $i = n - 1$ the result follows directly from *P3*(ii) and *P4*(ii). For $i = 0, 1, \ldots, n - 2$

$$C_i(x \vee y) = D_i(x \vee y)\overline{D_{i+1}(x \vee y)}$$

by Theorem 4.10

$$= (D_i(x) \vee D_i(y))\overline{D_{i+1}(x)}\,\overline{D_{i+1}(y)}$$

by Theorem 4.14 and Lemma 4.2(viii)

$$= C_i(x)\overline{D_{i+1}(y)} \vee C_i(y)\overline{D_{i+1}(x)}$$

by distributivity and Theorem 4.10

$$= C_i(x) \bigvee_{j=0}^{i} C_j(y) \vee C_i(y) \bigvee_{j=0}^{i} C_j(x)$$

using Definition 4.9

∎

THEOREM 4.16. A necessary and sufficient condition that $x \leq y$ is that $D_i(x) \leq D_i(y)$ for each $i = 1, 2, \ldots, n - 1$.

Proof. If $x \leq y$, then $x \vee y = y$ by Theorem 3.18(i) and $D_i(x) \vee D_i(y) = D_i(y)$ by Theorem 4.14, so $D_i(x) \leq D_i(y)$ by Theorem 3.18(i) for each $i = 1, \ldots, n - 1$. Conversely, if $D_i(x) \leq D_i(y)$ for each $i = 1, \ldots, n - 1$, then

$$x = \bigvee_{i=1}^{n-1} e_i D_i(x) \leq \bigvee_{i=1}^{n-1} e_i D_i(y) = y$$

by Theorem 4.13(ii) ∎

Applications for linearly ordered Post algebras of order n may be found in Chapter 2. Relevant tables are in Lemmas 2.2 and 2.3.

4.4   Duality and inversion

THEOREM 4.17.   A Post algebra of order n is isomorphic with its dual
under the mapping

$$(0) \qquad\qquad N(x) = \bigvee_{i=1}^{n-1} e_i \overline{D_{n-i}(x)}.$$

Let $\underline{A}$ denote the Post algebra of order n and let $\underline{A}^{\ddagger}$ denote its dual, while
$C_i^{\ddagger}$ and $e_i^{\ddagger}$ denote the operations of Postulates $P2$–$P6$ for $\underline{A}^{\ddagger}$ and $D_i^{\ddagger}$ denotes
the operations of Definition 4.9 for $\underline{A}^{\ddagger}$. These operations in $\underline{A}^{\ddagger}$ are given by
the following.

(i) $\qquad\qquad\qquad\qquad e_i^{\ddagger} = e_{n-i-1}$

(ii) $\qquad\qquad\qquad\qquad C_i^{\ddagger}(x) = \overline{C_{n-i-1}(x)}$

(iii) $\qquad\qquad\qquad\qquad D_i^{\ddagger}(x) = D_{n-i}(x).$

Proof.   Since $\overline{D_{n-j}(x)} \le \overline{D_{n-i}(x)}$ by Theorem 4.13(i), and Lemma 4.2(xiv)
applies for all $1 \le i \le j \le n-1$, Theorem 4.13(iii) yields

(iv) $\qquad\qquad\qquad\qquad D_i(N(x)) = \overline{D_{n-i}(x)}.$

Thus

(v) $\qquad\qquad\qquad\qquad N(N(z)) = z$

and it follows from Theorem 4.16 that

(vi) $\qquad\qquad\qquad x \le y$ if and only if $N(y) \le N(x).$

Consequently $\underline{A}^{\ddagger}$ is isomorphic with $\underline{A}$, so that $\underline{A}^{\ddagger}$ satisfies $P1$–$P6$. Since

$$\overline{D_{n-i}(x)} = \bigvee_{j=0}^{n-i-1} C_j(x)$$

and

$$\bigvee_{i=1}^{n-1} e_i \left(\bigvee_{j=0}^{n-i-1} C_j(x) \right) = \bigvee_{j=0}^{n-2} C_j(x) \left(\bigvee_{i=1}^{n-j-1} e_i \right) = \bigvee_{j=0}^{n-2} C_j(x) e_{n-j-1}$$

by Definition 4.9, $P3$, distributivity, and $e_1 \le \cdots \le e_{n-1}$,
setting $k = n - j - 1$ yields

$$(vii) \qquad\qquad\qquad N(x) = \bigvee_{k=1}^{n-1} e_k C_{n-k-1}(x).$$

Thus

$$(viii) \qquad\qquad\qquad e_i^{\ddagger} = N(e_i) = e_{n-i-1}$$

by uniqueness of the e_i, proving (i). Also

(ix) $$C_i(N(x)) = C_{n-i-1}(x)$$

by uniqueness of the disjoint operations C_i, and

(x) $$N(b) = C_0(b) = \bar{b}$$

whenever b is a complemented element by Theorem 4.6. Consequently

$$C_i^{\dagger}(x) = N(C_i(N(x))) \qquad \text{by the isomorphism}$$

$$= \overline{C_i(N(x))} \qquad \text{by } (x)$$

$$= \overline{C_{n-i-1}(x)} \qquad \text{for } i = 0, 1, \ldots, n-1 \text{ by (ix)}.$$

This proves (ii). Finally

$$D_i^{\dagger}(x) = N(D_i(N(x))) \qquad \text{by the isomorphism}$$

$$= \overline{D_i(N(x))} \qquad \text{by } (x)$$

$$= D_{n-i}(x) \qquad \text{by (iv)}.$$

This proves (iii) ∎

THEOREM 4.18. Some additional properties are given below.
(i) $N(x \vee y) = N(x)N(y)$
(ii) $N(xy) = N(x) \vee N(y)$
(iii) $xN(x) \leq y \vee N(y)$.

Proof of (i), (ii). These De Morgan identities follow from the isomorphism of Theorem 4.17.

Proof of (iii). Consider the two cases, n is odd and n is even.
   First, for odd n

$$y \vee N(y) = \bigvee_{i=1}^{n-1} e_i C_i(y) \vee \bigvee_{i=1}^{n-1} e_i C_{n-i-1}(y)$$

by $P6$ and Theorem 4.17(vii)

$$= \bigvee_{i=1}^{n-1} e_i(C_i(y) \vee C_{n-i-1}(y))$$

by distributivity

$$= e_{(n-1)/2} \bigvee_{i=(n-1)/2}^{n-1} (C_i(y) \vee C_{n-i-1}(y))$$

$$\vee \bigvee_{i=(n+1)/2}^{n-1} e_i(C_i(y) \vee C_{n-i-1}(y))$$

$$\text{using } e_1 \leq e_2 \leq \cdots \leq e_{n-1}$$

$$= e_{(n-1)/2} \vee \bigvee_{i=(n+1)/2}^{n-1} e_i(C_i(y) \vee C_{n-i-1}(y))$$

by *P3*(ii) and **V**-property

$$\geq e_{(n-1)/2}.$$

Hence

$$x \vee N(x) \geq e_{(n-1)/2}$$

$$N(x \vee N(x)) \leq N(e_{(n-1)/2})$$

by Theorem 4.17(vi)

$$xN(x) \leq e_{(n-1)/2}$$

by (i), Theorem 4.17(v), (viii) for odd n.

Thus

$$xN(x) \leq y \vee N(y).$$

Second, for even n, following the lines in the first part

$$y \vee N(y) = \bigvee_{i=1}^{n-1} e_i C_i(y) \vee \bigvee_{i=1}^{n-1} e_i C_{n-i-1}(y)$$

$$= \bigvee_{i=1}^{n-1} e_i(C_i(y) \vee C_{n-i-1}(y))$$

$$= e_{n/2} \bigvee_{i=n/2}^{n-1} (C_i(y) \vee C_{n-i-1}(y))$$

$$\vee \bigvee_{i=(n+2)/2}^{n-1} e_i(C_i(y) \vee C_{n-i-1}(y))$$

$$= e_{n/2} \vee \bigvee_{i=(n+2)/2}^{n-1} e_i(C_i(y) \vee C_{n-i-1}(y))$$

$$\geq e_{n/2}.$$

Hence

$$x \vee N(x) \geq e_{n/2}$$

$$N(x \vee N(x)) \leq N(e_{n/2})$$

by Theorem 4.17(vi).

$$xN(x) \leq e_{(n-2)/2}$$

by (i), Theorem 4.17(v), (viii) for even n.

Thus

$$xN(x) \le y \vee N(y)$$

since

$$e_{(n-2)/2} \le e_{n/2} \qquad \text{by } P2 \qquad \blacksquare$$

The following conjunctive form is a companion for the disjunctive form given in *P6*.

THEOREM 4.19. In a Post algebra of order n

$$x = \overline{C_0(x)}(e_1 \vee \overline{C_1(x)}) \cdots (e_{n-2} \vee \overline{C_{n-2}(x)}).$$

Proof.

$$x = N(N(x)) = N\left(\bigvee_{i=1}^{n-1} e_i C_{n-i-1}(x) \right)$$

by Theorem 4.17(v), (vii)

$$= \bigwedge_{i=1}^{n-1} (N(e_i) \vee N(C_{n-i-1}(x)))$$

by Theorem 4.18(i), (ii)

$$= \bigwedge_{i=1}^{n-1} (e_{n-i-1} \vee \overline{C_{n-i-1}(x)})$$

by Theorem 4.7(viii), (x) ∎

In a linearly ordered Post algebra of order n, Theorem 4.17(viii) gives the table for inversion as presented in Chapter 2. Relevant details are in Lemma 2.2(v), Lemma 2.3(vi), (vii), and Exercises E2.2–E2.6. The unary operations $C_i(x)$, $D_i(x)$, and $N(x)$ for the 5-element Post chain and the 6-element Post chain are shown by the tables in figure 4.2.

Inversion is an operation which occurs in many applications involving computer circuitry and systems. It plays a role in the K method described in Chapter 3, and is commonly used in fault diagnosis. Further, the isomorphism of a Post algebra of order n with its dual can ease certain proofs. An example is the proof of Theorem 4.19. Also, consider the proof of the following companion to Theorem 4.14.

THEOREM 4.20. $D_j(xy) = D_j(x)D_j(y)$ for $j = 1, 2, \ldots, n-1$.

Proof.

$$D_i(x \vee y) = D_i(x) \vee D_i(y), \quad i = 1, \ldots, n-1$$

(a) n = 5

x	$C_0(x)$	$C_1(x)$	$C_2(x)$	$C_3(x)$	$C_4(x) = D_4(x)$	$D_3(x)$	$D_2(x)$	$D_1(x)$	$N(x)$
0	4	0	0	0	0	0	0	0	4
1	0	4	0	0	0	0	0	4	3
2	0	0	4	0	0	0	4	4	2
3	0	0	0	4	0	4	4	4	1
4	0	0	0	0	4	4	4	4	0

(b) n = 6

x	$C_0(x)$	$C_1(x)$	$C_2(x)$	$C_3(x)$	$C_4(x)$	$C_5(x) = D_5(x)$	$D_4(x)$	$D_3(x)$	$D_2(x)$	$D_1(x)$	$N(x)$
0	5	0	0	0	0	0	0	0	0	0	5
1	0	5	0	0	0	0	0	0	0	5	4
2	0	0	5	0	0	0	0	0	5	5	3
3	0	0	0	5	0	0	0	5	5	5	2
4	0	0	0	0	5	0	5	5	5	5	1
5	0	0	0	0	0	5	5	5	5	5	0

Figure 4.2 Tables for unary operations in Post algebras of order (*a*) 5 and (*b*) 6.

by Theorem 4.14. Hence

$$D_{n-j}(N(x) \vee N(y)) = D_{n-j}(N(x)) \vee D_{n-j}(N(y)), \quad j = 1, \ldots, n-1$$
$$D_{n-j}(N(xy)) = D_{n-j}(N(x)) \vee D_{n-j}(N(y)), \quad j = 1, \ldots, n-1$$

by Theorem 4.18(ii)

$$\overline{D_j(xy)} = \overline{D_j(x)} \vee \overline{D_j(y)}, \quad j = 1, \ldots, n-1$$

by Theorem 4.17(iv)

$$D_j(xy) = D_j(x)D_j(y), \quad j = 1, \ldots, n-1$$

by Lemma 4.2(viii), (x) ∎

It follows from Theorems 4.14 and 4.20 that D_i for each $i = 1, 2, \ldots, n-1$ is a lattice homomorphism from A onto the center of A, with $b = D_i(b)$ for any element b in the center by Theorem 4.6 and Definition 4.9.

4.5 Normal forms for Postian functions

Full disjunctive or conjunctive normal forms are an important starting point for the expression or simplification of multiple-valued functions.

Definition 4.21. A Postian function of m variables $x_1, \ldots, x_m$ in the disjoint system of Post algebras of order n is a function which can be obtained from four kinds of construction.
(i) From the constant functions $E_i(x_1, \ldots, x_m) = e_i$.
(ii) From the identity functions $I_j(x_1, \ldots, x_m) = x_j$.
(iii) By a finite number of operations $\vee$, $\wedge$.
(iv) By a finite number of operations $C_0, C_1, \ldots, C_{n-1}$.
An important normal form result is the full disjunctive normal form (fdnf) theorem. The following definition and corollary is a preliminary to this theorem.

Definition 4.22. If m denotes the number of variables, then a *fundament* is a meet as follows

$$C_{i_1}(x_1)C_{i_2}(x_2) \cdots C_{i_m}(x_m)$$

where

$$0 \le i_j \le n-1.$$

Corollary 4.23. The following statements hold.
(i) There are n^m different fundaments of the m variables.
(ii) Distinct fundaments are disjoint.
(iii) The join of all the n^m fundaments is **V**.

Proof. Since there are n different possibilities for each subscript, and m different subscripts, the proof of (i) is clear. Statements (ii) and (iii) follow from $P3$ ∎

THEOREM 4.24. If f is a Postian function of m variables in the disjoint system of Post algebras of order n, then

$$f(x_1, \ldots, x_m) = \bigvee_{0 \le i_j \le n-1} f(e_{i_1}, \ldots, e_{i_m}) C_{i_1}(x_1) \cdots C_{i_m}(x_m).$$

Proof. It follows from Corollary 4.23(iii) that the theorem holds for the constant functions E_i. The theorem also holds for the identity functions I_j by $P6$. It is clear that if f and g satisfy the theorem, then $f \vee g$ satisfies the theorem. Using Corollary 4.23(ii), it is also clear that if f and g satisfy the theorem, then fg satisfies the theorem.

Finally, suppose that f is a Postian function satisfying the theorem. Each of $f(e_{i_1}, \ldots, e_{i_m})$ is equal to one of the e_j, by $P2$ and Theorem 4.7. Therefore

$$f(x_1, \ldots, x_m) = \bigvee_{k=0}^{n-1} e_k \left(\bigvee C_{i_1}(x_1) \cdots C_{i_m}(x_m) \right)$$

the inner join being extended over $(i_1, \ldots, i_m)$ for which $f(e_{i_1}, \ldots, e_{i_m}) = e_k$. Using Corollary 4.23(ii), (iii) and uniqueness of the disjoint operations, $C_k(f)$ is equal to the inner join for each k. Hence $C_k(f(x_1, \ldots, x_m))$ satisfies the theorem   ∎

There is a dual version of Theorem 4.24, called the full conjunctive normal form (fcnf) theorem.

THEOREM 4.25. If f is a Postian function of m variables in the disjoint system of Post algebras of order n, then

$$f(x_1, \ldots, x_m) = \bigwedge_{0 \le i_j \le n-1} (f(e_{i_1}, \ldots, e_{i_m}) \vee \overline{C_{i_1}(x_1)} \vee \cdots \vee \overline{C_{i_m}(x_m)}).$$

Proof. This follows from Theorems 4.17 and 4.24   ∎

The expression for f in Theorem 4.24 is called "full" because *all* the variables $x_1, \ldots, x_m$ appear in each meet. There is no such requirement for a disjunctive normal form (dnf). There are dual remarks for the expression in Theorem 4.25. With respect to the fcnf in Theorem 4.25, each join $\overline{C_{i_1}(x)} \vee \cdots \vee \overline{C_{i_m}(x_m)}$ is called a *dual fundament*. There are n^m different dual fundaments of the m variables. The join of two distinct dual fundaments is $\mathbf{V}$ and the meet of all the n^m dual fundaments is $\boldsymbol{\wedge}$.

Definition 4.26. A Postian function of m variables in the monotonic system of Post algebras of order n is obtained from the constructions (i)–(iii) in Definition 4.21, replacing the fourth construction with

(iv)'. A Postian function can be obtained by a finite number of operations $C_0, D_1, D_2, \ldots, D_{n-2}, D_{n-1}$.

It is easy to see that a Postian function in the disjoint system of Post algebras of order n can be written as a Postian function in the monotonic system of Post algebras of order n, and conversely, by Definition 4.9 and Theorem 4.10.

Definition 4.27. A Postian function of m variables in the disjoint system of Post algebras of order n with inversion, is a function which can be obtained by adding the construction

(v). A Postian function can be obtained by a finite number of operations, N, to (i)–(iv) of Definition 4.21.

Definition 4.28. A Postian function of m variables in the monotonic system of Post algebras of order n with inversion, is a function which can be obtained by adding the construction (v) of Definition 4.27 to (i)–(iii) of Definition 4.21 and (iv)' of Definition 4.26.

Postian functions in the disjoint system with inversion appear in the K method as presented in subsections 3.4.1–3.4.3. Postian functions in the monotonic system appear in Section 9.2. Postian functions in the monotonic system with inversion appear in Sections 9.3 and 9.4.

Any Postian function in the disjoint system with inversion can be expanded into a Postian function in the disjoint system through Theorem 4.17(vii). The K method in subsections 3.4.1–3.4.3 of Section 3.4 is a systematic way of simplifying a Postian function with a small number of variables in the disjoint system to a Postian function in the disjoint system with inversion. Any Postian function in the monotonic system with inversion can be expanded into a Postian function in the monotonic system through Theorem 4.17(0).

Any fdnf or fcnf may be simplified algebraically, but such simplifications may be difficult to find. It will be convenient for the presentation that follows to use one 3-valued function $h_1(x, y)$ whose fdnf is

$$h_1 = e_1 C_0(x) C_1(y) \vee e_1 C_1(x) C_1(y) \vee e_1 C_1(x) C_2(y) \vee C_0(x) C_2(y)$$
$$\vee C_2(x) C_1(y).$$

Recall that various dnf simplifications were given for this function, h_1, using the K method in subsections 3.4.1 and 3.4.4.

First

$$h_1 = e_1 C_1(y)[C_0(x) \vee C_1(x) \vee C_2(x)] \vee e_1 C_1(x)C_2(y) \vee C_0(x)C_2(y)$$
$$\vee C_2(x)C_1(y)$$

by absorption and distributivity

$$= e_1 C_1(y) \vee e_1 C_1(x)C_2(y) \vee C_0(x)C_2(y)$$
$$\vee C_2(x)C_1(y) \quad \text{by } P3(\text{ii}) \text{ and } \textbf{V}\text{-property.}$$

This is the Postian function in the disjoint system of Post algebras of order 3 given for h_1 in subsection 3.4.4(b).

Second, continuing from the last line for h_1,

$$h_1 = e_1 C_1(y) \vee e_1 C_1(x)[C_1(y) \vee C_2(y)] \vee C_0(x)C_2(y)$$
$$\vee C_2(x)C_1(y) \qquad\qquad \text{by absorption and distributivity}$$

$$= e_1 C_1(y) \vee e_1 C_1(x)D_1(y)$$
$$\vee C_0(x)C_2(y) \vee C_2(x)C_1(y)$$

by Definition 4.9. This is one of the simplified answers given for h_1 in subsection 3.4.4(c).

Third, from the given fdnf for h_1

$$h_1 = [e_1 C_1(x) \vee C_2(x)]C_1(y) \vee C_0(x)[e_1 C_1(y) \vee C_2(y)]$$
$$\vee e_1 C_1(x)C_2(y) \qquad\qquad \text{using distributivity}$$

$$= xC_1(y) \vee yC_0(x) \vee e_1 C_1(x)C_2(y) \qquad\qquad \text{by } P6.$$

This is the Postian function in the disjoint system of Post algebras of order 3 given by h_1 in subsection 3.4.4(a).

Fourth and last, from the given fdnf for h_1

$$h_1 = [e_1 C_1(x) \vee C_0(x)][e_1 C_1(y) \vee C_2(y)] \vee [e_1 C_1(x) \vee C_2(x)]C_1(y)$$

by idempotence and distributivity

$$= yN(x) \vee xC_1(y)$$

by $P6$ and Theorem 4.17(vii). This is one of the simplified answers in the disjoint system of Post algebras of order 3. with inversion given for h_1 in subsection 3.4.1.

4.6   Post algebras and special lattices

This section uses some of the special lattices discussed in Chapter 3 to find additional properties of Post algebras of order n.

THEOREM 4.29.   A Post algebra of order n is a B-algebra with $x \Rightarrow y$ given by

$$(0) \qquad x \Rightarrow y = C_0(x) \vee \bigvee_{i=1}^{n-1} (C_i(x)D_i(y)).$$

Proof.
(i)   For each $i = 1, \ldots, n-1$, $(C_i(x)e_i) \Rightarrow y$ exists and is equal to $\overline{C_i(x)} \vee D_i(y)$.
   This is shown in two parts. First

$$C_i(x)e_i[\overline{C_i(x)} \vee D_i(y)] = \boldsymbol{\Lambda} \vee C_i(x)e_i D_i(y)$$

$$= C_i(x)e_i D_i(y)$$

by distributivity, complementarity, and $\boldsymbol{\Lambda}$-property, and

$$C_i(x)e_i D_i(y) \le C_i(x)y \le y$$

using Theorem 4.13(ii). Second, suppose that $C_i(x)e_i b \le y$, where b is a complemented element.

$$D_i(C_i(x)e_i b) \le D_i(y)$$

$$\text{for each } i \text{ by Theorem 4.16}$$

$$D_i(C_i(x))D_i(e_i)D_i(b) \le D_i(y)$$

$$\text{by Theorem 4.20}$$

$$C_i(x)b \le D_i(y)$$

by Theorem 4.11, Theorem 4.6, and Definition 4.9. Thus

$$b \le \overline{C_i(x)} \vee b = \overline{C_i(x)} \vee C_i(x)b \le \overline{C_i(x)} \vee D_i(y)$$

using distributivity, complementarity, and $\boldsymbol{V}$-property.
(ii)   If $x \Rightarrow w$ and $y \Rightarrow w$ exist, then $(x \vee y) \Rightarrow w = (x \Rightarrow w)(y \Rightarrow w)$. This follows because the proof of Theorem 3.52(viii) applies.
(iii)   Finally,

$$[e_1 C_1(x) \vee \cdots \vee e_{n-1} C_{n-1}(x)] \Rightarrow y$$

$$= \bigwedge_{i=1}^{n-1} [(e_i C_i(x)) \Rightarrow y] = \bigwedge_{i=1}^{n-1} (\overline{C_i(x)} \vee D_i(y))$$

by (i) and (ii). Thus

$$x \Rightarrow y = \bigwedge_{i=1}^{n-1} [\overline{C_i(x)} \vee D_i(y)] \qquad\qquad \text{by } P6$$

and

$$x \Rightarrow y = C_0(x) \vee \bigvee_{i=1}^{n-1} C_i(x)D_i(y)$$

using Theorem 4.5, distributivity, $P3(i)$, Theorem 4.13(i) and absorption ∎

Corollary 4.30. A Post algebra of order n is a supplemented lattice with $!y = \mathbf{V} \Rightarrow y = D_{n-1}(y) = C_{n-1}(y)$.

Proof. From Theorem 4.29, Theorem 4.7 and Theorem 3.22 $!y = \mathbf{V} \Rightarrow y = D_{n-1}(y)$ and $C_{n-1}(y) = D_{n-1}(y)$ by Definition 4.9 ∎

THEOREM 4.31. A Post algebra of order n is a P-algebra.

Proof. After Theorem 4.29 it remains to prove that

(i) $\qquad\qquad (x \Rightarrow y) \vee (y \Rightarrow x) = \mathbf{V}.$

$$(x \Rightarrow y) \vee (y \Rightarrow x) = C_0(x) \vee \bigvee_{i=1}^{n-1} C_i(x)D_i(y)$$

$$\vee\, C_0(y) \vee \bigvee_{i=1}^{n-1} C_i(y)D_i(x)$$

$$= \bigvee_{i=0}^{n-1} C_i(x)[C_i(y) \vee \cdots \vee C_{n-1}(y)]$$

$$\vee \bigvee_{i=0}^{n-1} C_i(y)[C_i(x) \vee \cdots \vee C_{n-1}(x)]$$

$$= \bigvee_{0 \le i,j \le n-1} C_i(x)C_j(y)$$

$$= \mathbf{V}$$

by Corollary 4.23(iii) ∎

Corollary 4.32. The prime ideals of a Post algebra of order n lie in disjoint chains.

Proof. It is shown in Epstein and Horn (1974a) that the prime ideals of a P-algebra lie in disjoint chains. The result follows from Theorem 4.31 ∎

THEOREM 4.33. A Post algebra of order n is a Heyting algebra with
(i) $x \to y = (x \Rightarrow y) \vee y$.

Proof. This follows from Theorem 4.31 and Theorem 3.54(i) ∎

Corollary 4.34. A Post algebra of order n is a pseudo-complemented lattice with $\neg x = C_0(x) = x \Rightarrow \wedge$.

Proof. The result follows by substituting $\wedge$ for y in Theorems 4.29 and 4.33 using Theorem 4.11 ∎

Corollary 4.35. A Post algebra of order n is a Stone algebra.

Proof. $C_0(x) \vee D_1(x) = \mathbf{V}$, so $C_0(x) \vee C_0(C_0(x)) = \mathbf{V}$ ∎

THEOREM 4.36. A Post algebra of order n is an L-algebra.

Proof.

$$(x \to y) \vee (y \to x) = y \vee (x \Rightarrow y) \vee (y \Rightarrow x) \vee x$$

by Theorem 4.33

$$= y \vee \mathbf{V} \vee x$$

by Theorem 4.31

$$= \mathbf{V}$$

by $\mathbf{V}$-property ∎

THEOREM 4.37. A Post algebra of order n is a Kleene algebra with $\sim x = N(x)$.

Proof. This follows directly from Theorem 4.17(v) and 4.18(ii), (iii) ∎

THEOREM 4.38. The following hold in a Post algebra of order n.
(i) $D_i(y) = e_i \Rightarrow y$ for $i = 0, 1, \ldots, n-1$
(ii) $C_i(x) = (e_i \Rightarrow x)(x \Rightarrow e_i)$ for $i = 0, 1, \ldots, n-1$
(iii) $e_i \Rightarrow e_j = \wedge \quad$ for $i > j$
$ = \mathbf{V} \quad$ for $i \leq j$
(iv) $e_i \to e_j = e_j \quad$ for $i > j$
$ = \mathbf{V} \quad$ for $i \leq j$
(v) $!e_i = \wedge \quad$ for $i < n-1$
$!e_{n-1} = \mathbf{V}$
(vi) $\neg e_i = \wedge \quad$ for $i > 0$
$\neg e_0 = \mathbf{V}$.

Proof. To prove (i), set $x = e_i$ in Theorem 4.29(i).
(ii) follows through evaluation of $e_i \Rightarrow x$ and $x \Rightarrow e_i$ by Theorem 4.29. This

yields

$$(e_i \Rightarrow x)(x \Rightarrow e_i) = D_i(x)[C_0(x) \vee \cdots \vee C_i(x)]$$
$$= C_i(x) \text{ using Definition 4.9 and } P3(\text{i}).$$

(iii) follows from (i) and Theorem 4.11.
(iv) follows from (iii) and Theorem 4.33.
(v) follows from (iii) since $!e_i = e_{n-1} \Rightarrow e_i$.
(vi) follows from (iv) since $\neg e_i = e_i \rightarrow e_0$ ∎

Various elements in a Post algebra of order n may be computed easily using these results. Given y, for example, $D_i(y)$ or $C_i(y)$ for each $i = 0, 1, \ldots, n-1$ may be computed by Theorem 4.38(i) or (ii), respectively. Other computations can be made from Theorem 4.10 or Definition 4.9. Lastly, $N(y)$ follows from Theorem 4.17(0) or Theorem 4.17(vii).

An illustration is given in figure 4.3, which displays the Post algebra of order 3 with one free generator consisting of 27 elements. For the given y, the elements $C_0(y)$, $C_1(y)$, $C_2(y) = D_2(y)$, $D_1(y)$, $N(y)$ are shown, together with the chain of 3 elements, $\Lambda = e_0, e_1$, and $e_2 = V$. Computation proceeds easily. First, $C_0(y) = \neg y$ and $C_2(y) = D_2(y) = !y$. Second, for $n = 3$, $C_1(y) = \neg y \vee !y$, by $P3$. Third, $D_1(y) = C_1(y) \vee C_2(y)$ by Definition 4.9. Finally, $N(y) = e_1 C_1(y) \vee C_0(y)$ by Theorem 4.17(vii).

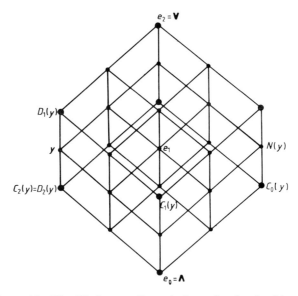

Figure 4.3   The 27-element Post algebra of order 3 with given y, showing the elements $e_0, e_1, e_2, C_0(y), C_1(y), C_2(y) = D_2(y), D_1(y)$, $N(y)$.

Applications for linearly ordered Post algebras of order n may be found in Chapter 2. Relevant tables may be found in Lemma 2.8.

4.7 Post algebras of order n and n-valued functions

This section gives a representation theory which uses n-valued functions. Examples are given where the number of different n-valued functions in the Post algebra is finite and equal to n^c, $n \geq 2$ and $c \geq 1$. The examples in this section include $n = 5$, $c = 2$ and $n = 4$, $c = 7$.

THEOREM 4.39. The Post algebra of order n, A, is isomorphic with the set of all continuous n-valued functions on a Stone space.

Proof. Details of a proof may be found in Section 6 of Epstein (1960). An introduction to Stone spaces may be found in pp 117–27 of Grätzer (1971) ∎

Corollary 4.40. The Post algebra of order n, A, is complete and atomic if and only if A is isomorphic with the set of all n-valued functions on a set S.

Proof. This follows from Theorem 4.39. Details are in Section 6 of Epstein (1960) ∎

The corollary below follows directly from Corollary 4.40, Theorem 3.14, and Theorem 3.20.

Corollary 4.41. The Post algebra of order n, A, contains a finite number of elements if and only if A is isomorphic with the set of all n-valued functions on a c-point set S, where c is the number of atoms of L.

This is discussed in the remainder of this section. It is immediate from Corollary 4.41 that the number of elements in A is n^c. This is illustrated in figure 4.1 for $c = 1$, $n = 2, 3, 4$; for $c = 2$, $n = 2, 3, 4$; and $c = 3$, $n = 2$. For $n = 3$, $c = 1, 2, 3$, see figure 3.26.

To furnish an additional example, figure 4.4 shows a lattice for $n = 5$, $c = 2$—that is, the $5^2 = 25$ 5-valued functions on a 2-point set.

To give a further example, consider the 4-valued function on a 7-point set. Here $n = 4$ and $c = 7$, so that the number of elements in this lattice is $4^7 = 16\,384$.

Observe that the n-valued functions take values $0, 1, 2, \ldots, n - 1$. The n elements e_i correspond to the n constant functions i, where $i = 0, 1, \ldots, n - 1$. If x corresponds to the n-valued function f, then $C_i(x)$ for each i corresponds to that function which has the value $n - 1$ at those points of S where f has the value i, and has the value 0 at the other points of S; $D_j(x)$ for each j

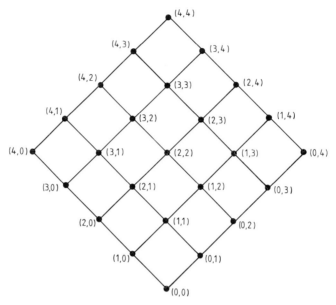

Figure 4.4   The 5-valued functions on a 2-point set ($n = 5$, $c = 2$).

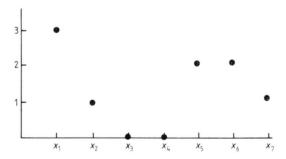

Figure 4.5   The 4-valued function $(3, 1, 0, 0, 2, 2, 1)$ on a 7-point set.

corresponds to that function which has the value $n - 1$ at those points of S where f has value $\geq j$, and has the value 0 at the other points of S. Finally, if x corresponds to the n-valued function f, then $N(x)$ corresponds to that function which has the value $n - 1 - i$ at those points of S where f has the value i, $0 \leq i \leq n - 1$.

To give a specific illustration, consider the 4-valued functions on a 7-point set and the element x corresponding to the function $(3, 1, 0, 0, 2, 2, 1)$ shown in figure 4.5. Then $C_0(x)$ corresponds to $(0, 0, 3, 3, 0, 0, 0)$, $C_1(x)$ corresponds to $(0, 3, 0, 0, 0, 0, 3)$, $C_2(x)$ corresponds to $(0, 0, 0, 0, 3, 3, 0)$, and $C_3(x)$ corresponds to $(3, 0, 0, 0, 0, 0, 0)$; $D_3(x)$ corresponds to $(3, 0, 0, 0, 0, 0, 0)$, $D_2(x)$ corresponds to $(3, 0, 0, 0, 3, 3, 0)$, and $D_1(x)$ corresponds to

$(3, 3, 0, 0, 3, 3, 3)$. $N(x)$ corresponds to $(0, 2, 3, 3, 1, 1, 2)$. The seven atoms are $(1, 0, 0, 0, 0, 0, 0)$, $(0, 1, 0, 0, 0, 0, 0)$, $(0, 0, 1, 0, 0, 0, 0)$, $(0, 0, 0, 1, 0, 0, 0)$, $(0, 0, 0, 0, 1, 0, 0)$, $(0, 0, 0, 0, 0, 1, 0)$, and $(0, 0, 0, 0, 0, 0, 1)$. The seven antiatoms are $(2, 3, 3, 3, 3, 3, 3)$, $(3, 2, 3, 3, 3, 3, 3)$, $(3, 3, 2, 3, 3, 3, 3)$, $(3, 3, 3, 2, 3, 3, 3)$, $(3, 3, 3, 2, 3, 3, 3)$, $(3, 3, 3, 3, 3, 2, 3)$, and $(3, 3, 3, 3, 3, 3, 2)$.

4.8 Post algebras of order n and prime ideals

THEOREM 4.42. Let L be the set of all n-valued functions on a set S consisting of c points, where $n \geq 2$ and $c \geq 1$. Then there are exactly $(n-1)c$ distinct prime ideals of the form $P_{si} = \{f : f(s) \leq i - 1\}$ for fixed s in S and $1 \leq i \leq n - 1$. That is, every maximal chain of properly ascending prime ideals in L consists of exactly $n - 1$ prime ideals, and every prime ideal is a member of one such chain.

Proof. It is easy to show that for any fixed $s \in S$, P_{si} is a prime ideal. First, if $g_1 \in P_{si}$ then $g_0 \leq g_1$ implies $g_0 \in P_{si}$ because $g_0(s) \leq g_1(s)$. Thus Definition 3.55(i) is satisfied. Second, let $g_2 \in P_{si}$. Then $g_1 \vee g_2 \in P_{si}$ because $g_1(s) \vee g_2(s) = \max(g_1(s), g_2(s))$. Thus Definition 3.55(ii) is satisfied, and P_{si} is an ideal. Third, if $g_1 \notin P_{si}$ and $g_2 \notin P_{si}$, then $g_1 g_2 \notin P_{si}$, because $g_1(s) g_2(s) = \min(g_1(s), g_2(s))$. Thus P_{si} is a prime ideal. It is obvious that there are exactly $(n-1)c$ distinct such prime ideals. By Corollary 4.32 every prime ideal must be of this form ∎

Example 4.1. Consider the lattice of 5-valued functions on a set S consisting of two points $\{0, 1\}$. The 25 functions are shown in the 25-element lattice of figure 4.4. By Theorem 4.42 there are exactly $(5 - 1)2 = 8$ distinct prime ideals called $P_{01}, P_{02}, P_{03}, P_{04}, P_{11}, P_{12}, P_{13}$, and P_{14}. These prime ideals are shown and labeled in figure 4.6.

Example 4.2. Consider the 27-element lattice of all 3-valued functions on a set S consisting of 3 points $\{0, 1, 2\}$ as shown in figure 3.26(iii). By Theorem 4.42 there are exactly $(3 - 1)3 = 6$ distinct prime ideals called $P_{01}, P_{02}, P_{11}, P_{12}, P_{21}$, and P_{22}. Note that P_{01}, P_{11}, and P_{21} each consists of 9 elements, and P_{02}, P_{12}, and P_{22} each consists of 18 elements.

THEOREM 4.43. Let L be a finite distributive lattice in which every maximal chain of properly ascending prime ideals consists of exactly $n - 1$ prime ideals, and every prime ideal is a member of exactly one such chain. Then L is a Post algebra of order n.

Proof. Denote the chains of prime ideals by $P_{s1} \subset P_{s2} \subset \cdots \subset P_{s(n-1)}$, where s ranges over some finite index set S. Let P_{s0} denote the empty set $\varnothing$ and let P_{sn} denote L.

For any $x \in L$ and any $s \in S$ there exists $i(s, x) = i$ such that x is in the set

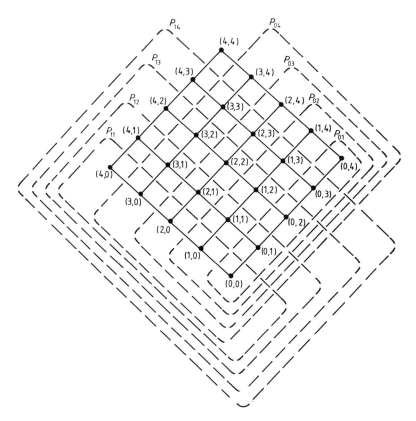

Figure 4.6 The eight prime ideals: $P_{01} \subset P_{02} \subset P_{03} \subset P_{04}$; $P_{11} \subset P_{12} \subset P_{13} \subset P_{14}$, for the lattice of 5-valued functions on a 2-point set $\{0, 1\}$.

difference $P_{s(i+1)} - P_{si}$. Hence

$$x \in \bigcap_{s \in S} (P_{s(i(s,x)+1)} - P_{si(s,x)}).$$

It can be shown that any such set intersection contains at most one element. Hence

$$\{x\} = \bigcap_{s \in S} (P_{s(i+1)} - P_{si}).$$

If $y \in L$ and $j(s, y) = j$, so that

$$\{y\} = \bigcap_{s \in S} (P_{s(j+1)} - P_{sj})$$

it follows that

(i) $$\{x \vee y\} = \bigcap_{s \in S} (P_{s(\max(i,j)+1)} - P_{s(\max(i,j))}),$$

(ii) $$\{xy\} = \bigcap_{s \in S} (P_{s(\min(i,j)+1)} - P_{s(\min(i,j))}).$$

Since L has a finite number of elements, it can be shown that for any $i(s)$

$$\bigcap_{s \in S} (P_{s(i(s)+1)} - P_{s(i(s))}) \neq \varnothing.$$

It follows that postulates $P1$–$P6$ are satisfied, with

(iii) $$\{e_i\} = \bigcap_{s \in S} (P_{s(i+1)} - P_{si})$$

and

(iv) $$\{C_j(x)\} = \bigcap_{x \in P_{s(j+1)} - P_{sj}} (L - P_{s(n-1)}) \cap \bigcap_{x \notin P_{s(j+1)} - P_{sj}} (P_{s1}).$$

To illustrate using figure 4.6, P_{04}–P_{03} is the line of points $\{(3, 0), (3, 1), (3, 2), (3, 3), (3, 4)\}$ and P_{14}–P_{13} is the line of points $\{(0, 3), (1, 3), (2, 3), (3, 3), (4, 3)\}$. The intersection of these two lines is obviously $\{(3, 3)\}$. That is

$$\{e_3\} = \{P_{04} - P_{03}\} \cap \{P_{14} - P_{13}\},$$

as given by Theorem 4.43(iii) for $n = 5$, $c = 2$, and $i = 3$.

Further developments relating to prime ideals may be found in Chang and Horn (1961), Traczyk (1968), Epstein and Horn (1974b), and Zarębski (1982).

4.9   Some completeness properties

There are certain completeness properties which hold in a Post algebra of order n, A. Some of these properties are given without proof below, where I represents an arbitrary index set. Details may be found in Section 7 of Epstein (1960).

THEOREM 4.44.   If

$$x = \bigvee_{i \in I} x_i$$

exists in A where $x_i \in A$ for all $i \in I$, then

$$\bigvee_{i \in I} D_j(x_i)$$

exists in B, the center of A, for each $j = 1, 2, \ldots, n - 1$. Conversely, if

$$\bigvee_{i \in I} D_j(x_i)$$

exists in B for each $j = 1, 2, \ldots, n - 1$ where $x_i \in A$ for all $i \in I$, then

$$\bigvee_{i \in I} x_i$$

exists in A and is equal to the element x which is determined by the formulas

$$D_j(x) = \bigvee_{i \in I} D_j(x_i)$$

in B. The dual statements are also true.

THEOREM 4.45. A is a complete lattice if and only if B, the center of A, is a complete lattice.

THEOREM 4.46.   The infinite distributive rule

$$y \bigvee_{i \in I} x_i = \bigvee_{i \in I} y x_i$$

is valid in A whenever

$$x = \bigvee_{i \in I} x_i$$

exists.

  The dual statement is also true.

THEOREM 4.47.   If

$$x = \bigvee_{i \in I} x_i$$

exists, then the following rules are valid.

$$C_{n-1}(x) = \bigvee_{i \in I} C_{n-1}(x_i)$$

$$C_k(x) = \bigvee_{i \in I} \left(\bigwedge_{j=k+1}^{n-1} \overline{C_j(x)} \right) C_k(x_i)$$

for $k = n - 2, n - 3, \ldots, 0$. Dually, if

$$y = \bigwedge_{i \in I} y_i$$

exists, then

$$C_0(y) = \bigvee_{i \in I} C_0(y_i)$$

$$C_k(y) = \bigvee_{i \in I} \left(\bigwedge_{j=0}^{k-1} \overline{C_j(y)} \right) C_k(y_i)$$

for $k = 1, 2, \ldots, n - 1$.

4.10 Overview

The formulation of Post algebras of order n given in Rosenbloom (1942) based on work in Post (1921) uses one unary operation, the prime operation illustrated in figure 2.14. A development for the disjoint system of Post algebras of order n may be found in Epstein (1960). Postulates consisting of identities for the monotonic system of Post algebras of order n are given in Traczyk (1964). Postulates consisting of identities for Post algebras of order n, using the monotonic system together with the binary operation $\rightarrow$ of a Heyting algebra, may be found in Rousseau (1969). Postulates consisting of identities for the disjoint system of Post algebras of order n are given in Epstein (1973).

The fdnf and fcnf results using disjoint operations are key results with respect to logic design. This is partially illustrated by the four simplifications of the fdnf for $h_1(x, y)$ in Section 4.5.

Representation theory for the case $n = 2$ appears in Stone (1936). See also Stone (1937), Kaplansky (1947), and Anderson and Blair (1961). Prime ideal characterizations for $n \geq 2$ are given in Epstein (1960) and Chang and Horn (1961). Post algebras of order n are discussed in Chapter 10 of Balbes and Dwinger (1974), Chapter 7 of Rasiowa (1974), and Chapter 4 of Muzio and Wesselkamper (1986).

Exercises

E4.1 Let H be a Stone algebra and a supplemented lattice in which $!(x \vee y) = !x \vee !y$ for all x, y in H. Let e be a fixed element of H such that $\neg e = !e = \mathbf{V}$ and $x = e \neg\neg x \vee !x$ for every x in H. Prove that H is a Post algebra of order 3.

E4.2 Prove the identities in:
(a) Lemma 4.2(iii)
(b) Lemma 4.2(x).

E4.3 Prove the identities in:
(a) Lemma 4.2(viii)
(b) Lemma 4.2(xiv).

E4.4 Simplify for all $i, j, 0 \leq i \leq n - 1, 1 \leq j \leq n - 1$:
(a) $C_i(D_j(x))$
(b) $D_j(C_i(x))$.

E4.5 In a Post algebra of order n, prove that e_{i+1} is the least dense element in the interval $[e_i, \mathbf{V}]$ for each $i < n - 1$.

E4.6 In a Post algebra of fixed order $n > 2$ prove that $e_{n-2}x = \mathbf{\Lambda}$ implies $x = \mathbf{\Lambda}$.

E4.7 In a Post algebra of order n prove that the interval $[e_i, e_{i+1}]$ is a Boolean interval for each $i \leq n - 2$.

E4.8 In a Post algebra of order n prove that $e_{i-1} \vee x = e_i$ implies $x = e_i$ for each i satisfying $0 < i < n - 1$.

E4.9 In a Post algebra of order n prove that $(x \Rightarrow y) \vee (N(x) \Rightarrow N(y)) = \mathbf{V}$.

E4.10 Give an algebraic simplification of the following using the fdnf for the 3-valued function h_2 in subsection 3.4.1 as a starting point.

$$h_2(x, y)e_1 C_0(x)C_1(y) \vee e_1 C_1(x)C_1(y) \vee e_1 C_2(x)C_1(y) \vee C_0(x)C_0(y)$$
$$\vee C_1(x)C_2(y) \vee C_2(x)C_0(y).$$

E4.11 Consider the 4-valued function

$$s(x, y) = C_1(x)[D_2(y) \vee e_1] \vee xy$$

(i) Use Theorem 4.24 to give the fdnf for $s(x, y)$.
(ii) Use Theorem 4.25 to give the fcnf for $s(x, y)$.

E4.12 Use Theorem 4.33 to prove that $!(x \rightarrow y) = (x \Rightarrow y)$.

E4.13 For the 16-element Post algebra of order 4 shown below, with the element x as shown, identify the elements $e_0, e_1, e_2, e_3, C_0(x), C_1(x), C_2(x), C_3(x), D_1(x), D_2(x), D_3(x), N(x)$. Confirm your answers through $P6$, Theorem 4.13(ii), and Theorem 4.17(0) or (vii).

E4.14 For the 16-element Post algebra of order 4 shown below, with the two elements x, y as shown, identify $x \to y$, $x \Rightarrow y$, $y \to x$, $y \Rightarrow x$. Confirm your answers through Definition 3.53 and Theorem 3.54(i), (ii).

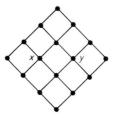

E4.15 In the 16-element Post algebra of order 4 with given element x shown in **E4.13**, identify all the prime ideals. Show that Theorem 4.43(iii) and (iv) are satisfied.

5 Sub-Post Algebras;
Double Heyting Algebras

The theory of sub-Post algebras, or P_2-lattices (Epstein and Horn 1974b), parallels the theory of Post algebras presented in Chapter 4. Because of this parallel, results in this chapter are given without proof. Explanatory comments are made where needed. The chapter ends with a discussion of double Heyting algebras with canonical dissection. These algebras share certain properties with sub-Post algebras.

5.1 Postulates for the disjoint system of sub-Post algebras of order n

The postulates of this section may be found in Section 5 of Epstein and Horn (1974b). They employ lattice operations $\wedge$, $\vee$; disjoint operations $C_0, C_1, \ldots, C_{n-1}$; and nullary operations $e_0, e_1, \ldots, e_{n-1}$. These postulates may be obtained from the postulates for Post algebras of order n given in Section 4.1 by simply dropping $P5$(iii). In this chapter A_0 denotes a sub-Post algebra of order n.

$P1$ (i) $x \vee y = y \vee x$
      (ii) $x \wedge y = y \wedge x$
      (iii) $(x \vee y) \vee z = x \vee (y \vee z)$
      (iv) $(x \wedge y) \wedge z = x \wedge (y \wedge z)$
      (v) $x \vee x = x$
      (vi) $x \wedge x = x$
      (vii) $(x \wedge y) \vee x = x$
      (viii) $(x \vee y) \wedge x = x$
      (ix) $x \wedge (y \vee z) = (x \wedge y) \vee (x \wedge z)$

$P2$ (i) $e_0 \vee x = x$
      (ii) $e_{i+1} \wedge e_i = e_i$ for $0 < i < n - 2$
      (iii) $x \wedge e_{n-1} = x$

$P3$ (i) $C_i(x) \wedge C_j(x) = e_0$ for $i \neq j$, $0 \leq i, j \leq n - 1$
      (ii) $C_0(x) \vee C_1(x) \vee \cdots \vee C_{n-2}(x) \vee C_{n-1}(x) = e_{n-1}$

P4 (i) $C_i(x \wedge y) = \{C_i(x) \wedge [C_i(y) \vee C_{i+1}(y) \vee \cdots \vee C_{n-1}(y)]\}$
$\vee \{C_i(y) \wedge [C_i(x) \vee C_{i+1}(x) \vee \cdots \vee C_{n-1}(x)]\}$
for $i = 0, 1, \ldots, n-1$

(ii) $C_{n-1}(x \vee y) = C_{n-1}(x) \vee C_{n-1}(y)$

P5 (i) $C_i(e_j) = e_0$ for $i \neq j$, $\quad 0 \leq i < n-1, 0 \leq j \leq n-1$

(ii) $C_{n-1}(e_0) = e_0$

P6 $\quad x = [e_1 \wedge C_1(x)] \vee [e_2 \wedge C_2(x)] \vee \cdots \vee [e_{n-1} \wedge C_{n-1}(x)].$

It follows from *P2* that A_0 is a bounded lattice in which $\boldsymbol{\Lambda} = e_0 \leq e_1 \leq \cdots \leq$ $e_{n-2} \leq e_{n-1} = \mathbf{V}$.

Any Post algebra of order n is obviously a sub-Post algebra of order n. For example, the Post algebra of order 3 consisting of 9 elements shown in figure 3.26(*b*) is a sub-Post algebra of order 3. Figure 5.1 shows a 6-element sub-Post algebra of order 3 which is not a Post algebra of order 3—this 6-element sub-Post algebra of order 3 may be viewed as the principal ideal generated by the element $(1, 2)$ in the 9-element Post algebra of order 3 given in figure 3.26(*b*). In figure 5.1 all elements of this ideal are labeled and the elements e_0, e_1, e_2 are identified.

The 9-element Post algebra of order 3 is a direct product of two chains of length 3, while the 6-element sub-Post algebra of order 3 is a direct product of a chain of length 2 with a chain of length 3.

Consider the 27-element Post algebra of order 3 shown in figure 3.26(*c*). Figure 5.2 shows a 12-element sub-Post algebra of order 3. It may be viewed as the principal ideal generated by the element $(1, 1, 2)$ in the 27-element Post algebra of order 3 shown in figure 3.26(*c*). In figure 5.2 all elements of this ideal are labeled and the elements e_0, e_1, e_2 are identified. The 12-element sub-Post algebra of order 3 shown in figure 5.2 is a direct product of two chains of length 2 and one chain of length 3. As a further example, figure

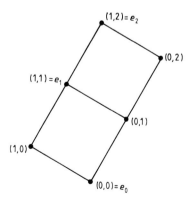

Figure 5.1 A 6-element sub-Post algebra of order 3.

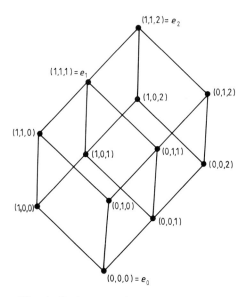

Figure 5.2   A 12-element sub-Post algebra of order 3.

5.3 shows an 18-element sub-Post algebra of order 3. It may be viewed as the principal ideal generated by the element $(2, 1, 2)$ in the 27-element Post algebra of order 3 shown in figure $3.26(c)$. In figure 5.3 all elements of this ideal are labeled and the elements e_0, e_1, e_2 are identified. The 18-element sub-Post algebra of order 3 is a direct product of one chain of length 2 with two chains of length 3.

The following remarks may be made. First, the postulates allow the degenerate case $e_0 = e_{n-1}$. Second, Boolean algebras coincide with sub-Post algebras of order 2. Third, it is straightforward to substitute $n = 3$ in the postulates, to obtain postulates for sub-Post algebras of order 3. Fourth, linearly ordered sub-Post algebras of order n coincide with linearly ordered Post algebras of order n. Fifth, the $C_i(x)$ and e_i, $i = 0, 1, \ldots, n - 1$, given by these postulates, are unique, and in the nondegenerate case the e_i are all distinct.

5.2   Basic properties in the disjoint system of sub-Post algebras of order n

In this section there are certain basic properties involving the disjoint operations C_i and the nullary operations e_i, $i = 0, 1, \ldots, n - 1$. Further properties are given later in this chapter.

Note that the property of Post algebras of order n given in Theorem 4.3

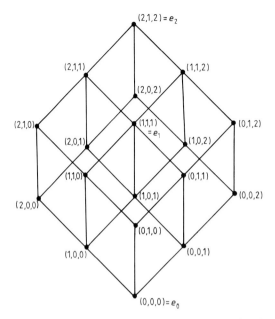

Figure 5.3 An 18-element sub-Post algebra of order 3.

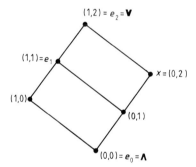

Figure 5.4 A sub-Post algebra of order $n = 3$ in which $x \vee e_1 = \mathbf{V}$ does not imply that $x = \mathbf{V}$.

does *not* hold in the class of sub-Post algebras of order n. This property of Post algebra of order n states that $x \vee e_{n-2} = \mathbf{V}$ implies that $x = \mathbf{V}$. To see that this does not have to hold in a sub-Post algebra, figure 5.4 shows a 6-element sub-Post algebra of order 3 with an element x such that $x \vee e_i = \mathbf{V}$ but $x \neq \mathbf{V}$.

THEOREM 5.1. $C_i(y)$ is a complemented element of the sub-Post algebra A_0.

THEOREM 5.2. For each i in the range $0 \leq i \leq n - 1$

$$C_{n-1}(C_i(x)) = C_i(x)$$

$$C_j(C_i(x)) = e_0 \qquad \text{for } 0 < j < n - 1$$

and

$$C_0(C_i(x)) = \bigvee_{k \neq i} C_k(x) = \overline{C_i(x)}.$$

THEOREM 5.3. If b is a complemented element of A_0, then $C_0(b) = \bar{b}$, $C_j(b) = e_0$ for $0 < j < n - 1$, and $C_{n-1}(b) = b$.

THEOREM 5.4. If $i \neq j$ and $i < n - 1$, then $C_i(e_j) = e_0$ and $C_i(e_i) = C_0(C_{n-1}(e_i))$.

THEOREM 5.5.

$$C_{n-1}(e_0) = e_0$$

and

$$C_{n-1}(e_{n-1}) = e_{n-1}.$$

THEOREM 5.6. If b_i are complemented elements of the sub-Post algebra A_0, $i = 1, 2, \ldots, n - 1$, and

$$x = \bigvee_{i=1}^{n-1} e_i b_i$$

then

$$x = \bigvee_{i=1}^{n-1} e_i \left(\bigvee_{j=i}^{n-1} b_j \right).$$

THEOREM 5.7. The following are valid for each $i = 0, 1, \ldots, n - 1$.

$$C_i(xy) = \left(C_i(x) \bigvee_{j=i}^{n-1} C_j(y) \right) \vee \left(C_i(y) \bigvee_{j=i}^{n-1} C_j(x) \right).$$

THEOREM 5.8. The following are valid for each $i = 0, 1, \ldots, n - 1$.

$$C_i(x \vee y) = \left(C_i(x) \bigvee_{j=0}^{i} C_j(y) \right) \vee \left(C_i(y) \bigvee_{j=0}^{i} C_j(x) \right).$$

5.3 Monotonic operations

The monotonic operations are developed as follows.

Definition 5.9. $D_j(x) = C_j(x) \vee C_{j+1}(x) \vee \cdots \vee C_{n-1}(x)$ for $j = 1, \ldots, n-1$. As a notational convenience $D_0(x)$ stands for $\mathbf{V}$.

THEOREM 5.10. $C_i(x) = D_i(x)\overline{D_{i+1}(x)}$ for $i = 0, 1, \ldots, n-2$ and $C_{n-1}(x) = D_{n-1}(x)$.

THEOREM 5.11. $D_i(e_j) = \mathbf{V}$ for $i \leq j$ and $D_i(e_j) = D_{n-1}(e_j)$ for $i > j$.

THEOREM 5.12. $D_i(D_j(x)) = D_j(x)$ for $1 \leq i, j \leq n-1$.

THEOREM 5.13.

(i) $$D_i(x) \leq D_j(x) \qquad \text{for } 1 \leq i \leq j \leq n-1$$

and

(ii) $$x = \bigvee_{i=1}^{n-1} e_i D_i(x).$$

(iii) If $b_i \geq b_j$ are complemented elements for all $1 \leq i \leq j \leq n-1$ and

$$x = \bigvee_{i=1}^{n-1} e_i b_i$$

then

$$b_i \leq D_i(x) \qquad \text{for all } i.$$

(iv) If $b_{n-1} = !x$ in (iii) above, then $b_i = D_i(x)$ for all i.

THEOREM 5.14. For each $i = 1, 2, \ldots, n-1$,
$$D_i(x \vee y) = D_i(x) \vee D_i(y).$$

THEOREM 5.15. A necessary and sufficient condition that $x \leq y$ is that $D_i(x) \leq D_i(y)$ for each $i = 1, 2, \ldots, n-1$.

THEOREM 5.16. For each $i = 1, 2, \ldots, n-1$
$$D_i(xy) = D_i(x)D_i(y).$$

5.4 Duality

THEOREM 5.17. Every sub-Post algebra A_0 of order n is isomorphic with its dual under the mapping N_0 given by

(0)
$$N_0(x) = \bigvee_{j=1}^{n-1} \overline{D_j(x)} f_{j-1} = \bigwedge_{j=1}^{n-1} (\overline{D_j(x)} \vee f_j)$$

where

$$f_i = \bigvee_{k=1}^{n-1-i} e_k \overline{D_{n-1}(e_{k+i-1})}, \qquad 0 \le i < n-1$$

and

$$f_{n-1} = \boldsymbol{\wedge}.$$

It may be surprising that the set of elements e_i, $i = 0, 1, \ldots, n-1$, and the set of elements f_i, $i = 0, \ldots, n-1$, can be different. Indeed, these two sets coincide if and only if the sub-Post algebra of order n is a Post algebra of order n. Figure 5.5 shows a 21-element sub-Post algebra of order 7 in which the two chains are different.

Properties involving N_0 are given below.

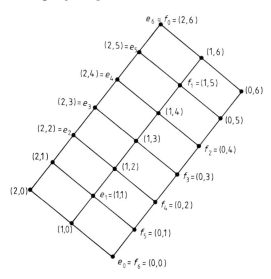

Figure 5.5   A 21-element sub-Post algebra of order 7 with the chains e_i, f_i, $i = 0, 1, 2, 3, 4, 5, 6$.

THEOREM 5.18.
(i) $N_0(N_0(x)) = x$
(ii) $x \le y$ if and only if $N_0(y) \le N_0(x)$

(iii) $N_0(x \vee y) = N_0(x) N_0(y)$
(iv) $N_0(xy) = N_0(x) \vee N_0(y)$
(v) $N_0(e_i) = f_i$
(vi) $N_0(f_i) = e_i$
(vii) $x N_0(x) \leq y \vee N_0(y)$
(viii) If b is a complemented element of A_0, then $N_0(b) = \bar{b}$.

5.5 A normal form theorem for sub-Postian functions

Definition 5.19. A sub-Postian function of m variables $x_1, \ldots, x_m$ in the disjoint system of sub-Post algebras of order n is a function which can be obtained through the same four kinds of constructions as given in Definition 4.21.

THEOREM 5.20. If f is a sub-Postian function of m variables $x_1, \ldots, x_m$, then

$$f(x_1, \ldots, x_m) = \bigvee_{0 \leq i_j \leq n-1} f(e_{i_1}, \ldots, e_{i_m}) C_{i_1}(x) \ldots C_{i_m}(x).$$

For Postian functions in Post algebras of order n, the $f(e_{i_1}, \ldots, e_{i_m})$ take the n values $e_0, e_1, \ldots, e_{n-1}$. However, sub-Postian functions in sub-Post algebras of order n take a number of additional values. To illustrate for $n = 3$, $f(e_{i_1}, \ldots, e_{i_m})$ may take any of the six following values: e_0, e_1, e_2, $C_2(e_1)$, $C_0(C_2(e_1))$, and $e_1 C_0(C_2(e_1))$.

5.6 Sub-Post algebras and special lattices

This section uses some of the special lattices introduced in Chapter 3 to find additional properties of sub-Post algebras of order n.

THEOREM 5.21. A sub-Post algebra of order n is a B-algebra with $x \Rightarrow y$ given by

$$x \Rightarrow y = C_0(x) \vee \bigvee_{i=1}^{n-1} (C_i(x) D_i(y)).$$

THEOREM 5.22. A sub-Post algebra of order n is a supplemented lattice with $!y = C_{n-1}(y) = D_{n-1}(y)$.

THEOREM 5.23. A sub-Post algebra of order n is a P-algebra.

THEOREM 5.24. The prime ideals of a sub-Post algebra of order n lie in disjoint chains.

THEOREM 5.25.   A sub-Post algebra of order n is a Heyting algebra with $x \to y = (x \Rightarrow y) \vee y$.

THEOREM 5.26.   A sub-Post algebra of order n is a Stone algebra with $\neg x = C_0(x) = x \Rightarrow \wedge$.

THEOREM 5.27.   A sub-Post algebra of order n is an L-algebra.

THEOREM 5.28.   A sub-Post algebra of order n is a Kleene algebra with $\sim x = N_0(x)$.

THEOREM 5.29.

(i) $\begin{aligned} e_i \Rightarrow e_j &= !e_j &&\text{for } i > j \\ &= \vee &&\text{for } i \leq j \end{aligned}$

(ii) $\begin{aligned} e_i \to e_j &= e_j &&\text{for } i > j \\ &= \vee &&\text{for } i \leq j \end{aligned}$

(iii) $!e_{n-1} = e_{n-1} = \vee$

(iv) $\begin{aligned} \neg e_i &= e_0 = \wedge &&\text{for } i > 0 \\ \neg e_0 &= e_{n-1} = \vee \end{aligned}$

(v) $D_i(x) = (e_i \Rightarrow x)$ for $i = 0, 1, \ldots, n-1$

(vi) $C_i(x) = (e_i \Rightarrow x)(x \Rightarrow e_i)(\overline{!(xe_i)})$ for $i = 0, 1, \ldots, n-2$.

5.7   Sub-Post algebras of order n and sub-Postian functions

This section gives a representation theory using functions whose maximum number of values is n.

THEOREM 5.30.   A sub-Post algebra of order n is order-isomorphic with a direct product of Post algebras of maximum order n.

Figure 5.1 gives an easy example. This figure shows the 6-element sub-Post algebra of order 3 which is a direct product of the 2-element Post algebra of order 2 with the 3-element Post algebra of order 3.

The above suggests a way around any difficulties for the logic designer posed by the fdnf theorem in sub-Post algebras as discussed in Section 5.5. If a digital system contains one portion which is binary and another portion which is ternary, say, the logic designer can simply treat each portion separately. An application of this kind may be found in Section 6.7.

There are a number of consequences of Theorem 5.30. Representation and completeness results follow. For example, every sub-Post algebra of order n is a principal ideal in some Post algebra of order n. As another example, a sub-Post algebra of order n is complete if and only if its center is complete. The following theorem applies for the case where the sub-Post algebra of order n has a finite number of elements.

THEOREM 5.31. If a nondegenerate sub-Post algebra A_0 of order n contains a finite number of elements then it is isomorphic with all the n_i-valued functions on a c-point set, where for each $i = 1, 2, \ldots, c$, n_i is a fixed integer in the range $2 \leq n_i \leq n$; for some i, $n_i = n$; and c is the number of atoms of A_0. At each i, the function takes values $0, 1, \ldots, n_i - 1$.

It is clear from Theorem 5.31 that the number of elements in A_0 is given

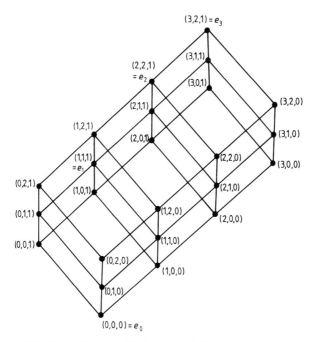

Figure 5.6 A $2 \times 3 \times 4 = 24$ element sub-Post algebra of order 4— for 3-tuple (c, b, a) entry a takes values $0, 1$ (as $n_1 = 2$), entry b takes values $0, 1, 2$ (as $n_2 = 3$), and entry c takes values $0, 1, 2, 3$ (as $n_3 = 4$).

by the product $n_1 n_2 \cdots n_c$. This is illustrated by the 24-element sub-Post algebra of order 4 in figure 5.6, with $n_1 = 2$, $n_2 = 3$, $n_3 = 4$; $n_1 n_2 n_3 = 24$; $c = 3$, $n = 4$.

As a further example, consider the n_i-valued functions on a 6-point set for a sub-Post algebra of order 4 where $n_1 = 2$, $n_2 = 3$, $n_3 = 2$, $n_4 = 4$, $n_5 = 2$, $n_6 = 3$. This is a direct product of Boolean algebra containing 8 elements with a Post algebra of order 3 containing 9 elements with a Post algebra of order 4 containing 4 elements. The total number of elements is $2^3 3^2 4 = 288$.

In this example, $e_0 = (0, 0, 0, 0, 0, 0)$, $e_1 = (1, 1, 1, 1, 1, 1)$, $e_2 = (1, 2, 1, 2, 1, 2)$, $e_3 = (1, 2, 1, 3, 1, 2)$. In this example, let $x = (0, 2, 1, 3, 1, 1)$ and $y = (1, 0, 0, 2, 1, 2)$. Clearly $x \vee y = (1, 2, 1, 3, 1, 2)$ and $xy = (0, 0, 0, 2, 1, 1)$. Also $(x \Rightarrow y) = (1, 0, 0, 0, 1, 2)$ and $x \rightarrow y = (1, 0, 0, 2, 1, 2)$. To obtain $D_1(x)$, $D_2(x)$, $D_3(x)$ use Theorem 5.29(v): $D_1(x) = (0, 2, 1, 3, 1, 2)$, $D_2(x) = (0, 2, 1, 3, 1, 0)$, $D_3(x) = (0, 2, 1, 3, 1, 0)$. To obtain $C_0(x)$, $C_1(x)$, $C_2(x)$ use Theorem 5.10: $C_0(x) = (1, 0, 0, 0, 0, 0)$, $C_1(x) = (0, 0, 0, 0, 0, 2)$, $C_2(x) = (0, 0, 0, 0, 0, 0)$. Since $C_3(x) = D_3(x)$ for $n = 4$, $C_3(x) = (0, 2, 1, 3, 1, 0)$.

5.8   Sub-Post algebras of order n and prime ideals

THEOREM 5.32.   For a given set S of c points and given $n_1, \ldots, n_c$, let L_0 be all the n_i-valued functions f as in Theorem 5.31. Then there are

$$\left(\sum_{i=1}^{c} n_i \right) - c$$

distinct prime ideals of the form $P_{si} = \{f : f(s) \leq i - 1\}$ for each s in S and $1 \leq i \leq n_s - 1$. Thus every maximal chain of properly ascending prime ideals in L_0 consists of at most $n - 1$ prime ideals, and every prime ideal is a member of one of these chains.

Consider as an example the 15-element sub-Post algebra of order 5 which is a direct product of a 3-element chain with a 5-element chain. Figure 5.7 shows the $(3 + 5) - 2 = 6$ prime ideals lying in two disjoint chains. One of these chains contains P_{01} and P_{02}, while the other chain contains P_{11}, P_{12}, P_{13}, and P_{14}.

THEOREM 5.33.   Let L_0 be a finite distributive lattice in which every maximal chain of properly ascending prime ideals consists of at most $n - 1$ prime ideals, there is at least one such chain which contains $n - 1$ prime ideals, and every prime ideal is a member of exactly one such chain. Then L_0 is a sub-Post algebra of order n.

For details concerning prime ideal representation in sub-Post algebras of order n, see Section 7 in Epstein and Horn (1974b).

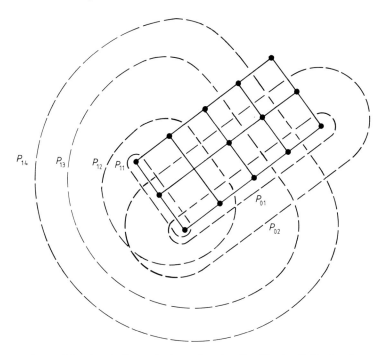

Figure 5.7 A sub-Post algebra of order 5 with six distinct prime ideals: $P_{01} \subset P_{02}$ and $P_{11} \subset P_{12} \subset P_{13} \subset P_{14}$.

5.9 The chain and the sublattice; double Heyting algebras

A sub-Post algebra of order n is a Heyting algebra by Theorem 5.25 and its dual is also a Heyting algebra by Theorem 5.17. In this section H denotes a Heyting algebra whose dual is a Heyting algebra. H is called a *double Heyting algebra*. As noted in subsection 3.6.10, any finite distributive lattice is a Heyting algebra, hence any finite distributive lattice is a double Heyting algebra. Consequently the results which follow hold for the class of finite distributive lattices.

A major interest in this section concerns the existence of a chain $\Lambda = e_0 \leq e_1 \leq \cdots \leq e_{n-2} \leq e_{n-1} = \mathbf{V}$, and elements $c_i(x)$ in a $\{\Lambda, \mathbf{V}\}$-sublattice of H, $c_1(x) \geq c_2(x) \geq \cdots \geq c_{n-1}(x)$, such that each element x in H has a representation of the form

$$x = \bigvee_{i=1}^{n-1} c_i(x)e_i.$$

This may be regarded as a generalization of the monotonic representations in Theorem 4.13(i), (ii) and Theorem 5.13(i), (ii).

Consider the following properties which hold in any sub-Post algebra of order n with respect to the chain $\Lambda = e_0 < e_1 < \cdots < e_{n-1} = V$.

(p1)   For each $i = 0, 1, \ldots, n-2$, e_{i+1} is the least dense element of the interval $[e_i, V]$.

(p2)   For each $i = 0, 1, \ldots, n-2$, $e_{i+1} \to e_i = e_i$.

(p3)   For each $i = 0, 1, \ldots, n-2$, $[e_i, e_{i+1}]$ is a Boolean interval.

All of these chain properties hold in sub-Post algebras of order n, and so also in Post algebras of order n—see Exercises E4.5, E4.7, and Theorem 5.29(ii). Further, for Stone algebras of order n see Katriňák and Mitschke (1972) and for P_1-lattices see Epstein and Horn (1974b). If H has a chain satisfying (p1)–(p3), then this chain is called the *canonical dissection* of H (Epstein and Horn 1983). Such a chain of length 8 is shown in the 46-element lattice of figure 5.8. In this figure, property (p3) may be illustrated by noting that the interval $[e_0, e_1]$ is an 8-element Boolean interval, the intervals $[e_4, e_5]$ and $[e_5, e_6]$ are 4-element Boolean intervals, and the intervals $[e_1, e_2]$, $[e_2, e_3]$, $[e_3, e_4]$, and $[e_6, e_7]$ are 2-element Boolean intervals.

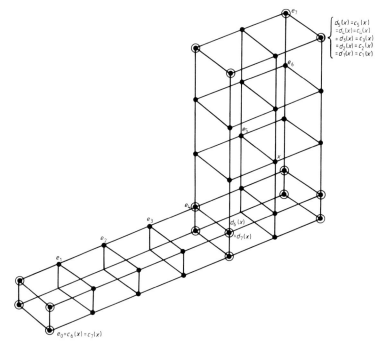

Figure 5.8   46-element lattice having 16-element exocenter and 8-element canonical chain. For the given x, the monotonic $c_i(x)$ and $d_i(x)$, $i = 1, 2, 3, 4, 5, 6, 7$, are shown,

It remains to find elements $c_i(x)$ for each x in H such that the above monotonic expansion is satisfied. Two solutions are given below. An illustration is given in figure 5.8.

An element c in H is called a *core point* if there exists an element x in H such that $x \to c = c = x \leftarrow c$. The set of all core points of H is called the *core* of H. The sublattice C generated by the core is called the *exocenter*. Since $\wedge$, $\vee$ are core points, the exocenter is a $\{\wedge, \vee\}$-sublattice of H. Indeed, each complemented element is a core point, so the exocenter contains the center of H. Further, the exocenter of a sub-Post algebra of order n coincides with its center. For every pair of elements x, y in H, if there is a greatest element d in the exocenter such that $xd \leq y$, let this element d be denoted by $x \rightarrow\!\!\!\!\bullet\ y$. This may be compared with the operation $\Rightarrow$ in a *B*-algebra, where $x \Rightarrow y$ denotes the greatest element b in the center such that $xb \leq y$. The two solutions below are given in Epstein and Horn (1983).

For the first solution, the elements $c_i(x)$ are selected from core points in the core of H. In particular these core points may be given for each $i = 1, 2, \ldots, n-1$ by

$$c_i(x) = (x \leftarrow e_i) \leftarrow (e_i \to x).$$

This yields a monotonic expansion for each x in H. However, the join or meet of two core points does not have to be a core point. While $c_i(xy) \leq c_i(x)c_i(y)$, equality does not have to hold. This first solution is illustrated for the 46-element lattice having 16-element exocenter in figure 5.8, with given element x. In this figure the 16 elements of the exocenter are circled; in addition to the 8-element chain, the 7 elements $c_i(x)$, $i = 1, 2, \ldots, 7$, are shown.

For the second solution, let $x \rightarrow\!\!\!\!\bullet\ y$ exist for every pair of elements x, y in H. Let $d_i(x)$ denote elements from the exocenter, C, such that each x in H has a monotonic expansion

$$x = \bigvee_{i=1}^{n-1} e_i d_i(x).$$

Then, a solution for these elements $d_i(x)$ is given by

$$d_i(x) = e_i \rightarrow\!\!\!\!\bullet\ x.$$

This may be compared with Theorem 5.29(v). It is left for the exercises at the end of this chapter to prove that $d_j(x) \leq d_i(x)$ for $1 \leq i \leq j \leq n-1$ and $d_i(xy) = d_i(x)d_i(y)$ for $i = 1, 2, \ldots, n-1$. These may be compared with Theorems 5.13(i), (ii) and 5.16. This solution is illustrated for the 46-element lattice in figure 5.8, where for given x the 7 elements $d_i(x)$, $i = 1, 2, \ldots, 7$, are shown. It can be easily seen from this figure that $c_7(x) \neq d_7(x)$, so the two solutions are different. It also follows that for any x, $c_i(x) \leq d_i(x)$ for each $i = 1, \ldots, n-1$. For additional discussion, see Bowen (1986).

5.10   Overview

Sub-Post algebras, also called P_2-lattices, are the strongest of the sequence P_0-lattices, P_1-lattices, P_2-lattices introduced in Epstein and Horn (1974b). Work on P_0-lattices is given in Traczyk (1963) with further developments in Traczyk (1977). Definitions of P_0-lattices and P_1-lattices may be found in the exercises at the end of this chapter.

Let A be a bounded distributive lattice with center B. Let Q be a $\{\wedge, \vee\}$-sublattice of A. If there is a greatest element q in Q such that $xq \leq y$ for all x, y in A, then A is said to be a *subresiduated lattice*, or *subresiduated with respect to* Q. For every x, y in A, this greatest element q in Q is denoted by $x \overset{Q}{\to} y$. Using this notation, with the center of A denoted by B

$$x \to y = x \overset{A}{\to} y \qquad \text{and} \qquad x \Rightarrow y = x \overset{B}{\to} y.$$

If A is a double Heyting algebra with exocenter C, then $x \blacktriangleright y = x \overset{C}{\to} y$. Some fundamental properties for $x \to y$, $x \Rightarrow y$, and $x \blacktriangleright y$ are properties which hold in the class of all subresiduated lattices. Special cases arise depending upon the relation of the sublattice Q to the center B or exocenter C. Some cases, and logics characterized by subresiduated lattices, may be found in Epstein and Horn (1976). For a case where the sublattice Q contains the exocenter, see Theorem 5.20 in Epstein and Horn (1983). For cases where the sublattice Q bears a relation to the center, see Epstein and Horn (1976).

Exercises

E5.1   Consider a sub-Post algebra of order n which consists of exactly the n elements $e_0 < e_1 \cdots < e_{n-1}$. Prove that this sub-Post algebra is a Post algebra of order n.

E5.2   How many nonisomorphic sub-Post algebras of order 6 are there which have 24 elements?

E5.3   How many nonisomorphic sub-Post algebras are there which have 24 elements?

In the following 4 problems consider the n_i-valued functions on a 9-point set for sub-Post functions of order 5 where $n_1 = 2$, $n_2 = 2$, $n_3 = 2$, $n_4 = 2$, $n_5 = 3$, $n_6 = 3$, $n_7 = 3$, $n_8 = 5$, $n_9 = 5$ and let $x = (0, 1, 0, 1, 2, 1, 2, 4, 3)$, $y = (1, 1, 0, 0, 0, 2, 2, 1, 4)$.

E5.4   Give $x \wedge y$, $x \vee y$, $x \Rightarrow y$, and $x \to y$.

E5.5   Give e_0, e_1, e_2, e_3, e_4, f_0, f_1, f_2, f_3, and f_4.

E5.6   Give $D_1(x)$, $D_2(x)$, $D_3(x)$, and $D_4(x)$.

E5.7   Give $C_0(x)$, $C_1(x)$, $C_2(x)$, $C_3(x)$, and $C_4(x)$.

E5.8   Prove that $N_0(x) = N(x)$ in any sub-Post algebra of order n which is a Post algebra of order n.

E5.9   In Theorem 4.43(iii) a prime ideal representation is given for e_i in a Post algebra of order n which has a finite number of elements. Give a prime ideal representation for e_i in a sub-Post algebra of order n which has a finite number of elements.

E5.10   Use Theorem 5.20 to obtain the fdnf for the function $g(x, y) = D_1(xy)$ where $n = 3$.

E5.11   Use Theorem 5.20 to obtain the fdnf for the function $h(x, y) = D_2(x \vee y)$ where $n = 4$.

Definition.   A P_0-*lattice* is a bounded distributive lattice A containing a chain $\wedge = e_0 \leq e_1 \leq \cdots \leq e_{n-1} = \vee$ such that each element x in A can be represented in the form

$$x = \bigvee_{i=1}^{n-1} e_i b_i(x)$$

where each $b_i(x)$, $i = 1, 2, \ldots, n-1$ is a complemented element of A. A P_0-lattice is said to be of order n if n is the smallest integer such that every element x in A has the above representation.

E5.12   Prove that every element x in a P_0-lattice A has a disjoint representation

$$x = \bigvee_{i=0}^{n-1} e_i k_i(x)$$

where each $k_i(x)$, $i = 1, \ldots, n-1$ is a complemented element with $k_i(x)k_j(x) = \wedge$ for all $i \neq j$ and

$$\bigvee_{i=0}^{n-1} k_i(x) = \vee.$$

E5.13   Let A be a P_0-lattice in which $e_i \Rightarrow e_0$ exists for all i. Prove that A is a Stone algebra.

Definition.   A P_1-*lattice* is a P_0-lattice A as defined above in which $e_{i+1} \rightarrow e_i$ exists and is equal to e_i for all i in the range $0 \leq i < n - 1$. (It follows that $e_i \rightarrow e_j = e_j$ for $i > j$ and $e_i \rightarrow e_j = \vee$ for $i \leq j$, so that $e_i \rightarrow e_j$ exists for all i, j.)

E5.14   Prove that a P_1-lattice is a Heyting algebra.

E5.15 Prove that a P_1-lattice is an L-algebra.

E5.16 Let A be a double Heyting algebra which is subresiduated with respect to its exocenter C. Prove the following analogues of Theorem 3.52(v) and (vii).
(a) If $x_1 \leq x_2$, then $x_2 \twoheadrightarrow y \leq x_1 \twoheadrightarrow y$
(b) $w \twoheadrightarrow (xy) = (w \twoheadrightarrow x)(w \twoheadrightarrow y)$.

E5.17 Prove that $c_i(x) \leq d_i(x)$ for each i, where the elements $c_i(x)$ and $d_i(x)$ are defined in Section 5.9.

E5.18 Using the results of **E5.16**, prove that $d_{i+1}(x) \leq d_i(x)$ and $d_i(xy) = d_i(x)d_i(y)$ for all i, where the elements $d_i(x)$ are defined in Section 5.9.

E5.19 Use the first solution in Section 5.9

$$x = \bigvee_{i=1}^{n-1} e_i c_i(x)$$

to prove the second solution in Section 5.9

$$x = \bigvee_{i=1}^{n-1} e_i d_i(x).$$

The elements $c_i(x)$ and $d_i(x)$ are defined in Section 5.9.

6 Arithmetic Operations

This chapter discusses rings and basic arithmetic operations such as addition and multiplication. Detailed logic designs are given for multi-digit full adders in the fixed radix case for the binary, ternary, and quaternary number systems; and in the mixed radix case for the factorial number system. Multi-digit full subtractors are treated in some of the exercises at the end of the chapter.

6.1 Preliminaries

In the logic diagram of an adder or subtractor each digit d_i in the number system representation given by Definition 2.11 normally resides in an n-stable device. It is assumed that there is a single input to this device, called Dd_i—it is the input to the delay device which holds d_i. It is also assumed that the device has, or can generate, n outputs $C_0(d_i), C_1(d_i), \ldots, C_{n-1}(d_i)$. These devices change under control of a synchronous clock which ticks at a regular rate. The interval between ticks is called the clock interval.

An adder or subtractor must be ready to assume new values at the end of each clock interval.

For $n = 2$ the delay device for x is called a delay flip–flop, pictured below.

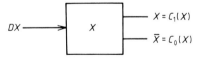

For $n = 3$ a delay 3-stable device for y is pictured below.

Recall that it is easy to secure a single n-valued output signal from this.

kind of device through use of postulate *P6*. To illustrate for $n = 3$, *P6* leads to

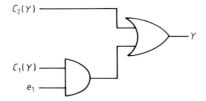

Digits a_i are used to designate values which reside in the n-stable devices of the accumulator or a-register within an adder. These digits represent the number a, as in the number representation of Definition 2.11, called the augend. Digits b_i are used to designate values which reside in the b-register of an adder. These digits represent the number b, called the addend.

A major concern of this chapter is the logic design of adders. The discussion can be modified to treat subtractors, as illustrated in some of the exercises at the end of this chapter. Multipliers and dividers within an arithmetic unit may use adders and subtractors to perform multiplication or division through sequences of additions or subtractions.

Figure 6.1 shows an 8-digit a-register and an 8-digit b-register for the binary case. This figure shows the augend 27 in its binary representation within the a-register and the addend 3 in its binary representation within the b-register.

One purpose of figure 6.1 is to lay the groundwork for a discussion of the addition of two 8-digit numbers. The digits a_i and b_i are said to be at stage i of the adder. Note that there are 8 stages in the 8-digit adder, from stage 0 at the right to stage 7 at the left. The least significant digits are at stage 0; the most significant digits are at stage 7. The greatest unsigned number which can be represented in 8 binary digits is decimal 255 (binary 11111111); the least number which can be represented is decimal 0 (binary 00000000).

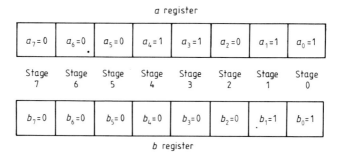

Figure 6.1 An 8-binary-digit augend in the a register and an 8-binary-digit addend in the b register.

6.2 Rings

Definition 6.1. A *ring* is an algebra $(R, \oplus, \otimes, 0)$ where $\oplus$ and $\otimes$ are binary operations and 0 is a nullary operation. If a, b are in the set R, then $a \oplus b$ and $a \otimes b$ are in R, while 0 is a fixed element of R called the *additive identity* or *zero*, with the following properties for all a, b, c in R.

(i) $(a \oplus b) \oplus c = a \oplus (b \oplus c)$
(ii) $a \oplus 0 = a$ for every a in R
(iii) For every a, there is a unique element $(-a)$ in R, called the additive inverse of a, such that $a \oplus (-a) = 0$
(iv) $a \oplus b = b \oplus a$
(v) $(a \otimes b) \otimes c = a \otimes (b \otimes c)$
(vi) $a \otimes (b \oplus c) = (a \otimes b) \oplus (a \otimes c)$
(vii) $(b \oplus c) \otimes a = (b \otimes a) \oplus (c \otimes a)$.

Definition 6.2. A commutative ring is a ring in which $\otimes$ is commutative:

$$a \otimes b = b \otimes a.$$

Definition 6.3. In any ring, $2a$ denotes $a \oplus a$, $3a$ denotes $a \oplus a \oplus a$, $4a$ denotes $a \oplus a \oplus a \oplus a$, etc. Further, a^2 denotes $a \otimes a$, a^3 denotes $a \otimes a \otimes a$, a^4 denotes $a \otimes a \otimes a \otimes a$, etc.

Definition 6.4. A ring with unit is a ring in which there is a fixed element 1 in R called the *multiplicative identity* or *unit* such that

$$a \otimes 1 = 1 \otimes a = a \text{ for every } a \text{ in } r.$$

Definition 6.5. If $a \neq 0$ and $b \neq 0$, with $a \otimes b = 0$, then a, b are each called a *proper divisor of zero*.

Definition 6.6. If a ring has a least positive integer q such that $qd = 0$ for all d in R, where qd is given in Definition 6.3, then R is said to have characteristic q—otherwise the ring is said to have characteristic 0.

Definition 6.7. A *field* is a commutative ring with unit in which: for every nonzero a, there is a unique element a^{-1} in R, called the multiplicative inverse of a, such that $a \otimes a^{-1} = a^{-1} \otimes a = 1$.
   A field is a commutative group with respect to $\oplus$ by (i)–(iv) of Definition 6.1, and a commutative group with respect to $\otimes$ by (v) and Definitions 6.2, 6.4, 6.7.

   Some basic results and key examples are given below to illustrate these concepts. The examples include the integers, the 2×2 real matrices, and the complex numbers. The final examples in this section treat the integer sets of figures 2.29–2.31 and 2.33.

THEOREM 6.8.   For any element a in a ring, $a \otimes 0 = 0 \otimes a = 0$.

Proof.

$$a^2 \oplus (-a^2) = (a \otimes (a \oplus 0)) \oplus (-a^2) \qquad \text{by Definition 6.1(ii)}$$

$$0 = (a^2 \oplus (a \otimes 0)) \oplus (-a^2) \qquad \text{by Definition 6.1(iii), (vi)}$$

$$0 = (a^2 \oplus (-a^2)) \oplus (a \otimes 0) \qquad \text{by Definition 6.1(i)}$$

$$0 = 0 \oplus (a \otimes 0) \qquad \text{by Definition 6.1(iii)}$$

$$0 = (a \otimes 0) \oplus 0 \qquad \text{by Definition 6.1(iv)}$$

$$0 = a \otimes 0 \qquad \text{by Definition 6.1(ii).}$$

There is a similar proof that $0 = 0 \otimes a$ ∎

THEOREM 6.9.   Let R be a commutative ring. The multiplicative cancellation rule

$$a \otimes b = a \otimes c \text{ implies } b = c \text{ for any } a, b, c \text{ in } R \text{ if } a \neq 0$$

holds in R if and only if R has no proper divisors of zero.

Proof.   If this cancellation rule holds in R, consider $a \otimes b = 0$. Then $a \otimes b = 0 = a \otimes 0 = 0 \otimes b$ by Theorem 6.8. If $a \neq 0$, then $b = 0$ by cancellation of a on the left; if $b \neq 0$, then $a = 0$ by cancellation of b on the right. Hence R has no proper divisors of 0. Conversely, if R has no proper divisors of zero, let $a \otimes b = a \otimes c$ where $a \neq 0$. Then

$$(a \otimes b) \oplus (-(a \otimes c)) = 0 \qquad \text{by Definition 6.1(iii)}$$

$$(a \otimes b) \oplus (a \otimes (-c)) = 0 \qquad \text{by uniqueness of the additive inverse in Definition 6.1(iii)}$$

$$a \otimes (b \oplus (-c)) = 0 \qquad \text{by Definition 6.1(vi).}$$

Since $a \neq 0$ and there are no proper divisors of zero in R, $b \oplus (-c) = 0$. Hence

$$c \oplus (b \oplus (-c)) = c \qquad \text{by Definition 6.1(ii)}$$

and

$$b = c \qquad \text{by Definition 6.1(i), (iv), (iii), (ii)} \quad ∎$$

Corollary 6.10.   A field has no proper divisors of zero.

Proof.   To prove that $b \otimes a = c \otimes a$ implies $b = c$ for any a, b, c, if $a \neq 0$

$$(b \otimes a) \otimes a^{-1} = (c \otimes a) \otimes a^{-1}$$

$$b \otimes (a \otimes a^{-1}) = c \otimes (a \otimes a^{-1}) \qquad \text{by Definition 6.1(v)}$$

$$b \otimes 1 = c \otimes 1 \qquad \text{by Definition 6.7}$$

$$b = c \qquad \text{by Definition 6.4.}$$

The result follows by Theorem 6.9 ∎

THEOREM 6.11. If the characteristic of a field is not 0, then it must be prime.

Proof. If the characteristic p has a factorization $p = qr$ then either q or r replaces p as characteristic. This is a contradiction unless $q = 1$ and $r = p$, or $q = p$ and $r = 1$ ∎

Example 6.1. If R is the set of all integers, then R is a commutative ring with unit. The ring zero is 0 and the ring unit is 1. The operation $\oplus$ is ordinary integer addition and the operation $\otimes$ is ordinary integer multiplication. There are no proper divisors of zero in this ring. The characteristic of r is 0.

Example 6.2. If R is the set of all real 2×2 matrices, then R is a ring with unit. The zero is

$$\begin{pmatrix} 0 & 0 \\ 0 & 0 \end{pmatrix}$$

and the unit is

$$\begin{pmatrix} 1 & 0 \\ 0 & 1 \end{pmatrix}$$

The operations $\oplus$, $\otimes$ are matrix addition and multiplication, respectively, where the entries are real numbers using real arithmetic operations as follows

$$\begin{pmatrix} a_1 & b_1 \\ c_1 & d_1 \end{pmatrix} \oplus \begin{pmatrix} a_2 & b_2 \\ c_2 & d_2 \end{pmatrix} = \begin{pmatrix} a_1 + a_2 & b_1 + b_2 \\ c_1 + c_2 & d_1 + d_2 \end{pmatrix}$$

and

$$\begin{pmatrix} a_1 & b_1 \\ c_1 & d_1 \end{pmatrix} \otimes \begin{pmatrix} a_2 & b_2 \\ c_2 & d_2 \end{pmatrix}$$

$$= \begin{pmatrix} a_1a_2 + b_1c_2 & a_1b_2 + b_1d_2 \\ c_1a_2 + d_1c_2 & c_1b_2 + d_1d_2 \end{pmatrix}$$

The additive inverse of a 2×2 matrix is given by

$$-\begin{pmatrix} a & b \\ c & d \end{pmatrix} = \begin{pmatrix} -a & -b \\ -c & -d \end{pmatrix}$$

A 2×2 matrix

$$\begin{pmatrix} a & b \\ c & d \end{pmatrix}$$

has a multiplicative inverse when $ad - bc \neq 0$, given by

$$\begin{pmatrix} a & b \\ c & d \end{pmatrix}^{-1} = \begin{pmatrix} d/(ad - bc) & b/(bc - ad) \\ c/(bc - ad) & a/(ad - bc) \end{pmatrix}$$

The proper divisors of zero together with

$$\begin{pmatrix} 0 & 0 \\ 0 & 0 \end{pmatrix}$$

are characterized by $ad = bc$, under this condition

$$\begin{pmatrix} a & b \\ c & d \end{pmatrix} \otimes \begin{pmatrix} d & -b \\ -c & a \end{pmatrix} = \begin{pmatrix} 0 & 0 \\ 0 & 0 \end{pmatrix}$$

This is an example of a ring which is not a commutative ring. An illustration is given below.

$$\begin{pmatrix} 0 & 1 \\ 2 & 0 \end{pmatrix} \otimes \begin{pmatrix} 0 & 3 \\ 1 & 0 \end{pmatrix} \neq \begin{pmatrix} 0 & 3 \\ 1 & 0 \end{pmatrix} \otimes \begin{pmatrix} 0 & 1 \\ 2 & 0 \end{pmatrix}$$

Example 6.3. If R is the set of complex numbers $a + bi$ with $i^2 = -1$ represented by real coordinates (a, b) in two dimensions, then R is a field. The zero is $(0, 0)$ and the unit is $(1, 0)$. The operations $\oplus, \otimes$ are given by

$$(a_1, b_1) \oplus (a_2, b_2) = (a_1 + a_2, b_1 + b_2)$$

and

$$(a_1, b_1) \otimes (a_2, b_2) = (a_1 a_2 - b_1 b_2, a_1 b_2 + b_1 a_2).$$

The additive inverse of (a, b) is $(-a, -b)$. If (a, b) is not $(0, 0)$, then the multiplicative inverse of (a, b) is given by $(a, b)^{-1} = (a/(a^2 + b^2), -b/(a^2 + b^2))$. There are no proper divisors of zero, by Corollary 6.10. The characteristic is 0.

Example 6.4. If R is the n-element integer set $\{0, 1, \ldots, n - 1\}$ for fixed $n \geq 2$ and the operations $\oplus, \otimes$ are defined as in Section 2.7, then R is a commutative ring with unit. It is clear that the ring zero is 0 and the ring unit is 1. The additive inverse of any nonzero d in R is given by $n - d$, also in R. Proper divisors of zero are discussed in the next example. The characteristic of R is n. For $n = 2$ see figure 2.30; for $n = 3$ see figure 2.31; for $n = 4$ see figure 2.33; for $n = 10$ see figure 2.29. These figures provide four illustrations for this example.

Example 6.5. If R is the p-element integer set $\{0, 1, \ldots, p - 1\}$ where p is a prime, otherwise satisfying the conditions of Example 6.4, then R is a field. The multiplicative inverse of any nonzero d in R is given by $c = d^{-1}$ in R, where $c \equiv d^{p-2} (\text{mod } p)$. A proof of this is left for some of the exercises at the end of this chapter. In this example, there are no proper divisors of zero, by Corollary 6.10. This is evident for $p = 2$ from figure 2.30 and for $p = 3$ from figure 2.31.

6.3 The binary case

Definition 6.12. A ring R in which $c^2 = c$ for all c in R is called a 2-*ring*. It is shown below that any such ring is a commutative ring, and R has characteristic 2.

THEOREM 6.13. In a 2-ring R, $(b \otimes a) \oplus (a \otimes b) = 0$ for all a, b in R.

Proof

$$(a \oplus b)^2 = a \oplus b \qquad \text{by Definition 6.12}$$

$$a^2 \oplus (b \otimes a) \oplus (a \otimes b) \oplus b^2 = a \oplus b \qquad \text{by Definition 6.1(vi), (vii)}$$

$$a \oplus (b \otimes a) \oplus (a \otimes b) \oplus b = a \oplus b \qquad \text{by Definition 6.12}$$

$$(-a) \oplus a \oplus (b \otimes a) \oplus (a \otimes b) \oplus b \oplus (-b) = (-a) \oplus a \oplus b \oplus (-b)$$

$$0 \oplus (b \otimes a) \oplus (a \otimes b) \oplus 0 = 0 \oplus 0 \qquad \text{by Definition 6.1(iv), (iii)}$$

$$(b \otimes a) \oplus (a \otimes b) = 0 \qquad \text{by Definition 6.1(iv), (ii)} \qquad ■$$

Corollary 6.14. A 2-ring R has characteristic 2.

Proof. To prove $a \oplus a = 0$ for all a in R, substitute a for b in Theorem 6.13, then use Definition 6.12 ■

Consequently $-a = a$, by the uniqueness of the additive inverse in Definition 6.1(iii)

Corollary 6.15. A 2-ring is a commutative ring.

Proof. Using Theorem 6.13,

$$(b \otimes a) \oplus (b \otimes a) \oplus (a \otimes b) = (b \otimes a)$$

$$0 \oplus (a \otimes b) = (b \otimes a) \qquad \text{by Corollary 6.14}$$

$$a \otimes b = b \otimes a \qquad \text{by Definition 6.1(iv), (ii)} \qquad ■$$

THEOREM 6.16

(i) A 2-ring with unit is a Boolean algebra, where

$a \wedge b = a \otimes b$

$a \vee b = a \oplus (a \otimes b) \oplus b$

$\bar{a} = a \oplus 1$

$\wedge = 0$

$\vee = 1$.

(ii) A Boolean algebra is a 2-ring with unit, where

$a \otimes b = a \wedge b$

$a \oplus b = (a \wedge \bar{b}) \vee (\bar{a} \wedge b)$

$0 = \wedge$

$1 = \vee$.

Proof. To prove (i), it must be shown that the thirteen conditions of Definition 3.30 are satisfied. These verifications are straightforward. To illustrate, the expression for $a \vee b$ in (i) as a ring polynomial on the right hand side may be obtained as follows. A ring polynomial for $a \vee b$ in $2^2 = 4$ undetermined binary coefficients k_0, k_1, k_2, k_3 may be written as follows

$$a \vee b = k_0 \oplus (k_1 \otimes b) \oplus (k_2 \otimes a) \oplus (k_3 \otimes (a \otimes b)).$$

Substituting 0, 1 values for each of a, b in the above yields $2^2 = 4$ equations

$$0 = 0 \vee 0 = k_0$$

$$1 = 0 \vee 1 = k_0 \oplus k_1$$

$$1 = 1 \vee 0 = k_0 \oplus k_2$$

$$1 = 1 \vee 1 = k_0 \oplus k_1 \oplus k_2 \oplus k_3.$$

Since $k_0 = 0$ by the first of these four equations, $k_1 = 1$ by the second equation and $k_2 = 1$ by the third equation. The fourth equation becomes $1 = 0 \oplus 1 \oplus 1 \oplus k_3$. Hence $k_3 = 1$. This yields the result in (i), $a \vee b = b \oplus a \oplus (a \otimes b)$.

To prove (ii), it must be shown that the conditions of Definition 6.1(i)–(iv), Definitions 6.4 and 6.12 are satisfied. Some details are left for exercises at the end of this chapter ■

Consider now the addition of two 8-digit binary numbers, as illustrated in Example 2.7. At the ith column of the addition, or the ith stage of an adder which implements this 8-binary-digit addition, a_i denotes the augend digit, b_i denotes the addend digit, and c_i denotes the carry. So the stage immediately to the left has augend digit a_{i+1}, addend digit b_{i+1}, with carry from the ith stage denoted by c_{i+1}. The sum digit at the ith stage is denoted by S_i. Binary arithmetic operations $\oplus$, $\otimes$ are given in figure 2.30. The 8-row tables for S_i and c_{i+1} in terms of a_i, b_i, and c_i are shown in figure 6.2.

a_i	b_i	c_i	S_i	c_{i+1}
0	0	0	0	0
0	0	1	1	0
0	1	0	1	0
0	1	1	0	1
1	0	0	1	0
1	0	1	0	1
1	1	0	0	1
1	1	1	1	1

Figure 6.2   8-row tables for binary sum and carry.

The fdnf from Theorem 4.25 using $n = 2$ yields

$$S_i = \bar{a}_i \bar{b}_i c_i \vee \bar{a}_i b_i \bar{c}_i \vee a_i \bar{b}_i \bar{c}_i \vee a_i b_i c_i$$

and likewise

$$c_{i+1} = \bar{a}_i b_i c_i \vee a_i \bar{b}_i c_i \vee a_i b_i \bar{c}_i \vee a_i b_i c_i.$$

This last equation may be simplified by algebraic means or Karnaugh map to

$$c_{i+1} = a_i b_i \vee a_i c_i \vee b_i c_i$$

so

$$c_{i+1} = a_i b_i \vee (a_i \vee b_i) c_i.$$

by lattice distributivity.

Next, consider the design of an 8-stage *full adder* (a full adder refers to the fact that a full addition is being performed including carries). As mentioned earlier, this allows the addition of numbers where the maximum value is 255. The adder is shown in figure 6.3.An a-register augend and a b-register addend, each stage i of which uses a_i, b_i, c_i and S_i, c_{i+1}, $i = 0, 1, 2, 3, 4, 5, 6, 7$, are shown in figure 6.3(a). This full binary adder forms a sum digit S_i at the ith stage and a carry c_{i+1} for the next stage at the left. These eight stages are connected in tandem from stage 0 at the right to stage 7 at the left. The initial carry c_0 for an addition is fixed at 0. If c_8 at the completion of an addition is equal to 0, then the 8-stage sum is a binary number ≤ 255. If c_8 at the completion of an addition is equal to 1, then the sum is equal to 256 plus the value of the binary number given by this 8-digit sum. Thus the sum is given by

$$(c_8)2^8 + \sum_{i=0}^{7} S_i 2^i.$$

The 8-digit binary adder of figure 6.3 requires that a_i, b_i be obtained from delay flip-flops or some such 2-valued source. Thus $\bar{a}_i$, $\bar{b}_i$ might already be available to the adder, but for the sake of completeness in figure 6.3(a) these values $\bar{a}_i$, $\bar{b}_i$ are generated. The 8 sum digits S_i, $i = 0, 1, 2, 3, 4, 5, 6, 7$, may feed any 8-digit register, such as the a-register.

The 8-digit adder of figure 6.3 is sometimes called a *ripple adder* because the carry "ripples" through the consecutive stages one at a time from right to left. This is indicated in figure 6.3(b). From figure 6.3(b) it may be seen that the gate depth of this adder is 18—this maximum number of gates occurs on a path from c_0 at the right to S_7 at the left. The speed of the adder is measured by the total delay through these 18 gates, and this total delay must be less than the clock interval. Further, it is clear that for an m-digit binary ripple adder of this kind, the gate depth is $2(m - 1) + 4 = 2(m + 1)$.

A feature of this adder is that the fan-out of c_i at each ith stage, $i = 1, 2, 3, 4, 5, 6$, is only 2. So at each ith stage, the carry to the next stage, c_{i+1}, is obtained from c_i without use of an amplifier for c_i.

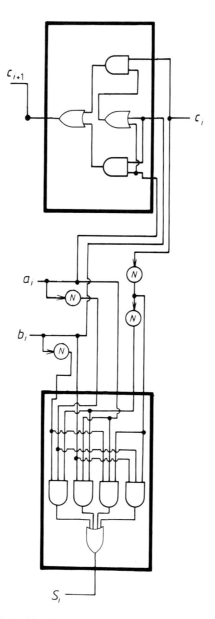

Figure 6.3(a)   Single stage i of full binary adder: 3 inputs a_i, b_i, c_i; 2 outputs S_i, c_{i+1}, where $i = 0, 1, 2, 3, 4, 5, 6, 7$.

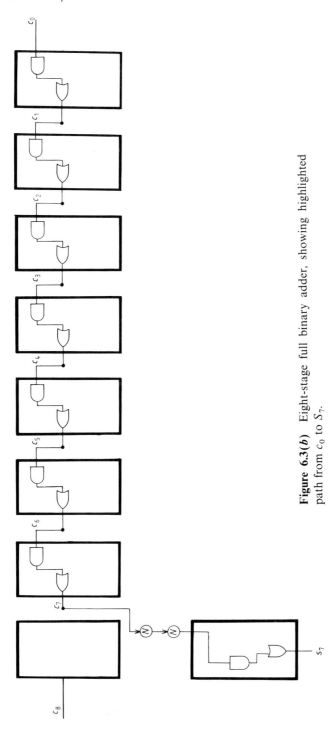

Figure 6.3(b) Eight-stage full binary adder, showing highlighted path from c_0 to S_7.

6.4   The ternary case

Definition 6.17.   A ring R in which $c^3 = c$ and $3c = 0$ for all c in R is called a 3-ring.

THEOREM 6.18.   A 3-ring R is a commutative ring.

Proof

$$(a \oplus b)^3 = a \oplus b$$

so that

$$(a \otimes b^2) \oplus (b^2 \otimes a) \oplus (b \otimes a \otimes b) \oplus (a \otimes b \otimes a) \oplus (a^2 \otimes b) \oplus (b \otimes a^2) = 0$$

using Definition 6.17. It follows that

$$(a \otimes b^2) \oplus (b^2 \otimes a) \oplus (b \otimes a \otimes b) = 0.$$

Hence

$$0 = b \otimes [(a \otimes b^2) \oplus (b^2 \otimes a) \oplus (b \otimes a \otimes b)]$$
$$= (b \otimes a) \oplus (b \otimes a \otimes b^2) \oplus (b^2 \otimes a \otimes b)$$

and

$$0 = [(a \otimes b^2) \oplus (b^2 \otimes a) \oplus (b \otimes a \otimes b)] \otimes b$$
$$= (a \otimes b) \oplus (b^2 \otimes a \otimes b) \oplus (b \otimes a \otimes b^2)$$

using Definition 6.17. Consequently

$$b \otimes a = a \otimes b \qquad\blacksquare$$

Since $c \oplus c \oplus c = 0$ in a 3-ring by Definition 6.17, it follows that the additive inverse $-c$ in a 3-ring is given by $-c = 2c$.

THEOREM 6.19.

(i) A Post algebra of order 3 is a 3-ring with ring zero e_0 and ring unit e_1, where

$$a \oplus b = e_1 C_0(a) C_1(b) \vee e_1 C_1(a) C_0(b)$$
$$\vee e_1 C_2(a) C_2(b) \vee C_1(a) C_1(b)$$
$$\vee C_0(a) C_2(b) \vee C_2(a) C_0(b)$$

and

$$a \otimes b = e_1 C_1(a) C_1(b) \vee e_1 C_2(a) C_2(b)$$
$$\vee C_1(a) C_2(b) \vee C_2(a) C_1(b).$$

The expressions for $a \oplus b$ and $a \otimes b$ are fdnf's from figure 2.31 and yield a ring according to Definition 6.1. It is straightforward to verify from these expressions that

$$c \oplus e_0 = e_0 \oplus c = c$$

$$c \otimes e_1 = e_1 \otimes c = c$$

with

$$c \oplus c \oplus c = e_0 \quad \text{and} \quad c \otimes c \otimes c = c.$$

This shows that a Post algebra of order 3 is a 3-ring R with unit.

(ii) A 3-ring with unit is a Post algebra of order 3, where

$$a \vee b = a \oplus b \oplus (a^2 \otimes b) \oplus 2(a \otimes b) \oplus (a^2 \otimes b^2) \oplus (a \otimes b^2)$$

$$a \wedge b = 2(a^2 \otimes b) \oplus (a \otimes b) \oplus 2(a^2 \otimes b^2) \oplus 2(a \otimes b^2)$$

and, writing 2 for 2(1) in R

$$C_0(a) = (a \oplus 1) \otimes (a \oplus 2)$$

$$C_1(a) = a \otimes (a \oplus 1)$$

$$C_2(a) = a \otimes (a \oplus 2),$$

$$e_0 = 0, \ e_1 = 1, \text{ and } e_2 = 2.$$

The conditions in subsection 4.1.2 may be verified, because the ring-theoretic functions on the right hand side are chosen to satisfy the defining tables for the lattice-theoretic functions in a Post algebra of order 3 on the left hand side. In particular, the ring polynomials for $a \vee b$ and $a \wedge b$ on the right hand side can each be determined by solving $3^2 = 9$ equations in $3^2 = 9$ undetermined coefficients, and the ring polynomials for $C_i(a)$, $i = 0, 1, 2$, on the right hand side can each be determined by solving 3 equations in 3 undetermined coefficients.

Finally, consider the addition of two 5-digit ternary numbers. Such an adder is comparable to the 8-digit binary adder of Section 6.3 in the following sense. While the maximum number representable in an 8-digit adder is $2^8 - 1 = 255$, the maximum number representable in a 5-digit ternary adder is $3^5 - 1 = 242$. Thus if the maximum number size in a particular application were 240, say, then either a 5-digit ternary adder or an 8-digit binary adder could be used.

The same conventions are used for the a-register augend and the b-register addend as in Section 6.3, using a_i, b_i, c_i, and S_i, $i = 0, 1, 2, 3, 4$. Each a_i and b_i provides 3 outputs for use in the adder: $C_0(a_i)$, $C_1(a_i)$, $C_2(a_i)$ and $C_0(b_i)$, $C_1(b_i)$, $C_2(b_i)$, $i = 0, 1, 2, 3, 4$. The ternary adder forms a sum digit S_i at the ith stage and a carry c_{i+1} for the next stage at the left. The initial carry c_0 is 0. The final carry c_5 represents the overflow value. If c_5 is 0 at the end of an addition, the sum does not exceed 242. The correct sum at the end of the

a_i	b_i	c_i	S_i	c_{i+1}
0	0	0	0	0
0	1	0	1	0
0	2	0	2	0
1	0	0	1	0
1	1	0	2	0
1	2	0	0	1
2	0	0	2	0
2	1	0	0	1
2	2	0	1	1
0	0	1	1	0
0	1	1	2	0
0	2	1	0	1
1	0	1	2	0
1	1	1	0	1
1	2	1	1	1
2	0	1	0	1
2	1	1	1	1
2	2	1	2	1

Figure 6.4   18-row tables for ternary sum and carry.

addition is given by

$$c_5 3^5 + \sum_{i=0}^{4} S_i 3^i.$$

Ternary arithmetic operations $\oplus$, $\otimes$ are given in figure 2.31. Figure 6.4 shows 18-row logic tables for S_i and c_{i+1}. The 9 rows in which $c_i = 2$ do not appear in this table because the initial carry c_0 is equal to 0 and carries at subsequent stages are ≤ 1. Consequently, these 9 dropped rows yield don't-cares (DC) for S_i and c_{i+1}. Appropriate selection of 0, 1 values for these DC yields the following logic equations for the case $n = 3$.

$$S_i = e_1 C_0(a_i) C_1(b_i) C_0(c_i)$$
$$\vee \; e_1 C_1(a_i) C_0(b_i) C_0(c_i)$$
$$\vee \; e_1 C_2(a_i) C_2(b_i) C_0(c_i)$$
$$\vee \; e_1 C_0(a_i) C_0(b_i) C_1(c_i)$$
$$\vee \; e_1 C_1(a_i) C_2(b_i) C_1(c_i)$$
$$\vee \; e_1 C_2(a_i) C_1(b_i) C_1(c_i)$$

$$\vee\ C_0(a_i)C_2(b_i)C_0(c_i)$$

$$\vee\ C_1(a_i)C_1(b_i)C_0(c_i)$$

$$\vee\ C_2(a_i)C_0(b_i)C_0(c_i)$$

$$\vee\ C_0(a_i)C_1(b_i)C_1(c_i)$$

$$\vee\ C_1(a_i)C_0(b_i)C_1(c_i)$$

$$\vee\ C_2(a_i)C_2(b_i)C_1(c_i)$$

$$c_{i+1} = e_1[C_1(a_i)C_2(b_i)$$

$$\vee\ C_2(a_i)C_1(b_i)\ \vee\ C_2(a_i)C_2(b_i)]$$

$$\vee\ c_i[C_2(b_i)\ \vee\ C_1(a_i)C_1(b_i)\ \vee\ C_2(a_i)].$$

Next, consider the construction of a 5-digit ternary adder. This consists of five identical stages, where the details for each stage are shown in figure 6.5(a). Stage i has three inputs a_i, b_i, c_i and two outputs S_i and c_{i+1}, where $i = 0, 1, 2, 3, 4$. Leads labeled e_1 denote for this ternary case the supply voltage corresponding to the intermediate constant e_1. These stages are connected in tandem from stage 0 at the right to stage 4 at the left.

In figure 6.5(a) the three values $C_0(a_i)$, $C_1(a_i)$, $C_2(a_i)$ are generated, but these might already be available as the outputs of a 3-stable device or some such source. There is a similar remark for $C_0(b_i)$, $C_1(b_i)$, $C_2(b_i)$. The five sum values S_i, $i = 0, 1, 2, 3, 4$ may be connected as inputs to any 5-ternary-digit register, such as the accumulator.

As in Section 6.3, the carry in this adder ripples over the stages, one by one from right to left. The gate depth of this adder may be computed from a path which traverses a maximum number of gates as highlighted in figure 6.5(b). From figure 6.5(b) it may be seen that the gate depth of this adder is 11—this occurs on a path from c_0 at the right to S_4 at the left. Further it is clear that for an m-digit ternary ripple adder of this kind, the gate depth is $2(m - 1) + 3 = 2m + 1$.

Thus the speed of this ternary adder may be faster than the speed of the binary adder, provided that the ternary and binary gates have comparable speed. The equipment costs depend on the relative costs of the ternary and binary equipment.

Finally, it can be easily seen from figure 6.5(a) that the fan-in to the OR-gate which provides each sum output is 12. This can be reduced using distributivity, as illustrated below.

$$S_i = e_i[C_0(a_i)C_1(b_i)C_0(c_i)$$

$$\vee\ C_1(a_i)C_0(b_i)C_0(c_i)$$

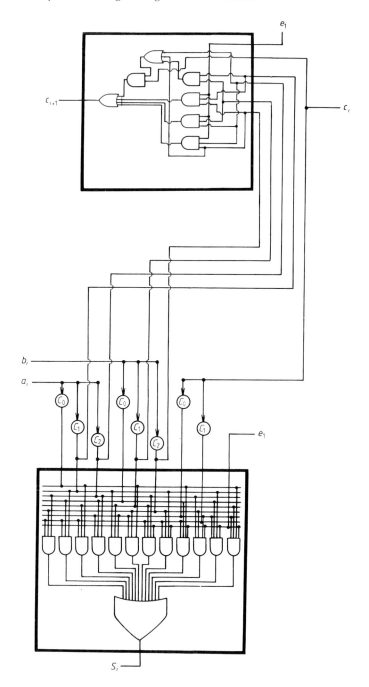

Figure 6.5(a)   Single stage i of full ternary adder: 3 inputs a_i, b_i, c_i; 2 outputs S_i, c_{i+1}, where $i = 0, 1, 2, 3, 4$.

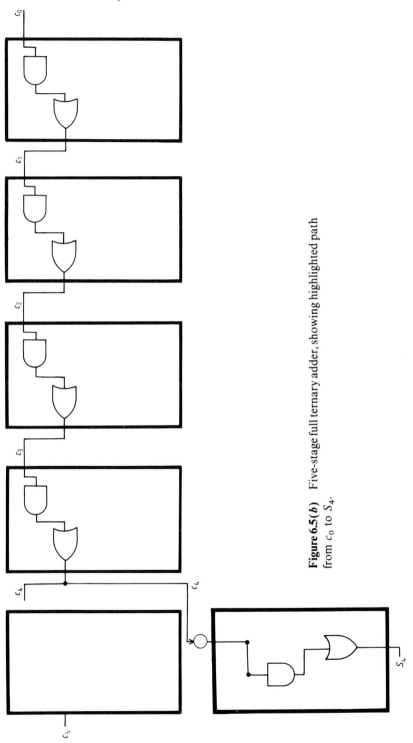

Figure 6.5(*b*) Five-stage full ternary adder, showing highlighted path from c_0 to S_4.

$$\vee \ C_2(a_i)C_2(b_i)C_0(c_i)$$
$$\vee \ C_0(a_i)C_0(b_i)C_1(c_i)$$
$$\vee \ C_1(a_i)C_2(b_i)C_1(c_i)$$
$$\vee \ C_2(a_i)C_1(b_i)C_1(c_i)]$$
$$\vee \ C_0(a_i)C_2(b_i)C_0(c_i)$$
$$\vee \ C_1(a_i)C_1(b_i)C_0(c_i)$$
$$\vee \ C_2(a_i)C_0(b_i)C_0(c_i)$$
$$\vee \ C_0(a_i)C_1(b_i)C_1(c_i)$$
$$\vee \ C_1(a_i)C_0(b_i)C_1(c_i)$$
$$\vee \ C_2(a_i)C_2(b_i)C_1(c_i).$$

An implementation corresponding to this expression reduces the fan-in from 12 to 7. However, this decrease in fan-in at the OR-gate which provides S_4 leads to a slight increase in the adder's gate depth.

6.5 The quaternary case

THEOREM 6.20.   A Post algebra of order 4 is a commutative ring R with unit having characteristic 4, where

$$a \oplus b = e_1 C_0(a)C_1(b) \vee e_1 C_1(a)C_0(b)$$
$$\vee \ e_1 C_2(a)C_3(b) \vee e_1 C_3(a)C_2(b)$$
$$\vee \ e_2 C_0(a)C_2(b) \vee e_2 C_2(a)C_0(b)$$
$$\vee \ e_2 C_1(a)C_1(b) \vee e_2 C_3(a)C_3(b)$$
$$\vee \ C_0(a)C_3(b) \vee C_1(a)C_2(b)$$
$$\vee \ C_2(a)C_1(b) \vee C_3(a)C_0(b)$$
$$a \otimes b = e_1 C_1(a)C_1(b) \vee e_1 C_3(a)C_3(b)$$
$$\vee \ e_2 C_1(a)C_2(b) \vee e_2 C_2(a)C_1(b)$$
$$\vee \ e_2 C_2(a)C_3(b) \vee e_2 C_3(a)C_2(b)$$
$$\vee \ C_1(a)C_3(b) \vee C_3(a)C_1(b).$$

Proof.   The expressions for $a \oplus b$ and $a \otimes b$ are fdnf's from figure 2.33 and yield a commutative ring with ring zero e_0 and ring unit e_1 having characteristic 4. The following come directly from these expressions.

(i) $a \oplus e_0 = e_0 \oplus a = a$
(ii) $a \otimes e_1 = e_1 \otimes a = a$
(iii) $a \otimes b = b \otimes a$
(iv) $a \oplus a \oplus a \oplus a = e_0$

It follows from (iv) that the additive inverse of a is given by $-a = a \oplus a \oplus a$.

However, it is *not* the case that $a^4 = a$ for all a. Consider the element e_2. By the above expression for $a \otimes b$, $(e_2 \otimes e_2) = e_0$. Hence $[e_2]^4 = [e_2]^2 \otimes [e_2]^2 = e_0 \otimes e_0 = e_0$. Hence $[e_2]^4 \neq e_2$ in nondegenerate Post algebras of order 4.

The following development for binary-encoded quaternary addition is different from the development given for binary addition and ternary addition in Sections 6.3 and 6.4.

It is obvious that addition of two 4-digit quaternary numbers matches the addition of two 8-digit binary numbers in the sense that each can represent the addition of two decimal numbers between 0 and 255.

It is instructive here to consider binary-encoded quaternary numbers, where each quaternary value 0, 1, 2, 3, is represented by its 2-digit binary equivalent, 00, 01, 10, 11, respectively. With this encoding, each quaternary value in the a-register or b-register can be realized by a binary pair of flip–flops, and each quaternary output sum can be represented by a pair of lines. The corresponding 32-row logic tables for sum and carry are shown in figure 6.6. Here each carry c_j is combined with a_{2j+1}, a_{2j}, b_{2j+1}, b_{2j} to produce the 2-binary-digit sum represented by S_{2j+1}, S_{2j}. Resulting logic equations from figure 6.6 are given below.

$$c_{j+1} = a_{2j+1}b_{2j+1} \vee (a_{2j+1} \vee b_{2j+1})a_{2j}b_{2j} \vee c_j(a_{2j} \vee b_{2j})(a_{2j+1} \vee b_{2j+1})$$

$$S_{2j} = a_{2j}\overline{c_j}\,\overline{b_{2j}} \vee \overline{a_{2j}}\,c_j\overline{b_{2j}} \vee \overline{a_{2j}}\,\overline{c_j}b_{2j} \vee a_{2j}c_jb_{2j}$$

$$S_{2j+1} = \overline{c_j}(a_{2j+1}\overline{b_{2j+1}}\,\overline{a_{2j}}$$

$$\vee\, a_{2j+1}\overline{b_{2j+1}}\,\overline{b_{2j}} \vee \overline{a_{2j+1}}b_{2j+1}\overline{a_{2j}}$$

$$\vee\, \overline{a_{2j+1}}b_{2j+1}\overline{b_{2j}}) \vee a_{2j+1}b_{2j+1}\,\overline{a_{2j}}\,\overline{b_{2j}}$$

$$\vee\, \overline{a_{2j+1}}\overline{b_{2j+1}}a_{2j}b_{2j}$$

$$\vee\, \overline{a_{2j+1}}b_{2j+1}\overline{a_{2j}}b_{2j}$$

$$\vee\, a_{2j+1}\overline{b_{2j+1}}a_{2j}b_{2j}$$

$$\vee\, c_j(\overline{a_{2j+1}}\,\overline{b_{2j+1}}a_{2j} \vee \overline{a_{2j+1}}\,\overline{b_{2j+1}}b_{2j}$$

$$\vee\, a_{2j+1}b_{2j+1}a_{2j} \vee a_{2j+1}b_{2j+1}b_{2j}).$$

The adder which uses these logic equations is shown in figure 6.7. While

a_{2j+1}	a_{2j}	b_{2j+1}	b_{2j}	c_j	S_{2j+1}	S_{2j}	c_{j+1}
0	0	0	0	0	0	0	0
0	0	0	0	1	0	1	0
0	0	0	1	0	0	1	0
0	0	0	1	1	1	0	0
0	0	1	0	0	1	0	0
0	0	1	0	1	1	1	0
0	0	1	1	0	1	1	0
0	0	1	1	1	0	0	1
0	1	0	0	0	0	1	0
0	1	0	0	1	1	0	0
0	1	0	1	0	1	0	0
0	1	0	1	1	1	1	0
0	1	1	0	0	1	1	0
0	1	1	0	1	0	0	1
0	1	1	1	0	0	0	1
0	1	1	1	1	0	1	1
1	0	0	0	0	1	0	0
1	0	0	0	1	1	1	0
1	0	0	1	0	1	1	0
1	0	0	1	1	0	0	1
1	0	1	0	0	0	0	1
1	0	1	0	1	0	1	1
1	0	1	1	0	0	1	1
1	0	1	1	1	1	0	1
1	1	0	0	0	1	1	0
1	1	0	0	1	0	0	1
1	1	0	1	0	0	0	1
1	1	0	1	1	0	1	1
1	1	1	0	0	0	1	1
1	1	1	0	1	1	0	1
1	1	1	1	0	1	0	1
1	1	1	1	1	1	1	1

Figure 6.6　32-row table for sum and carry, $n = 4$.

this adder uses binary signals throughout, it does not use ripple carries over each binary stage, as in figure 6.3. The adder in figure 6.7 forms only 4 carries, while the ripple adder in figure 6.3 forms 8 carries. Specifically, each carry in figure 6.7 jumps across 2 binary stages, corresponding to the width of each quaternary value. The details of each quaternary stage are shown in figure 6.7(a). It is said that the carries "look-ahead-2". The adder in figure 6.7 is almost twice as fast as the adder in figure 6.3. The gate depth in figure 6.7 is 10—this occurs on a path from c_0 to S_7, as indicated in figure 6.7(b).

Carry look-aheads are an important technique for speeding up adder designs. For example, an octal ($n = 8$) adder following lines of the above design incorporates look-ahead-3 carry propagation. Other adders may use staggered look-aheads—that is, look-ahead-2 over some stages, look-ahead-3 over some stages, etc.

6.6 p-rings

Definition 6.21. A p-ring is a ring in which $pa = 0$ and $a^p = a$ for every a in the ring.

It follows that a p-ring is a commutative ring. This result is in Sections 6.3 and 6.4 for the cases $p = 2$ and $p = 3$, respectively. A proof for $p = 5$ which leads to the generalized result may be found in Chapter 7 of McCoy (1948).

A Post algebra of order n is a commutative ring with unit having characteristic n. The ring operations $a \oplus b$ and $a \otimes b$ may be obtained in fdnf's from tables, as in Section 6.3 for $n = 2$ using the tables in figure 2.30, in Section 6.4 for $n = 3$ using the tables in figure 2.31, and in Section 6.5 for $n = 4$ using the tables in figure 2.33. The results may be stated explicitly as follows. The ring zero is e_0 and the ring unit is e_1, where $a \oplus b$ and $a \otimes b$ are given by

$$a \oplus b = \bigvee_{i=1}^{n-1} e_j \left(\bigvee_{j \oplus k = i} C_j(a) C_k(b) \right)$$

$$a \otimes b = \bigvee_{i=1}^{n-1} e_i \left(\bigvee_{j \otimes k = i} C_j(a) C_k(b) \right).$$

For given n, $j \oplus k$ and $j \otimes k$ in the above are defined in Section 2.7. Since n is finite, the joins in the above expressions are finite. A generalization of this may be found in Epstein and Rasiowa (1991). If n is not prime, there exists an element c such that $c^n \neq c$. If n is equal to a prime p, then $c^p = c$ for all c, and the Post algebra of order p is a p-ring.

Conversely, a p-ring is a Post algebra of order p. The lattice operations $a \vee b, a \wedge b, C_i(a), i = 0, \ldots, p - 1$, may be obtained as for $p = 2$ in Section 6.3 and for $p = 3$ in Section 6.4. First, $a \vee b$ and $a \wedge b$ may each be obtained as a ring polynomial through the solution of p^2 equations in p^2 undetermined coefficients. Second, $C_i(a), i = 0, \ldots, p - 1$, may be given explicitly by

$$C_i(a) = \prod_{j \neq p - i} (a \oplus j)$$

where j stands for $j(1)$ and the product stands for circle-product in the ring. Third, e_0 is the ring zero, e_1 is the ring unit, and $e_j = j$ for $0 \leq j \leq p - 1$.

Finally, it follows from Theorem 5.30 that the direct product of t p_i-rings, $i = 1, \ldots, t$, where p_i are distinct primes, is a sub-Post algebra of order q,

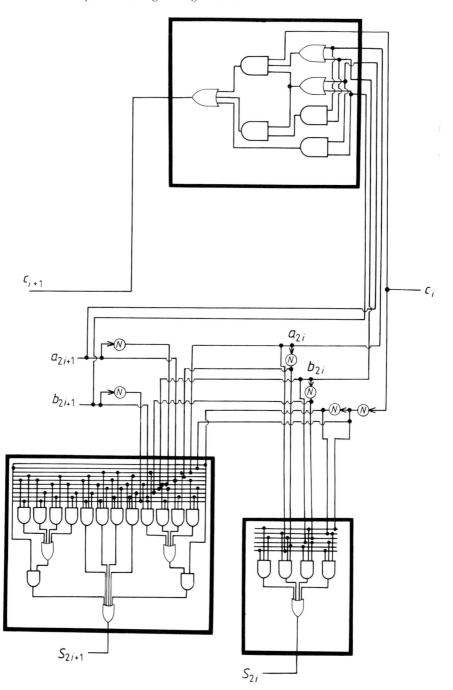

Figure 6.7(a)   Single stage i of full quaternary adder: 5 inputs a_{2i}, a_{2i+1}, b_{2i}, b_{2i+1}, c_i; 3 outputs S_{2i}, S_{2i+1}, c_{i+1}.

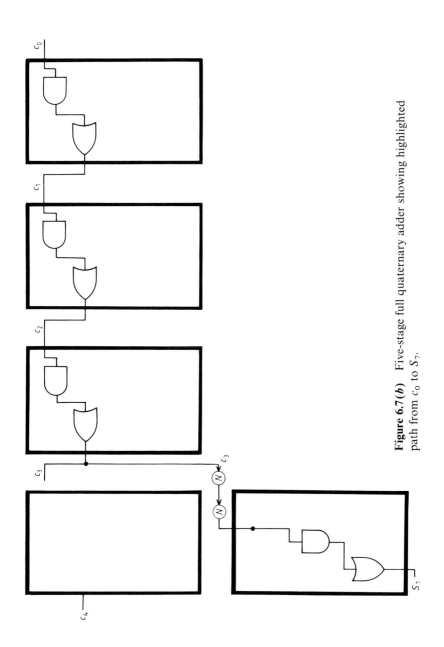

Figure 6.7(b) Five-stage full quaternary adder showing highlighted path from c_0 to S_7.

where q is the largest of these primes. As stated in Epstein and Horn (1974b), a ring with unit is a direct product of t rings each of which is a p_i-ring, $i = 1, \ldots, t$, if and only if R satisfies

(i) $a^m = a$ where $m = 1 + \text{LCM}\dagger\,(p_1 - 1, \ldots, p_t - 1)$
(ii) $p_1 p_2 \ldots p_t a = 0$
(iii) $\left(\prod_{j \neq i} p_j\right)(a^{p_i}) = \left(\prod_{j \neq i} p_j\right)a, \quad 1 \leq i \leq t.$

These three conditions are partially illustrated using the 6-element sub-Post algebra of order 3 shown in figure 5.4. Note that ring operations of addition and multiplication are performed component-wise on the pairs in this figure. Since the first component of the pair is binary, binary addition and multiplication are performed on this component; since the second component of the pair is ternary, ternary addition and multiplication are performed on this component.

First, let $a = (1, 2)$, the lattice unit, in figure 5.4. Then, $(1, 2) \otimes (1, 2) = (1, 1)$; and so $(1, 2) \otimes (1, 2) \otimes (1, 2) = (1, 2)$, as required by (i), since $1 + \text{LCM}\,((2 - 1), (3 - 1)) = 1 + 2 = 3 = m$.

Second, consider $e_1 = (1, 1)$, the ring unit. Then $(1, 1) \oplus (1, 1) = 2(1, 1) = (0, 2)$; $3(1, 1) = (1, 0)$; $4(1, 1) = (0, 1)$; $5(1, 1) = (1, 2)$; $6(1, 1) = (0, 0)$, as required by (ii). At the first step, $(0, 2) = e_1 \oplus e_1 \neq e_2 = (1, 2)$, unlike the situation in Post algebras of order n for $n \geq 3$, where $e_1 \oplus e_1 = e_2$.

Third, let $a = (1, 2)$. Then $a^2 = (1, 1)$, and $3(1, 1) = (1, 0) = 3(1, 2)$; also $2(a^3) = 2a$ follows directly from (i). This illustrates (iii), since here $t = 2$ with $p_1 = 2$ and $p_2 = 3$.

The next section discusses an adder where the register length is 3. The rightmost digit at stage 0 is binary, taking values 0, 1, the middle digit at stage 1 is ternary, taking values 0, 1, 2, and the leftmost digit at stage 2 is quaternary, taking values 0, 1, 2, 3. Consequently, the $4! = 24$ possible values which may occur can be shown as a sub-Post algebra of order 4 having 24 elements; see figure 5.6. Indeed, each 3-tuple (c, b, a) shown in figure 5.6 corresponds with the 3-digit register representation just described.

6.7 The mixed radix case

A main concern in this section is the mixed radix case, using the factorial number system. In the mixed radix case each t digit number x is represented by

$$x = \sum_{i=0}^{t-1} x_i r(i)$$

† Least-common-multiple.

where $r(i)$ may vary with i. An important example is the factorial number system, in which $r(i) = (i + 1)!$ and each x_i is a non-negative integer in the range $0 \le x_i \le (i + 1)$. The main example in this section uses 3-digit numbers, so that $t = 3$ and the register length is 3. Once again the least significant digit of the adder is at the rightmost stage and the most significant digit is at the leftmost stage. Thus the digit x_0 appears at stage 0, the digit x_1 appears at stage 1, and the digit x_2 appears at stage 2.

According to the above representation for x, using $t = 3$,

$$x = x_2(3!) + x_1(2!) + x_0(1!) = 6x_2 + 2x_1 + x_0.$$

The minimum such number is $6(0) + 2(0) + 1(0) = 0$, whose register representation is the triple $(0, 0, 0)$. The maximum such number is $6(3) + 2(2) + 1(1) = 23$, whose register representation is the triple $(3, 2, 1)$. These 24 register triples are shown in figure 5.6 as a sub-Post algebra of order 4, where the rightmost digit is binary, the middle digit is ternary, and the leftmost digit is quaternary.

Consider the logic design of a mixed radix adder for such 3-digit numbers in the factorial number system. A separate logic design will be given for each stage. Resulting logic equations are given below.

The sum and carry binary logic equations for stage 0 from figure 6.8 are given below, where here it is understood that $j = 0$.

$$c_{j+1} = a_j b_j$$
$$S_j = a_j \overline{b_j} \vee \overline{a_j} b_j \qquad \text{where} \qquad c_0 = 0.$$

a_j	b_j	S_j	c_{j+1}
0	0	0	0
0	1	1	0
1	0	1	0
1	1	0	1

Figure 6.8 The binary stage 0 of a 3-digit factorial number system adder.

The sum and carry ternary logic equations for stage 1 from figure 6.9 are given below, where here it is understood that $j = 1$. Also, figure 6.9 shows a table of 18 rows that represents a table of 27 rows in which the last 9 rows have been dropped. These 9 dropped rows, in which $c_j = 2$, are not shown because each carry is at most 1 if the initial carry c_0 is equal to 0. There are DCs for S_j and c_{j+1} at each of these 9 rows. Appropriate selection of values for these DCs yields the following.

$$c_{j+1} = e_1[C_1(a_j)C_2(b_j)$$
$$\vee\; C_2(a_j)C_1(b_j) \vee C_2(a_j)C_2(b_j)]$$
$$\vee\; c_j[C_2(b_j) \vee C_1(a_j)C_1(b_j) \vee C_2(a_j)]$$

$$S_j = e_1 C_0(a_j) C_1(b_j) C_0(c_j)$$
$$\vee\ e_1 C_1(a_j) C_0(b_j) C_0(c_j)$$
$$\vee\ e_1 C_2(a_j) C_2(b_i) C_0(c_j)$$
$$\vee\ e_1 C_0(a_j) C_0(b_j) C_1(c_j)$$
$$\vee\ e_1 C_1(a_j) C_2(b_j) C_1(c_j)$$
$$\vee\ e_1 C_2(a_j) C_1(b_j) C_1(c_j)$$
$$\vee\ C_0(a_j) C_2(b_j) C_0(c_j)$$
$$\vee\ C_1(a_j) C_1(b_j) C_0(c_j)$$
$$\vee\ C_2(a_j) C_0(b_j) C_0(c_j)$$
$$\vee\ C_0(a_j) C_1(b_j) C_1(c_j)$$
$$\vee\ C_1(a_j) C_0(b_j) C_1(c_j)$$
$$\vee\ C_2(a_j) C_2(b_j) C_1(c_j).$$

a_j	b_j	c_j	S_j	c_{j+1}
0	0	0	0	0
0	1	0	1	0
0	2	0	2	0
1	0	0	1	0
1	1	0	2	0
1	2	0	0	1
2	0	0	2	0
2	1	0	0	1
2	2	0	1	1
0	0	1	1	0
0	1	1	2	0
0	2	1	0	1
1	0	1	2	0
1	1	1	0	1
1	2	1	1	1
2	0	1	0	1
2	1	1	1	1
2	2	1	2	1

Figure 6.9   The ternary stage 1 of a 3-digit factorial number system adder.

Finally, the sum and carry logic equations from figure 6.10 at stage $j = 2$ of the adder use $n = 4$ and are given below. Figure 6.10 shows a table of 32 rows that represents a table of 64 rows in which the last 32 rows have been dropped. Specifically, the 16 rows in which $c_j = 2$ and the 16 rows in which

a_j	b_j	c_j	S_j	c_{j+1}
0	0	0	0	0
0	1	0	1	0
0	2	0	2	0
0	3	0	3	0
1	0	0	1	0
1	1	0	2	0
1	2	0	3	0
1	3	0	0	1
2	0	0	2	0
2	1	0	3	0
2	2	0	0	1
2	3	0	1	1
3	0	0	3	0
3	1	0	0	1
3	2	0	1	1
3	3	0	1	1
0	0	1	1	0
0	1	1	2	0
0	2	1	3	0
0	3	1	0	1
1	0	1	2	0
1	1	1	3	0
1	2	1	0	1
1	3	1	1	1
2	0	1	3	0
2	1	1	0	1
2	2	1	1	1
2	3	1	2	1
3	0	1	0	1
3	1	1	1	1
3	2	1	2	1
3	3	1	3	1

Figure 6.10 The quaternary stage 2 of a 3-digit factorial number adder.

$c_j = 3$ are not shown because each carry is at most 1 if the initial carry c_0 is equal to 0. There are DCs for S_j and c_{j+1} at each of these dropped rows. Appropriate selection of values for these DCs yields the following.

$$c_{j+1} = e_1[C_1(a_j)C_3(b_j)$$
$$\lor\ C_2(a_j)C_2(b_j) \lor C_2(a_j)C_3(b_j)$$
$$\lor\ C_3(a_j)C_1(b_j) \lor C_3(a_j)C_2(b_j)$$
$$\lor\ C_3(a_j)C_3(b_j)] \lor c_j[C_3(b_j) \lor C_1(a_j)C_2(b_j)$$
$$\lor\ C_2(a_j)C_1(b_j) \lor C_2(a_j)C_2(b_j) \lor C_3(a_j)]$$

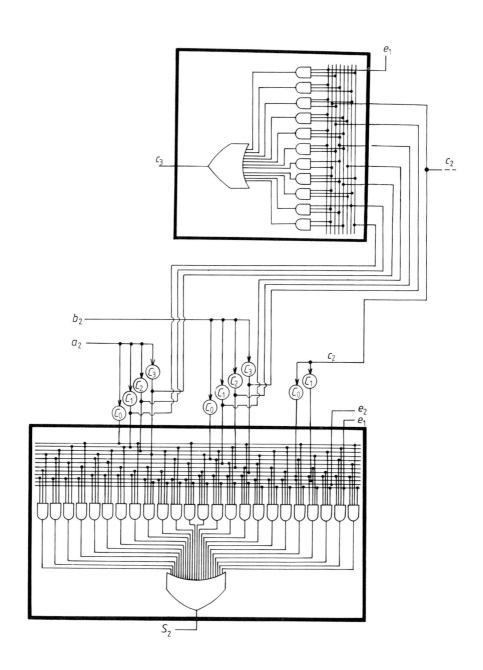

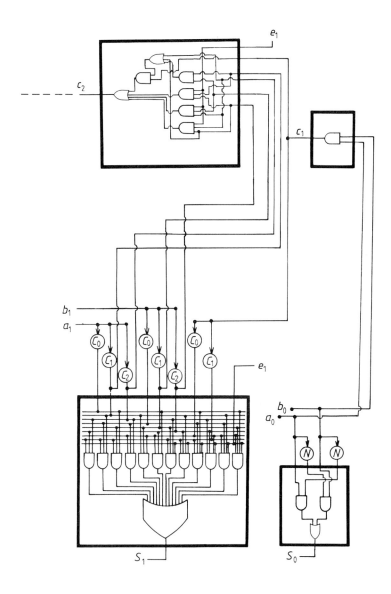

Figure 6.11 3-digit adder, factorial number system.

$$S_j = e_1 C_0(a_j)C_1(b_j)C_0(c_j)$$
$$\lor\ e_1 C_1(a_j)C_0(b_j)C_0(c_j)$$
$$\lor\ e_1 C_2(a_j)C_3(b_j)C_0(c_j)$$
$$\lor\ e_1 C_3(a_j)C_2(b_j)C_0(c_j)$$
$$\lor\ e_1 C_0(a_j)C_0(b_j)C_1(c_j)$$
$$\lor\ e_1 C_1(a_j)C_3(b_j)C_1(c_j)$$
$$\lor\ e_1 C_2(a_j)C_2(b_j)C_1(c_j)$$
$$\lor\ e_1 C_3(a_j)C_1(b_j)C_1(c_j)$$
$$\lor\ e_2 C_0(a_j)C_2(b_j)C_0(c_j)$$
$$\lor\ e_2 C_1(a_j)C_1(b_j)C_0(c_j)$$
$$\lor\ e_2 C_2(a_j)C_0(b_j)C_0(c_j)$$
$$\lor\ e_2 C_3(a_j)C_3(b_j)C_0(c_j)$$
$$\lor\ e_2 C_0(a_j)C_1(b_j)C_1(c_j)$$
$$\lor\ e_2 C_1(a_j)C_0(b_j)C_1(c_j)$$
$$\lor\ e_2 C_2(a_j)C_3(b_j)C_1(c_j)$$
$$\lor\ e_2 C_3(a_j)C_2(b_j)C_1(c_j)$$
$$\lor\ C_0(a_j)C_3(b_j)C_0(c_j)$$
$$\lor\ C_1(a_j)C_2(b_j)C_0(c_j)$$
$$\lor\ C_2(a_j)C_1(b_j)C_0(c_j)$$
$$\lor\ C_3(a_j)C_0(b_j)C_0(c_j)$$
$$\lor\ C_0(a_j)C_2(b_j)C_1(c_j)$$
$$\lor\ C_1(a_j)C_1(b_j)C_1(c_j)$$
$$\lor\ C_2(a_j)C_0(b_j)C_1(c_j)$$
$$\lor\ C_3(a_j)C_3(b_j)C_1(c_j).$$

The logic equations given above are used in the 3-digit mixed radix adder in figure 6.11, using the factorial number system. The correct sum at the end of the addition is given by

$$c_3(4!) + \sum_{j=0}^{2} S_j(j+1)!$$

There are possible applications for mixed radix number systems when the numerical data is represented in a form which uses varying radices, as discussed on pp 175–6 in Knuth (1969).

It should be evident from figure 6.11 that the complexity of an adder using the factorial number system increases sharply as the number of digits increases. There are mixed radix number systems where this does not hold. An example may be found in one of the exercises at the end of this chapter. This example involves a 5-digit mixed radix adder, where 2 of the 5 digits are binary and the other 3 digits are quaternary.

6.8 Overview

Rings and fields are discussed in textbooks on modern algebra such as Birkhoff and MacLane (1965) and Herstein (1975). Some topics in these books appear as exercises at the end of this chapter. These topics include the little Fermat theorem, and quaternions. p-rings are in McCoy and Montgomery (1937). Post algebras of order n are discussed in Rosenbloom (1942). Connections between Post algebras and rings are studied in Wade (1945).

A major purpose of this chapter is to introduce the subject of adders. The subject of subtractors may be found in exercises at the end of this chapter. The logic design of an adder in a given application will depend on the actual circuits which are available for the primitive operations. The logic designer may play a role in the design of these circuits.

There is a wide variety of adders and arithmetic units which have been devised since the early 1950s. The following is a nonexhaustive sampling of related work during the period 1980–90: Kabat and Wojcik (1981); Ling (1981); Wheaton and Current (1981); Mouftah and Garba (1984); Kawahito *et al* (1986); Razavi and Bou-Ghazale (1987); Diawuo and Mouftah (1987); Manzoul and Bommireddy (1988); Wakui and Tanaka (1989); and Manzoul *et al* (1989).

Exercises

E6.1 For $n = 2$, using the expressions in Theorem 6.16(i) which give lattice operations in terms of ring operations, prove that $a \vee (b \vee c) = (a \vee b) \vee c$.

E6.2 For $n = 2$, using the expressions in Theorem 6.16(i) which give lattice operations in terms of ring operations, prove that $a \wedge (b \vee c) = (a \wedge b) \vee (a \wedge c)$.

E6.3 For $n = 2$, using the expressions in Theorem 6.16(ii) which give ring operations in terms of lattice operations, prove that

$$a \oplus (b \oplus c) = (a \oplus b) \oplus c.$$

E6.4 For $n = 2$, using the expressions in Theorem 6.16(ii) which give ring operations in terms of lattice operations, prove that $a \oplus a = 0$.

E6.5 Let $R = \{0, 1, \ldots, p - 1\}$, where p is a prime. Following Example 6.4, R is a commutative ring with unit. If a is any nonzero element in R, show that $a^p = a$ in R by proving the little Fermat theorem: for any integer q and prime p, $q^p \equiv q \pmod{p}$.

E6.6 Give an example of a commutative ring which has no unit element and no proper divisors of 0.

E6.7 Let $R = \{0, 1, \ldots, p - 1\}$, where p is a prime. Prove that R is a field, as stated in Example 6.5.

E6.8 Let R be the set of *quaternions* $a + bi + cj + dk$ with i, j, k distinct elements satisfying $i^2 = j^2 = k^2 = -1$, $ij = -ji = k$, $jk = -kj = i$, $ki = -ik = j$ and each quaternion is represented by real coordinates (a, b, c, d) in four dimensions. The operations are given by

$$(a_1, b_1, c_1, d_1) \oplus (a_2, b_2, c_2, d_2) = (a_1 + a_2, b_1 + b_2, c_1 + c_2, d_1 + d_2)$$

and

$$(a_1, b_1, c_1, d_1) \otimes (a_2, b_2, c_2, d_2) = (a_1 a_2 - b_1 b_2 - c_1 c_2 - d_1 d_2,$$
$$a_1 b_2 + b_1 a_2 + c_1 d_2 - d_1 c_2,$$
$$a_1 c_2 + c_1 a_2 + d_1 b_2 - b_1 d_2,$$
$$a_1 d_2 + d_1 a_2 + b_1 c_2 - c_1 b_2).$$

R is a ring with zero $(0, 0, 0, 0)$ and unit $(1, 0, 0, 0)$. The additive inverse of (a, b, c, d) is $(-a, -b, -c, -d)$. However, R is not a commutative ring.

(a) Show that the quaternion $q = 1 + 2i + 3j + 4k$ has a multiplicative inverse by giving q^{-1}.
(b) Prove that every quaternion $q \neq 0$ has a multiplicative inverse, so R has no proper divisors of zero.
(c) State a relation between quaternions in four dimensions and complex numbers in two dimensions.

E6.9 Let R be the set of *ternions* $A + Bj + Ck$ with $j \neq -1$ and $k \neq -1$ distinct elements satisfying $j^3 = k^3 = -1$, $j^2 = -k$, $k^2 = -j$, $jk = kj = 1$, and each ternion is represented by real coordinates (A, B, C) in three dimensions. The operations are given by

$$(A_1, B_1, C_1) \oplus (A_2, B_2, C_2) = (A_1 + A_2, B_1 + B_2, C_1 + C_2)$$

and

$$(A_1, B_1, C_1) \otimes (A_2, B_2, C_2)$$
$$= (A_1 A_2 + B_1 C_2 + C_1 B_2,$$
$$B_1 A_2 + A_1 B_2 - C_1 C_2,$$
$$A_1 C_2 + C_1 A_2 - B_1 B_2).$$

R is a commutative ring with zero $(0, 0, 0)$ and unit $(1, 0, 0)$. The additive inverse of (A, B, C) is $(-A, -B, -C)$.

(a) Show that $2 + j + k$ is a proper divisor of zero.
(b) Show that $t = 1 + 2j + 3k$ has a multiplicative inverse by giving t^{-1}.
(c) If $T = A + Bj + Ck$ has a multiplicative inverse, give an expression for T^{-1}.
(d) Characterize the proper divisors of zero together with $(0, 0, 0)$ in three dimensions, using lines, planes, etc. as needed.
(e) State a relation between ternions in three dimensions and complex numbers in two dimensions.

E6.10 For the binary case, construct an 8-row table for a full subtractor. Show three input columns for a_i, b_i, BOR_i at the left and two output columns DIF_i, BOR_{i+1} at the right. Here b_i is to be subtracted from a_i, where DIF_i is the difference at the ith stage, BOR_i is the borrow at the ith stage, and BOR_{i+1} is the borrow for the stage at the immediate left.

E6.11 Using **E6.10** above, give a logic diagram for a full subtractor, where $n = 2$ and $m = 8$. The initial borrow BOR_0 should be taken equal to 0. To what extent is your logic diagram similar to the logic diagram for the full adder where $n = 2$, $m = 8$ in figure 6.3?

E6.12 For $n = 3$, using the expressions in Theorem 6.19(i) which give ring operations in terms of lattice operations, prove that

$$a \otimes e_1 = e_1 \otimes a = a.$$

E6.13 For $n = 3$, using the expressions in Theorem 6.19(i) which give ring operations in terms of lattice operations, prove that

$$a \oplus a = e_2 \otimes a.$$

E6.14 For $n = 3$, using the expressions in Theorem 6.19(ii) which give lattice operations in terms of ring operations, prove that

$$a \vee a = a.$$

E6.15 For the ternary number system construct a table for a full subtractor. The column headings for this table should have the same format as in **E6.10**.

E6.16 Referring to **E6.15** above and assuming that the initial borrow BOR_0 is taken equal to 0, explain the entries for the rows in which $BOR_i = 2$.

E6.17   For the quaternary number system construct a table for a full adder. For this quaternary table, entries take values from 0, 1, 2, 3. This contrasts with the table in figure 6.6, where all the entries are binary.

E6.18   How does the table of **E6.17** above depend on the value of the initial carry c_0? Contrast the initial condition $c_0 = 0$ with the initial condition $c_0 = 3$.

E6.19   In British imperial measure

   1 pint = 4 gills
   1 quart = 2 pints
   1 gallon = 4 quarts
   1 peck = 2 gallons
   1 bushel = 4 pecks.

A corresponding word of length 5 is shown below, where stage 0 holds a quaternary digit for gills, stage 1 holds a binary digit for pints, stage 2 holds a quaternary digit for quarts, stage 3 holds a binary digit for gallons, and stage 4 holds a quaternary digit for pecks. In a corresponding adder which uses such a word, as shown below, an overflow carry at the left represents 1 bushel.

Peck	Gallon	Quart	Pint	Gill
Quaternary digit	Binary digit	Quaternary digit	Binary digit	Quaternary digit
Stage 4	Stage 3	Stage 2	Stage 1	Stage 0

To illustrate, the maximum amount which can be represented with such a word is

3	1	3	1	3

that is, 3 pecks, 1 gallon, 3 quarts, 1 pint, and 3 gills.

(a) Give a logic diagram for a 5-digit mixed radix adder for this case having sum outputs S_4, S_3, S_2, S_1, S_0. For the quaternary stages, see the table of **E6.17**.
(b) In this part each quaternary digit is represented by a pair of binary digits, as in Section 6.5. The result is a word length of 8 *binary* digits

Stage 7	Stage 6	Stage 5	Stage 4	Stage 3	Stage 2	Stage 1	Stage 0

Give a logic diagram for this 8-binary-digit adder. For each quaternary pair of binary digits, see figures 6.6 and 6.7.

7 Finite State Diagrams

7.1 An introduction to finite state diagrams

Finite state diagrams (FSDs) are used to help analyse or design digital structures. The usual textbook emphasis is on binary hardware structures. Here a general approach is given for $n = 2, 3, \ldots$, with concentration on the binary and ternary cases.

An example of a ternary FSD is shown in figure 7.1 where there are two circled states, called q_0 and q_1. Finite state diagrams may show states of a machine, states of a program, or even states of a human mind. The inputs are IN1, IN2, ..., INj and the outputs are OUT1, OUT2, ..., OUTk. Between states there are directed edges labelled IN1, IN2, ..., INj/OUT1, OUT2, ..., OUTk, denoting the values of the j n-valued inputs at the left of the slash, and the values of the k n-valued outputs at the right of the slash. In figure 7.1, $n = 3$, so that all signal values are 0, 1, 2, and $j = 1, k = 2$. If a synchronous finite state machine is pictured by a state diagram, it is assumed that all changes of states, inputs, and outputs are initiated by a *clock tick* which occurs at regular intervals. Such an interval is called the *clock interval*—for example, the clock interval between two consecutive clock ticks might be 1 microsecond. The clock interval must be sufficiently large so that all changes in states, inputs, and outputs are completed *during* the ensuing clock interval, *prior* to the next clock tick.

Some details may be remarked upon in figure 7.1. While in state q_0, an input of either IN1 $= 0$ or IN1 $= 1$ will result, at the next clock tick, in no change in state and outputs OUT1 $= 0$, OUT2 $= 2$. On the other hand, while in state q_0, an input IN1 $= 2$ will result, at the next clock tick, in a change of state from q_0 to q_1 and outputs OUT1 $= 1$, OUT2 $= 1$. The FSD is clearly a pictorial way of displaying all states and the state transitions and outputs that correspond to different inputs. This chapter treats the completely specified case, in which all possibilities are taken into account, so that each state will have precisely n^j arrows leaving it. In figure 7.1 there are $3^1 = 3$ edges leaving each state (the 3 edges bear input labels 0, 1, 2, occurring in each edge label at the left of the slash).

An alternative to the FSD is the finite state table (FST). While an FSD gives a graphical representation, an FST gives a tabular representation. See table 7.1 for an example of the FST corresponding to the ternary FSD shown in

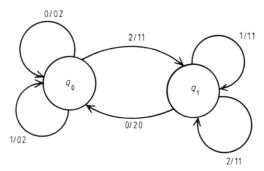

Figure 7.1 Example of ternary finite state diagram.

Table 7.1 Finite state table for ternary FSD of figure 7.1.

Current state	IN1 = 0	IN1 = 1	IN1 = 2
q_0	$q_0, 02$	$q_0, 02$	$q_1, 11$
q_1	$q_0, 20$	$q_1, 11$	$q_1, 11$

figure 7.1. Consider the first row of the finite state table in table 7.1. The "Current state" entry in this first row is q_0. Under each of the two headings IN1 = 0 and IN1 = 1 at this first row, the next state entry is q_0, to the left of the comma under each heading. To the right of the comma under each of these headings are the output values OUT1 = 0, OUT2 = 2. Consider next at this same first row, the heading IN1 = 2. The next state entry is q_1, to the left of the comma under this heading. To the right of this comma the output values are OUT1 = 1, OUT2 = 1. There is a similar treatment for the second row.

The details for table 7.1 are the same as those for figure 7.1. It is easy to see that the displayed results are the same whether FSDs or FSTs are used. In the rest of this chapter FSDs will be used because of their pictorial advantage, but FSTs will also be used when the occasion warrants.

In this chapter all combinatorial circuits are built from AND-gates, OR-gates, input-signals, constants e_i, and disjoint gates $C_i, i = 0, 1, \ldots, n - 1$. For $n = 2$, the C_0 gate appears as an inverter and C_1 is not used because $x = C_1(x)$. For memory elements, synchronous n-valued delay n-stable devices are used. All such memory elements are controlled by a synchronous clock. These memory elements are referred to as D (delay) n-stable devices. Such a device x has a single n-valued Dx input and n decisive outputs $C_0(x)$, $C_1(x), \ldots, C_{n-1}(x)$. For $n = 2$, such delay 2-stable devices are called D flip–flops (delay flip–flops).

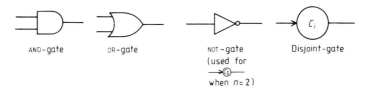

Figure 7.2 Basic combinational circuits.

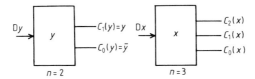

Figure 7.3 n-stable devices for $n = 2$ and $n = 3$.

Basic combinational circuits are shown in figure 7.2. n-stable devices are shown in figure 7.3. Consider the 3-stable device of figure 7.3. Let $Dx = 0$. Then at the next tick of the clock, $C_0(x)$ becomes 2 while $C_1(x)$ and $C_2(x)$ each become 0. Next, suppose $Dx = 1$. At the next tick of the clock $C_1(x)$ becomes 2 while $C_0(x)$ and $C_2(x)$ each become 0. Last, let $Dx = 2$. At the next tick of the clock $C_2(x)$ becomes 2 while $C_0(x)$ and $C_1(x)$ each become 0.

This chapter is concerned with clock mode sequential circuits using the Mealy model. In a Mealy model, outputs depend on the current state and the inputs. Other variants exist—see for example Hill and Peterson (1981).

7.2   Analysis

This section deals with the analysis of given logic circuits through the use of FSDs. With an FSD it is possible to gain a pictorial understanding of the logic circuit at hand. First, a finite state table may be constructed for the given logic circuit. Next, an FSD may be drawn with the aid of this table. For elementary examples, it may be possible to obtain an FSD without forming a state table.

7.2.1   Analysis of a binary mystery machine

Consider a binary 'mystery' machine, as presented in figure 7.4. What is the action of this mystery machine?

A finite state table for the binary machine of figure 7.4 is given as table 7.2. Note that the logic circuit for this machine shows two D flip–flops $X1$ and $X2$. There is, one input, IN1, and three outputs, OUT1, OUT2, OUT3. The flip–flop names $X1$, $X2$ are identified with the top $X1$, $X2$ outputs of the flip–flops, respectively. Corresponding to these top exiting values of the

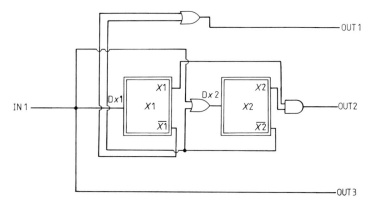

Figure 7.4   Binary mystery machine.

Table 7.2   Finite state table for binary mystery machine.

Current state	$X1$	$X2$	$IN1 = 0$	$IN1 = 1$
q_0	0	0	$q_1, 100$	$q_3, 101$
q_1	0	1	$q_0, 100$	$q_3, 101$
q_2	1	0	$q_1, 100$	$q_3, 101$
q_3	1	1	$q_0, 010$	$q_3, 011$

flip–flops, $X1$ and $X2$, the four rows of the state table are given in increasing binary order: q_0 is given by $X1 = 0$, $X2 = 0$; q_1 is given by $X1 = 0$, $X2 = 1$; q_2 is given by $X1 = 1$, $X2 = 0$; q_3 is given by $X1 = 1$, $X2 = 1$. This information is shown in the first three columns of table 7.2.

Consider the first row of table 7.2. This row states that if $X1 = 0$ and $X2 = 0$, then an input of $IN1 = 0$ will result at the next clock tick in next state q_1 (to the left of the comma in column 4 of the first row) and outputs $OUT1 = 1$, $OUT2 = 0$, $OUT3 = 0$ (to the right of the comma in column 4 at the first row). Recall that q_1 stands for $X1 = 0$, $X2 = 1$, as shown in the second row. A similar analysis may be applied at the first row using column 5, in which $IN1 = 1$. There are similar treatments at each of the rows 2, 3, and 4, corresponding to the different values of the flip–flops $X1$, $X2$ shown in columns 2 and 3.

The details for table 7.2 follow from the logic circuit in figure 7.4. Corresponding to the first row of table 7.2, consider $X1 = X2 = 0$. Corresponding to column 4 let $IN1 = 0$. At the next clock tick, the action of the logic circuit is as follows. Obviously $OUT3 = 0$ because $IN1$ is connected directly to $OUT3$. Since $X1 = 0$, it is clear that $OUT2 = 0$, because $OUT2$ results from an AND-gate which has $X1$ as an input. Also, $OUT1 = 1$, because $OUT1$ results from an OR-gate which has $\overline{X1}$, $\overline{X2}$ as inputs. Finally, $DX1 = 0$

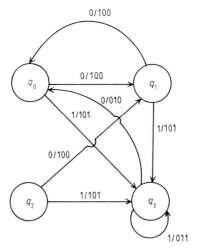

Figure 7.5 Finite state diagram for binary mystery machine.
Some observations:
  (i) A constant 0 input stream causes the machine to oscillate between
      states q_0 and q_1.
 (ii) An input of 1 results in state q_3.
(iii) q_2 cannot be reached from any other state.
 (iv) Except for state q_3, IN1 = 0 input yields the same OUT1, OUT2,
      OUT3 outputs (i.e., 100), and IN1 = 1 input yields the same
      OUT1, OUT2, and OUT3 outputs (i.e., 101),

because IN1 is connected directly to the D input of flip–flop $X1$—hence
$X1$ will become 0 at the next clock tick; also $DX2 = 1$ because $DX2$ results
from an OR-gate one of whose inputs is $\overline{X2} = 1$. Thus the corresponding
entry to the left of the comma in column 4 of row 1 is q_1. Other details for
table 7.2 follow from the logic circuit of figure 7.4 in similar fashion.

From table 7.2 it is easy to draw an FSD. The state table shows four states,
q_0, q_1, q_2, q_3; in the FSD of figure 7.5 these are shown circled.

The FSD in figure 7.5 uses labeled directed edges to show state transitions.
For example, using table 7.2, consider row 1. While in state q_0, if input
IN1 = 0, then at the next clock tick there is a change of state from q_0 to q_1,
with outputs OUT1 = 1, OUT2 = 0, OUT3 = 0. This is shown in the FSD
of figure 7.5 by the directed edge from q_0 to q_1, labeled 0/100. The 0 to the
left of the slash is the value of IN1. The triple 100 to the right of the slash
are the outputs OUT1, OUT2, OUT3. All remaining instances are treated
similarly. The resulting FSD in figure 7.5 may be regarded as a pictorial
representation of table 7.2.

A number of observations may be made from the FSD. For example, if the
machine were to start in state q_0 with a constant input stream of 0s, the FSD
clearly shows that the machine would oscillate between states q_0 and q_1 with

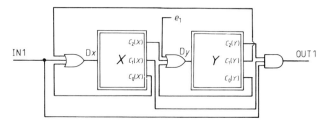

Figure 7.6   Ternary mystery machine.

Table 7.3   Finite state table for ternary mystery machine.

Current state	X	Y	IN1 = 0	IN1 = 1	IN1 = 2
q_0	0	0	$q_2, 0$	$q_5, 0$	$q_8, 0$
q_1	0	1	$q_8, 0$	$q_8, 0$	$q_8, 0$
q_2	0	2	$q_2, 0$	$q_5, 0$	$q_8, 0$
q_3	1	0	$q_1, 0$	$q_4, 1$	$q_7, 2$
q_4	1	1	$q_7, 0$	$q_7, 0$	$q_7, 0$
q_5	1	2	$q_2, 0$	$q_5, 0$	$q_8, 0$
q_6	2	0	$q_7, 0$	$q_7, 0$	$q_7, 0$
q_7	2	1	$q_7, 0$	$q_7, 0$	$q_7, 0$
q_8	2	2	$q_8, 0$	$q_8, 1$	$q_8, 2$

constant outputs OUT1 = 1, OUT2 = 0, OUT3 = 0. This observation may be found among others stated in the bottom half of figure 7.5.

7.2.2   Analysis of a ternary mystery machine

Finite state diagrams can be constructed for the *n*-valued case, for any fixed 2, 3, ... An analysis for the binary case is given in subsection 7.2.1. In this subsection an analysis is given for the ternary case, using the logic circuit shown in figure 7.6. For this ternary mystery machine, there is one ternary input IN1 and one ternary output OUT1, with two delay 3-stable devices, *X* and *Y*. The delay input for *X* is D*X* and the decisive outputs for the 3-stable device *X* are $C_0(X)$, $C_1(X)$, $C_2(X)$. The delay input for the 3-stable device *Y* is D*Y* and the decisive outputs for the 3-stable device *Y* are $C_0(Y)$, $C_1(Y)$, $C_2(Y)$.

Once again a state table is formed which captures in a tabular way the operation of this ternary machine. As a result, table 7.3 shows, for any state of the machine, what the next state will be for any given input (i.e. IN1 = 0, IN1 = 1, or IN1 = 2) and what the output will be. In table 7.3 there are nine rows, corresponding to the nine possible ternary values of *X* and *Y*. These values are shown in columns 2 and 3. The corresponding nine state names

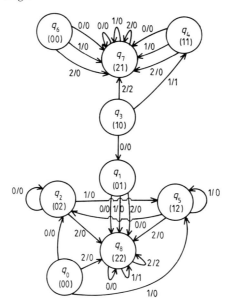

Figure 7.7 Finite state diagram for ternary mystery machine.
Some observations:

(i) A constant 2 input stream starting from any state causes the machine to go to a trap state, q_7 or q_8.

(ii) q_3 is the only state that you can start at and result in either trap state.

(iii) q_3 and q_8 are the only states that can output a 1 or a 2.

are shown in column 1. Increasing ternary order has been chosen for these entries as a matter of convenience.

The state table is derived from the logic circuit of figure 7.6 in a manner similar to the 2-valued case treated in subsection 7.2.1. In this subsection the 3-valued case is being used.

From table 7.3 it is easy to draw a ternary FSD. The table shows nine states, q_i, $i = 0, 1, \ldots, 8$, shown circled in the FSD of figure 7.7.

Figure 7.7 uses labeled directed edges to show state transitions, just as the binary FSD does. A difference is that a ternary FSD for the completely specified case has three directed edges leaving each state, while a binary FSD has two. Of course, all values in the ternary case are 0, 1, 2, whereas all values in the binary case are 0, 1. The FSD in figure 7.7 comes from the state table in a straightforward way, as when $n = 2$.

In figure 7.7, it can be seen that there are two states, q_7 and q_8, each of which have the property that there is no exiting edge. A state with this property is called a *trap state*. The FSD shows that a fixed input stream $IN1 = 2$ starting from any state will eventually lead to one of these two trap states. Other observations may be found in figure 7.7.

7.3   Synthesis

The combining of parts or strategies to make a whole is known as synthesis. For the logic designer, synthesis is the art of taking a description or specifications of some task and converting this into a logic structure.

7.3.1   From a job to an FSD

Assume that a CUSTOMER comes to a DESIGNER with a job description and specifications. The CUSTOMER asks if the DESIGNER will take the job. The CUSTOMER does not expect the DESIGNER to perform the job in isolation. Interaction and dialogue are expected between the CUSTOMER and DESIGNER, to assure that the structure develops in an appropriate way.

Four sample jobs and dialogues are given below. Each of these jobs will be discussed in various stages of the synthesis process in the subsections which follow. Throughout the rest of this section, input or output streams indicate inputs or outputs from right to left. For example, the input stream 011 indicates that the first input is 1, the second input is 1, and the third input is 0. The state q_0 in each FSD denotes the initial state.

Job 1

CUSTOMER: I need a binary logic circuit with binary input stream which detects three consecutive alternating 0s and 1s and outputs a single unit pulse when this is detected.

DESIGNER: So input stream 010 should output a single unit pulse?

CUSTOMER: Correct.

DESIGNER: And input stream 101 should also output a single unit pulse?

CUSTOMER: Correct.

DESIGNER: And if the input stream were 0110 or 10011?

CUSTOMER: The output stream should be 0 continually.

DESIGNER: My design for this job will be a synchronous one, using an internal clock with a 1 microsecond interval between clock ticks. So the single unit pulse output will be equal to 1 with a duration of 1 microsecond. Is that satisfactory?

CUSTOMER: No. The rest of the system requires that this output pulse be 2 microseconds in duration. However, your logic circuit does not have to be synchronized with the rest of the system.

DESIGNER: How about voltage levels or current requirements?

CUSTOMER: We will take care of that at our end. You may use binary logic circuit parameters as you like.

To obtain an FSD for such a job, it is often helpful to make a first pass of the diagram layout. This first pass is a first attempt at·an FSD for the problem. It may omit, temporarily, a number of details in an effort to achieve the required outputs. Such a first pass for Job 1, missing a number of details, is shown in figure 7.8.

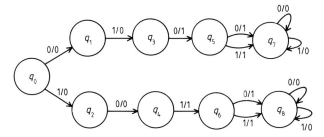

Figure 7.8 First pass in pursuit of binary FSD for Job 1.

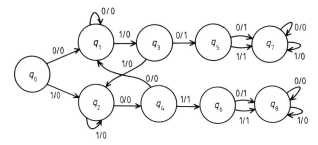

Figure 7.9 Second pass in pursuit of binary FSD for Job 1.

At the second pass, the missing details of figure 7.8 are supplied in figure 7.9. Recall that binary FSDs have exactly two labeled directed edges leaving each circled state. The missing directed edges of figure 7.8 are shown in figure 7.9. Care must be taken that such additional edges do not allow operation which is contrary to the required job at hand. The FSD in figure 7.9 satisfies the requirements of Job 1.

There is no guarantee that the result of this second pass shown by the FSD in figure 7.9 is an FSD with a minimum number of states. There is a systematic method for making a third pass which ensures such a minimum-state FSD. This systematic method will be applied for each of the four jobs in subsection 7.3.2.

Job 2
CUSTOMER: I need a ternary logic circuit whose output is 2 as long as the ternary input stream is …0210210, but otherwise the output goes to 0 and stays at 0 thereafter.

DESIGNER: So for the output to be 2 at the beginning, the first input must be 0?

CUSTOMER: Correct.

DESIGNER: You realize that for a random ternary input stream, the output will not stay at 2 for very long?

CUSTOMER: I realize that.

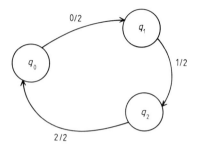

Figure 7.10 First pass in pursuit of ternary FSD for Job 2.

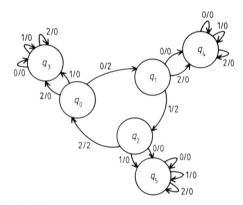

Figure 7.11 Second pass in pursuit of ternary FSD for Job 2.

DESIGNER (thinking about the job): Let's see—I need to make a first pass for this FSD. At the very least, this first pass should correctly show the required output. Missing details can be supplied at the second pass.

A first pass for the FSD of Job 2 is shown in figure 7.10. It takes into account only the input ...210210.

DESIGNER (thinking about the job): In the desired FSD, each circled state must have three departing edges, corresponding to possible inputs 0, 1, 2. I'll supply these labelled directed edges and introduce three trap states.

The resulting second pass for this FSD is shown in figure 7.11. It is a correct FSD for Job 2. To apply a third pass and obtain an FSD which has a minimum number of states, see subsection 7.3.2.

Job 3

CUSTOMER: I need a binary logic circuit that outputs a 1 and stays at 1 afterwards, when any 3 binary digits of a 4-digit input sequence are each equal to 1.

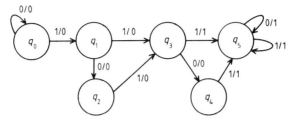

Figure 7.12   First (incorrect) pass in pursuit of binary FSD for Job 3.

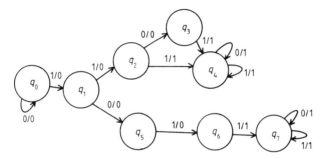

Figure 7.13   New first pass in pursuit of binary FSD for Job 3.

DESIGNER: So the input stream 1011 should output 1 and stay at 1 after the fourth input digit is received?
CUSTOMER: Correct.
DESIGNER: And the input stream 110101 should output 1 and stay at 1 after the sixth input digit is received, but not before?
CUSTOMER: Correct, no matter what input digits are received after the sixth input digit.
DESIGNER: Let me be sure that I understand. If and when this logic circuit outputs a 1, the circuit must output 1 forever afterward.
CUSTOMER: That is correct.
DESIGNER (thinking about the job): Well, let's see what 4-digit sequences need to be detected. They are 0111, 1011, 1101, 1110, and 1111. The first and the last of these 5 sequences may be detected at the same time, after three consecutive 1s are received. Let me try a test first pass which attempts to correspond to this.

A test first pass corresponding to this approach is shown in figure 7.12. However, this test first pass is incorrect! It incorrectly outputs a 1 for the input stream 10101. This flaw is easily corrected, and a resulting next pass is shown in figure 7.13.

At the last pass, the missing directed edges are supplied, leading to the FSD in figure 7.14. It is easily seen that the FSD in figure 7.14 has two trap states, q_4 and q_7. This FSD in figure 7.14 is a correct FSD for Job 3.

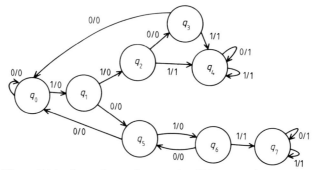

Figure 7.14   Second pass in pursuit of binary FSD for Job 3.

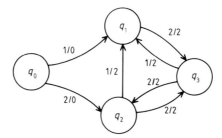

Figure 7.15   First pass in pursuit of ternary FSD for Job 4.

Job 4

CUSTOMER: I need a ternary logic circuit whose output is 2 if the last two received ternary input digits have a ternary sum of 3 or more.

DESIGNER: You mean that the only times the output will be 2 is when the last two input digits of the received ternary input stream are 12, 21, or 22, since these are the only instances of two ternary digits which sum to 3 or more.

CUSTOMER: Why, is that really true?

DESIGNER: Yes, if I am understanding you correctly.

CUSTOMER: I hadn't thought of it that way before. Yes, that is indeed what I want.

DESIGNER: I am not clear about the output you want after the output goes to 2 the first time.

CUSTOMER: The output should be 2 each time there is an instance of the last two received ternary digits summing to 3 or more. At all other times the output should be 0.

DESIGNER: Thank you.

The DESIGNER's first pass focuses on the required outputs, and is shown in figure 7.15. At the second pass, the DESIGNER fills in the missing directed edges and pays close attention to the effect that these additional edges have

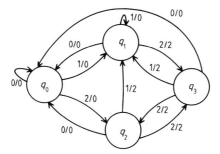

Figure 7.16 Second pass in pursuit of ternary FSD for Job 4.

on the outputs. This second pass yields a correct FSD for Job 4, as shown in figure 7.16. In subsection 7.3.2, which immediately follows, a systematic method is presented, called the HM method, which yields an FSD with a minimum number of states.

7.3.2 From an FSD to a minimum state FSD
Although FSDs given in subsection 7.3.1 for the four jobs of that subsection may lead to correct logic circuits, there is no guarantee that each such FSD has a minimum number of states, and hence the corresponding logic circuit may not be minimal. It is possible that the DESIGNER may have *tried* to achieve an FSD with a minimum number of states. Such an approach might be fine for the experienced DESIGNER who knows something about minimum-state FSDs, but for others, a systematic method that finds the minimum-state FSD for a given job can be very helpful. A minimum number of states can save hardware and design time. For example, it might be found that a ternary FSD drawn with four states could be redrawn with only three states. In such an event, only one 3-stable device would be needed, because only one 3-stable device is needed to handle 3 states. On the other hand, two 3-stable devices would be needed to realize the ternary FSD having four states. In other words, a minimum number of states can lead to a cheap logic circuit.

To achieve the minimum number of states, a systematic method is used called the HM method, after work for $n = 2$ in Huffman (1954), Mealy (1955), and Moore (1956). This method finds a minimum number of state equivalence classes. This leads to a minimum-state FSD. Logic designs based upon these minimum-state FSDs for the jobs illustrated in this section may be found in subsection 7.3.3.

Job 1
Recall that the job description of Job 1 calls for a binary logic circuit with binary input stream that detects 3 consecutive alternating 0s and 1s in the input stream and outputs a pulse of two 1s when this input is detected. The

Table 7.4 State table for Job 1's second pass (see figure 7.9).

Current state	IN1 = 0	IN1 = 1
q_0	$q_1, 0$	$q_2, 0$
q_1	$q_1, 0$	$q_3, 0$
q_2	$q_4, 0$	$q_2, 0$
q_3	$q_5, 1$	$q_2, 0$
q_4	$q_1, 0$	$q_6, 1$
q_5	$q_7, 1$	$q_7, 1$
q_6	$q_8, 1$	$q_8, 1$
q_7	$q_7, 0$	$q_7, 0$
q_8	$q_8, 0$	$q_8, 0$

Table 7.5 HM method—four classes; nine states (Job 1).

Class	a					b		c	d
States	q_0	q_1	q_2	q_7	q_8	q_5	q_6	q_3	q_4
Next class	a a	a c	d a	a a	a a	a a	a a	b a	a b

starting point for this subsection is the 9-state FSD in figure 7.9. Corresponding to this FSD is table 7.4.

The HM method consists of two basic steps. At the first step, states are grouped according to similar input–output combinations. In a binary job with single input and single output like Job 1, there are 4 possibilities for the outputs in the last two columns of table 7.4: 00, 01, 10, and 11. Class **a** consists of those states whose rows have output 00: $\{q_0, q_1, q_2, q_7, q_8\}$. Class **b** consists of those states whose rows have outputs 11; $\{q_5, q_6\}$. Class **c** consists of the one state whose row has outputs 10: $\{q_3\}$. Class **d** consists of the one state whose row has outputs 01: $\{q_4\}$.

The second step involves a number of iterations, starting from the result of the first step just described. For the binary case with single input, the next class is determined by where a state will go to after an input of 0 or 1. For the ternary case with single input, the next class is determined by where a state will go to after an input of 0, 1, or 2. For general $n \geq 2$ with single input, the next class is determined by where a state will go to after an input of 0, 1, ..., or $n - 1$. The first iteration for Job 1 is shown in table 7.5. Two classes appear under each state in this table. Each state at the top changes to a state in the lower leftmost class for input 0; each state at the top changes to a state in the lower rightmost class for input 1. For the ternary case, the lower leftmost class would be the result for input 0, the lower center class

Table 7.15 State table for Job 3's second pass (see figure 7.14).

Current state	IN1 = 0	IN1 = 1
q_0	$q_0, 0$	$q_1, 0$
q_1	$q_5, 0$	$q_2, 0$
q_2	$q_3, 0$	$q_4, 1$
q_3	$q_0, 0$	$q_4, 1$
q_4	$q_4, 1$	$q_4, 1$
q_5	$q_0, 0$	$q_6, 0$
q_6	$q_5, 0$	$q_7, 1$
q_7	$q_7, 1$	$q_7, 1$

Table 7.16 HM method—intermediate step (Job 3).

Class	a			b			c	
States	q_0	q_1	q_5	q_2	q_3	q_6	q_4	q_7
Next class								

Table 7.17 HM method—three classes; eight states (Job 3).

Class	a			b			c	
States	q_0	q_1	q_5	q_2	q_3	q_6	q_4	q_7
Next class	a a	a b	a b	b c	a c	a c	c c	c c

Table 7.18 HM method—intermediate step (Job 3).

Class	a		b		c		d	e
States	q_1	q_5	q_3	q_6	q_4	q_7	q_0	q_2
Next class								

Table 7.19 HM method—five classes; eight states (Job 3).

Class	a		b		c		d	e
States	q_1	q_5	q_3	q_6	q_4	q_7	q_0	q_2
Next class	a e	d b	d c	a c	c c	c c	d a	b c

Table 7.20 HM method—intermediate step (Job 3).

Class	a	b	c		d	e	f	g
States Next class	q_1	q_3	q_4	q_7	q_0	q_2	q_5	q_6

Table 7.21 HM method—seven classes; eight states (Job 3).

Class	a	b	c		d	e	f	g
States	q_1	q_3	q_4	q_7	q_0	q_2	q_5	q_6
Next class	f e	d c	c c	c c	d a	b c	d g	f c

Table 7.22 HM method—seven classes; seven states (Job 3).

Class	a	b	c	d	e	f	g
States	*B*	*K*	*E*	*A*	*J*	*F*	*G*
Next class	f e	d c	c c	d a	b c	d g	f c

Table 7.23 Minimum-state table for Job 3 (see figure 7.19).

Current state	IN1 = 0	IN1 = 1
A	*A*, 0	*B*, 0
B	*F*, 0	*J*, 0
J	*K*, 0	*E*, 1
K	*A*, 0	*E*, 1
E	*E*, 1	*E*, 1
F	*A*, 0	*G*, 0
G	*F*, 0	*E*, 1

Using table 7.19, it may be seen that two new classes must be created, as follows. In class **a**, q_1 must be distinguished from q_5. In class **b**, q_3 must be distinguished from q_6. This leads to the partial table shown as table 7.20. This third iteration is completed in table 7.21.

There are seven equivalence classes in table 7.21, and the iteration procedure halts. The minimum number of states is seven. In table 7.22, state names *A*, *B*, *J*, *K*, *E*, *F*, *G* are used, with corresponding state table shown as table 7.23. The corresponding minimum-state FSD is given in figure 7.19. This uses one less state than the FSD for Job 3 in figure 7.14.

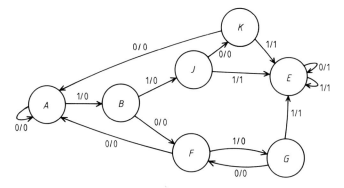

Figure 7.19 Minimum-state FSD for Job 3.

Table 7.24 State table for Job 4's second pass (see figure 7.16).

Current state	IN1 = 0	IN1 = 1	IN1 = 2
q_0	$q_0, 0$	$q_1, 0$	$q_2, 0$
q_1	$q_0, 0$	$q_1, 0$	$q_3, 2$
q_2	$q_0, 0$	$q_1, 2$	$q_3, 2$
q_3	$q_0, 0$	$q_1, 2$	$q_2, 2$

Table 7.25 HM method—four classes; four states (Job 4).

Class	a	b	c	
States	q_0	q_1	q_2	q_3
Next class	a b c	a b c	a b c	a b c

Job 4

The CUSTOMER for Job 4 requires a ternary logic circuit that outputs 2 whenever the last two received ternary digits in the input stream have a sum of 3 or more, and outputs 0 otherwise. An FSD for this job is shown in figure 7.16. A corresponding state table is table 7.24. Are the four states of figure 7.16 a minimum for Job 4? Application of the HM method, as indicated below, answers this question.

The first step and first iteration of the second step of the method yield table 7.25. It follows from this table that no further iterations are required. There are three equivalence classes in this table and so the minimum number

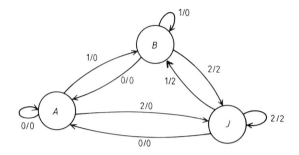

Figure 7.20   Minimum-state FSD for Job 4.

Table 7.26   Final table for HM method— three classes; three states (Job 4).

Class	a	b	c
States	*A*	*B*	*J*
Next class	**a b c**	**a b c**	**a b c**

Table 7.27   Minimum-state table for Job 4 (see figure 7.20).

Current state	IN1 = 0	IN1 = 1	IN1 = 2
A	*A*, 0	*B*, 0	*J*, 0
B	*A*, 0	*B*, 0	*J*, 2
J	*A*, 0	*B*, 2	*J*, 2

of states is 3. The FSD of figure 7.16 has four states and is *not* a minimum-state FSD. In the minimum-state FSD of figure 7.20, the following state names are used for the equivalence classes of table 7.25: *A* for **a**, *B* for **b**, and *J* for **c**. This is shown in table 7.26, with corresponding state table shown as table 7.27. The minimum-state FSD in figure 7.20 uses one less state than the FSD for Job 4 in figure 7.16.

7.3.3   The assignment of state names, with resulting D logic equations and logic circuits

This subsection discusses the assignment of names to states in a minimum-state FSD, and corresponding realization by delay *n*-stable devices. Delay D logic equations are given for the inputs of these devices. To achieve this, K-maps and preassignment equations are used.

Each state name will be a p-tuple of n-valued digits, where $p \geq 1$ and $n \geq 2$. For example, 2012 is a 4-tuple for case $n = 3$. The p-tuple has a realization in a logic circuit which uses p n-stable devices. Thus in the previous subsection, each state of an FSD for a job is assigned a name which is a p-tuple of n-valued digits, and the corresponding logic circuit uses p n-stable devices. The value of p is determined as follows. Suppose the number of states in the FSD is q. Then p cannot be less than the least integer $\geq \log_n q$. As an example, consider the situation for Job 4 described in subsection 7.3.2. The initial FSD has four states, the minimum-state FSD has only three states. So the initial FSD requires two 3-stable devices, because the least integer $\geq \log_3 4$ is equal to 2, but the minimum-state FSD requires only one 3-stable device, because the least integer $\geq \log_3 3$ is equal to 1.

The problem is to assign n^p-tuple names to the q states. Each such name influences the resulting logic equations and logic circuits. What approach should be taken to optimize the logic equations and circuits?

One approach is to make these assignments randomly, without consideration for the cost of the resulting logic circuits. If technology costs are low, this is a possibility. However, the treatment of such logic equations and circuits may be cumbersome. A second approach is to make assignments such that all D logic equations are in fdnf with a minimum number of total conjuncts over all the logic equations. A third approach is to make assignments such that all D logic equations are in dnf with a minimum number of total conjuncts over all the logic equations and a minimum number of total input terms to all these conjuncts. Finally, a fourth approach is to allow other considerations, such as factoring and sharing. In this last approach, the logic equations do not have to be in dnf.

For an introductory presentation, the rest of this section uses a combination of the second and third approaches. This is accomplished through the use of two rules, given below.

Rule 1. Search the FSD for the most-transferred-to state, i.e. the state with the most incoming arrows. Assign to this state the name which consists of all 0s. If a tie occurs, choose one of the states meeting this requirement for the assignment. Look for the next most-transferred-to state. Assign to this state a name which consists of the next most number of 0s. If a tie occurs at any time after the first assignment, apply the guidelines in Rule 2.

Rule 2. Following application of Rule 1, form K-maps for all delay logic equation inputs DX_i and outputs s_j. Using preassignment equations, attempt to place conjunctive players optimally over all these maps. By definition, preassignment equations are logic equations in which state letters may appear prior to assignment of names to these states. Conjunctive players may be placed on all these K-maps by exhaustion (where possible), or by the use of heuristics.

Rule 1 gives an elementary rule for the assignment of p-tuple names to the states of an FSD. For example, the first assignment is simply the assignment of p 0s to a state which has the maximum number of incoming arrows. Rule 1 minimizes the total number of conjuncts in all the fdnf's for the D input logic equations. While this need not lead to optimal logic equations, it does lead to a straightforward approach which exposes some of the design considerations which are involved.

Rule 2 attempts to minimize these fdnf's using preassignment equations and K-maps for the D input, and output logic equations. Preassignment equations are logic equations in which state letters are allowed to appear. Certain of these state letters have been assigned p-tuple names. The other state letters represent states to which p-tuple names have not yet been assigned. These preassignment equations capture the meaning of the FSD and show the consequences of assigning potential p-tuple names to unassigned states. These consequences are displayed on K-maps for all the D input, and output logic equations.

Jobs 1–4 are used to illustrate this approach.

Job 1

In subsection 7.3.1 Job 1 was transformed into an FSD. In subsection 7.3.2 the HM method was applied to obtain a minimum-state FSD. Job 1's minimum-state FSD is reproduced from figure 7.17 as figure 7.21, for ease of use in this subsection. It remains to assign a unique numeric name to each state. Since the number of states in the FSD of figure 7.21 is seven and $7 \leq 2^3$, there are eight possible names. These eight binary names are: 000, 001, 010, 011, 100, 101, 110, and 111. Since there are seven states, only seven of these names will be used, and one name will be unused.

Rule 1 assigns the name 000 to state G, because G is the state with the

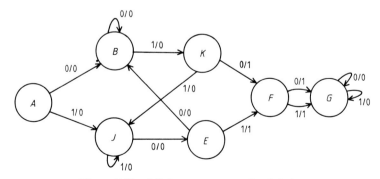

Figure 7.21   Minimum state FSD for Job 1.

Table 7.28 State name assignments after applying Rule 1 (Job 1).

Number of inputs to state	State	State assignment name
4	G	000
3	B	001
3	J	010
2	F	100
1	K	?
1	E	?
0	A	111

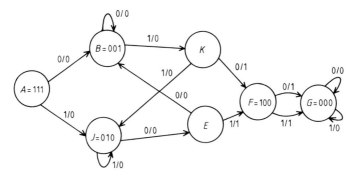

Figure 7.22 The partial state assignments for Job 1.

maximum number of incoming arrows, four. At the other extreme, state *A* is assigned the name with the least number of 0s, 111, because there are no incoming arrows to state *A*. This dispenses with six of the eight possible names. Three of the six possible names have two 0s in their names: 001, 010, and 100. Since states *B* and *J* tie for the next most number of incoming arrows, three, they each receive one of these names. State *B* is assigned the name 001 and state *J* is assigned the name 010. State *F* follows with the next most number of incoming arrows, two, and is assigned the remaining name with two 0s, 100. This leaves states *K* and *E* to be assigned names from the remaining three possible names: 011, 101, and 110. The situation at this point is summarized in table 7.28 and figure 7.22.

Rule 2 is applied to determine names for states *K* and *E* as follows. There are six possible assignments for the two states *K* and *E*, namely, 011 and 110, 101 and 011, 101 and 110, 110 and 011, 011 and 101, 110 and 101. Since the names for states *K* and *E* are interchangeable, this reduces to three possible assignments for the two states *K* and *E*: 101 and 011, 011 and 110, 101 and 110.

For the three binary digit names in Job 1, variable names for the flip–flops will be $X_1 = w$, $X_2 = x$, and $X_3 = y$. Each 3-tuple name assigned to a state corresponds to a conjunct in the logic equations. For example, 010, which is assigned to state J in this job, corresponds to the conjunct $\bar{w}x\bar{y}$. Let the input be denoted by z and the output be denoted by s.

From figure 7.22, the preassignment equations for the inputs to the delay flip–flops w, x, and y may be determined as follows.

(1) $Dw = K\bar{z} \vee Ez \vee \{Bz\}_{K \text{ has } w=1} \vee \{J\bar{z}\}_{E \text{ has } w=1}$

(2) $Dx = Az \vee Jz \vee Kz \vee \{J\bar{z}\}_{E \text{ has } x=1} \vee \{Bz\}_{K \text{ has } x=1}$

(3) $Dy = E\bar{z} \vee A\bar{z} \vee B\bar{z} \vee \{Bz\}_{K \text{ has } y=1} \vee \{J\bar{z}\}_{E \text{ has } y=1}$

In these equations each variable z corresponds to input 1 in some edge-label at the left of a slash in the FSD, and each variable $\bar{z}$ corresponds to input 0 in some edge-label at the left of a slash in the FSD. The bracket notation, such as $\{Bz\}_{K \text{ has } w=1}$, in the first logic equation for Dw denotes that this conjunct does not appear if the assigned name for state K has $w = 0$, but does appear if the assigned name for state K has $w = 1$.

Since there are three different assignments of names to the pair of states K, E, three solutions follow. Note that the 2-valued Karnaugh maps which follow are the 4 × 4 variants mentioned in Section 3.3.

$K = 101$, $E = 011$

Figure 7.22 and (1)–(3) lead to the four Karnaugh maps in figure 7.23. Application of the Karnaugh method leads to the following equations.

(4) $Dw = \bar{w}yz \vee w\bar{x}y\bar{z}$

(5) $Dx = wyz \vee \bar{w}x\bar{y}$

(6) $Dy = \bar{w}\bar{x}y \vee xy\bar{z} \vee \bar{w}x\bar{z}$

(7) $s = w\bar{x}\bar{y} \vee w\bar{x}\bar{z} \vee \bar{w}xyz.$

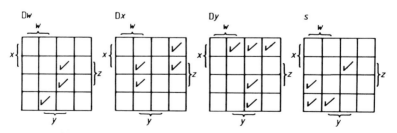

Figure 7.23   Karnaugh maps for Job 1 where $K = 101$, $E = 011$.

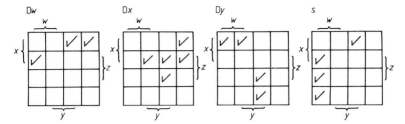

Figure 7.24   Karnaugh maps for Job 1 where $K = 011$, $E = 110$.

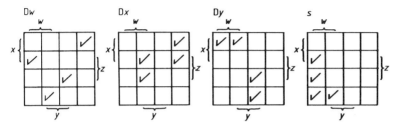

Figure 7.25   Karnaugh maps for Job 1 where $K = 101$, $E = 110$.

Each equation is in dnf. In this solution there are a total of 10 conjuncts in all the equations, and a total of 32 terms in all these conjuncts.

$K = 011, E = 110$
Figure 7.22 and (1)–(3) lead to the four Karnaugh maps in figure 7.24. Application of the Karnaugh method leads to the following equations.

(8) $Dw = \bar{w}x\bar{z} \lor wx\bar{y}z$

(9) $Dx = \bar{w}x\bar{y} \lor xyz \lor \bar{w}yz$

(10) $Dy = wx\bar{z} \lor \bar{w}\bar{x}y$

(11) $s = \bar{w}xy\bar{z} \lor w\bar{y}z \lor w\bar{x}\bar{y}.$

In this solution there are a total of 10 conjuncts in all the equations, and a total of 32 terms in all these conjuncts.

$K = 101, E = 110$
Figure 7.22 and (1)–(3) lead to the four Karnaugh maps in figure 7.25. Application of the Karnaugh method leads to the following equations.

(12) $Dw = \bar{w}x\bar{y}\bar{z} \lor wx\bar{y}z \lor \bar{w}\bar{x}yz \lor w\bar{x}y\bar{z}$

(13) $Dx = \bar{w}x\bar{y} \lor wyz$

(14) $Dy = wx\bar{z} \lor \bar{w}\bar{x}y$

(15) $s = w\bar{x}\bar{z} \lor w\bar{y}z.$

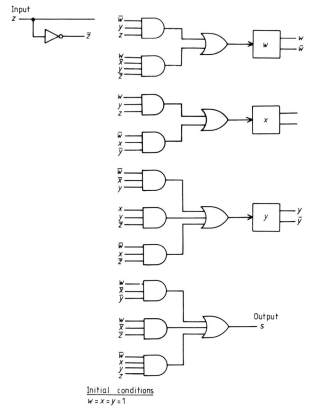

Figure 7.26 A logic circuit for Job 1 corresponding to logic equations (4)–(7).

In this solution there are a total of 10 conjuncts in all the equations, and a total of 34 terms in all these conjuncts.

It should be noted in each of the above solutions that the output, s, is determined by states with outgoing arrows that bear a label with a 1 to the right of the slash.

Of these three solutions, the first and second are the least expensive and the third is the most expensive. A logic circuit corresponding to the first solution, (4)–(7), may be found in figure 7.26. In this logic circuit the initial condition is $w = x = y = 1$, because the initial state q_0 is equal to $A = 111$.

Job 2

The minimum-state FSD for Job 2 given in figure 7.18 is reproduced in figure 7.27. Since $n = 3$ and the number of states in figure 7.27 is 4, it follows that there are nine possible ternary names: 00, 01, 02, 10, 11, 12, 20, 21, 22. Since

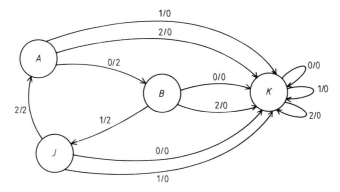

Figure 7.27 Minimum-state FSD for Job 2.

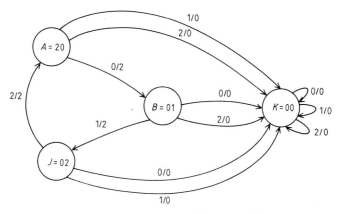

Figure 7.28 FSD for Job 2 with state assignments.

there are four states in the FSD of figure 7.27, only four of these nine names will be used, and five names will be unused.

Rule 1 assigns the name 00 to state K, because K is the state with the maximum number of incoming arrows, six. The names 20, 02, 01, and 10 remain for assignment to states A, B, and J. The names 20 and 02 are preferred, to minimize appearances of the term e_1 in the logic equations, so the name 20 is assigned to state A and the name 02 is assigned to state J. Finally, the name 01 is assigned to state B. This is shown in figure 7.28.

For the 2-ternary-digit names in Job 2, variable names for the 3-stable devices will be $X_1 = w$, $X_2 = y$. Each 2-tuple name assigned to a state corresponds to a conjunct in the logic equations. For example, the name 20, which is assigned to state A in this job, corresponds to the conjunct $C_2(w)C_0(y)$. The input is denoted by z and the output is denoted by s.

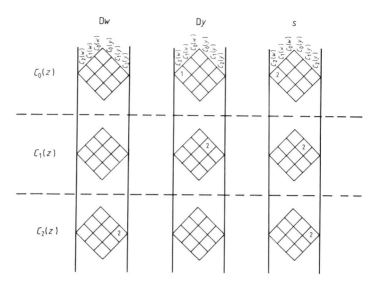

Figure 7.29   The three K-maps for Job 2.

From figure 7.28, the following fdnf equations are obtained.

(16) $Dw = C_0(w)C_2(y)C_2(z)$

(17) $Dy = e_1 C_2(w)C_0(y)C_0(z) \vee C_0(w)C_1(y)C_1(z)$

(18) $s = C_2(w)C_0(y)C_0(z) \vee C_0(w)C_1(y)C_1(z) \vee C_0(w)C_2(y)C_2(z).$

These equations lead to the three K-maps in figure 7.29. Application of the K method shows that the only conjunctive players which may be placed on each of these maps are single cell players. In other words, the logic equations (16)–(18) cannot be simplified by the K method. A logic circuit corresponding to this solution can be found in figure 7.30. In this logic circuit the initial condition is $w = 2$, $y = 0$, because the initial state q_0 is equal to $A = 20$.

Job 3

The minimum-state FSD for Job 3 given in figure 7.19 is reproduced as figure 7.31. Since the number of states in figure 7.31 is seven, it follows that there are eight possible names: 000, 001, 010, 011, 100, 101, 110, and 111. Seven of these names will be used.

Rule 1 assigns the name 000 to state E, because E is the state with the maximum number of incoming arrows, five. The name 010 is assigned to state A which has three incoming arrows, and the name 001 is assigned to state F which has two incoming arrows. This leaves the names 100, 011, 101, and 110 for assignments to states B, J, K, and G, each of which has one

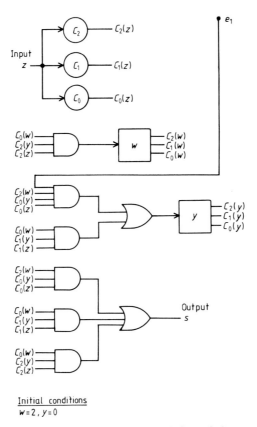

Initial conditions
w = 2, y = 0

Figure 7.30 A logic circuit for Job 2.

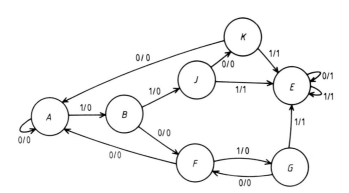

Figure 7.31 Minimum-state FSD for Job 3.

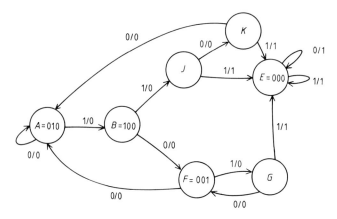

Figure 7.32   The partial state assignments for Job 3.

incoming arrow. Arbitrarily assign 100 to state B. This leaves names 011, 101, and 110 for assignment to states J, K, and G. This is shown in figure 7.32.

The variable names in this job will be the same as in Job 1 of this subsection. The preassignment equations from figure 7.32 for the inputs to the D flip–flops w, x, and y are given below.

(19) $Dw = Az \vee \{Bz\}_{J \text{ has } w=1} \vee \{J\bar{z}\}_{K \text{ has } w=1} \vee \{Fz\}_{G \text{ has } w=1}$

(20) $Dx = A\bar{z} \vee K\bar{z} \vee F\bar{z} \vee \{Bz\}_{J \text{ has } x=1} \vee \{J\bar{z}\}_{K \text{ has } x=1} \vee \{Fz\}_{G \text{ has } x=1}$

(21) $Dy = B\bar{z} \vee G\bar{z} \vee \{Bz\}_{J \text{ has } y=1} \vee \{J\bar{z}\}_{K \text{ has } y=1} \vee \{Fz\}_{G \text{ has } y=1}.$

Using these preassignment equations and either Karnaugh maps or algebraic simplification, it follows that the name for G should have $x = 1$ and the name for J should have $y = 1$. Under such conditions, in the logic equation for Dx, $F\bar{z} \vee \{Fz\}_{G \text{ has } x=1}$ simplifies to F, and in the logic equation for Dy, $B\bar{z} \vee \{Bz\}_{J \text{ has } y=1}$ simplifies to B. Consequently the remaining possible assignments are as follows. The name 110 is assigned to G and the name 011 is assigned to J, with the name 101 assigned to K; 011 is assigned to G and 101 is assigned to J, with 110 assigned to K; 110 is assigned to G and 101 is assigned to J, with 011 assigned to K.

Hence there are three solutions, as follows.

$G = 110$, $J = 011$, $K = 101$
Figure 7.32 and (19)–(21) lead to the four Karnaugh maps in figure 7.33. Application of the Karnaugh method leads to the following equations.

(22) $Dw = \bar{w}xy\bar{z} \vee \bar{w}x\bar{y}z \vee \bar{w}\bar{x}yz$

(23) $Dx = \bar{w}x\bar{y}\bar{z} \vee w\bar{x}\bar{y}z \vee \bar{w}\bar{x}y \vee \bar{x}y\bar{z}$

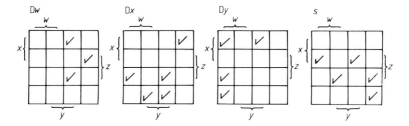

Figure 7.33 Four Karnaugh maps for Job 3 where $G = 110, J = 011,$ $K = 101.$

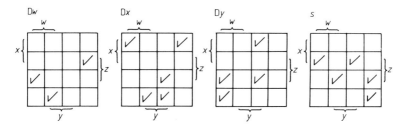

Figure 7.34 Four Karnaugh maps for Job 4 where $G = 011, J = 101,$ $K = 110.$

$$(24) \qquad Dy = \bar{w}xy\bar{z} \vee wx\bar{y} \vee w\bar{y}\bar{z}$$

$$(25) \qquad s = wx\bar{y}z \vee \bar{w}xyz \vee w\bar{x}yz \vee \bar{w}\bar{x}\bar{y}.$$

In this solution there are a total of 14 conjuncts in all the equations, and a total of 51 terms in all these conjuncts.

$G = 011, J = 101, K = 110$

Figure 7.32 and (19)–(21) lead to the four Karnaugh maps in figure 7.34. Application of the Karnaugh method leads to the following equations.

$$(26) \qquad Dw = \bar{w}x\bar{y}z \vee w\bar{x}\bar{y}z \vee w\bar{x}y\bar{z}$$

$$(27) \qquad Dx = x\bar{y}\bar{z} \vee \bar{w}\bar{x}y \vee \bar{x}y\bar{z}$$

$$(28) \qquad Dy = w\bar{x}\bar{y} \vee \bar{w}\bar{x}yz \vee \bar{w}xy\bar{z}$$

$$(29) \qquad s = \bar{w}\bar{x}\bar{y} \vee wx\bar{y}z \vee \bar{w}xyz \vee w\bar{x}yz.$$

In this solution there are a total of 13 conjuncts in all the equations, and a total of 47 terms in all these conjuncts.

$G = 110, J = 101, K = 011$

Figure 7.32 and (19)–(21) lead to the four Karnaugh maps in figure 7.35. Application of the Karnaugh method leads to the following equations.

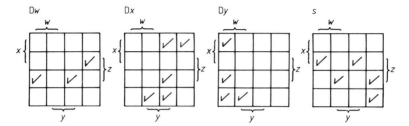

Figure 7.35   Four Karnaugh maps for Job 3 where $G = 110$, $J = 101$, $K = 0.11$.

(30) $$Dw = \bar{w}x\bar{y}z \vee w\bar{x}\bar{y}z \vee \bar{w}\bar{x}yz$$

(31) $$Dx = \bar{w}x\bar{z} \vee \bar{w}\bar{x}y \vee \bar{x}y\bar{z}$$

(32) $$Dy = w\bar{x}\bar{y} \vee w\bar{x}\bar{z} \vee w\bar{y}\bar{z}$$

(33) $$s = \bar{w}\bar{x}\bar{y} \vee wx\bar{y}z \vee \bar{w}xyz \vee w\bar{x}yz.$$

In this solution there are a total of 13 conjuncts in all the equations, and a total of 45 terms in all these conjuncts.

Of these three solutions, the first is the most expensive and the last is the least expensive. A logic circuit corresponding to this last solution (30)–(33) may be found in figure 7.36. In this logic circuit the initial condition is $w = y = 0$, $x = 1$, because the initial state q_0 is equal to $A = 010$.

Job 4

The minimum-state FSD for Job 4 given in figure 7.20 is reproduced as figure 7.37. Since there are three states in the ternary FSD of figure 7.37, it follows that there are exactly three one-digit names for these states: 0, 1, and 2.

There are three incoming arrows to each of the three states, so 0 is assigned to state A, 1 is assigned to state B, and 2 is assigned to state J, arbitrarily. This is shown in figure 7.37. The one 3-stable device will be denoted by $X_1 = x$, the input will be denoted by z and the output will be denoted by s.

Figure 7.37 leads to the following logic equations.

(34) $$Dx = e_1C_1(x)C_1(z) \vee e_1C_0(x)C_1(z) \vee e_1C_2(x)C_1(z)$$
$$\vee\, C_0(x)C_2(z) \vee C_1(x)C_2(z) \vee C_2(x)C_2(z)$$

(35) $$s = C_1(x)C_2(z) \vee C_2(x)C_1(z) \vee C_2(x)C_2(z).$$

The corresponding two K-maps are given in figure 7.38. Application of the K method yields the following solution.

(36) $$Dx = z$$

(37) $$s = C_1(x)C_2(z) \vee C_2(x)C_1(z) \vee C_2(x)C_2(z).$$

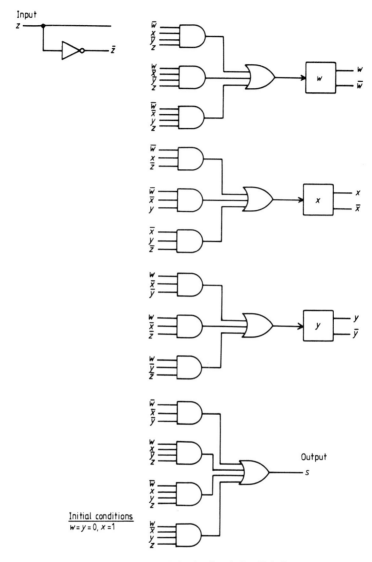

Figure 7.36 A logic circuit for Job 3.

Note that (36) is a considerable simplification of (34). This is a consequence of the K method applied to the K-map for Dx, in which the conjunctive-1-player z is easily recognized.

A logic circuit for the solution (36)–(37) may be found in figure 7.39. Obviously x must be set equal to 0 initially.

With respect to the designs for Job 1 and Job 4, the CUSTOMER should be informed of the following detail. At the start of any clock interval in which

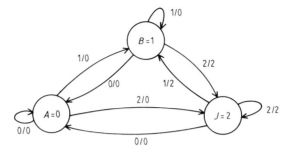

Figure 7.37 Minimum-state FSD for Job 4.

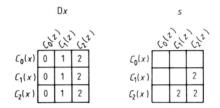

Figure 7.38 Two Karnaugh maps for Job 4.

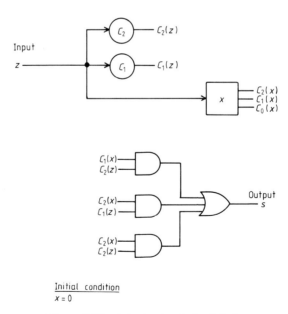

Figure 7.39 A logic circuit for Job 4.

the output s moves from 0 to 1, or from 1 to 0, the duration of the new value of s will be slightly less than the duration of the clock interval, as indicated in figure 2.15. Hence in Job 1 or Job 4 there may be a slight lag or shortening in certain output values of s. This may not be serious in Job 2 or Job 3, because in each of these jobs there is only one transition for the output s.

7.4 From a job to a logic circuit without use of finite state diagrams

The method described in the previous section for deriving a logic circuit corresponding to a minimal number of states in an FSD can be quite time consuming. In this section certain short cuts and basic designs, such as shift registers and counters, are used to go directly from the job description to a logic circuit, bypassing the FSD.

To start with, it is important to read and fully understand the job description. Try to formulate exactly what the CUSTOMER is asking and apply this to the design of the logic circuit. This is done below for Jobs 1–4.

Job 1

In this binary job the output s is initially 0. The output s goes to 1 the first time alternating 0s and 1s is seen through a window three digits in length. The output s stays at 1 for one extra clock interval afterward, then returns to 0 and stays at 0 thereafter.

For the window, a shifting register is used at the input. The input z shifts into flip–flop A, which in turn shifts into flip–flop B. The window is the triple z, A, B. Consider the first three inputs, with first input at z. The second input appears at z as the first input shifts into A. The third input appears at z as the second input shifts into A and the first input shifts into B. This three-digit window must be inspected continually for the first occurrence of input sequence 010 or 101. Hence $s_0 = \bar{z}A\bar{B} \vee z\bar{A}B$ detects such occurrence, in that s_0 goes to 1 when the input sequence is either 010 or 101, and is 0 otherwise. For initial conditions, A and B are each set equal to the value of the first input at z. This assures that $s_0 = 0$ initially—that is, for the first two inputs of the input stream at z. Hence s_0 may go to 1 at the third input or afterwards, but not before.

It remains to exploit s_0 and output accordingly. This is shown in the logic circuit of figure 7.40. A modified shift register consisting of flip–flops P, Q is used as a counter. Initially P and Q are each set equal to 0. s_0 shifts into P, P in turn shifts into Q as long as $Q = 0$; should $Q = 1$, then Q remains at 1 thereafter. This is a consequence of the OR-gate at the input to the delay

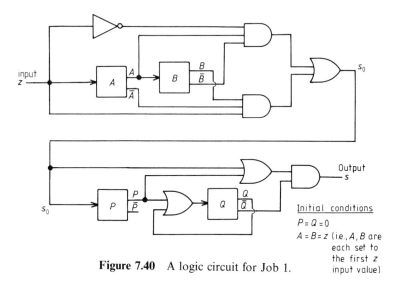

Figure 7.40   A logic circuit for Job 1.

Initial conditions
$P = Q = 0$
$A = B = z$ (ie., A, B are
each set to
the first z
input value)

flip–flop Q. The gating at the output s completes the job. The logic equations are given below.

(1) $$s_0 = \bar{z}A\bar{B} \vee z\bar{A}B$$

(2) $$DA = z$$

(3) $$DB = A$$

(4) $$DP = s_0$$

(5) $$DQ = P \vee Q$$

(6) $$s = (s_0 \vee P)\bar{Q}.$$

The logic circuit for Job 1 in figure 7.40 requires one more flip–flop than the logic circuit in figure 7.26.

Job 2

In this ternary job the output s is initially 2. The output s remains at 2 until the input pattern ... 10210210 is violated, upon which s goes to 0 and remains at 0 thereafter. The input is shifted into a shift register consisting of the single 3-stable device A. The window in this job is the pair z, A. The detection signal for this job is $s_0 = C_0(z)C_2(A) \vee C_1(z)C_0(A) \vee C_2(z)C_1(A)$. This signal remains at 2 as long as there is no violation in the input pattern. The signal goes to 0 at the first violation of the desired pattern. For correct operation, it is required that A be set equal to 2 initially.

The logic circuit in figure 7.41 detects the first time that s_0 goes to 0, using a 3-stable device P which is initially set equal to 2. The output s is 2 as long

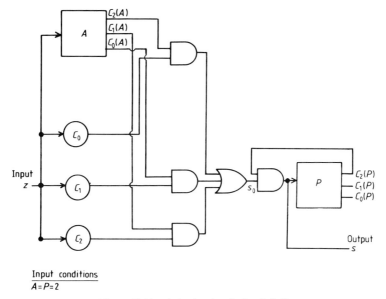

Figure 7.41 A logic circuit for Job 2.

as s_0 is 2. When s_0 goes to 0 the first time, s changes to 0 and at the next tick P goes to 0 and remains at 0 thereafter. Thus s remains at 0 thereafter.

The logic equations are given below.

(7) $$s_0 = C_0(z)C_2(A) \vee C_1(z)C_0(A) \vee C_2(z)C_1(A)$$

(8) $$DA = z$$

(9) $$DP = s_0 C_2(P)$$

(10) $$s = s_0 C_2(P).$$

Note that the logic circuit for Job 2 in figure 7.41 has the same number of 3-stable devices as the logic circuit in figure 7.30.

Job 3

This job requires a 4-digit window. There are 3 flip–flops A, B, J in the shift register so that the window is the 4-tuple z, A, B, J. To detect the first occurrence of three 1s in this 4-digit window, the detection signal is given by the expression $zAB \vee zAJ \vee zBJ$. Initially A, B, and J are each set equal to 0. Hence this detection signal is initially 0, and goes to 1 the first time that there are three 1s in the window.

The logic circuit is shown in figure 7.42. There are some minor details which are clarified by the logic equations below. In particular, note that the output s uses the detection signal in an evident way.

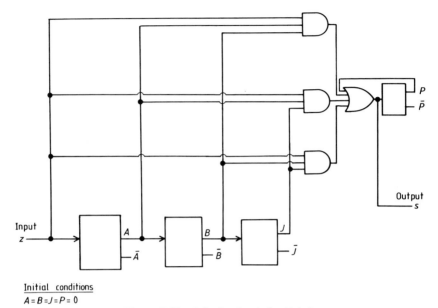

Initial conditions
$A = B = J = P = 0$

Figure 7.42   A logic circuit for Job 3.

(11) $DA = z$

(12) $DB = A$

(13) $DJ = B$

(14) $DP = zAB \vee zAJ \vee zBJ \vee P$

(15) $s = zAB \vee zAJ \vee zBJ \vee P$

The logic circuit for Job 3 in figure 7.42 requires one more flip–flop than the logic circuit in figure 7.36.

Job 4
This is a ternary job. The output s is to be 2 whenever the sum of two ternary digits in the window is 3 or more; the output s is to be 0 whenever the sum of these two digits is 2 or less. The shift register at the input consists of a single 3-stable device, A. The window is the pair z, A. The required detection signal and output is given by $s = C_1(z)C_2(A) \vee C_2(z)C_1(A) \vee C_2(z)C_2(A)$. It is obvious that A should be set equal to 0 initially. The resulting logic circuit is shown in figure 7.43, with corresponding logic equations below.

(16) $DA = z$

(17) $s = C_1(z)C_2(A) \vee C_2(z)C_1(A) \vee C_2(z)C_2(A)$

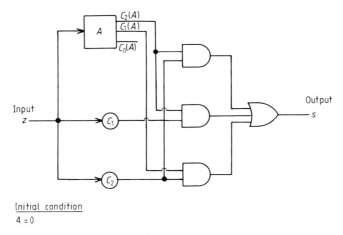

Figure 7.43 A logic circuit for Job 4.

This is identical with the solution for this job in the previous section. A different solution for this job may be found in one of the exercises at the end of this chapter.

7.5 Software structures

Sections 7.3 and 7.4 are concerned with ways to obtain a logic circuit from a job description. The logic design of the circuit may be implemented in hardware, for example, by fabricating an integrated circuit chip. Sometimes logic designers want to know how a hardware design compares with a similar software design in a program. It may be more efficient to debug the program than to build the hardware then debug the logic circuit. Further, a logic circuit and a program for the same job may reveal some underlying aspects of the job which might not otherwise be apparent, especially with respect to speed and cost.

Both hardware and software design seek to implement algorithms and systematic procedures in order to make jobs more manageable. For the former, finite state diagrams may be used. For the latter, flow charts may be used. While finite state diagrams and flow charts both have incoming and outgoing arrows, flow charts symbolically represent programming conventions, so differ in this extent from finite state diagrams.

A PASCAL program is given below for each of the four jobs under discussion in this chapter. For each of these jobs the input and output streams will be represented by input and output sequential files prepared for use in the program by RESET and REWRITE, respectively.

Job 1

The PASCAL program in figure 7.44 initializes at the input through the three lines

```
READ(datalin,z);
a:=z;
b:=z;
```

This comes from the initial conditions for the logic circuit in figure 7.40. The program in figure 7.44 uses a flag which is initially set equal to 0. While this

```
0
1
0                      (* contents of input file called datalin *)
1
0
0
0
0
*********************************************************************************
PROGRAM prog1 (datalin, datalout, OUTPUT);

VAR
  z,a,b,flag:
    INTEGER;
  datalin, datalout:    (* program will be using binary data *)
    TEXT;

BEGIN (* prog1 *)
  RESET(datalin);        (* Prepare input data file *)
  REWRITE(datalout);     (* Prepare output data file *)
  flag := 0;             (* Set 'flag to recognize pattern occurrence' to zero *)
  READ(datalin,        z); (* z is set to the 1st input *)
  a := z          ;
  b := z          ;
  WHILE NOT EOF(datalin) DO
    BEGIN
      IF ((z = 1) AND (a = 0) AND (b = 1) AND (flag <> 1))
      OR ((z = 0) AND (a = 1) AND (b = 0) AND (flag <> 1))
      THEN
        BEGIN
          WRITELN(datalout, '1');
          WRITELN(datalout, '1');
          flag := 1
        END
      ELSE
        WRITELN(datalout, '0');
      b := a;
      a := z;
      READ(datalin, z)
    END
END.  (* prog1 *)

*********************************************************************************
0
0
1                      (* contents of output file called datalout *)
1
0
0
0
0
```

Figure 7.44 A PASCAL program for Job 1.

flag is equal to 0, the same detection signal s_0 is used as in the description of Job 1 in Section 7.4. Upon detection the two lines

```
WRITELN(data1out, '1');
WRITELN(data1out, '1');
```

give the required output pulse for Job 1. The flag is set equal to 1 and remains at 1 thereafter, assuring that the output is 0 thereafter. The shifting at the

```
0
1
2
0                    (* contents of an input file called data2in *)
1
0
1
2

****************************************************************************

PROGRAM prog2 (data2in, data2out, OUTPUT);

VAR
   z, i:      (* z is input, i is counter *)
     INTEGER;
   data2in, data2out:    (* data should only be ternary values: 0,1,2 *)
     TEXT;

BEGIN (* prog2 *)
   RESET(data2in);     (* Prepare input data file *)
   REWRITE(data2out);  (* Prepare output data file *)
   i := 0;
   WHILE NOT EOF(data2in) DO
     BEGIN
       READ(data2in, z);
       IF z = i
         THEN
           WRITELN(data2out, '2')
         ELSE
           BEGIN
             WRITELN(data2out, '0');
             WHILE NOT EOF(data2in) OO
               BEGIN
                 READ(data2in, z);
                 WRITELN(data2out, '0')
               END
           END;
       i := ( i+1 ) MOD 3 (* MOD gives the remainder of a division *)
     END
END. (* prog2 *)

****************************************************************************

2
2
2                    (* contents of an output file called data2out *)
2
2
0
0
0
```

Figure 7.45 A PASCAL program for Job 2.

```
0
1
1
0
0           (* contents of input file called data3in *)
1
1
1
0
0

*********************************************************************

PROGRAM prog3 (data3in, data3out, OUTPUT);

VAR
 z,a,b,c,flag:  INTEGER;
 data3in, data3out:  TEXT;

BEGIN  (* prog3 *)
  RESET(data3in);        (* Prepare input data file *)
  REWRITE(data3out);     (* Prepare output data file*)
  a := 0;
  b := 0;
  j := 0;
  flag := 0;
  READ(data3in, z);
  WHILE NOT EOF(data3in) DO
    BEGIN
      READ(data3in, z);
      IF flag = 1
        THEN
          WRITELN(data3out, '1')
        ELSE
          BEGIN
            IF ( z = 1 ) AND
              ( (( a = 1 ) AND ( b = 1 )) OR
                (( a = 1 ) AND ( j = 1 )) OR
                (( b = 1 ) AND ( j = 1 )) )
              THEN
                BEGIN
                  WRITELN(data3out, '1');
                  flag := 1
                END
              ELSE
                WRITELN(data3out, '0');
            j := b;
            b := a;
            a := z
          END
    END
END.  (* prog3 *)

*********************************************************************

0
0
0
0
0           (* contents of output file called data3out *)
0
0
1
1
1
```

Figure 7.46 A PASCAL program for Job 3.

input is performed by the three lines

```
b:=a;
a:=z;
READ(data1in, z)
```

Job 2

The PASCAL program in figure 7.45 uses a single digit ternary counter initialized at 0 to generate the desired pattern of this job at the input:...210210. The line

```
i:=0;
```

performs the initialization, and the line

```
i:=(i+1)  MOD 3
```

performs the ternary counting. While the z input values match the value of

```
2
1
0
2              (* contents of an input file called data4in *)
2
1
2
0

*************************************************************

PROGRAM prog4 (data4in, data4out, OUTPUT);

VAR
  z,a:
    INTEGER;
  data4in, data4out:    (* data should be ternary *)
    TEXT;

BEGIN  (* prog4 *)
  RESET(data4in);       (* Prepare  input  data  file *)
  REWRITE(data4out);    (* Prepare output data file *)
  a := 0
  WHILE NOT EOF(data4in) DO
    BEGIN
      READ(data4in, z);
      IF (z + a) >= 3          (* assuming ternary data *)
        THEN
          WRITELN(data4out, '2')
        ELSE
          WRITELN(data4out, '0');
      a := z
    END
END.  (* prog4 *)

*************************************************************

0
2
0
0              (* contents of an output file called data4out *)
2
2
2
0
```

Figure 7.47   A PASCAL program for Job 4.

this counter, the output is 2. This match is performed by the line

```
IF z = i
```

with output printed by the line

```
WRITELN(data2out, '2')
```

When this match fails, each of the remaining outputs is set equal to 0.

Job 3
With the exception of a flag and output, the PASCAL program in figure 7.46
comes from Job 3 in Section 7.4. In the program of figure 7.46, a flag is used
to help provide the desired output. This flag is initialized to 0 and remains
at 0 until the detection signal becomes true, after which the output and the
flag each become equal to 1. Finally, the flag remains at 1 and each of the
resulting outputs is set equal to 0 through the lines

```
IF flag = 1
  THEN
    WRITELN(data3out, '1')
```

Job 4
The PASCAL program in figure 7.47 comes from Job 4 in Section 7.4, except
that the logic expression s in Job 4 of Section 7.4 here becomes the
logico-arithmetic expression $(z + a) >= 3$. It is obvious that these expressions are logically equivalent.

7.6   Overview

Any concrete digital computer must be a finite state machine, hence must
have a finite state diagram (FSD). The large number of states in such an FSD
may be subdivided into units such as the control and logico-arithmetic units
shown in figure 1.3. Further subdivisions may be made into known designs
such as shift registers and counters. This occurs in Section 7.4. Basic designs
having general application include read only memories (ROMs) and programmable logic arrays (PLAS). The latter are discussed in Chapter 10. Also
discussed in Chapter 10 are feedback shift registers.

   In Section 7.3, Rule 1 is easy to apply but does not guarantee an optimal
solution. In general, an algorithm for optimal state assignments depends on
the kind of n-stable devices which are being used. To illustrate for $n = 2$,
other kinds of flip–flops besides the D flip–flop are the R–S flip–flop and
the J–K flip–flop. These flip–flops are defined in Section 9.2 of Hill and
Peterson (1981). The state assignment problem for these flip–flops is discussed
in Section 10.10 of the same book.

Improvements on some results in this chapter have been described for the binary case. The HM method is improved in Hopcroft (1971). The state assignment problem has been discussed since the 1950s. An algorithm for optimal state assignment when the number of states is large may be found in Varma and Trachtenberg (1988).

Exercises

E7.1 Give an FSD for the binary logic circuit below.

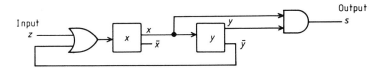

E7.2 Give an FSD for the ternary logic circuit below.

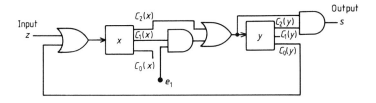

E7.3 Give a finite state table for **E7.1**.

E7.4 Give a finite state table for **E7.2**.

E7.5 Consider the binary FSD below, with two binary inputs and two binary outputs. Give a finite state table for this FSD.

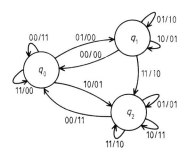

E7.6   Consider the quaternary FSD below, with one quaternary input and one quaternary output. Give a finite state table for this FSD.

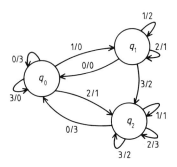

E7.7   The correspondence between **E7.5** and **E7.6** is obvious. However, since the former is binary and the latter is quaternary, a logic circuit for the former, in which $n = 2$, will differ from a logic circuit for the latter, in which $n = 4$.

(a) Give a binary logic circuit for **E7.5**.
(b) Give a quaternary logic circuit for **E7.6**.

E7.8   Apply the HM method to the ternary FSD below in order to determine a minimum-state FSD.

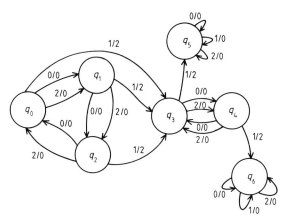

E7.9   Give a ternary logic circuit corresponding to the minimum-state FSD of **E7.8**.

E7.10   Consider the following ternary job, using a single ternary input z and a single ternary output s. The output s is equal to 0 at the start of the input stream z, and remains 0 until three consecutive nonzero input digits are all the same. At the third such digit, s becomes equal to 2 and remains at 2 thereafter. Hence for example 202211122 at the input yields 222220000 at the output. For this job, give a ternary logic circuit.

E7.11 Consider the following binary job, using a single binary input z and a single binary output s. The output s is equal to 0 at the start of the input stream at z, and remains 0 until a five-digit window at the input contains three 1s. At the first such occurrence of three 1s in this window, s becomes equal to 1 and remains at 1 thereafter. Hence for example 11100110000100011 at the input yields 11100000000000000 at the output.

(a) Use the HM method to give a minimum-state FSD for this job.
(b) Give a binary logic circuit corresponding to this minimum-state FSD.
(c) Use Section 7.4 to give a logic circuit. In this approach the 5-digit window requires a 4 flip–flop shift register at the input.
(d) Contrast the designs in (b) and (c).

E7.12 A logic circuit for Job 4 was obtained in figure 7.39 by assigning 0 to state A, 1 to state B, and 2 to state J in figure 7.37. Suppose 0 were assigned to state J, 1 were assigned to state B, and 2 were assigned to state A. What would the resulting solution be? Contrast the expense of this solution with the solution in figure 7.39.

E7.13 In Job 3, the three solutions of subsection 7.3.3 depended on the arbitrary assignment of 100 to state B. Suppose 100 were assigned to state G instead. This would leave names 011, 101, 110 for assignment to states B, J, and K. Give all the resulting solutions.

E7.14 For Job 4, the logic circuit in figure 7.39 and the solution in **E7.12** are two of $3! = 6$ possible circuits corresponding to possible assignments of the names 0, 1, 2 to states A, B, J. Give the four solutions corresponding to the other four assignments. Contrast the expense of these six solutions.

E7.15 Give a PASCAL program using input and output files as in Section 7.5 which performs (a) the ternary job in **E7.10** and (b) the binary job in **E7.11**.

8 Axiomatic Propositional Calculi

In this chapter a sequence of propositional calculi is presented, building from the implicational calculus C5 in Section 2.5. First, a propositional calculus is given which is characterized by the class of all P algebras. Second, an n-valued propositional calculus is given which is characterized by the class of all sub-Post algebras of order n. Third, an n-valued propositional calculus is given which is characterized by the class of all Post algebras of order n. Certain of the results are illustrated by means of implementations which use three basic logic circuits: the AND-gate, OR-gate, and binary differential amplifier or comparator.

8.1 Preliminaries

An axiomatic propositional calculus is a system for generating new *well-formed formulas* from given ones. These formulas involve propositional letters $A_1, A_2, \ldots$, nullary operations such as $\mathbf{F}$ and $\mathbf{T}$, unary operations such as $\sim$, and the binary operations $\&$, $\vee$, and $\supset$.

Well-formed formulas of the first propositional calculus of this chapter are defined below.

Definition 8.1. A well-formed formula of the first propositional calculus of this chapter is given by finitely many applications of the rules below.
(i) $\mathbf{F}$, $\mathbf{T}$, or a propositional letter A_i by itself is a well-formed formula.
(ii) If A is a well-formed formula, then $\sim(A)$ and $\square(A)$ are well-formed formulas.
(iii) If A and B are well-formed formulas, then $(A)\&(B)$, $(A)\vee(B)$, and $(A)\supset(B)$ are well-formed formulas.

Well-formed formulas of the remaining propositional calculi in this chapter are defined by expanding the well-formed formulas of Definition 8.1 as follows, for fixed $n \geq 2$.

Definition 8.2. A well-formed formula is given by finitely many applications of the rules of Definition 8.1, expanded as follows.
To (i) of Definition 8.1, add the well-formed formulas:

$$\mathbf{E}_0, \mathbf{E}_1, \ldots, \mathbf{E}_{n-1},$$

where $\mathbf{E}_0$ is written for $\mathbf{F}$ and $\mathbf{E}_{n-1}$ is written for $\mathbf{T}$.

To (ii) of Definition 8.1, where A is a well-formed formula, add the well-formed formulas: $D_1(A), D_2(A), \ldots, D_{n-2}(A), C_1(A), C_2(A), \ldots, C_{n-2}(A)$.

Certain conventions exist for the dropping of parentheses in well-formed formulas. Here it is sufficient to drop parentheses around single occurrences of propositional letters or $\mathbf{E}_0, \mathbf{E}_1, \mathbf{E}_2, \ldots, \mathbf{E}_{n-2}, \mathbf{E}_{n-1}$.

Example 8.1. Consider the well-formed formula

$$((A_1) \vee ((A_2) \supset (A_3))) \supset ((\mathbf{T}) \& (A_2))$$

obtained from (i) and (iii) of Definition 8.1. Parentheses may be dropped to yield $(A_1 \vee (A_2 \supset A_3)) \supset (\mathbf{T} \& A_2)$.

An axiomatic propositional calculus consists of a set of axioms and a set of inference rules. Each axiom is a well-formed formula.

A well-formed formula is provable, or a provable formula, if there exists a finite sequence of well-formed formulas $F_1, F_2, \ldots, F_p$ such that each F_i is either an axiom or generated from preceding formulas in the sequence by one of the rules of inference, and F_p is the resulting formula F. Such a sequence is a proof of F. In particular, each axiom is a provable formula, as there is a one-step proof of it. For each of the propositional calculi in this chapter, there are two rules of inference, given below.

(Ri) Rule of substitution.
A well-formed formula α may be substituted for a propositional letter A_j in a formula F_i, provided that all occurrences of A_j in F_i are replaced by α.

(Rii) Rule of detachment.
If F_j is a provable formula and $F_j \supset F_k$ is a provable formula, then F_k is a provable formula.

The well-formed formulas which involve $\supset$ alone are called I formulas in Section 2.5. Axioms for the implicational calculus C5 of Section 2.5 are used as a starting point for the propositional calculi of this chapter. Since the rules of inference (Ri) and (Rii) in Section 2.5 are identical with the rules of inference given here, the provable formulas of C5 are provable formulas in each of the propositional calculi which follow.

This section concludes with the following definition.

Definition 8.3. In a given propositional calculus, if α and β are well-formed formulas such that $\alpha \supset \beta$ and $\beta \supset \alpha$ are each provable formulas, then α and β are said to be *logically equivalent*.

8.2 The three basic logic circuits

Consider real-valued signals r in the real interval $R = [0, 1]$, as shown in figure 8.1. In the chain of figure 8.1, the top value 1 corresponds with logical

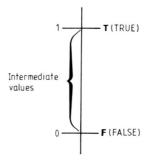

Figure 8.1   Scaled real values $R = [0, 1]$.

T (TRUE) and the bottom value 0 corresponds with logical **F** (FALSE). All
values are scaled between 0 and 1. This kind of scaling is common in many
applications.

The three basic two-place logic operations are: $A \& B$, $A \vee B$, and $A \supset B$.
Implementations for conjunction, disjunction, and real-valued decisive
implications are

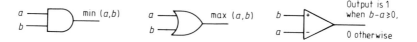

respectively. The output of an AND-gate is the minimum of the inputs. The
output of an OR-gate is the maximum of the inputs. The binary differential
comparator has two possible outputs: 0, 1. Some details for these logic circuits
are given in Section 2.4.

It will be helpful to define tautologous networks as follows.

Definition 8.4.   A tautologous network with respect to R is a network built
from a finite number of the three logic circuits given above, whose output
is 1 for all possible inputs in R.

Example 8.2.   The easiest example of a tautologous network is a binary
differential comparator whose inputs are tied together.

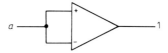

Obviously for any input a, $a - a \geq 0$, so the output is 1 for all a in R.

Example 8.3. This example reflects the linearity of the reals a, b in R.

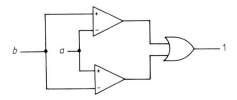

For any real inputs a, b either $a \leq b$ or $b \leq a$. Hence the top comparator has output 1 or the bottom comparator has output 1. If $a = b$, then both comparators have output 1. Since at least one input to the OR-gate is 1, the output of the OR-gate is 1 for all a, b in R.

8.3 PC

The propositional calculus of this section is called PC, as given in Epstein and Horn (1976). Axioms for PC are listed below.

Ax 1 $A_1 \supset A_1$

Ax 2 $(A_1 \supset (A_2 \supset A_3)) \supset ((A_1 \supset A_2) \supset (A_1 \supset A_3))$

Ax 3 $(A_2 \supset A_3) \supset (A_1 \supset (A_2 \supset A_3))$

Ax 4 $(((A_1 \supset A_2) \supset A_3) \supset (A_1 \supset A_2)) \supset (A_1 \supset A_2)$

Ax 5 $(A_1 \,\& A_2) \supset A_1$

Ax 6 $(A_1 \,\& A_2) \supset A_2$

Ax 7 $(A_1 \supset A_2) \supset ((A_1 \supset A_3) \supset (A_1 \supset (A_2 \,\& A_3)))$

Ax 8 $A_1 \supset (A_1 \vee A_2)$

Ax 9 $A_2 \supset (A_1 \vee A_2)$

Ax 10 $(A_3 \supset A_1) \supset ((A_2 \supset A_1) \supset ((A_3 \vee A_2) \supset A_1))$

Ax 11 $(A_1 \,\& (A_2 \vee A_3)) \supset ((A_1 \,\& A_2) \vee (A_1 \,\& A_3))$

Ax 12 $(A_2 \supset A_3) \vee (A_3 \supset A_2)$

Ax 13 $\mathbf{F} \supset A_1$

Ax 14 $A_1 \supset \mathbf{T}$

Ax 15 $(\sim(A_1)) \supset (A_1 \supset \mathbf{F})$

Ax 16 $(A_1 \supset \mathbf{F}) \supset (\sim(A_1))$

Ax 17 $(\square(A_1)) \supset (\mathbf{T} \supset A_1)$

Ax 18 $(\mathbf{T} \supset A_1) \supset (\square(A_1))$

Observe that Ax 1–Ax 4 coincide with axioms (C1)–(C4) for the implicational calculus C5 in Section 2.5. Ax 5–Ax 7 introduce conjunction (&) and Ax 8–Ax 10 introduce disjunction ($\vee$). Ax 1–Ax 10 are not sufficient to guarantee distributivity, but may be of interest in quantum logics, or denotational semantics, where distributivity need not hold. Ax 11 assures distributivity. Ax 12 guarantees that values are linearly ordered, as shown in Example 8.3. Ax 12 is logically equivalent with the I formula of Theorem 2.9, and may be replaced by this I formula if desired.

Two examples of proofs in this propositional calculus are given below.

Example 8.4. This example demonstrates that $(B \vee A) \supset (A \vee B)$ is a provable formula. To exploit the detachment rule, try substitutions which place this formula at the far right-hand side of a provable formula. Of various such substitutions, try the following substitutions into Ax 10: $A \vee B$ for A_1, A for A_2, and B for A_3. The result is the provable formula

$$(B \supset (A \vee B)) \supset ((A \supset (A \vee B)) \supset ((B \vee A) \supset (A \vee B))).$$

The proof follows easily. In Ax 9 substitute A for A_1 and B for A_2. The result is the provable formula which is at the far left-hand side of the formula above. By detachment, the result is the provable formula

$$(A \supset (A \vee B)) \supset ((B \vee A) \supset (A \vee B))$$

where the outermost parentheses are dropped for brevity. Finally, in Ax 8 substitute A for A_1 and B for A_2. A final detachment yields the desired formula

$$(B \vee A) \supset (A \vee B).$$

This completes the proof. It can also be seen, through substitution of A for B, and B for A in this last formula, that $(A \vee B) \supset (B \vee A)$, hence $A \vee B$ is logically equivalent with $B \vee A$.

Example 8.5. This example demonstrates that $(A \& (A \supset B)) \supset B$ is a provable formula.

Repeating the strategy of the previous example, try a substitution which places this formula at the far right of a provable formula. Of various such substitutions try the following substitution into Ax 2: $A \& (A \supset B)$ for A_1 and B for A_3. This achieves the placement just mentioned, but no substitution is yet made for A_2, as shown below.

$$((A \& (A \supset B)) \supset (A_2 \supset B)) \supset (((A \& (A \supset B))$$
$$\supset A_2) \supset ((A \& (A \supset B)) \supset B)).$$

Of various substitutions which might be made for A_2 in this formula, substitute A for A_2, yielding the provable formula

$$((A \& (A \supset B)) \supset (A \supset B)) \supset (((A \& (A \supset B)) \supset A) \supset ((A \& (A \supset B)) \supset B)).$$

The proof follows easily. In Ax 6 substitute A for A_1 and $A \supset B$ for A_2. Detachment yields

$$((A \& (A \supset B)) \supset A) \supset ((A \& (A \supset B)) \supset B).$$

Finally, in Ax 5 substitute A for A_1 and $A \supset B$ for A_2. Detachment yields

$$(A \& (A \supset B)) \supset B$$

the desired result.

Observe that Ax 13 and Ax 14 lead to the correspondence of **F** with 0 and **T** with 1 shown in figure 8.1. From Ax 15 and Ax 16, $\sim(A)$ is logically equivalent with $(A \supset \mathbf{F})$; from Ax 17 and Ax 18, $\square(A)$ is logically equivalent with $(\mathbf{T} \supset A)$.

An implementation corresponding to Ax 13 shows the bottom input fixed at 0.

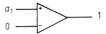

This implementation is a tautologous network because $0 \le a_1$ for all a_1 in R.

An implementation corresponding to Ax 14 shows the top input fixed at 1.

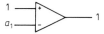

This implementation is a tautologous network because $a_1 \le 1$ for all a_1 in R.

An implementation for $\sim(A_1)$ is shown below—the output is shown as the pseudo-complement of a_1 in R.

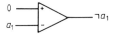

An implementation for $\square(A_1)$ is shown below—the output is shown as the supplement of a_1 in R.

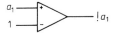

THEOREM 8.5. A formula is provable in PC if and only if the corresponding network is a tautologous network with respect to R.

Proof. It has been shown above that Ax 1, Ax 12, Ax 13, and Ax 14 each correspond to a tautologous network. It is not difficult to show that each of the remaining axioms corresponds to a tautologous network. Since applications of substitution and detachment generate only formulas which correspond to tautologous networks, it follows that every provable formula corresponds to a tautologous network with respect to R. Conversely, consider a network of AND-gates, OR-gates, and binary differential comparators which is a tautologous network. It must be shown that the corresponding propositional formula is provable from Ax 1–Ax 18 using substitution and detachment. This may be accomplished by introducing equivalence classes of propositional formulas, as in Epstein and Horn (1976)   ■

To confirm that $(B \lor A) \supset (A \lor B)$ of Example 8.4 is a provable formula, it is clear that the implementation below is a tautologous network—the output is 1 for all inputs a, b.

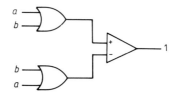

To confirm that $(A \& (A \supset B)) \supset B$ of Example 8.5 is a provable formula, it is clear that the implementation below is a tautologous network, since the output of the AND-gate is $\leq b$ for all inputs a, b in R.

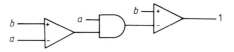

8.4 Characterizations

Consider a propositional calculus with symbols $\&$, $\lor$, $\supset$ for conjunction, disjunction, and implication, and possibly other symbols such as $\sim$ for negation and $\square$ for affirmation. Consider assignments to the propositional letters which take values in a B-algebra, L. This leads to a valuation val(A) for each formula A by the valuation rules:

val$(A \& B) = $ val$(A) \land$ val(B)
val$(A \lor B) = $ val$(A) \lor$ val(B)
val$(A \supset B) = $ val$(A) \Rightarrow$ val(B)
val$(\sim(A)) = $ val$(A) \Rightarrow 0$
val$(\square(A)) = 1 \Rightarrow$ val(A).

The formula F is said to be valid in L if val$(F) = 1$ for every assignment in L. A propositional calculus is said to be characterized by a class K of B-algebras if it consists of those formulas which are valid in every member of the class K.

Consider the real interval $R = [0, 1]$. Note that R is a B-algebra with $\wedge = 0$ and $\vee = 1$. Using R, values of $a \land b$, $a \lor b$, $a \Rightarrow b$ are given by the output values of the AND-gate, OR-gate, and binary differential comparator, respectively. It follows from Example 8.3 that R is a P-algebra.

The propositional calculus PC is characterized by the class of all P-algebras (Epstein and Horn 1976). It follows from Theorem 4.6 in Epstein and Horn (1974a) that an equation holds identically in the class of all P-algebras if it holds in the real interval $R = [0, 1]$.

8.5   Sub-Postian propositional calculus for fixed $n \geq 2$

The following theorem gives sub-Post algebras of order n in P-algebraic terms.

THEOREM 8.6.   Consider a P-algebra with n elements $e_0, e_1, \ldots, e_{n-1}$ where e_0 is the zero element and e_{n-1} is the unit element, and the following are satisfied

(i) $$e_i \leq e_j \qquad \text{for } 0 < i \leq j < n - 1$$

(ii) $$e_{i+1}(e_i \Rightarrow e_j) \leq e_j \qquad \text{for } 0 \leq j < i < n - 1$$

(iii) $$x = \bigvee_{k=1}^{n-1} (e_k(e_k \Rightarrow x)).$$

Then this P-algebra is a sub-Post algebra of order n.

Proof.   It must be shown that $P1$–$P6$ of Section 5.1 are satisfied. To accomplish this, set $D_i(x) = e_i \Rightarrow x$ for $0 \leq i \leq n - 1$ and let $C_i(x) = D_i(x)\overline{D_{i+1}(x)}$ for $0 \leq i < n - 1$, with $C_{n-1}(x) = D_{n-1}(x)$. This leads at once to $P1$–$P3$, $P5$(ii), and $P6$. From Theorem 3.52(vii) and Theorem 3.54(viii), $D_i(xy) = D_i(x)D_i(y)$ and $D_i(x \vee y) = D_i(x) \vee D_i(y)$. Hence $P4$ follows. $P5$(i) is equivalent to $(e_i \Rightarrow e_j) = (e_{i+1} \Rightarrow e_j)$ for $i \neq j$, $i < n - 1$. This is obvious for $i < j$, and follows from (ii) for $i > j$ ∎

Next, consider a P-algebra which contains $e_0 \leq e_1 \leq \ldots \leq e_{n-1}$ such that e_0 is the zero element and e_{n-1} is the unit element. In the propositional calculus, $\mathbf{E}_i$ is used to correspond with e_i.

The sub-Postian propositional calculus of this section is obtained by adding to Ax 1–Ax 18 the following.

Ax 19 $\mathbf{E}_i \supset \mathbf{E}_j$ $\qquad\qquad$ for $0 < i \leq j < n - 1$

Ax 20 $(\mathbf{E}_{i+1} \& (\mathbf{E}_i \supset \mathbf{E}_j)) \supset \mathbf{E}_j$ $\qquad$ for $0 \leq j < i < n - 1$

Ax 21 $A \supset ((\mathbf{E}_1 \& (\mathbf{E}_1 \supset A)) \vee (\mathbf{E}_2 \& (\mathbf{E}_2 \supset A)) \vee \cdots$
$\qquad\qquad \vee (\mathbf{E}_{n-1} \& (\mathbf{E}_{n-1} \supset A)))$

Ax 22 $((\mathbf{E}_1 \& (\mathbf{E}_1 \supset A)) \vee (\mathbf{E}_2 \& (\mathbf{E}_2 \supset A)) \vee \cdots$
$\qquad\qquad \vee (\mathbf{E}_{n-1} \& (\mathbf{E}_{n-1} \supset A))) \supset A.$

The number of formulas required by Ax 19 and Ax 20 depends on n. To give an easy example for $n = 3$, the number of additional formulas needed by Ax 19 is 0 and the number of additional formulas needed by Ax 20 is 1.

The propositional calculus Ax 1–Ax 22 is characterized by the class of all sub-Post algebras of order n. This follows from Theorem 8.6.

It follows from the proof of Theorem 8.6 that monotonic and disjoint operations can be added to the propositional calculus as shown below.

Ax 23 $D_i(A_1) \supset (\mathbf{E}_i \supset A_1)$ for $1 \le i < n - 1$

Ax 24 $(\mathbf{E}_i \supset A_1) \supset D_i(A_1)$ for $1 \le i < n - 1$

Ax 25 $C_i(A_1) \supset (D_i(A_1) \& (\sim (D_{i+1}(A_1))))$ for $0 < i < n - 1$

Ax 26 $(D_i(A_1) \& (\sim (D_{i+1}(A_1)))) \supset C_i(A_1)$ for $0 < i < n - 1$.

Here $C_0(A_1)$, $C_{n-1}(A_1)$, and $D_{n-1}(A_1)$ do not appear because $\sim (A_1)$ plays the role of $C_0(A_1)$, while $\square(A_1)$ plays the role of $D_{n-1}(A_1)$ and $C_{n-1}(A_1)$.

8.6   Postian propositional calculus for fixed $n \ge 2$

A Postian n-valued propositional calculus is obtained by adding to Ax 1–Ax 26 the single axiom below.

Ax 27 $(\mathbf{E}_{n-1} \supset \mathbf{E}_{n-2}) \supset \mathbf{E}_0$.

This propositional calculus, whose axioms are Ax 1–Ax 27, is characterized by the class of all Post algebras of order n. It follows from Ax 27 and Ax 13 that $\mathbf{E}_{n-1} \supset \mathbf{E}_{n-2}$ is logically equivalent with $\mathbf{E}_0$. The result follows by using Ax 23 and Ax 24, as it has been shown in Chapters 4 and 5 that Post algebras of order n are obtained by adding the single condition $D_{n-1}(e_{n-2}) = e_0$ to sub-Post algebras of order n.

Next, let E denote the n element chain $e_0 \le e_1 \le \cdots \le e_{n-1}$. The following implementations are consequences of Section 4.1.3 and Theorem 4.38.

For input values in E, conjunction, disjunction, and n-valued decisive implication correspond to the three basic logic circuits respectively, shown below. Here the binary differential comparator has two possible outputs: e_0,

e_{n-1}. The chain E is a P-algebra with values of $a \wedge b$, $a \vee b$, and $a \Rightarrow b$ given by the outputs of the AND-gate, OR-gate, and binary digital comparator shown above. This chain E is a linearly-ordered Post algebra of order n, with $D_i(a)$

and $C_i(a)$ for $i = 0, 1, \ldots, n - 2$ given by implementations

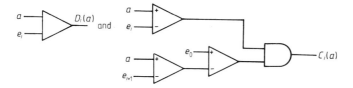

respectively. An alternative implementation for $C_i(a)$ by Theorem 4.38(ii) is shown below.

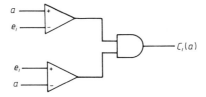

Definition 8.7. A tautologous network with respect to E is a network built from a finite number of the three basic logic circuits given above, whose output is e_{n-1} over all inputs in E.

This leads to the following theorem.

THEOREM 8.8. A formula is provable in the Postian propositional calculus whose axioms are Ax 1–Ax 27 if and only if the corresponding network is a tautologous network with respect to E.

To illustrate Theorem 8.8, consider $\sim(e_i \supset e_j)$ for $i > j$. This is a provable formula in the Postian propositional calculus, as shown by the tautologous network below.

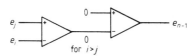

This formula, $\sim(e_i \supset e_j)$ for $i > j$, is an example of a formula which is provable from Ax 1–Ax 27, but is not provable from Ax 1–Ax 26.

Definition 8.9. The Postian propositional calculus for $n = 2$ is commonly called the 2-valued propositional calculus. The axioms for the 2-valued propositional calculus can be simplified considerably. For example, in the 2-valued propositional calculus $\square(A_1)$ is logically equivalent with A_1, and $\sim(\sim(A_1))$ is logically equivalent with A_1. Three axioms for the implicational fragment of the 2-valued propositional calculus are given in Section 2.5.

8.7 Overview

The Postian propositional calculus whose axioms are Ax 1–Ax 27 uses an implication $A \supset B$ which valuates to $a \Rightarrow b$, where $\Rightarrow$ is the implicative operation of B-algebras. In linearly ordered Post algebras of order n, this double arrow operation is called n-valued decisive implication. A Postian propositional calculus for $n \geq 2$ whose implication $A \supset' B$ valuates to $a \rightarrow b$, where $\rightarrow$ is the implicative operation of Heyting algebras, appears in Chapter 14 of Rasiowa (1974). This builds upon work in Rousseau (1969 and 1970). In linearly-ordered Post algebras of order n, this single arrow operation is called n-valued intuitionist implication.

It has been shown that n-valued decisive implication is given by a single binary differential comparator:

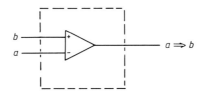

where input values a, b are in E. However, n-valued intuitionist implication requires

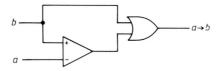

where input values a, b are in E.

The Postian propositional calculus in Section 8.5 has two rules of inference: substitution and detachment. The Postian propositional calculus in Rasiowa (1974) has three rules of inference: substitution, detachment, and a rule of necessitation. For some additional details, see Section 4 in Epstein and Horn (1976).

Exercises

E8.1   Use substitution, detachment, and Ax 1–Ax 7 to give a proof that

$$(B \& A) \supset (A \& B).$$

E8.2   Use substitution, detachment, and Ax 1–Ax 11 to give a proof that

$$(A \vee (A \& B)) \supset A.$$

E8.3 Use substitution, detachment, and Ax 1–Ax 11 to show that $(A \,\&\, B) \vee (A \,\&\, C)$ is logically equivalent with $A \,\&\, (B \vee C)$.

E8.4 Use substitution, detachment, and Ax 1–Ax 3 to give a proof that

$$(A \supset B) \supset ((C \supset A) \supset (C \supset B)).$$

E8.5 Use substitution, detachment, and Ax 1–Ax 7 to give a proof that

$$((A \supset B) \,\&\, (B \supset C)) \supset (A \supset C).$$

E8.6 Describe the propositional calculus which results by adding the axiom

$$(\Box(A_1)) \vee (\sim(A_1))$$

to the axioms for PC.

E8.7 Describe the propositional calculus which results by adding the axiom

$$(\Box(A_1)) \vee (A_1 \supset A_2) \vee (\sim(A_2))$$

to the axioms for PC.

E8.8 Display a tautologous network corresponding to Ax 2.

E8.9 Display a tautologous network corresponding to Ax 3.

E8.10 Display a tautologous network corresponding to Ax 7.

E8.11 Display a tautologous network corresponding to Ax 11.

E8.12 Show that the networks corresponding to Ax 20 in the Postian propositional calculus for fixed $n \geq 2$ are tautologous networks using the n-element chain E.

9 Special Functions

Certain functions occur frequently within a wide variety of design problems, or are fundamental within a particular range of applications. The special multiple-valued functions discussed in this chapter include the following: symmetric functions, positive and monotone increasing functions, negative and monotone decreasing functions, unate functions, and threshold functions. Results are applied for $n \geq 2$.

It should be noted that the presentation for these functions uses certain n-valued operations discussed previously. For example, the discussion of n-valued symmetric functions uses m variables x_j, $j = 1, 2, \ldots, m$, binary operations $\wedge$, $\vee$, , unary operations C_i and constants e_i, $i = 0, 1, \ldots, n - 1$. These are functions in the disjoint system of Post algebras of order n.

In this chapter e_i will be identified with i for $i = 0, 1, \ldots, n - 1$. Functions in Post algebras of order n have m variables $x_1, x_2, \ldots, x_m$, where $n \geq 2$, $m \geq 1$. Consequently, when the variables are assigned values in the range $0, 1, \ldots, n - 1$, any such Post function valuates to an integer in this range. Recall that such a function is called a decisive function if it takes only two possible values $\{0, n - 1\}$ for all possible n-valued assignments to the variables $x_1, \ldots, x_m$.

9.1 Symmetric functions

Definition 9.1. An n-valued function $f(x_1, \ldots, x_m)$ is *symmetric in the variables* x_i *and* x_j if $f(x_1, \ldots, x_i, \ldots, x_j, \ldots, x_m) = f(x_1, \ldots, x_j, \ldots, x_i, \ldots, x_m)$. An n-valued function is *symmetric* if it is symmetric in all pairs of its variables chosen two at a time from $x_1, \ldots, x_m$.

A *decisive symmetric function* is a symmetric function which is a decisive function.

Definition 9.2. For given m, there are m *simple symmetric functions* τ_j, $j = 1, 2, \ldots, m$, defined as follows (for notational convenience, boundary values are given for τ_0 and τ_{m+1}).

$$\tau_0 = (n - 1)$$

$$\tau_1 = x_1 \lor x_2 \lor \cdots \lor x_m$$

$$\tau_2 = x_1 x_2 \lor x_1 x_3 \lor \cdots \lor x_1 x_m \lor \cdots \lor x_{m-1} x_m$$

$$\vdots$$

$$\tau_m = x_1 x_2 \ldots x_m$$

$$\tau_{m+1} = 0.$$

The simple symmetric function τ_j is the join of all meets of variables taken j at a time. These simple symmetric functions are used for the case $n = 2$ in Epstein (1958). Such functions appear as *voter functions* in fault-tolerant computers.

Example 9.1. For $n = 2$, the six simple symmetric functions of four variables w, x, y, z are

$$\tau_0 = 1$$

$$\tau_1 = w \lor x \lor y \lor z$$

$$\tau_2 = wx \lor wy \lor wz \lor xy \lor xz \lor yz$$

$$\tau_3 = wxy \lor wxz \lor wyz \lor xyz$$

$$\tau_4 = wxyz$$

$$\tau_5 = 0.$$

Definition 9.3. A *fundamental symmetric function* is a decisive symmetric function for which there is an n-tuple $\{\alpha_0, \ldots, \alpha_{n-1}\}$ such that the function valuates to $n - 1$ if and only if for each i in the range $1 \le i \le m$, α_i of its arguments are assigned the value i; in all other cases the function valuates to 0. Clearly

$$\sum_{i=0}^{n-1} \alpha_i = m.$$

A fundamental symmetric function is denoted by

$$f_{\alpha_0 \ldots \alpha_{n-1}}.$$

Example 9.2. For $n = 2$, the five fundamental symmetric functions of four variables w, x, y, z are

$$f_{40} = \bar{w}\bar{x}\bar{y}\bar{z}$$

$$f_{31} = \bar{w}\bar{x}\bar{y}z \lor \bar{w}\bar{x}y\bar{z} \lor \bar{w}x\bar{y}\bar{z} \lor w\bar{x}\bar{y}\bar{z}$$

$$f_{22} = \bar{w}\bar{x}yz \lor \bar{w}x\bar{y}z \lor \bar{w}xy\bar{z} \lor w\bar{x}\bar{y}z \lor w\bar{x}y\bar{z} \lor wx\bar{y}\bar{z}$$

$$f_{13} = \bar{w}xyz \lor w\bar{x}yz \lor wx\bar{y}z \lor wxy\bar{z}$$

$$f_{04} = wxyz.$$

Note for example that the function f_{13} valuates to 1 if and only if one of its arguments is assigned the value 0 and the other three arguments are assigned the value 1.

Example 9.3.
(i) f_{04} is an example of a fundamental symmetric function which is also a simple symmetric function, namely τ_4.
(ii) f_{13} is an example of a fundamental symmetric function which is *not* a simple symmetric function.

Example 9.4.   Consider f_{102}. Since there are three subscripts, the value of n must be 3. The number of variables is $1 + 0 + 2 = 3$, say $w = x_1$, $x = x_2$, $y = x_3$. By definition, this function is given by

$$f_{102} = C_0(w)C_2(x)C_2(y)$$
$$\vee\ C_2(w)C_0(x)C_2(y) \vee C_2(w)C_2(x)C_0(y).$$

This function valuates to 2 if and only if one of its arguments is assigned the value 0 and the other two arguments are assigned the value 2.

Example 9.5.   Consider f_{0400}. This is a 4-valued function of four variables x_1, x_2, x_3, x_4. This fundamental symmetric function is given by

$$f_{0400} = C_1(x_1)C_1(x_2)C_1(x_3)C_1(x_4).$$

This function valuates to 3 if and only if each of the four arguments is assigned the value 1.

In this section the emphasis is on decisive symmetric functions. A canonical representation theorem is given for fundamental symmetric functions. It is shown that a decisive symmetric function is a join of fundamental decisive functions. Next it is explained how such joins may be simplified using a pictorial method (Epstein *et al* 1977).

There is immediate application to arbitrary n-valued symmetric functions, where such functions need not be decisive. For any n-valued function f, it follows from Chapter 4 that f has the representation

$$f = \bigvee_{i=1}^{n-1} e_i C_i(f).$$

If f is symmetric, then so is each decisive function $C_i(f)$, $i = 1, 2, \ldots, n - 1$. Using methods which are discussed in subsections 9.1.1–9.1.3, each $C_i(f)$ may be simplified individually. Further simplifications are discussed in subsection 9.1.4.

9.1.1 A canonical representation for fundamental symmetric functions

Recall that

$$C_i(x) = \begin{cases} n - 1 & \text{if } x = i \\ 0 & \text{otherwise} \end{cases}$$

for each i in the range $0 \leq i \leq n - 1$, where x is assigned integer values in the range $0 \leq x \leq n - 1$.

Since the simple symmetric functions τ_i are the basic building blocks for the canonical representation given below, the following observations will be useful. First, it is clear that τ_i takes the value j for $1 \leq i \leq m$, $0 \leq j \leq n - 1$ if and only if at least i variables have values greater than $j - 1$ and at most $i - 1$ variables have values greater than j. Second, it follows that, if $1 \leq k \leq p \leq m$, then $\tau_k \geq \tau_p$. Third, it follows that $\tau_i \vee \tau_j = \tau_k$ where k is the smaller of i, j, and $\tau_i \tau_j = \tau_k$ where k is the larger of i, j. Consequently, expressions of the form $\tau_i \vee \tau_j$, $\tau_i \tau_j$ may be simplified and need never appear in a canonical representation. Fourth, the term $C_i(\tau_j) = n - 1$ if and only if at least j variables have values greater than $i - 1$ and at most $j - 1$ variables have values greater than i. Hence if $i > j$ and $k > p$, then $C_k(\tau_i)C_p(\tau_j) = 0$ since $\tau_i \leq \tau_j$.

Consider a fundamental symmetric function $f_{\alpha_0 \cdots \alpha_{n-1}}$. It will be convenient to define a new $(n + 1)$-tuple $\{\beta_0, \ldots, \beta_n\}$ as follows:

$$\beta_n = 0$$

$$\beta_i = \beta_{i+1} + \alpha_i \text{ for each } i \text{ in the range } 0 \leq i \leq n - 1.$$

These tuples are used in the canonical representation theorem below.

THEOREM 9.4 (Canonical Representation Theorem). Any fundamental symmetric function may be expressed as a meet of at most $2n - 2$ terms of the form $C_i(\tau_j)$ as follows:

(i)
$$f_{\alpha_0 \cdots \alpha_{n-1}} = \bigwedge_{\substack{i=0 \\ \alpha_i \neq 0}}^{n-1} C_i(\tau_{\beta_i})C_i(\tau_{\beta_{i+1}} + 1).$$

Proof. Clearly each side of (i) takes either the value 0 or the value $n - 1$. Suppose that

$$f_{\alpha_0 \cdots \alpha_{n-1}} = n - 1.$$

Consider one term of the right-hand side of (i), say

$$C_i(\tau_{\beta_i})C_i(\tau_{\beta_{i+1}} + 1), \quad \alpha_i \neq 0.$$

By definition β_i variables have values greater than $i - 1$ and β_{i+1} variables have values greater than i. It follows that

$$C_i(\tau_{\beta_i})C_i(\tau_{\beta_{i+1}} + 1)$$

takes the value $n - 1$. This is true for all i, $0 \leq i \leq n - 1$, with $\alpha_i \neq 0$ and hence the right-hand side of (i) takes the value $n - 1$. Conversely, suppose that

$$\bigwedge_{\substack{i=0 \\ \alpha_i \neq 0}}^{n-1} C_i(\tau_{\beta_i})C_i(\tau_{\beta_{i+1}} + 1) = n - 1.$$

It follows that

$$C_i(\tau_{\beta_i})C_i(\tau_{\beta_{i+1}} + 1) = n - 1$$

for each i, $0 \leq i \leq n - 1$. Since

$$C_i(\tau_{\beta_i}) = n - 1$$

at least β_i variables have values greater than $i - 1$. Since

$$C_i(\tau_{\beta_{i+1}} + 1) = n - 1$$

at most β_{i+1} variables have values greater than i. Hence at least $\beta_i - \beta_{i+1} = \alpha_i$ variables have the value i. Since this holds for all i, $0 \leq i \leq n - 1$, $\alpha_i \neq 0$, it follows that exactly α_i variables have the value i for each i, $0 \leq i \leq n - 1$, and so $f_{\alpha_0 \cdots \alpha_n}$ takes the value $n - 1$.

Finally, if $\alpha_0 \neq 0$, then

$$C_0(\tau_{\beta_0})C_0(\tau_{\beta_1} + 1)$$

can be simplified to

$$C_0(\tau_{\beta_1} + 1)$$

because

$$\beta_0 \geq \beta_1 + 1 \quad \text{and} \quad \tau_{\beta_0} \leq \tau_{\beta_1} + 1.$$

If $\alpha_{n-1} \neq 0$, then

$$C_{n-1}(\tau_{\beta_{n-1}})C_{n-1}(\tau_{\beta_n} + 1)$$

can be simplified to

$$C_{n-1}(\tau_{\beta_{n-1}})$$

because

$$\beta_{n-1} \geq \beta_n + 1 \quad \text{and} \quad \tau_{\beta_{n-1}} \leq \tau_{\beta_n} + 1.$$

These follow by postulate $P4$(i). This completes the proof—any fundamental symmetric function is a meet of at most $2n - 2$ terms of the form $C_i(\tau_j)$. A final simplification should be noted with respect to (i). If $\alpha_i = 1$

$$\beta_i = \beta_{i+1} + 1, \quad \text{and} \quad C_i(\tau_{\beta_i})C_i(\tau_{\beta_{i+1}} + 1)$$

simplifies to

$$C_i(\tau_{\beta_i}) \qquad\qquad \blacksquare$$

Example 9.6. Application of the canonical representation theorem in Theorem 9.4 yields the following representations for each of the five binary fundamental symmetric functions of Example 9.2, where $n = 2$.

$$f_{40} = \overline{(w \lor x \lor y \lor z)}$$

$$f_{31} = (w \lor x \lor y \lor z)\overline{(wx \lor wy \lor wz \lor xy \lor xz \lor yz)}$$

$$f_{22} = (wx \lor wy \lor wz \lor xy \lor xz \lor yz)\overline{(wxy \lor wxz \lor wyz \lor xyz)}$$

$$f_{13} = (wxy \lor wxz \lor wyz \lor xyz)\overline{(wxyz)}$$

$$f_{04} = wxyz.$$

9.1.2 The simplification of decisive symmetric functions

It is straightforward that any decisive symmetric function f can be expressed as a join of certain fundamental symmetric functions. The result for $n = 2$ comes from Shannon (1938), and the result for general n uses the same kind of argument where $n \geq 2$. Given a defining logic table for f, it is easy to obtain the required fundamental symmetric functions.

Example 9.7. Consider the 3-valued function of two variables, $f = D_1(xy)$. A K-map for this function is given below.

f	$C_0(y)$	$C_1(y)$	$C_2(y)$
$C_0(x)$	0	0	0
$C_1(x)$	0	2	2
$C_2(x)$	0	2	2

Clearly this function is $f(x, y) = f_{020} \lor f_{011} \lor f_{002}$.

It is more difficult to simplify joins of fundamental symmetric functions for $n \geq 3$ than it is to simplify joins of fundamental symmetric functions for $n = 2$.

Example 9.8. Consider the 4-valued fundamental symmetric function f_{1101} in 3 variables w, x, y. This function is

$$f_{1101} = C_0(w)C_1(x)C_3(y) \lor C_0(w)C_3(x)C_1(y)$$
$$\lor C_0(x)C_1(w)C_3(y) \lor C_0(x)C_3(w)C_1(y)$$
$$\lor C_0(y)C_1(w)C_3(x) \lor C_0(y)C_3(w)C_1(x).$$

By Theorem 9.4, this function has the simplified canonical representation

$$f_{1101} = C_0(\tau_3)C_1(\tau_2)C_3(\tau_1)$$

where $\tau_1 = w \vee x \vee y$, $\tau_2 = wx \vee wy \vee xy$, $\tau_3 = wxy$.

Example 9.9.   For $n = 2$, the simplification of $f_{31} \vee f_{22}$ proceeds as follows.

$$f_{31} \vee f_{22} = C_1(\tau_1)C_0(\tau_2) \vee C_1(\tau_2)C_0(\tau_3)$$

$$= \tau_1 \bar{\tau}_2 \vee \tau_2 \bar{\tau}_3$$

by the canonical representation theorem

$$= \tau_1 \bar{\tau}_3$$

where the last simplification for $n = 2$ is given in Epstein (1958).

In the next subsection there is a pictorial method for obtaining such simplifications for $n \geq 2$.

9.1.3   A pictorial simplification method

A fundamental symmetric function will be pictured as a step function on a graph where the x-axis has the n coordinate values $0, 1, 2, \ldots, n - 1$, and the y-axis has m coordinate variables $0, 1, \ldots, m$. Each point of the step function is defined by the number of variables required to assume values less than or equal to the x-coordinate for the function to assume the value $n - 1$. For example, f_{2032} has seven variables and takes values $\{0, 1, 2, 3\}$. This function is pictured in figure 9.1. For convenience, the values taken by the β_i may be read from the column immediately to the left of the value column at the y-axis. The β column is simply the inverse of the y column.

The step function may be defined as the following sequence of pairs

$$(0, \beta_0), (0, \beta_1), (1, \beta_1), (1, \beta_2), \ldots, (i - 1, \beta_k), (i, \beta_i), (i, \beta_{i+1}), \ldots, (n - 1, \beta_n).$$

From the example in figure 9.1, this sequence of pairs for f_{2032} is:

$$(0, 7), (0, 5), (1, 5), (1, 5), (2, 5), (2, 2), (3, 2), (3, 0).$$

It will be convenient in what follows to drop the value column at the y-axis. The y-axis will be shown with the β column as coordinates at its immediate left. The function of figure 9.1 is repeated in figure 9.2 with each $C_j(\tau_k)$ identified by name. There will always be a single vertical at horizontal coordinate j, between lower β coordinate k and upper β coordinate $k - 1$. The canonical representation of f_{2032} is obtained quite easily from figure 9.2 as

$$f_{2032} = C_0(\tau_6)C_2(\tau_5)C_2(\tau_3)C_3(\tau_2).$$

For each vertical step in the step function, as shown in figure 9.2, there is a corresponding meet $C_i(\tau_j)C_i(\tau_k)$, as illustrated in figure 9.3. If there is a single vertical step, then this simplifies to a single term, $C_i(\tau_j)$. Each of the steps at $i = 0$ or $i = n - 1$ of the step function also reduces to a single term, as

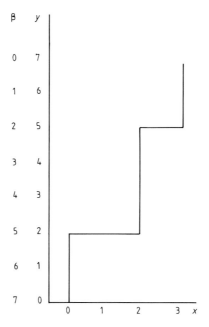

Figure 9.1 f_{2032} pictured with β column to the left of the *y*-axis.

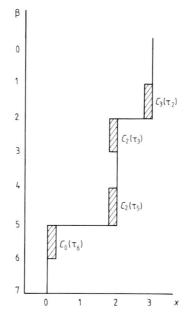

Figure 9.2 A picture of the canonical representation for f_{2032}.

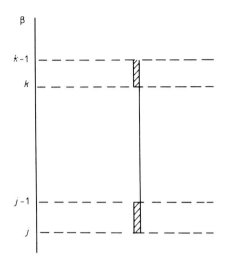

Figure 9.3 The vertical segment for $C_i(\tau_j)C_i(\tau_k)$.

illustrated in figure 9.2. These last kinds of simplification are discussed in the last paragraph of the proof of Theorem 9.4.

Consider next the case $n = 3$, $m = 2$ and a 3-valued decisive symmetric function of two variables. For this case there are six different fundamental symmetric functions. Theorem 9.4 yields the canonical representations below.

Example 9.10. The six fundamental symmetric functions for $n = 3, m = 2$ are

$$f_{200} = C_0(\tau_1)$$
$$f_{020} = C_1(\tau_2)C_1(\tau_1)$$
$$f_{002} = C_2(\tau_2)$$
$$f_{110} = C_0(\tau_2)C_1(\tau_1)$$
$$f_{101} = C_0(\tau_2)C_2(\tau_1)$$
$$f_{011} = C_1(\tau_2)C_2(\tau_1).$$

It follows from subsection 9.1.2 that there are $2^6 = 64$ 3-valued decisive symmetric functions of two variables. Each of these may be simplified using the pictorial method described above.

Example 9.11. Three of the 64 simplified 3-valued decisive symmetric functions for $n = 3$, $m = 2$ are given below.

(i) $f_{200} \vee f_{020} = C_0(\tau_1) \vee C_1(\tau_2)C_1(\tau_1)$
(ii) $f_{020} \vee f_{110} = C_1(\tau_1)$
(iii) $f_{200} \vee f_{020} \vee f_{110} = C_0(\tau_1) \vee C_1(\tau_1).$

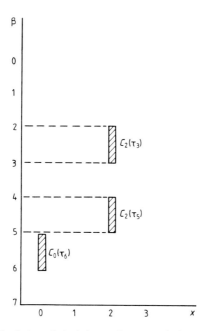

Figure 9.4 Omitting $C_3(\tau_2)$ from the canonical representation for f_{2032}.

Certain joins of fundamental symmetric function may be expressed as a meet of $C_i(\tau_j)$ terms. Consider the meet $C_0(\tau_6)C_2(\tau_5)C_2(\tau_3)$ obtained by dropping the term $C_3(\tau_2)$ from the meet given above for f_{2032}. There are three $C_i(\tau_j)$ functions in the resulting meet, and these are shown by the three bars in figure 9.4. It remains to display the various step functions which may be drawn to include these three bars. There are exactly three such functions: f_{2032}, f_{2041}, and f_{2050}, as shown in figure 9.5.

Given any join of fundamental symmetric functions, the corresponding step functions may be displayed graphically, and a simplified meet using terms $C_i(\tau_j)$ may be obtained.

Example 9.12. A simplification of $f_{2032} \vee f_{2041} \vee f_{2050}$ may be given immediately as a result of the above discussion

$$f_{2032} \vee f_{2041} \vee f_{2050} = C_0(\tau_6)C_2(\tau_5)C_2(\tau_3).$$

The final topic in this subsection concerns joins of fundamental symmetric functions which do not allow any simplifications of the kind just described. The study of this topic will tell the worst case that can occur in the implementation of decisive symmetric functions using fundamental symmetric functions.

First, consider a 2-valued decisive function of m variables. There are $m + 1$

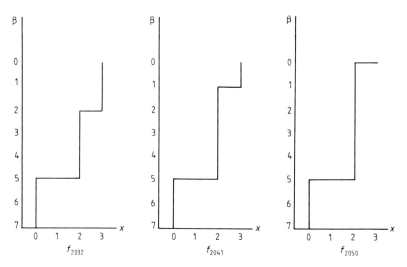

Figure 9.5   A picture showing $C_0(\tau_6)C_2(\tau_5)C_2(\tau_3) = f_{2032} \vee f_{2041} \vee f_{2050}$.

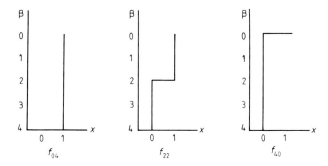

Figure 9.6   For $n = 2, m = 4$, $f_{04} \vee f_{22} \vee f_{40}$ allows no simplification.

fundamental decisive functions for $n = 2$: $f_{m0}, f_{(m-1)1},...,f_{0m}$. The pictorial method shows that there are a maximum of

$$\lceil (m + 1)/2 \rceil$$

of these which can be ·pictured without yielding any simplification, where $\lceil (m + 1)/2 \rceil$ denotes the *ceiling* of $(m + 1)/2$—that is, the least integer $\geq (m + 1)/2$. To illustrate, for $m = 4$ there are five fundamental symmetric functions $f_{40}, f_{31}, f_{22}, f_{13}, f_{04}$. The maximum number of fundamental symmetric functions whose join does not allow any simplification is three: the decisive symmetric function $f_{04} \vee f_{22} \vee f_{40}$ allows no simplification, as shown in figure 9.6. The ratio of the maximum number of fundamental symmetric functions which can be joined without allowing any simplification to the total number of fundamental symmetric functions is 3/5. To extend

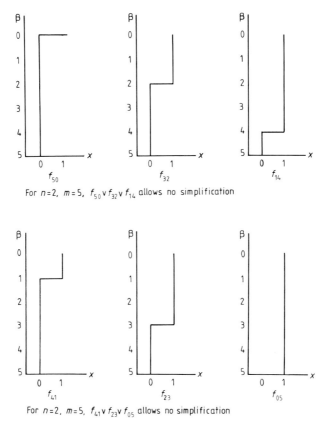

For $n = 2$, $m = 5$, $f_{50} \vee f_{32} \vee f_{14}$ allows no simplification

For $n = 2$, $m = 5$, $f_{41} \vee f_{23} \vee f_{05}$ allows no simplification

Figure 9.7 For $n = 2$, $m = 5$, two decisive symmetric functions which do not simplify.

the illustration to $m = 5$, there are six fundamental symmetric functions: f_{50}, f_{41}, f_{32}, f_{23}, f_{14}, f_{05}. The maximum number of fundamental symmetric functions which can be joined together without allowing any simplification is three. This occurs in different ways. The decisive symmetric functions $f_{50} \vee f_{32} \vee f_{14}$ and $f_{41} \vee f_{23} \vee f_{05}$ are shown in figure 9.7. The ratio of the maximum number of fundamental symmetric functions which can be joined without allowing any simplification to the total number of fundamental symmetric functions is $3/6 = 1/2$. To summarize for the case $n = 2$, when m is odd this ratio is $1/2$ and when m is even this ratio is $(1/2) + (1/2)(m + 1)$. An algebraic proof of these results for $n = 2$ is given in Epstein (1958).

Second, consider the case of 3-valued decisive symmetric functions of four variables. There are 15 fundamental symmetric functions:

$$f_{004}, f_{040}, f_{400}, f_{031}, f_{013}, f_{301}, f_{103}, f_{310}, f_{130}, f_{022}, f_{220}, f_{202}, f_{112}, f_{121}, f_{211}.$$

There is a maximum of nine of these whose join allows no simplification.

This can be done in different ways. One such join is:

$$f_{004} \vee f_{103} \vee f_{202} \vee f_{301} \vee f_{400} \vee f_{022} \vee f_{040} \vee f_{220} \vee f_{121}.$$

Note that the ratio here is $9/15 = (1/2) + (1/10)$.

Third, consider the case of 4-valued decisive symmetric functions of four variables. It is straightforward to compute that there are 35 fundamental symmetric functions. In this case there is a maximum of 19 of these whose join allows no simplification. This can be done in a number of different ways. One such join is:

$$f_{0004} \vee f_{0040} \vee f_{0022} \vee f_{0103} \vee f_{0400} \vee f_{4000} \vee f_{2200}$$

$$\vee f_{3010} \vee f_{0121} \vee f_{0202} \vee f_{1012} \vee f_{0220} \vee f_{1030} \vee f_{0301}$$

$$\vee f_{2020} \vee f_{2101} \vee f_{2002} \vee f_{1210} \vee f_{1111}.$$

Note that the ratio here is $19/35 = (1/2) + (3/70)$.

The last two ratios were obtained with J C Muzio. It is proved in Muzio (1990) that these ratios approach $1/2$ as the number of variables increases for each of the cases $n = 3$ and $n = 4$. A proof for $n \geq 2$ is given in Butler and Schueller (1991).

9.1.4 Symmetric functions

While it is possible to simplify an n-valued symmetric function f through simplification of each its disjoint elements, $C_i(f)$, $i = 1, 2, \ldots, n - 1$, there may be further simplifications because of certain redundancies which may occur among the $C_i(f)$. Methods have been developed for finding such redundancies and making these further simplifications in Epstein *et al* (1980) and Muzio *et al* (1983). An example is shown below.

Example 9.13. Consider the simplification of

(i) $$g(w, x, y) = e_1(f_{012} \vee f_{030}) \vee f_{021}.$$

Here $C_2(g) = f_{021}$ is a join of three fundaments and $C_1(g) = f_{012} \vee f_{030}$ is a join of four fundaments. From elementary properties given in Chapter 4, it follows that

(ii) $$g(w, x, y) = e_1(f_{012} \vee f_{030} \vee f_{021}) \vee f_{021}.$$

However, the pictorial simplification of g using (ii) is preferable to the pictorial simplification of g using (i).

First, $f_{021} = C_2(g) = C_1(\tau_3)C_1(\tau_2)C_2(\tau_1)$, by the canonical representation theorem. It is easy to see from figure 9.8 that $C_1(g) = f_{012} \vee f_{030}$ allows no simplification, with the result

(iii) $$g = e_1[C_1(\tau_3)C_2(\tau_2) \vee C_1(\tau_3)C_1(\tau_1)] \vee [C_1(\tau_3)C_1(\tau_2)C_2(\tau_1)].$$

Second, the pictorial simplification of $f_{012} \vee f_{030} \vee f_{021}$ in figure 9.9 yields

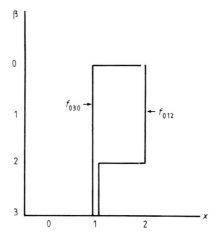

Figure 9.8 For $n = 3$, $m = 3$, $f_{012} \vee f_{030}$ allows no simplification.

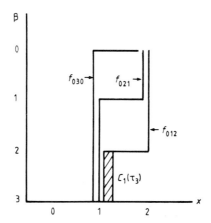

Figure 9.9 For $n = 3$, $m = 3$, $f_{012} \vee f_{030} \vee f_{021}$ simplifies to $C_1(\tau_3)$.

$f_{012} \vee f_{030} \vee f_{021} = C_1(\tau_3)$. The result using (ii) is

(iv) $\qquad g = [e_1 C_1(\tau_3)] \vee [C_1(\tau_3)C_1(\tau_2)C_2(\tau_1)].$

It is clear that (iv) is an improvement over (iii).
   Alternatively, (iv) may be written

$$g = C_1(\tau_3)[e_1 \vee C_1(\tau_2)C_2(\tau_1)]$$

using distributivity.

9.2   Positive functions

Definition 9.5.   An *n-valued positive function of m variables* is a logic function which can be realized by a logic circuit with inputs selected from $x_1, x_2, \ldots, x_m$ whose allowed operations are $\wedge$, $\vee$, $D_1, D_2, \ldots, D_{n-1}$ and constants e_0, $e_1, \ldots, e_{n-1}$.

Owing to the basic properties in Chapter 4, any *n*-valued positive function of *m* variables can be expressed in dnf using operations $\wedge$, $\vee$, with arguments selected from $D_i(x_j)$, $i = 1, 2, \ldots, n - 1$, $j = 1, 2, \ldots, m$, and e_0, $e_1, \ldots, e_{n-1}$. Thus a positive function is a Postian function which can be expressed in the monotonic system of Post algebras of order *n* without use of the pseudo-complement operation C_0.

Example 9.14,   *n* = 3, *m* = 2. $g_1 = xy$ is a 3-valued positive function of two variables *x*, *y*. Here $x = x_1$ and $y = x_2$. A dnf of the form mentioned above for g_1 may be obtained as follows.

$$g_1 = (e_1 D_1(x) \vee D_2(x))(e_1 D_1(y) \vee D_2(y))$$

by Theorem 4.13(ii)

$$= e_1 D_1(x)D_1(y) \vee e_1 D_1(x)D_2(y)$$

$$\vee e_1 D_2(x)D_1(y) \vee D_2(x)D_2(y) \qquad \text{by distributivity.}$$

A simplified dnf for g_1 is given below, using distributivity and Theorem 4.13(i).

$$g_1 = e_1 D_1(x)D_1(y) \vee D_2(x)D_2(y).$$

Example 9.15,   *n* = 2, *m* = 3. $g_2 = w(x \vee \bar{x}y)$ is a 2-valued positive function of three variables *w*, *x*, *y*. Here $x = x_1$, $y = x_2$, and $w = x_3$.

It follows that

$$g_2 = w(x \vee \bar{x})(x \vee y) \qquad \text{by distributivity}$$

$$= w \mathbf{V}(x \vee y) \qquad \text{by complementarity}$$

$$= w(x \vee y) \qquad \text{by } \mathbf{V}\text{-property}$$

$$= wx \vee wy \qquad \text{by distributivity.}$$

The last line shows g_2 as a positive function in dnf—recall that for $n = 2$, $x = D_1(x)$, $y = D_1(y)$, and $w = D_1(w)$.

Example 9.16,   *n* = 4,   *m* = 2. $g_3 = (e_1 \vee C_0(C_0(x)))(e_2 \vee D_2(y))$ is a 4-valued positive function of two variables *x*, *y*.

It follows that

$$g_3 = (e_1 \vee D_1(x))(e_2 \vee D_2(y)) \qquad \text{by Theorem 4.5 and Definition 4.9}$$

$$= e_1 \vee e_2 D_1(x) \vee D_1(x)D_2(y)$$

by distributivity, *P2*(ii), and absorption.

The last line shows g_3 as a positive function in dnf.

Figure 9.10 The three 2-valued positive functions of one variable x.

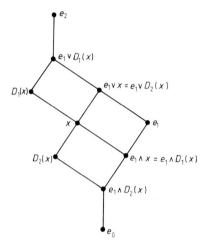

Figure 9.11 The ten 3-valued positive functions of one variable x.

Let ψ_{nm} denote the number of distinct n-valued positive functions of m variables. For the case of one variable, it is shown in Epstein and Liu (1982) that

$$\psi_{n1} = \binom{2n-1}{n-1}.$$

There are three different 2-valued positive functions of one variable shown in figure 9.10 and ten different 3-valued positive functions of one variable shown in figure 9.11.

However, there has been little success in obtaining other enumeration formulas for positive functions. Dedekind's problem of determining an enumeration formula for ψ_{2m} has remained an open problem since 1897. The case $\psi_{22} = 6$ is shown in figure 9.12 and the case $\psi_{23} = 20$ is shown in figure 9.13. For four variables, $\psi_{24} = 168$ (Dedekind 1897). For five variables, $\psi_{25} = 7581$ (Church 1940). For six variables, $\psi_{26} = 7\,828\,354$ (Ward 1946). For seven variables, $\psi_{27} = 2\,414\,682\,040\,998$ (Church 1965).

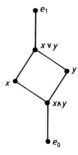

Figure 9.12   The six positive functions for $n = 2$, $m = 2$.

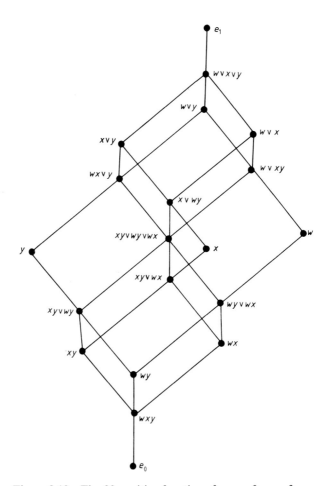

Figure 9.13   The 20 positive functions for $n = 2$, $m = 3$.

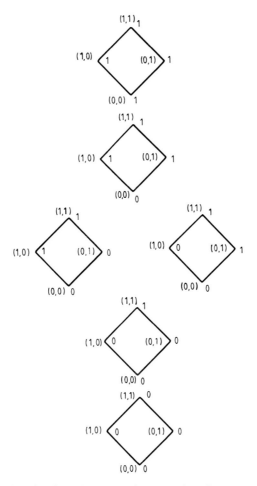

Figure 9.14   The six order-preserving mappings for $n = 2$, $m = 2$.

For $n > 2$, the following are known. For the 3-valued, 2-variable case, $\psi_{32} = 175$ (Epstein and Liu 1982). For the 3-valued, 3-variable case, $\psi_{33} = 252\,853$; for the 4-valued, 2-variable case, $\psi_{42} = 24\,696$; for the 5-valued, 2-variable case, $\psi_{52} = 16\,818\,516$ (Epstein *et al* 1985). Finally, $\psi_{62} = 55\,197\,331\,332$ and $\psi_{72} = 872\,299\,918\,503\,728$ were computed by R S Jones and M A Neerincx with the author in 1991.

Consider next the *monotone increasing n-valued functions* of m variables. These may be viewed as order-preserving mappings from the lattice which is a direct product of m n-element chains, into an n-element chain denoted by $0 < 1 < 2 < \cdots < (n-1)$. Such a function f satisfies the monotone increasing property: for every $a \le b$ in the lattice, $f(a) \le f(b)$. An illustration for $n = 2$, $m = 2$ is given in figure 9.14.

It will be shown below that the monotone increasing n-valued functions of m variables have a one-to-one correspondence with the n-valued positive functions of m variables. For an easy example using the case $n = 2$, $m = 2$, compare the six order-preserving mappings in figure 9.14 with the six positive functions in figure 9.12.

THEOREM 9.6.   An n-valued positive function of m variables is expressible as a monotone increasing Postian function of m variables in Post algebras of order n. Conversely, a monotone increasing Postian function of m variables in Post algebras of order n is expressible as an n-valued positive function.

Proof.   Consider any n-valued positive function of m variables. First, each variable and each constant by itself is clearly a monotone increasing function. Second, if f is a monotone increasing function, then $D_i(f)$ for each $i = 1, 2, \ldots, n-1$ is also a monotone increasing function. Third, if f, g are each monotone increasing functions, then so are fg and $f \vee g$. This completes the proof of the first part.

For the converse, let f be a monotone increasing Postian function of m variables in Post algebras of order n. By the fdnf theorem in Chapter 4, f may be expanded as a join of terms of the form $e_i C_{i_1}(x_1) \ldots C_{i_m}(x_m)$. Consider any term $e_i C_{j_1}(x_1) \ldots C_{j_m}(x_m)$ where $j_r \geq i_r$ for each $r = 1, \ldots, m$. Since f is a monotone increasing function, all such terms may be joined to the join expansion of f. As a consequence, each term $e_i C_{i_1}(x_1) \ldots C_{i_m}(x_m)$ may be replaced by the term $e_i D_{i_1}(x_1) \ldots D_{i_m}(x_m)$.

This completes the proof   ∎

Example 9.17.   Consider the case $n = 3$, $m = 1$. The ten 3-valued positive functions of one variable for this case are given in figure 9.11. The corresponding ten monotone increasing functions for this case are tabulated in figure 9.15. It is easy to see that each of the ten functions in figure 9.11 is a positive function. It is also easy to see that each of the ten functions in figure 9.15 is a monotone increasing function.

Example 9.18.   Consider the 3-valued positive function of two variables x, y, $f_0(x, y) = e_1 D_1(x) \vee D_2(y)$. In figure 9.16 the direct product of two 3-element chains is shown as a pair (x, y) at the left of each of the nine elements in the lattice and the value of the function f_0 at that element is shown at the right. Inspection of this figure shows that f_0 is a monotone

x	f_1	f_2	f_3	f_4	f_5	f_6	f_7	f_8	f_9	f_{10}
2	0	1	1	1	2	2	2	2·	2	2
1	0	0	1	1	0	1	2	1	2	2
0	0	0	0	1	0	0	0	1	1	2

Figure 9.15   The ten monotone increasing functions for $n = 3$, $m = 1$.

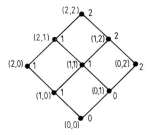

Figure 9.16 The monotone increasing function
$$f_0(x, y) = e_1 D_1(x) \vee D_2(y), \quad n = 3, \ m = 2.$$

increasing function. Application of Theorem 9.6 and elementary properties in Chapter 4 yields

$$\begin{aligned}
f_0 &= e_1 C_1(x)C_0(y) \vee e_1 C_2(x)C_0(y) \\
&\quad \vee e_1 C_1(x)C_1(y) \vee e_1 C_2(x)C_1(y) \\
&\quad \vee C_0(x)C_2(y) \vee C_1(x)C_2(y) \vee C_2(x)C_2(y) \\
&= e_1 D_1(x)D_0(y) \vee e_1 D_2(x)D_0(y) \\
&\quad \vee e_1 D_1(x)D_1(y) \vee e_1 D_2(x)D_1(y) \\
&\quad \vee D_0(x)D_2(y) \vee D_1(x)D_2(y) \vee D_2(x)D_2(y) \\
&= e_1 D_1(x) \vee e_1 D_2(x) \vee e_1 D_1(x)D_1(y) \\
&\quad \vee e_1 D_2(x)D_1(y) \vee D_2(y) \vee D_1(x)D_2(y) \\
&\quad \vee D_2(x)D_2(y) \\
&= e_1 D_1(x) \vee D_2(y).
\end{aligned}$$

This simplified dnf may be read directly from figure 9.16.

Example 9.19. Consider the 3-valued ACTION function $A_1(V, W)$ shown by the 9-row table in figure 2.4. This is redrawn as a logic function A_1 on a 3×3 lattice in figure 9.17. It is evident from figure 9.17 that A_1 is a monotone increasing function. It follows from Theorem 9.6 that a simplified dnf for the positive function A_1 is

$$\begin{aligned}
A_1(V, W) = e_1 D_2(V) &\vee e_1 D_1(V)D_1(W) \\
&\vee e_1 D_2(W) \vee D_2(V)D_1(W) \vee D_1(V)D_2(W).
\end{aligned}$$

This simplified dnf may be read directly from figure 9.17.

Example 9.20. Consider the 4-valued ACTION function A_2 shown by the 16-row table in figure 2.5. This is redrawn as a logic function A_2 on a 4×4 lattice in figure 9.18. It is evident from this figure that A_2 is a monotone

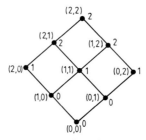

Figure 9.17 The ACTION function A_1 on a 3×3 lattice.

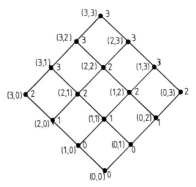

Figure 9.18 The ACTION function A_2 on a 4×4 lattice.

increasing function. It follows from Theorem 9.6 that a simplified dnf for the positive function A_2 is

$$A_2(V, W) = e_1 D_2(V) \vee e_1 D_1(V) D_1(W)$$
$$\vee e_1 D_2(W) \vee e_2 D_0(V) \vee e_2 D_2(V) D_1(W)$$
$$\vee e_2 D_1(V) D_2(W) \vee e_2 D_3(W)$$
$$\vee D_3(V) D_1(W) \vee D_1(V) D_3(W).$$

This simplified dnf may be read directly from figure 9.18.

Definition 9.7. A Postian function f of m variables x_i, $i = 1, \ldots, m$, in Post algebras of order n is said to be monotone increasing in x_i for some fixed i if f is a monotone increasing function in the single variable x_1 for each possible assignment of values from $0, 1, \ldots, n - 1$ to the remaining $m - 1$ variables.

THEOREM 9.8. A Postian function $f(x_1, \ldots, x_m)$ in Post algebras of order n is a positive function if and only if f is monotone increasing in x_i for each $i = 1, 2, \ldots, m$.

Proof. This is a consequence of Theorem 9.6 ∎

Example 9.21. Consider the 3-valued positive function f_0 of two variables $x_1 = x$, $x_2 = y$ given below and shown in figure 9.16.

$$f_0(x_1, x_2) = e_1 D_1(x_1) \vee D_2(x_2).$$

f_0 is monotone increasing in x_1 because the possible assignments for x_2 yield $f_0(x_1, 0) = e_1 D_1(x)$, $f_0(x_1, 1) = e_1 D_1(x)$, $f_0(x_1, 2) = e_2$. Each of these is a positive function in the single variable x_1, hence f_0 is a monotone increasing function in x_1 by Theorem 9.6. On the other hand, f_0 is monotone increasing in x_2 because the possible assignments for x_1 yield $f_0(0, x_2) = D_2(y)$, $f_0(1, x_2) = e_1 \vee D_2(x_2)$, $f_0(2, x_2) = e_1 \vee D_2(x_2)$. Each of these is a positive function in the single variable x_2, hence f_0 is a monotone increasing function in x_2 by Theorem 9.6. Thus $f_0(x_1, x_2)$ is a positive function by Theorem 9.8. It is evident immediately from figure 9.16 that f_0 is monotone increasing in x for each of the assignments $y = 0$, $y = 1$, $y = 2$, and monotone increasing in y for each of the assignments $x = 0$, $x = 1$, $x = 2$.

9.3 Negative functions

Definition 9.9. An n-valued negative function of m variables is a logic function which can be realized by a logic circuit with inputs selected from $N(y_1), N(y_2), \ldots, N(y_m)$ with allowed operations $\wedge$, $\vee$, $D_1, D_2, \ldots, D_{n-1}$ and constants $e_0, e_1, \ldots, e_{n-1}$.

Because of basic properties in Chapter 4, any n-valued negative function of m variables can be expressed in dnf using operations $\wedge$, $\vee$, with arguments selected from $D_i(N(y_j))$, $i = 1, 2, \ldots, n - 1$, $j = 1, 2, \ldots, m$, and e_0, $e_1, \ldots, e_{n-1}$. It is evident that there is a correspondence between n-valued positive functions of m variables and n-valued negative functions of m variables. A positive function in m variables $x_1, \ldots, x_m$ becomes a negative function in m variables $y_1, \ldots, y_m$ by setting $x_j = N(y_j)$ for each $j = 1, 2, \ldots, m$. Conversely, a negative function in m variables $y_1, \ldots, y_m$ becomes a positive function in m variables $x_1, \ldots, x_m$ by setting $y_j = N(x_j)$ for each $j = 1, 2, \ldots, m$. It follows that the number of distinct n-valued negative functions of m variables is equal to ψ_{nm}.

Consider next the *monotone decreasing n-valued functions* of m variables. These may be viewed as order inverting mappings from the lattice which is a direct product of m n-element chains into an n-element chain denoted by $0 < 1 < 2 < \ldots < (n - 1)$. Such a function f satisfies the monotone decreasing property: for every $a \leq b$ in the lattice, $f(b) \leq f(a)$.

The following theorem may be obtained through modification of Theorem 9.6.

THEOREM 9.10. An n-valued negative function of m variables is expressible as a monotone decreasing Postian function of m variables in Post algebras

y	g_1	g_2	g_3	g_4	g_5	g_6	g_7	g_8	g_9	g_{10}
0	0	1	1	1	2	2	2	2	2	2
1	0	0	1	1	0	1	2	1	2	2
2	0	0	0	1	0	0	0	1	1	2

Figure 9.19   The ten monotone decreasing functions for $n = 3, m = 1$.

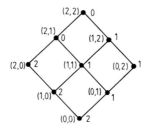

Figure 9.20   The monotone decreasing function
$$g_0(y_1, y_2) = e_1 D_1(N(y_1)) \vee D_2(N(y_2)), \quad n = 3, m = 2.$$

of order n. Conversely, any monotone decreasing Postian function of m variables in Post algebras of order n is expressible as an n-valued negative function of m variables.

Example 9.22.   The six 2-valued negative functions of two variables x, y are: $0, \bar{x}\bar{y}, \bar{x}, \bar{y}, \bar{x} \vee \bar{y}, 1$. The six corresponding positive functions are shown in figure 9.12.

Example 9.23.   The ten 3-valued negative functions of one variable are: e_0, $e_1 D_2(N(y)), D_2(N(y)), e_1 N(y), N(y), e_1, e_1 \vee N(y), D_1(N(y)), e_1 \vee D_1(N(y))$, e_2. The ten corresponding positive functions are shown in figure 9.11. The ten 3-valued, monotone decreasing functions of one variable are tabulated in figure 9.19. This may be contrasted with the ten 3-valued monotone increasing functions of one variable tabulated in figure 9.15.

Example 9.24.   Consider the 3-valued negative function of two variables y_1, y_2 shown below.

$$g_0(y_1, y_2) = e_1 D_1(N(y_1)) \vee D_2(N(y_2)).$$

This comes from Example 9.18 by setting $x = x_1 = N(y_1)$, and $y = x_2 = N(y_2)$. It is clear from figure 9.20 that this function g_0 is monotone decreasing. Suppose, on the other hand, that g_0 were given by the diagram in figure 9.20. Transformation of variables by $y_1 = N(x_1)$ and $y_2 = N(x_2)$ leads to figure 9.16, and the result $f_0(x_1, x_2) = e_1 D_1(x_1) \vee D_2(x_2)$ by Theorem 9.6. Hence the inverse transformation of variables $x_1 = N(y_1)$ and $x_2 = N(y_2)$

Given pairs
(y_1, y_2) for g_0:

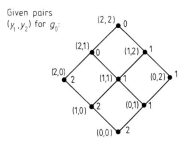

$y_1 = N(x_1), y_2 = N(x_2)$ leads to pairs (x_1, x_2) for f_0:

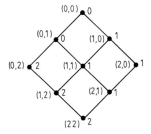

which may be redrawn as the monotone
increasing function

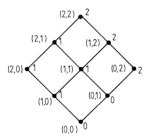

so $f_0(x_1, x_2) = e_1 D_1(x_1) \vee D_2(x_2)$ by Theorem 9.6.
Hence $x_1 = N(y_1), x_2 = N(y_2)$ leads to $g_0(y_1, y_2) =$
$e_1 D_1(N(y_1)) \vee D_2(N(y_2))$.

Figure 9.21 Obtaining a dnf for a monotone decreasing function g_0.

yields $g_0(y_1, y_2) = e_1 D_1(N(y_1)) \vee D_2(N(y_2))$. These details are shown in figure 9.21.

Example 9.25. The n-valued function $C_0(y)$ of one variable y is a negative function. Since $C_0(y) = N(D_1(y))$ by Theorem 4.5, Definition 4.9, and Theorem 4.17(x), and since $N(D_1(y)) = D_{n-1}(N(y))$ by Theorem 4.17(iv), the result follows.

The total number of different n-valued logic functions of m variables which are either positive or negative is $2\psi_{nm} - n$. This follows easily from the fact that the only functions which are both positive and negative are the n constants $e_0, \ldots, e_{n-1}$.

Definition 9.11. A Postian function f of m variables x_i, $i = 1, \ldots, x_m$ in Post algebras of order n is said to be monotone decreasing in x_i for some fixed i if f is a monotone decreasing function in the single variable x_1 for each possible assignment of values from $0, 1, \ldots, n-1$ to the remaining $m-1$ variables.

THEOREM 9.12. A Postian function $f(x_1, \ldots, x_m)$ in Post algebras of order n is a negative function if and only if f is monotone decreasing in x_i for each $i = 1, 2, \ldots, m$.

Proof. This is a consequence of Theorem 9.10 ∎

9.4 Unate functions

Definition 9.13. An n-valued unate function of m variables $x_1, \ldots, x_m$ is a logic function which can be realized by a logic circuit with inputs selected from $w_1, \ldots, w_m$ where for each $j = 1, 2, \ldots, m$ either $w_j = x_j$ or $w_j = N(x_j)$, with allowed operations $D_1, D_2, \ldots, D_{n-1}$ and constants $e_0, e_1, \ldots, e_{n-1}$.

Owing to the basic properties in Chapter 4, any n-valued unate function of m variables $x_1, \ldots, x_m$ can be expressed in dnf using operations $\wedge$, $\vee$, with arguments selected from $D_i(w_j)$, $i = 1, 2, \ldots, n-1$, $j = 1, \ldots, m$ and e_0, $e_1, \ldots, e_{n-1}$, where for each j either $w_j = x_j$ or $w_j = N(x_j)$.

An n-valued positive function of m variables $x_1, \ldots, x_m$ is a unate function where $w_j = x_j$ for each $j = 1, 2, \ldots, m$. An n-valued negative function of m variables $y_1, \ldots, y_m$ is a unate function where $w_j = N(y_j)$ for each $j = 1, 2, \ldots, m$.

Example 9.26, $n = 2$, $m = 3$. $h_1 = x\bar{y} \vee \overline{(y \vee z)}$ is a 2-valued unate function of three variables. A dnf for h_1 is

$$h_1 = x\bar{y} \vee \bar{y}\bar{z} \qquad \text{by Lemma 4.2(viii)}.$$

Thus $w_1 = x$, $w_2 = \bar{y} = N(y)$, $w_3 = \bar{z} = N(z)$.

Example 9.27, $n = 3$, $m = 2$. $h_2 = e_1 D_2(x) \vee N(D_2(y))$ is a 3-valued unate function of two variables.

A dnf for h_2 is

$$h_2 = e_1 D_2(x) \vee D_1(N(y)) \qquad \text{by Theorem 4.17(iv), (x)}.$$

Thus $w_1 = x$ and $w_2 = N(y)$.

Example 9.28. There are 14 different 2-valued unate functions of two variables. According to the previous section, there are $2\psi_{22} - 2 = 10$ different functions which are either positive or negative—namely, 0, xy, x, y, $x \vee y$, $\bar{x}\bar{y}$, $\bar{x}$, $\bar{y}$, $\bar{x} \vee \bar{y}$, 1. Each of these is unate. The four additional unate functions for this example are $x\bar{y}$, $\bar{x}y$, $x \vee \bar{y}$, $\bar{x} \vee y$.

This last example leads to some observations concerning the enumeration of unate functions. First, consider the following partition of the n-valued positive functions of m variables into $m + 1$ classes. Class i for $i = 0, 1, \ldots, m$ consists of those n-valued positive functions of m variables which require a minimum of i variables for each function to be realized. Let $\psi_{nm:i}$ denote the number of positive functions in class i. Consequently

$$\psi_{nm} = \sum_{i=0}^{m} \psi_{nm:i}$$

For example, $\psi_{22:0} = 2$ (the constants 0, 1), $\psi_{22:1} = 2$ (the functions x, y), and $\psi_{22:2} = 2$ (the functions xy, $x \vee y$). For another example, $\psi_{23:0} = 2$ (the constants 0, 1), $\psi_{23:1} = 3$ (the functions w, x, y), $\psi_{23:2} = 6$ (the functions $w \vee x, w \vee y, x \vee y, wx, wy, xy$), and $\psi_{23:3} = 9$ (the functions $w \vee xy, x \vee wy$, $y \vee xw, wx \vee wy, xw \vee xy, yx \vee yw, wx \vee wy \vee xy, w \vee x \vee y, wxy$). Lastly, $\psi_{32:0} = 3$ (the constants 0, 1, 2), $\psi_{32:1} = 14$ (the functions $e_1 D_2(x), D_2(x)$, $e_1 x, x, e_1 \vee x, D_1(x), e_1 \vee D_1(x), e_1 D_2(y), D_2(y), e_1 y, y, e_1 \vee y, D_1(y)$, $e_1 \vee D_1(y)$), and $\psi_{32:2} = 158$.

Let η_{nm} denote the total number of distinct n-valued unate functions of m variables. Since each w_j of a unate function is either x_j or $N(x_j)$ by Definition 9.13, it follows that

$$\eta_{nm} = \sum_{i=0}^{m} 2^i \psi_{nm:i} \, .$$

For example

$$\eta_{22} = (1)(2) + (2)(2) + (4)(2) = 14,$$

$$\eta_{23} = (1)(2) + (2)(3) + (4)(6) + (8)(9) = 104,$$

and

$$\eta_{32} = (1)(3) + (2)(14) + (4)(158) = 663.$$

Other enumerations which follow are

$$\eta_{42} = 98\,648,$$

$$\eta_{62} = 220\,789\,323\,486,$$

and

$$\eta_{33} = 2\,020\,781.$$

It has been indicated in Section 9.2 that the ACTION functions of Chapter 2 are positive functions. Thus these ACTION functions are unate

V	X	A_0
0	0	1
0	1	0
0	2	0
1	0	2
1	1	1
1	2	0
2	0	2
2	1	2
2	2	1

Figure 9.22 The 3-valued unate ACTION function A_0 of two variables V, X.

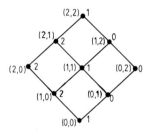

Figure 9.23 The unate function A_0 on a 3 × 3 lattice, using pairs (V, X).

functions. An application for an ACTION function which is *not* a positive function is given below.

Example 9.29. For the ACTION function A_0 of this section, the same argument V is used as in the ACTION function A_1 of figure 2.4. The function A_0 uses arguments V and X, where the 3-valued argument X is defined as follows. Let X be the distance of an aircraft raid from the defense system, quantized in 3 values. If the raid is 0–24 miles from the defense system, let $X = 0$. If the raid is 25–75 miles from the defense system, let $X = 1$. If the raid is greater than 75 miles from the defense system, let $X = 2$. Here, a low value of X indicates that the raid is more of a threat to a defensive system than a high value of X. Recall that a high value of the 3-valued argument V indicates that the raid is more of a threat to a defensive system than a low value of V. A possible ACTION function A_0 for this situation is given in figure 9.22. The 9-row table of this figure is redrawn in figure 9.23 as a function on a 3 × 3 lattice. It can be seen from figure 9.23 that this function A_0 is a unate function. In particular, this function has been chosen to bear an easy relation with the positive ACTION function A_1—namely, $A_1(V, W) = A_0(V, N(W)) = A_0(V, X)$.

THEOREM 9.14. An n-valued Post function $f(x_1, \ldots, x_m)$ is a unate function if and only if f is monotone increasing or monotone decreasing in x_i for each $i = 1, \ldots, m$.

Proof. From Definition 9.13, f is a positive function in the variables $w_1, \ldots, w_m$. Hence f regarded as a function in the variables $w_1, \ldots, w_m$ is monotone increasing in w_i for each $i = 1, \ldots, m$, by Theorem 9.6. For $w_i = x_i$, f is monotone increasing in x_i; for $w_i = N(x_i)$, f is monotone decreasing in x_i ∎

9.5 Threshold functions

Definition 9.15. Let f be an n-valued function of m arguments $x_1, \ldots, x_m$. The function f is an n-valued threshold function of m arguments if there are fixed real thresholds T_j, fixed real weights W_k, and a function S satisfying

$$S = \sum_{k=1}^{m} W_k x_k$$

such that either

(a) $\quad S \geq T_{n-1}$ $\qquad$ if and only if $f = n - 1$

$\quad T_{j+1} > S \geq T_j$ $\quad$ if and only if $f = j$ $(j = 1, 2, \ldots, n - 2)$

$\quad T_1 > S$ $\qquad\qquad$ if and only if $f = 0$

or

(b) $\quad S \geq T_{n-1}$ $\qquad$ if and only if $f = 0$

$\quad T_{j+1} > S \geq T_j$ $\quad$ if and only if $f = n - 1 - j$ $(j = 1, 2, \ldots, n - 2)$

$\quad T_1 > S$ $\qquad\qquad$ if and only if $f = n - 1$.

Thus the thresholds satisfy $T_1 < T_2 < \cdots < T_{n-1}$. It is understood in this definition that any condition involving $f = k$ is dropped if there are no values of the m arguments such that $f = k$. C Moraga has observed that this definition leads directly to the following theorem.

THEOREM 9.16. If f is an n-valued threshold function of m arguments, then $N(f)$ is an n-valued threshold function of m arguments.

Proof. Using Theorem 4.17(viii), f satisfies Definition 9.15(a) implies that $N(f)$ satisfies Definition 9.15(b), and f satisfies Definition 9.15(b) implies that $N(f)$ satisfies Definition 9.15(a) ∎

THEOREM 9.17. Let f be a threshold function with weights W_i and thresholds T_j, where $1 \leq i \leq m$ and $1 \leq j \leq n - 1$. Let k be any positive real number. Then f is a threshold function with weights kW_i and thresholds kT_j, where $1 \le i \le m$ and $1 \le j \le n - 1$.

Proof.   This is immediate from Definition 9.15   ∎

THEOREM 9.18.   Every threshold function is a unate function.

Proof.   This follows from Definitions 9.7, 9.11, 9.13, and 9.15   ∎

To illustrate the statement of Definition 9.15 for $n = 2$, $f(x_1, \ldots, x_m)$ is a 2-valued threshold function if there exists a fixed real threshold T_1, fixed real weights W_k, and a function

$$S = \sum_{k=1}^{m} W_k x_k$$

such that either

(a) $S \ge T_1$ if and only if $f = 1$

and

                    $T_1 > S$ if and only if $f = 0$

or

(b) $S \ge T_1$ if and only if $f = 0$

                    $T_1 > S$ if and only if $f = 1$.

Example 9.30.   The 2-valued simple symmetric function $f_1(x_1, x_2, x_3) = x_1 x_2 \lor x_1 x_3 \lor x_2 x_3$ is a 2-valued threshold function by Definition 9.15(a) with weights $W_1 = W_2 = W_3 = 1$ and $T_1 = 1.5$. For these weights,

$$S = x_1 + x_2 + x_3.$$

Since $f_1(1, 1, 1) = f_1(0, 1, 1) = f_1(1, 0, 1) = f_1(1, 1, 0) = 1$ and $f_1 = 0$ for other arguments, it follows that $S \ge 1.5$ for $f_1 = 1$ and $1.5 > S$ for $f_1 = 0$.

To illustrate the statement of Definition 9.15 for $n = 3$, $f(x_1, \ldots, x_m)$ is a 3-valued threshold function if there exist fixed real thresholds T_1 and T_2, fixed real weights W_k, and a function

$$S = \sum_{k=1}^{m} W_k x_k$$

such that either

(a) $S \ge T_2$ if and only if $f = 2$

                    $T_2 > S \ge T_1$ if and only if $f = 1$

                    $T_1 > S$ if and only if $f = 0$

or

(b)

$$S \geq T_2 \qquad \text{if and only if } f = 0$$

$$T_2 > S \geq T_1 \qquad \text{if and only if } f = 1$$

$$T_1 > S \qquad \text{if and only if } f = 2.$$

Example 9.31. The 3-valued function

$$g(x_1, x_2) = x_1 C_0(x_2) \vee C_2(x_1)(e_1 \vee C_1(x_2))$$

is a 3-valued threshold function of two arguments by Definition 9.15(a), using weights $W_1 = 1$ and $W_2 = -0.5$ with thresholds $T_1 = 0.8$ and $T_2 = 1.2$.

Here $g(2, 0) = g(2, 1) = 2$, $g(1, 0) = g(2, 2) = 1$, and $g = 0$ for other arguments. For these weights, $S = x_1 - (0.5)x_2$. It is straightforward to confirm the conditions in Definition 9.15(a).

Example 9.32. The 3-valued function

$$h(x_1, x_2) = C_0(x_1) \vee e_1 C_2(x_2) \vee C_1(x_1)(e_1 \vee D_1(x_2))$$

is a 3-valued threshold function of two arguments.

Inspection of the logic tables for g and h in Examples 9.31 and 9.32 shows that $h = N(g)$. Hence h is a 3-valued threshold function of two arguments by Theorem 9.16. The conditions in Definition 9.15(b) may be verified using the same weights and thresholds as given in Example 9.31.

Example 9.33. For each $n \geq 2$, n-valued decisive implication $x_1 \Rightarrow x_2$ is an n-valued threshold function of two arguments by Definition 9.15(a), using weights $W_1 = -1$ and $W_2 = 1$, with thresholds $T_1 = -0.7$ and $T_{n-1} = -0.3$.

Since n-valued decisive implication $x_1 \Rightarrow x_2$ takes only the values 0 and $n - 1$, only the top and bottom conditions in Definition 9.15(a) apply. The result follows by observing from the table for n-valued decisive implication that $x_1 \Rightarrow x_2$ takes the value $n - 1$ if and only if $x_1 \leq x_2$—that is, $-x_1 + x_2 \geq 0$, while $x_1 \Rightarrow x_2$ takes the value 0 if and only if $x_1 > x_2$—that is, $-1 \geq -x_1 + x_2$.

Example 9.34. For each $n \geq 2$, the n-valued function f of four arguments given by $f = x_1 x_2 \vee x_3 x_4$ is *not* an n-valued threshold function of four arguments.

Using (a) in Definition 9.15, $f(0, 0, n - 1, n - 1) = f(n - 1, n - 1, 0, 0) = n - 1$, so that $(W_3 + W_4)(n - 1) \geq T_{n-1}$ and $(W_1 + W_2)(n - 1) \geq T_{n-1}$. Hence $(W_1 + W_2 + W_3 + W_4)(n - 1) \geq 2T_{n-1}$. On the other hand, $f(0, n - 1, 0, n - 1) = f(n - 1, 0, n - 1, 0) = 0$, so that $(W_3 + W_4)(n - 1) < T_1$ and $(W_1 + W_3)(n - 1) < T_1$. Hence $(W_1 + W_2 + W_3 + W_4)(n - 1) < 2T_1$. Thus $T_{n-1} \leq (W_1 + W_2 + W_3 + W_4)(n - 1)/2 < T_1$. This contradicts $T_1 < T_{n-1}$ in Definition 9.15.

There is a similar demonstration using Definition 9.15(b). The same argument values again lead to $T_{n-1} < T_1$, and once again this contradicts $T_1 < T_{n-1}$.

The following enumerations are known for n-valued threshold functions of m arguments.

For $n = 2$,

m	Number of 2-valued threshold functions of m arguments
1	4
2	14
3	104
4	1 882
5	94 572
6	15 028 134
7	8 378 070 864
8	17 561 539 552 946

These enumerations may be found in Muroga *et al* (1970).

For $n = 3$, the number of 3-valued threshold functions of one argument is 17, the number of 3-valued threshold functions of two arguments is 471, and the number of 3-valued threshold functions of three arguments is 85 629 (Aibara and Akagi 1970).

For $n = 4$, the number of 4-valued threshold functions of one argument is 66, and the number of 4-valued threshold functions of two arguments is 18 184 (Moraga and Schulte-Ontrop 1982).

9.6   Overview

Simple symmetric functions in bounded distributive lattices are analogous to elementary symmetric functions in commutative rings with unit (see van der Waerden 1953). Each simple symmetric function τ_i in the former is a join of all possible meets of the variables taken i at a time. Each elementary symmetric function σ in the latter is a sum of all possible products of the variables taken i at a time.

The presentation of symmetric functions in Section 9.1 is based on work in Epstein *et al* (1977 and 1980) and Muzio *et al* (1983).

The development in Sections 9.2–9.4 extends work on positive functions in Epstein and Liu (1982) to negative functions and unate functions. It should be mentioned here that positive functions are a positive fragment of the n-valued functions given in Traczyk (1964). The problems of finding enumeration formulas for ψ_{2m} and ψ_{n2} have remained open for a number of years.

For work on 2-valued threshold functions see, for example, Muroga (1971). For work on 3-valued threshold functions, see Hanson (1963), Merrill (1964), Mine and Fujita (1970), and Moraga (1977).

For work on n-valued threshold functions, see Nomura (1973) and Moraga (1989). There are many variants of n-valued threshold functions. For example, linear separable, polynomial separable, bilinear separable, and adaptive separable functions are defined in Moraga and Schulte-Ontrop (1982). Disjointly separable functions are defined in Epstein *et al* (1984) and use disjoint operations C_i, $i = 0, 1, \ldots, n - 1$.

Exercises

E9.1 Prove that the number of different n-valued fundamental symmetric functions of m variables is

$$\binom{n + m - 1}{m}.$$

E9.2 For $n = 4$, $m = 2$, express the decisive symmetric function $C_1(xy)$ as a join of fundamental symmetric functions.

E9.3 For $n = 2$, $m = 4$, letting ab denote $a \wedge b = a \otimes b$, the simple symmetric functions are

$$\tau_0 = 1$$

$$\tau_1 = w \vee x \vee y \vee z$$

$$\tau_2 = wx \vee wy \vee wz \vee xy \vee xz \vee yz$$

$$\tau_3 = wxy \vee wxz \vee wyz \vee xyz$$

$$\tau_4 = wxyz$$

$$\tau_5 = 0$$

the fundamental symmetric functions are

$$f_{40} = \bar{w}\bar{x}\bar{y}\bar{z}$$

$$f_{31} = \bar{w}\bar{x}\bar{y}z \vee \bar{w}\bar{x}y\bar{z} \vee \bar{w}x\bar{y}\bar{z} \vee w\bar{x}\bar{y}\bar{z}$$

$$f_{22} = \bar{w}\bar{x}yz \vee \bar{w}x\bar{y}z \vee \bar{w}xy\bar{z} \vee w\bar{x}\bar{y}z \vee w\bar{x}y\bar{z} \vee wx\bar{y}\bar{z}$$

$$f_{13} = \bar{w}xyz \vee w\bar{x}yz \vee wx\bar{y}z \vee wxy\bar{z}$$

$$f_{04} = wxyz$$

and the elementary symmetric functions are

$$\sigma_0 = 1$$

$$\sigma_1 = w \oplus x \oplus y \oplus z$$

$$\sigma_2 = wx \oplus wy \oplus wz \oplus xy \oplus xz \oplus yz$$

$$\sigma_3 = wxy \oplus wxz \oplus wyz \oplus xyz$$

$$\sigma_4 = wxyz.$$

(a) Express each σ_i as a join of fundamental symmetric functions.
(b) Express each τ_i as a join of fundamental symmetric functions.
(c) Express each fundamental symmetric function as a ring sum of elementary symmetric functions.
(d) Express each simple symmetric function as a ring sum of elementary symmetric functions.

E9.4   In a 3-ring consider

$$g(a, b, c) = \sigma_1 \oplus \sigma_2 = a \oplus b \oplus c \oplus (a \otimes b) \oplus (a \otimes c) \oplus (b \otimes c).$$

Express g in the form $g = e_1 C_1(g) \vee C_2(g)$ where $C_1(g)$ and $C_2(g)$ are each expressed as a join of fundamental symmetric functions.

E9.5   In a 2-ring prove that each symmetric function of four variables may be expressed as a sum of elementary symmetric functions. The elementary symmetric functions for $n = 2$, $m = 4$ are detailed in **E9.3** above.

E9.6   Use Theorem 9.4 to express the 6-valued fundamental symmetric function f_{320102} of eight variables as a simplified meet of terms of the form $C_i(\tau_j)$.

E9.7   Draw a graph of the step function corresponding to the fundamental symmetric function f_{320102} of **E9.6.**

E9.8   Show that the 175 3-valued positive functions of two variables x, y can be expressed as joins of terms in the form

$$e_i, \quad e_i D_j(x), \quad e_i D_k(y), \quad e_i D_j(x) D_k(y)$$

where $0 \le i \le 2$ and $1 \le j, k \le 2$ in each term.

E9.9   Of the 175 monotone increasing 3-valued functions of variables x, y, written as pairs (x, y), how many satisfy $f(i, i) = i$ for each $i = 0, 1, 2$? In other words, how many different ways are there to assign function values to the remaining six points in the lattice below such that the resulting function is a monotone increasing function?

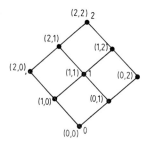

E9.10 Consider the 4-valued monotone decreasing function $F(x, y)$ shown below, using pairs (x, y). Give this function as a negative function according to Definition 9.9.

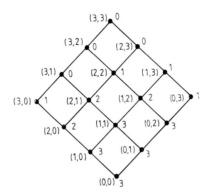

E9.11 How many 3-valued symmetric functions of two variables x, y are positive functions?

E9.12 How many 2-valued symmetric functions using exactly three variables w, x, y are positive or negative functions?

E9.13 For $n = 2$, $m = 4$, give $\psi_{24:0}$, $\psi_{24:1}$, $\psi_{24:2}$, $\psi_{24:3}$, $\psi_{24:4}$. Give η_{24}, the number of 2-valued unate functions of 4 variables.

E9.14 Give the two 2-valued functions of two variables x, y which are *not* unate functions.

E9.15 How many 3-valued functions of two variables are not unate functions?

E9.16 Prove that the 3-valued positive function $D_1(x_1) \vee D_1(x_2)$ is a 3-valued threshold function of two variables x_1, x_2.

E9.17 Prove that the 3-valued function $C_0(y) \vee e_1 C_2(x) \vee (e_1 \vee D_1(x))C_1(y)$ is a 3-valued threshold function of two variables x, y.

E9.18 Give an example of a 4-valued unate function of four variables which is not a positive function, not a negative function, and not a threshold function.

10   Special Applications

In this chapter there is a discussion of special applications, including programmable logic arrays (PLAS) and linear feedback shift registers (LFSRS). There is also a discussion of built-in self-test (BIST), as related to PLAS and LFSRS.

10.1   Programmable logic arrays

PLAS are building blocks which occur in the design of digital integrated circuits. These arrays are highly regular and modular structures which provide simple interconnections, with a small number of uniform components. These structures may be modified in an easy way to realize arbitrary functions. This allows both flexibility and efficient mass production. Typical applications include control logic functions, special arithmetic functions, and combinational logic functions for finite state machines. For example, binary microprocessors such as the Motorola MC 68020, Intel 80386, AT&T WE 32100, and IBM Micro 1370 use PLAS for the implementation of control logic functions.

To overcome design complexity and testability problems in VLSI technology, subsystems having regular and modular structure such as programmable logic arrays (PLAS) and read only memories (ROMS) are often used. While present day applications are mainly for the case $n = 2$, there are also applications for $n \geq 2$. For example, for $n = 4$, there are 4-valued ROMS as discussed in Rich et al (1985). In general, there are applications within any multiple-valued subsystem. A feature of the Type 2 PLAS described below for $n \geq 2$, is that the PLA internal arrays are binary throughout, regardless of the value of n.

Figure 10.1 shows the basic AND array, OR array structure of a PLA. The AND array, OR array **are** also called MIN array, MAX array, respectively, because of the definition of AND, OR in a Post chain of order n. It may be seen from figure 10.1 that the inputs are at the left of the AND array, and the outputs are at the right of the OR array.

In what follows, two types of PLAS are presented, following Sasao (1986). In Type 1 PLAS, the top rows of the AND array are the $n - 2$ constants e_1, $e_2, \ldots, e_{n-2}$. In Type 2 PLAS there are no such top rows. As a consequence, a Type 1 PLA allows intermediate logic values within the AND, OR arrays, while a Type 2 PLA does not. Other than intermediate logic values, inputs to the AND array of a Type 1 or Type 2 PLA are decisively decoded input variables. Thus for the ternary case, if there were two disjointly decoded inputs x, y, an input representation would be as follows.

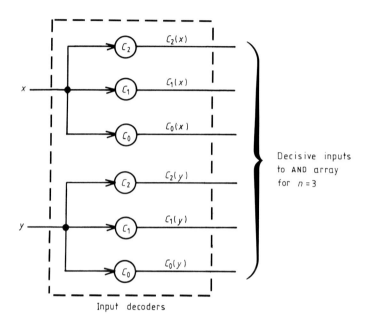

Input decoders

For the binary case, if there were two inputs x, y, disjoint decoding would be represented as follows.

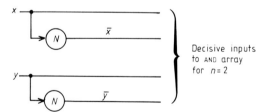

The general form of a Type 1 PLA is shown in figure 10.2. The general form of a Type 2 PLA is shown in figure 10.3. In these figures, m n-valued inputs are shown, with q n-valued outputs. For each input x_i, $i = 1, 2, \ldots, m$, there are a certain number of decisively decoded inputs to the AND array, depending on the kind of decoding. This will be illustrated below for $n = 3$, $m = 2$, $q = 1$—that is, for one 3-valued function of two variables x, y, and one 3-valued output.

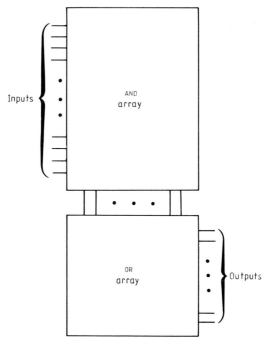

Figure 10.1   General structure of a PLA.

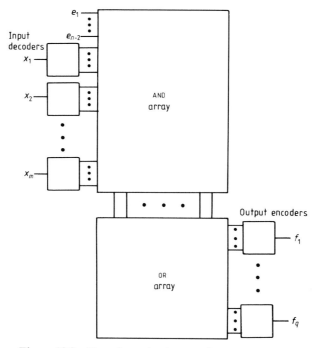

Figure 10.2   Type 1 n-valued PLA, m inputs, q outputs.

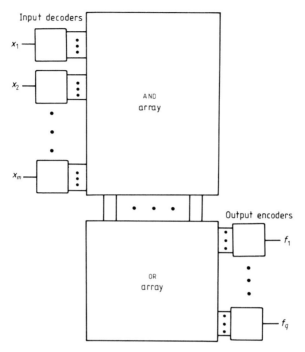

Figure 10.3 Type 2 *n*-valued PLA, *m* inputs, *q* outputs.

Consider the function *g* given by the logic table in figure 10.4. The fdnf for *g* may be written in the following form

$$g = e_1 C_1(g) \vee C_2(g)$$
$$= e_1[C_0(x)C_1(y) \vee C_1(x)C_0(y) \vee C_2(x)C_0(y)]$$
$$\vee C_0(x)C_2(y) \vee C_1(x)C_1(y) \vee C_1(x)C_2(y) \vee C_2(x)C_1(y) \vee C_2(x)C_2(y).$$

x	y	g
0	0	0
0	1	1
0	2	2
1	0	1
1	1	2
1	2	2
2	0	1
2	1	2
2	2	2

Figure 10.4 Table for 3-valued function $g(x, y)$.

Note that $C_1(g)$ is a disjunction of three fundaments and $C_2(g)$ is a disjunction of five fundaments. To minimize for PLA implementation using the operations appearing in these expressions, first note that $C_1(g)$ cannot be simplified directly. However, any fundament of $C_2(g)$ may be joined to $C_1(g)$ because of fundamental properties in Chapter 4. Further, $C_2(g)$ may be simplified directly. The results are shown below.

$$C_2(g) = C_1(x)C_1(y) \vee C_2(x)C_1(y) \vee [C_0(x) \vee C_1(x) \vee C_2(x)]C_2(y)$$
$$= C_1(x)C_1(y) \vee C_2(x)C_1(y) \vee C_2(y)$$
$$b_1(g) = C_1(g) \vee C_1(x)C_1(y) \vee C_2(x)C_1(y) \vee C_1(x)C_2(y) \vee C_2(x)C_2(y)$$
$$= [C_0(x) \vee C_1(x) \vee C_2(x)]C_1(y) \vee C_1(x)[C_0(y) \vee C_1(y) \vee C_2(y)]$$
$$\vee C_2(x)[C_0(y) \vee C_1(y) \vee C_2(y)]$$
$$= C_1(y) \vee C_1(x) \vee C_2(x)$$

with

$$g = e_1 b_1(g) \vee C_2(g)$$
$$= e_1[C_1(y) \vee C_1(x) \vee C_2(x)] \vee C_1(x)C_1(y) \vee C_2(x)C_1(y) \vee C_2(y).$$

It should be noted that x, y, $N(x)$, $N(y)$ are not allowed as primitives in the simplification because PLA inputs must be decisive.

The resulting implementation for a Type 1 PLA is shown in figure 10.5, and that for a Type 2 PLA is shown in figure 10.6. All signals within the AND, OR arrays of a Type 2 PLA for the 3-valued function in figure 10.6 are decisive, taking the values 0, 2 alone. It should be noted that the 3-valued output encoding for g is based on the two decisive lines for $b_1(g)$ and $C_2(g)$ coming from the OR array. In this case the output encoding for g is neither a disjoint encoding nor a monotonic encoding, because $b_1(g) \neq C_1(g)$ and $b_1(g) \neq D_1(g)$.

Efficient implementations for PLAS may also depend upon the kind of input decoding and output encoding. Such considerations may reduce not only the chip area, but also propagation delay and power dissipation. The example for the 3-valued function $h(x, y)$ in figure 10.7 shows one kind of savings which can be made with respect to input decoding. It is clear from the depiction of h on the 3×3 lattice in figure 10.7 that h is a monotone increasing function, hence h is a positive function by Theorem 9.6. It follows from Section 9.2 that h may be realized from two decisive inputs, $D_1(x)$ and $D_2(x)$, used as a monotonic decoding for variable x and two decisive inputs $D_1(y)$ and $D_2(y)$ used as a monotonic decoding for variable y. There are two decisive outputs from the OR array for h, as follows.

$$D_2(h) = D_1(x)D_1(y) \vee D_2(y)$$
$$D_1(h) = D_1(x) \vee D_1(y)$$

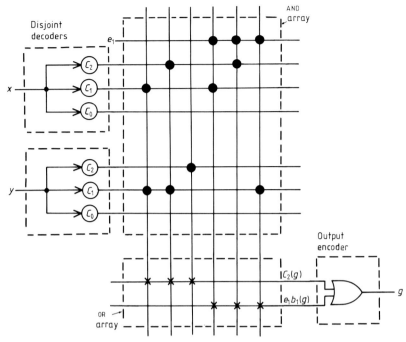

Figure 10.5   Type 1 PLA for the 3-valued function $g(x, y)$.

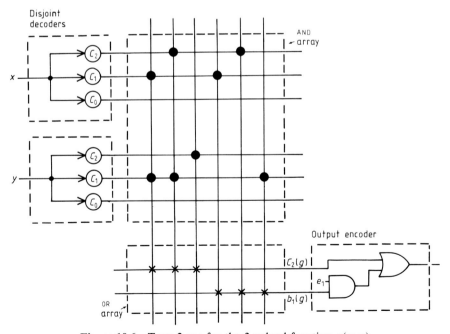

Figure 10.6   Type 2 PLA for the 3-valued function $g(x, y)$.

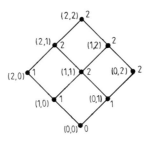

Figure 10.7   The 3-valued function $h(x, y)$ is a monotone increasing function on pairs (x, y).

with

$$h = e_1 D_1(h) \vee D_2(h) = e_1[D_1(x) \vee D_1(y)] \vee D_1(x)D_1(y) \vee D_2(y).$$

The Type 1 PLA for h is shown in figure 10.8. The Type 2 PLA for h is shown in figure 10.9. Type 2 arrays are attractive for PLA implementation because of their decisive array structure. For certain difficulties with implementations using Type 1 arrays, see Sections 3.2–3.3 of Sasao (1986). For some further remarks on decisive codings, see Sasao (1988).

Clearly Karnaugh or algebraic methods are limited to a small number of variables and low values of n. Different algorithms have been studied for the simplification of n-valued functions in PLAS. An example of work in this area

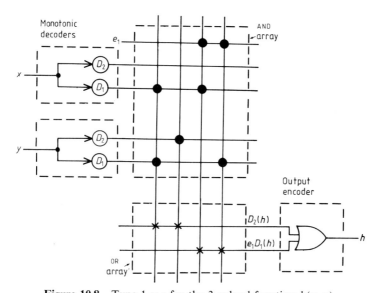

Figure 10.8   Type 1 PLA for the 3-valued function $h(x, y)$.

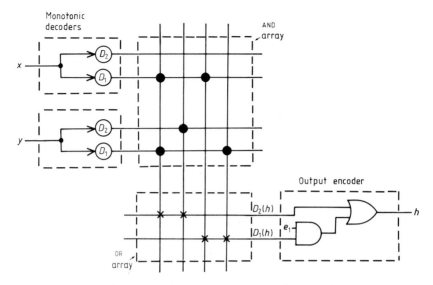

Figure 10.9 Type 2 PLA for the 3-valued function $h(x, y)$.

is Rudell and Sangiovanni-Vincentelli (1987). A comparative analysis of seven minimization algorithms for n-valued functions in PLAs may be found in Tirumalai and Butler (1988).

10.2   Linear feedback shift registers

An LFSR is a shift register of m n-stable devices $a_1, \ldots, a_m$ satisfying

$$(1) \qquad\qquad Da_i = a_{i+1}, \quad i = 1, 2, \ldots, m-1$$

with a linear function f_0 for the initial n-stable device a_m

$$(2) \qquad\qquad Da_m = f_0(a_1, \ldots, a_m).$$

The linear function f_0 by definition is a function which is expressible using the addition operation $\oplus$ and the multiplication operation $\otimes$ of Chapter 6, together with constants $e_i = i$, $i = 0, 1, \ldots, n-1$. Where there is no chance of confusion, $a + b$ is written for $a \oplus b$ and ab is written for $a \otimes b$. In other words, f_0 satisfies

$$(3) \qquad\qquad f_0 = \sum_{i=1}^{m} (k_i a_i)$$

where each k_i, $i = 1, 2, \ldots, m$, is an integer satisfying $0 \le k_i \le n-1$. Feedback is said to occur for those a_i for which $k_i \ne 0$.

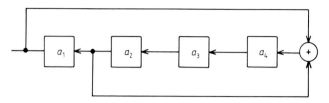

Figure 10.10   An LFSR for $n = 2$, $m = 4$ with primitive polynomial $1 + x + x^4$.

An example for $n = 2$ is shown in figure 10.10 and one for $n = 3$ is shown in figure 10.11. In figure 10.10, $n = 2$, $m = 4$, $k_1 = 1$, $k_2 = 1$, $k_3 = 0$, $k_4 = 0$, so $Da_4 = f_0 = a_1 \oplus a_2$, and feedback is from a_1, a_2. In figure 10.11, $n = 3$, $m = 3$, $k_1 = 2$, $k_2 = 0$, $k_3 = 1$, so $Da_3 = f_0 = (2 \otimes a_1) \oplus (a_3)$ and feedback is from a_1, a_3. There will be further discussion of these two examples later in this section.

The operation of an LFSR may be depicted using an $m \times m$ matrix **M** as a linear transform

$$(4) \qquad \begin{bmatrix} a_1 \\ a_2 \\ \vdots \\ a_{m-1} \\ a_m \end{bmatrix} \leftarrow \begin{bmatrix} 0 & 1 & 0 & 0 & \cdots & 0 & 0 & 0 \\ 0 & 0 & 1 & 0 & \cdots & 0 & 0 & 0 \\ 0 & 0 & 0 & 1 & \cdots & 0 & 0 & 0 \\ \vdots & \vdots & \vdots & \vdots & \vdots & \vdots & \vdots & \vdots \\ 0 & 0 & 0 & 0 & \cdots & 0 & 1 & 0 \\ 0 & 0 & 0 & 0 & \cdots & 0 & 0 & 1 \\ k_1 & k_2 & k_3 & k_4 & \cdots & k_{m-2} & k_{m-1} & k_m \end{bmatrix} \begin{bmatrix} a_1 \\ a_2 \\ \vdots \\ a_{m-1} \\ a_m \end{bmatrix}$$

$$\underbrace{\hspace{6cm}}_{\text{The } m \times m \text{ matrix } \mathbf{M}}$$

Here arithmetic operations $\oplus$, $\otimes$ are used for the linear transform operations. It may be seen easily that (4) is equivalent to (1)–(3). An $m \times m$ matrix **M**

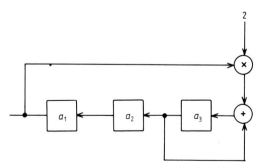

Figure 10.11   An LFSR for $n = 3$, $m = 3$ with primitive polynomial $1 + 2x^2 + x^3$.

of the form shown above is called the companion matrix of the minimal polynomial

(5) $$g(x) = (n - k_1) + (n - k_2)x + \cdots + (n - k_m)x^{m-1} + x^m.$$

The polynomial $g(x)$ in (5) is the monic polynomial (that is, a polynomial whose leading coefficient is equal to 1) of least degree with $g(\mathbf{M}) = 0$. If the k_i, $i = 1, 2, \ldots, m$ in $\mathbf{M}$ are chosen so that

(6) $$\mathbf{M}^{(n^m - 1)} = 1$$

and no less power of $\mathbf{M}$ is equal to 1, where 1 at the right of (6) denotes the identity matrix, then $g(x)$ is called a *primitive polynomial*. Examples of primitive polynomials are given in figures 10.10 and 10.11.

Definition 10.1. Consider polynomials whose coefficients are members of a given number system having fixed base $n \geq 2$. A sum or product of two such polynomials may be formed in the usual way, then each coefficient of the sum or product may be reduced modulo n, as in Section 2.7. Such polynomials are called *polynomials over a number system having fixed base n*.

The three examples which follow use the two polynomials $g(x) = x^4 + x^2 + x + 1$ and $h(x) = x^3 + x^2 + x + 1$. The usual polynomial sum is

$$g(x) + h(x) = s(x) = x^4 + x^3 + 2x^2 + 2x + 2$$

and the usual polynomial product is

$$g(x)h(x) = p(x) = x^7 + x^6 + 2x^5 + 3x^4 + 3x^3 + 3x^2 + 2x + 1.$$

Example 10.1. Consider the binary number system. Then $g(x) + h(x) = s(x) = x^4 + x^3$ and $g(x)h(x) = p(x) = x^7 + x^6 + x^4 + x^3 + x^2 + 1$, because $2 \equiv 0 \pmod 2$ and $3 \equiv 1 \pmod 2$.

Example 10.2. Consider the ternary number system. Then

$$g(x) + h(x) = s(x) = x^4 + x^3 + 2x^2 + 2x + 2$$

and

$$g(x)h(x) = p(x) = x^7 + x^6 + 2x^5 + 2x + 1,$$

because $3 \equiv 0 \pmod 3$.

Example 10.3. Consider the balanced ternary number system. Then

$$g(x) + h(x) = s(x) = x^4 + x^3 - x^2 - x - 1$$

and

$$g(x)h(x) = p(x) = x^7 + x^6 - x^5 - x + 1,$$

because $2 \equiv (-1) \pmod 3$ and $3 \equiv 0 \pmod 3$.

The following theorem is an easy consequence of the above.

THEOREM 10.2. For given $n \geq 2$, let $F[x]$ denote the polynomials in x over a number system having base n, under addition and multiplication as discussed above. Then $F[x]$ is a commutative ring with unit of characteristic n.

An *irreducible polynomial* is a polynomial which cannot be factored. For fixed n, any primitive polynomial is an irreducible polynomial. In each of Examples 10.1–10.3, $p(x)$ is a polynomial which is *not* an irreducible polynomial, hence *not* a primitive polynomial. There are irreducible polynomials which are *not* primitive polynomials. Specifically, an irreducible polynomial in x of degree m is a primitive polynomial if and only if the polynomial divides $x^s - 1$ for no s less than $n^m - 1$.

Consider once again the examples shown in figures 10.10 and 10.11. In figure 10.10, the matrix form corresponding to (4) is

$$\begin{bmatrix} a_1 \\ a_2 \\ a_3 \\ a_4 \end{bmatrix} \leftarrow \begin{bmatrix} 0 & 1 & 0 & 0 \\ 0 & 0 & 1 & 0 \\ 0 & 0 & 0 & 1 \\ 1 & 1 & 0 & 0 \end{bmatrix} \begin{bmatrix} a_1 \\ a_2 \\ a_3 \\ a_4 \end{bmatrix}$$

The 4×4 matrix **M** above is the companion matrix for the minimal polynomial $1 + x + x^4$. This is one of two primitive polynomials for the case $n = 2$, $m = 4$, the other being $1 + x^3 + x^4$. The only other irreducible polynomial for this case is the polynomial $1 + x + x^2 + x^3 + x^4$. However, this polynomial is not a primitive polynomial because it divides $x^5 - 1$.

It is easy to establish that this **M** satisfies

$$\mathbf{M}^{(2^4 - 1)} = \mathbf{M}^{15}$$

and no less power of **M** is equal to 1. Consider successive application of **M** to the 4-tuple a given by $a_1 = 1$, $a_2 = 0$, $a_3 = 0$, $a_4 = 0$ as shown in figure 10.12. It may be seen from this figure that a cycle of 15 states is obtained, starting with any 4-tuple a whose entries are not all 0. In other words, $\mathbf{M}^{15}a = a$, and $\mathbf{M}^{15} = 1$. A cycle of 1 is obtained starting with the tuple whose entries are all 0 (this holds for all LFSRs, regardless of n, m). A state diagram for this is shown in figure 10.13.

In figure 10.11, the matrix form corresponding to (4) is

$$\begin{bmatrix} a_1 \\ a_2 \\ a_3 \end{bmatrix} \leftarrow \begin{bmatrix} 0 & 1 & 0 \\ 0 & 0 & 1 \\ 2 & 0 & 1 \end{bmatrix} \begin{bmatrix} a_1 \\ a_2 \\ a_3 \end{bmatrix}$$

The 3×3 matrix **M** above is the companion matrix for the minimum polynomial

$$1 + 2x^2 + x^3.$$

	a_1	a_2	a_3	a_4
a	1	0	0	0
$\mathbf{M}a$	0	0	0	1
$\mathbf{M}^2a$	0	0	1	0
$\mathbf{M}^3a$	0	1	0	0
$\mathbf{M}^4a$	1	0	0	1
$\mathbf{M}^5a$	0	0	1	1
$\mathbf{M}^6a$	0	1	1	0
$\mathbf{M}^7a$	1	1	0	1
$\mathbf{M}^8a$	1	0	1	0
$\mathbf{M}^9a$	0	1	0	1
$\mathbf{M}^{10}a$	1	0	1	1
$\mathbf{M}^{11}a$	0	1	1	1
$\mathbf{M}^{12}a$	1	1	1	1
$\mathbf{M}^{13}a$	1	1	1	0
$\mathbf{M}^{14}a$	1	1	0	0
$\mathbf{M}^{15}a$	1	0	0	0

Figure 10.12   The 15 states for an LFSR with $n = 2, m = 4$ and primitive polynomial $1 + x + x^4$.

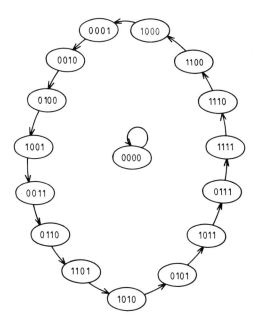

Figure 10.13   State diagram for an LFSR with $n = 2$, $m = 4$ and primitive polynomial $1 + x + x^4$.

This is a primitive polynomial with

$$\mathbf{M}^{(3^3-1)} = \mathbf{M}^{26} = 1$$

and no less power of $\mathbf{M}$ is equal to 1. This is shown in figure 10.14, in which $\mathbf{M}$ is applied successively to the 3-tuple $a_1 = 1$, $a_2 = 0$, $a_3 = 0$. From figure 10.14 it may be seen that a cycle of 26 is obtained starting with any 3-tuple a whose entries are not all 0. In other words, $\mathbf{M}^{26}a = a$ and $\mathbf{M}^{26} = 1$. A cycle of 1 is obtained starting with the 3-tuple whose entries are all 0. A state diagram for this is shown in figure 10.15.

In the remainder of this section, two applications of LFSRS are discussed: (i) counters, and (ii) pseudo-random generators.

An LFSR has the capability of generating $n^m - 1$ states. Since partial tabulations exist of primitive polynomials, it is an easy matter to obtain

	a_1	a_2	a_3
a	1	0	0
$\mathbf{M}a$	0	0	2
$\mathbf{M}^2a$	0	2	2
$\mathbf{M}^3a$	2	2	2
$\mathbf{M}^4a$	2	2	0
$\mathbf{M}^5a$	2	0	1
$\mathbf{M}^6a$	0	1	2
$\mathbf{M}^7a$	1	2	2
$\mathbf{M}^8a$	2	2	1
$\mathbf{M}^9a$	2	1	2
$\mathbf{M}^{10}a$	1	2	0
$\mathbf{M}^{11}a$	2	0	2
$\mathbf{M}^{12}a$	0	2	0
$\mathbf{M}^{13}a$	2	0	0
$\mathbf{M}^{14}a$	0	0	1
$\mathbf{M}^{15}a$	0	1	1
$\mathbf{M}^{16}a$	1	1	1
$\mathbf{M}^{17}a$	1	1	0
$\mathbf{M}^{18}a$	1	0	2
$\mathbf{M}^{19}a$	0	2	1
$\mathbf{M}^{20}a$	2	1	1
$\mathbf{M}^{21}a$	1	1	2
$\mathbf{M}^{22}a$	1	2	1
$\mathbf{M}^{23}a$	2	1	0
$\mathbf{M}^{24}a$	1	0	1
$\mathbf{M}^{25}a$	0	1	0
$\mathbf{M}^{26}a$	1	0	0

Figure 10.14   The 26 states for an LFSR with $n = 3$, $m = 3$ and primitive polynomial $1 + 2x^2 + x^3$.

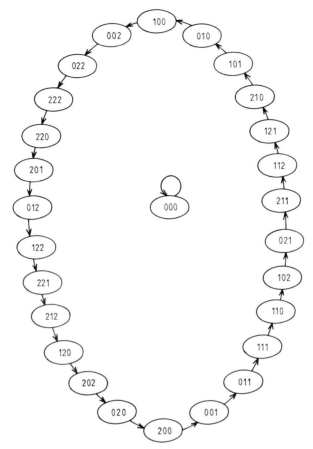

Figure 10.15 State diagram for an LFSR with $n = 3$, $m = 3$ and primitive polynomial $1 + 2x^2 + x^3$.

corresponding LFSRs. Partial tabulations of primitive polynomials for $n \leq 19$, $m \leq 19$ may be found in Gulliver *et al* (1988). Other tabulations may be found in Church (1935), Marsh (1957), Peterson and Weldon (1972), Serra (1986), and Bardell *et al* (1987). From such tabulations, sample logical equations are given below for the initial n-stable device a_m of an LFSR of m n-stable devices which generates $n^m - 1$ states.

$\underline{n = 2}$

$m = 2$: $Da_2 = a_1 + a_2$

$m = 3$: $Da_3 = a_1 + a_2$

$m = 4$: $Da_4 = a_1 + a_2$

$m = 5$: $Da_5 = a_1 + a_3$ (*continued overleaf*)

$m = 6$: $Da_6 = a_1 + a_2$
$m = 7$: $Da_7 = a_1 + a_2$
$m = 8$: $Da_8 = a_1 + a_2 + a_4 + a_6$
$m = 9$: $Da_9 = a_1 + a_5$
$m = 10$: $Da_{10} = a_1 + a_4$
$m = 11$: $Da_{11} = a_1 + a_3$.

$n = 3$

$m = 2$: $Da_2 = a_1 + a_2$
$m = 3$: $Da_3 = (2a_1) + a_3$
$m = 4$: $Da_4 = a_1 + a_4$
$m = 5$: $Da_5 = (2a_1) + a_5$
$m = 6$: $Da_6 = a_1 + a_6$
$m = 7$: $Da_7 = (2a_1) + a_3$
$m = 8$: $Da_8 = a_1 + a_7$
$m = 9$: $Da_9 = 2(a_1 + a_2 + a_3 + a_6 + a_8 + a_9)$
$m = 10$: $Da_{10} = a_1 + a_8 + a_{10}$
$m = 11$: $Da_{11} = 2(a_1 + a_8 + a_{10} + a_{11})$

$n = 5$

$m = 2$: $Da_2 = (3a_1) + (4a_2)$
$m = 3$: $Da_3 = (3a_1) + (4a_3)$
$m = 4$: $Da_4 = (3a_1) + a_2 + (4a_4)$
$m = 5$: $Da_5 = (2a_1) + (3a_2) + (4a_3) + (4a_5)$
$m = 6$: $Da_6 = (3a_1) + (4a_6)$
$m = 7$: $Da_7 = (3a_1) + (4a_7)$
$m = 8$: $Da_8 = (3a_1) + (4a_2) + (4a_3) + (4a_8)$
$m = 9$: $Da_9 = (2a_1) + a_2 + (4a_9)$
$m = 10$: $Da_{10} = (2a_1) + (3a_2) + (4a_{10})$
$m = 11$: $Da_{11} = (3a_1) + (4a_{11})$.

$n = 7$

$m = 2$: $Da_2 = (4a_1) + (6a_2)$
$m = 3$: $Da_3 = (5a_1) + (6a_2) + (6a_3)$
$m = 4$: $Da_4 = (4a_1) + (6a_2) + (6a_4)$
$m = 5$: $Da_5 = (3a_1) + (6a_5)$
$m = 6$: $Da_6 = (2a_1) + (5a_2) + (6a_3) + (6a_6)$
$m = 7$: $Da_7 = (3a_1) + a_2 + (6a_7)$.

$n = 11$

$m = 2$: $Da_2 = (4a_1) + (10a_2)$
$m = 3$: $Da_3 = (8a_1) + (10a_3)$
$m = 4$: $Da_4 = (3a_1) + (10a_4)$
$m = 5$: $Da_5 = (7a_1) + (10a_2) + (10a_5)$
$m = 6$: $Da_6 = (4a_1) + (10a_2) + (10a_6)$
$m = 7$: $Da_7 = (7a_1) + (10a_7)$.

n = 13

$m = 2$: $Da_2 = (11a_1) + (12a_2)$

$m = 3$: $Da_3 = (11a_1) + (12a_3)$

$m = 4$: $Da_4 = (11a_1) + (12a_2) + (12a_4)$

$m = 5$: $Da_5 = (7a_1) + (12a_2) + (12a_5)$

$m = 6$: $Da_6 = (7a_1) + (11a_2) + (12a_6)$

$m = 7$: $Da_7 = (2a_1) + (9a_2) + (12a_7)$.

n = 17

$m = 2$: $Da_2 = (14a_1) + (16a_2)$

$m = 3$: $Da_3 = (10a_1) + (16a_3)$

$m = 4$: $Da_4 = (10a_1) + (16a_2) + (16a_4)$

$m = 5$: $Da_5 = (12a_1) + (16a_5)$

$m = 6$: $Da_6 = (14a_1) + (16a_6)$

$m = 7$: $Da_7 = (15a_1) + (16a_7)$.

n = 19

$m = 2$: $Da_2 = (17a_1) + (18a_2)$

$m = 3$: $Da_3 = (13a_1) + (18a_3)$

$m = 4$: $Da_4 = (17a_1) + (18a_4)$

$m = 5$: $Da_5 = (14a_1) + (18a_5)$

$m = 6$: $Da_6 = (4a_1) + (18a_6)$

$m = 7$: $Da_7 = (14a_1) + (18a_7)$.

It is not possible to achieve n^m states with an LFSR. However, given an LFSR which generates $n^m - 1$ states, it is possible to replace the linear function f_0 in (2) with a nonlinear function g_0 so that the all-0 state is included and n^m states are generated. It is straightforward to modify f_0 to obtain g_0, as illustrated below.

First, consider the function f of figures 10.10 and 10.12 where $n = 2$, $m = 4$ and $f = a_1 \oplus a_2$. The all-0 state, 0000. may be inserted between the state $a_1 = 1$, $a_2 = 0$, $a_3 = 0$, $a_4 = 0$ and the state $a_1 = 0$, $a_2 = 0$, $a_3 = 0$, $a_4 = 1$ by changing $Da_4 = f$ to $Da_4 = g$, where

$$g = a_1 \oplus a_2 \oplus (\bar{a}_2 \wedge \bar{a}_3 \wedge \bar{a}_4).$$

While g is nonlinear and somewhat more complicated than f, $2^4 = 16$ states are generated using g.

Second, consider the function f of figures 10.11 and 10.14 $f = (2 \otimes a_1) \oplus (a_3)$. The all-0 state 000 may be inserted between the state $a_1 = 1$, $a_2 = 0$, $a_3 = 0$ and the state $a_1 = 0$, $a_2 = 0$, $a_3 = 2$ by changing $Da_3 = f$ to $Da_3 = g$, where

$$g = (2 \otimes a_1) \oplus a_3 \oplus (N(a_1) \wedge C_0(a_2) \wedge C_0(a_3)).$$

Alternatively, the all-0 state 000 could be inserted between the state $a_1 = 2$, $a_2 = 0$, $a_3 = 0$ and the state $a_1 = 0$, $a_2 = 0$, $a_3 = 1$.

Next, an LFSR which generates $n^m - 1$ states has the property that the generated single values of a_i for any fixed i simulate, to a certain extent, randomly generated digits $d_i = 0, 1, \ldots, n - 1$ using uniform distribution of these digits. For example, consider the 26 consecutive values of a_1, starting with the first row of figure 10.14, where $n = 3$, $m = 3$. These 26 values are 1, 0, 0, 2, 2, 2, 0, 1, 2, 2, 1, 2, 0, 2, 0, 0, 1, 1, 1, 0, 2, 1, 1, 2, 1, 0. In this sequence of ternary digits there are 9 twos, 9 ones, and 8 zeros. Pseudo-random properties of such sequences become clear as m increases. For a review of these properties and further discussion, see Hortensius *et al* (1989).

There are many uses of LFSRS, for example they may occur in signal processing and cryptography. For a use of the LFSR to detect faults in combinational circuits, see Section 10.5.

10.3   Built-in self-test, register and circuit faults

The term BIST refers to the self-testing of internal circuitry through the addition of extra internal equipment whose function is to test the internal circuitry and also the extra internal equipment. This allows for the testing of circuitry in its normal environment. In particular, in the VLSI environment, pins are scarce and BIST is attractive, especially if the amount of extra internal test equipment can be kept low. This is clear when extra internal equipment uses up scarce chip area.

An easy example is afforded by the detection of a single fault in an n-valued word contained in a register of r digits. This may be done by expanding the register to $r + 1$ digits. In addition to the extra register digit, circuitry is introduced to form the arithmetic sum (mod n) of the digits. This uses the $\oplus$ operation of Chapter 6. If s denotes the arithmetic sum (mod n) of the original r digits, the extra digit is set to $n - s$, so that the arithmetic sum (mod n) of all $r + 1$ digits is equal to 0. This is called even parity checking when $n = 2$. Below are examples for $n = 5$ and $r = 8$.

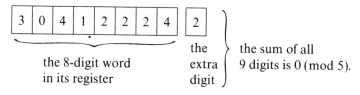

| 3 | 0 | 4 | 1 | 2 | 2 | 2 | 4 | | 2 |

the 8-digit word in its register

the extra digit

the sum of all 9 digits is 0 (mod 5).

The sum of the original 8 digits is 18, which is 3 (mod 5). Thus the extra register digit is set to 2, as shown above. It is clear that a single error anywhere within this 9-digit register will cause a like error in the arithmetic sum (mod 5) of all 9 digits. For example, if the fourth digit from the left has an error of $+2$, then the sum of all 9 digits has an error of $+2$, as shown below.

3	0	4	3	2	2	2	4		2

$\underbrace{}$ the sum of all
$+2$ the   9 digits is 2 (mod 5).
error   extra
      digit

A single error in the extra register digit is also detected. For example, if the extra digit has an error of $+1$, then the sum of all 9 digits has an error of $+1$, as shown below.

3	0	4	1	2	2	2	4		3

$+1$ the sum of all
error   9 digits is 1 (mod 5).

While single faults will be detected by this parity checker, multiple faults need not be detected. In the above example, suppose that the fourth digit from the left has an error of $+1$, the fifth digit from the left has an error of $+2$, and the sixth digit from the left has an error of $+2$. The resulting sum of all 9 digits is 0, and the three errors are undetected. This is shown below.

3	0	4	2	4	4	2	4		2

triple fault   the sum of all
     9 digits is 0 (mod 5).

This last example shows that a single extra register digit added to a register of 8 digits is insufficient to detect a triple fault for $n = 5$. Detection of multiple faults requires additional digits. For a theory of detection and correction of errors in digital words see Peterson and Weldon (1972).

Some basic faults occurring in digital circuits are described below. A *fault* is a physical defect within a circuit. A *logical fault* causes a change in the logic function which corresponds to the circuit. A *parametric fault* causes a change in the magnitude of a circuit parameter, such as circuit voltage or speed. An *intermittent fault* is a fault which occurs at certain moments of time and is absent at other moments of time. A *permanent fault* is a fault which is constantly present, and whose nature is unchanged during testing.

The faults discussed below are logical and permanent faults.

An *s-a-d fault* ($0 \leq d \leq n - 1$) is a fault which occurs when a signal line is stuck at (hence 's-a') the logical value d, for fixed $d = 0, 1, \ldots$, or $n - 1$. For example, an s-a-0 fault is a fault where a single line is stuck at zero. This causes an error when the signal is supposed to take nonzero values. For $n = 2$, there are two kinds of s-a-d faults corresponding to $d = 0$ or $d = 1$—namely, s-a-0 faults or s-a-1 faults.

A *bridging fault* is a fault which occurs when two signal lines are shorted. The net effect of such a fault depends on the implementation—the short circuit may result in an AND of the two lines, an OR of the two lines, or even a feedback path that changes a combinational circuit into a noncombinational circuit which has memory delays.

In a PLA, a *crosspoint fault* is a fault caused within the AND array or OR array by an extra or a missing connecting device.

10.4 Built-in self-test, PLAs

Since the AND array and OR array of Type 2 PLAs are decisive, they may be tested exploiting known techniques for the testing of binary PLAs. In this section, such testing techniques are used for the Type 2 PLA of figure 10.6, where $n = 3$. The approach given in this section is general and holds for $n \geq 2$. The approach for $n = 2$ is described in Section 7.4 of Fujiwara (1985). See also Hong and Ostapko (1980). To test the decisive arrays of a Type 2

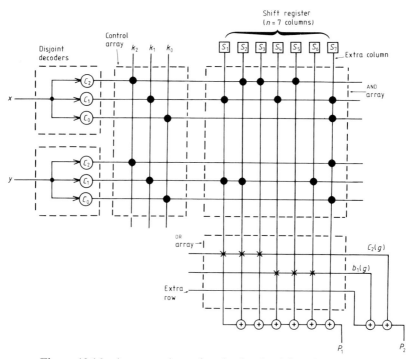

Figure 10.16 Augmented PLA for the 3-valued function $g(x, y)$ of figure 10.6.

PLA using disjoint decoding, the following equipment is built in: one extra binary parity column, one extra binary parity row, two cascades of $\oplus$ (binary arithmetic sum) gates, one binary shift register, and n extra control lines, k_0, $k_1, \ldots, k_{n-1}$ for fixed $n \geq 2$. The $n \times nm$ array between the input decoders and the AND array is called the control array. For given $n \geq 2$, this extra equipment is independent of the n-valued function which is realized by the PLA. The resulting structure is called an augmented PLA and is shown in figure 10.16, using the 3-valued function g having arguments $x_1 = x$, $x_2 = y$ in figure 10.6.

The shift register selects column t by setting $S_t = T$ and $S_r = F$ for all other values of r. One extra column is built in at the far right so that each row of the AND array has an odd number of connection devices. One extra row is built in at the bottom of the OR array so that each column in the OR array has an odd number of connection devices. Extra control lines $k_0, \ldots, k_{n-1}$ are built in so that each row of the AND array can be selected, as follows. The row $C_i(x_j)$ is selected by setting k_i equal to T and each other control line equal to F, while setting x_j equal to i and each other input unequal to i. The two $\oplus$ cascades at the bottom of figure 10.16 are used as parity checkers to detect any odd weight errors (that is, single binary error, triple binary error, etc).

Since the AND and OR arrays are decisive, the augmented PLA may be tested by an extension of the universal test set given in Table 7.1 of Fujiwara (1985). This extended test set does not depend on the logic functionality of the PLA—further, these are the only tests which have to be applied in order to detect all binary stuck-at faults and crosspoint faults in the remainder of the PLA.

10.5   Built-in self-test, combinational circuits

The addition of an LFSR to a combinational circuit for the purpose of stimulating and testing the circuit is ideal from the standpoint that an LFSR requires little additional logic. Besides the m n-stable devices of the shift register, the only additional logic is the logic required for the implementation of the linear input function to a_m. To illustrate for $n = 2$, it may be seen from the partial tabulation in Section 10.2, that the amount of this additional logic is low for each m in the ranges $2 \leq m < 8$ or $8 < m \leq 11$, but is somewhat higher for $m = 8$. Similar observations may be made for increasing values of n, m. For $n = 2$, $m \leq 300$; see Bardell *et al* (1987).

The example below treats a 2-valued combinational circuit with four inputs. An LFSR of four flip–flops is built in for the purpose of circuit stimulation. An LFSR of three flip–flops is built in for the purpose of data compaction and testing.

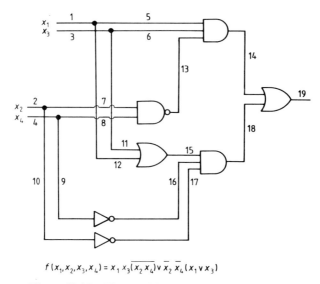

$$f(x_1,x_2,x_3,x_4) = x_1\,x_3\overline{(x_2\,x_4)}\vee \bar x_2\,\bar x_4\,(x_1\vee x_3)$$

Figure 10.17   The combinational circuit under test.

The combinational circuit under test is shown in figure 10.17. Key points within the circuit are numbered from 1 to 19. The inputs have the variable names x_1, x_2, x_3, x_4, and the output f is

$$f = x_1 x_3 \overline{(x_2 x_4)} \vee \bar x_2 \bar x_4 (x_1 \vee x_3).$$

A 16-row table for f is shown in figure 10.18.

x_1	x_2	x_3	x_4	f
0	0	0	0	0
0	0	0	1	0
0	0	1	0	1
0	0	1	1	0
0	1	0	0	0
0	1	0	1	0
0	1	1	0	0
0	1	1	1	0
1	0	0	0	1
1	0	0	1	0
1	0	1	0	1
1	0	1	1	1
1	1	0	0	0
1	1	0	1	0
1	1	1	0	1
1	1	1	1	0

Figure 10.18   Table for $f(x_1, x_2, x_3, x_4)$.

The 4 flip–flop LFSR *stimulator* is the one shown in figure 10.10, with corresponding primitive polynomial $1 + x + x^4$. This LFSR generates 15 test states as shown in figures 10.12 and 10.13. Assuming correct operation, the combinational circuit is stimulated by the four flip–flops of this LFSR as shown in figure 10.19. The resulting consecutive 15 values of f are injected into the 3 flip–flop LFSR shown in figure 10.20, through $Db_3 = b_1 \oplus b_2 \oplus f$. Initially $b_1 = b_2 = b_3 = 0$. This 3 flip–flop LFSR is called a *data compactor* (Serra 1987). The data is compacted or compressed into the digits b_1, b_2, b_3. The data compaction is shown in full in figure 10.21. The resulting 3-tuple sequence in this LFSR after 15 stimulations of the circuit, $b_1 = 0$, $b_2 = 1$, $b_3 = 1$, at the bottom of figure 10.21 is called the *signature* for the data compaction. An error is detected when the signature is incorrect.

Suppose, for example, that there is an s-a-1 fault in this combinational circuit at line 13. The 4 flip–flop LFSR stimulator generates consecutive values of f as shown at the left of figure 10.22. Consequently, the 3 flip–flop LFSR compactor takes consecutive 3-tuple values as shown at the right of figure 10.22. At the bottom line of figure 10.22 the 3-tuple 110 in the LFSR is unequal to the 3-tuple 011 at the bottom line of figure 10.21. Hence the error is detected.

There may be a fault in the circuit such that the resulting signature is

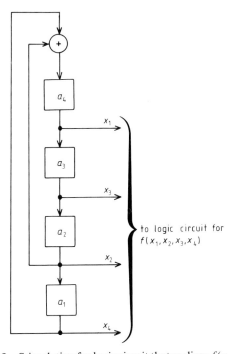

Figure 10.19 Stimulation for logic circuit that realizes $f(x_1, x_2, x_3, x_4)$.

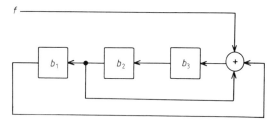

Figure 10.20   Data compaction.

a_1	a_2	a_3	a_4	f		b_1	b_2	b_3
1	0	0	0	0	→	0	0	0
0	0	0	1	1	→	0	0	1
0	0	1	0	1	→	0	1	1
0	1	0	0	0	→	1	1	1
1	0	0	1	0	→	1	1	0
0	0	1	1	1	→	1	0	1
0	1	1	0	0	→	0	1	1
1	1	0	1	0	→	1	1	1
1	0	1	0	0	→	1	1	0
0	1	0	1	0	→	1	0	0
1	0	1	1	1	→	0	0	0
0	1	1	1	1	→	0	0	1
1	1	1	1	0	→	0	1	0
1	1	1	0	0	→	1	0	1
1	1	0	0	0	→	0	1	1

Figure 10.21   Result of data compaction for circuit of figure 10.17.

nevertheless correct. This *aliasing* may be a consequence of the data compaction, and is discussed in Williams *et al* (1988).

It should be noted that an LFSR stimulator does not stimulate a random generation of m-digit test patterns because of its shifting nature. The consecutive 4-bit patterns of figure 10.12 are clearly correlated because of the shifting. Other kinds of registers, such as the cellular registers in Serra *et al* (1988) and Hortensius *et al* (1989), may be more suitable if random m-digit patterns are desired for stimulation of the m-input circuit under test. However, an LFSR stimulator which generates $n^m - 1$ states is appropriate for certain applications, such as the detection of stuck-at faults. Cellular or other registers may be appropriate for the partial generation of less than $n^m - 1$ states, for example if the number of circuit inputs is large, or when the faults cause memory or time delays within the circuit.

a_1	a_2	a_3	a_4	f with line 13 s-a-1		b_1	b_2	b_3
1	0	0	0	0	→	0	0	0
0	0	0	1	1	→	0	0	1
0	0	1	0	1	→	0	1	1
0	1	0	0	0	→	1	1	1
1	0	0	1	0	→	1	1	0
0	0	1	1	1	→	1	0	1
0	1	1	0	0	→	0	1	1
1	1	0	1	0	→	1	1	1
1	0	1	0	0	→	1	1	0
0	1	0	1	0	→	1	0	0
1	0	1	1	1	→	0	0	0
0	1	1	1	1	→	0	0	1
1	1	1	1	1	→	0	1	1
1	1	1	0	0	→	1	1	1
1	1	0	0	0	→	1	1	0

Figure 10.22 Result of data compaction with line 13 of circuit stuck-at-1.

While certain digital applications lend themselves to binary designs, LFSRS afford an example where n-valued designs for $n > 2$ may be preferable to 2-valued designs. Multiple-valued LFSRS may be built in as testers for binary or nonbinary circuits. It is shown in Serra (1987) that for various examples, taking into account hardware and aliasing, ternary LFSRS perform at least as well as binary LFSRS.

10.6 Overview

Of various applications for multiple-valued logic, the applications in this chapter use basic concepts introduced in this book. There are other applications—see, for example, optical computing applications in Arrathoon (1986).

There are other important applications, such as n-valued orthogonal functions and transforms. See, for example, work on block functions in Epstein and Loka (1985a,b) and work on Chrestenson functions in Moraga (1987). Seminal work for $n = 2$ can be found in Walsh (1923) and for $n \geq 2$ in Chrestenson (1955). Current applications of orthogonal functions and transforms include error detection and correction, analysis of digital systems, and pattern processing— see Hurst *et al* (1985) and Karpovsky (1985).

There has been considerable work on PLAS since their introduction in the

1970s. Among a number of references in the 1970s for the binary case is Fleisher and Maissel (1976). For the n-valued case, $n \geq 2$, Type 1 and Type 2 PLAs appear in Sasao (1986). Coding for the inputs or outputs of a PLA is discussed in Sasao (1988). Function minimization for PLA implementation is discussed in Tirumalai and Butler (1988). Substantial reductions in the size of PLAS can be made through appropriate coding and minimization.

The augmented PLA and corresponding universal test set for $n = 2$ are discussed in Fujiwara (1985) and Miller (1990).

The linear feedback shift sequences used in LFSRS are discussed in Golomb (1967). LFSRS are developed in Peterson and Weldon (1972). The multiple-valued LFSRS of this chapter are called Type 2 LFSRS in Serra and Muzio (1986). Both Type 1 and Type 2 LFSRS are studied in Peterson and Weldon (1972) and Serra and Muzio (1986).

Data compaction techniques and analysis are widely studied—see, for example, Smith (1980), Williams *et al* (1986), and Saxena (1987). Multiple-valued compactors are used in Serra (1987) to test multiple-valued logic circuits for $n \geq 2$.

Exercises

E10.1   Consider the following 3-valued function $q(x, y)$.

$$q(x, y) = e_1[C_1(x)C_1(y) \vee C_2(x)C_1(y) \vee C_1(x)C_2(y) \vee C_2(x)C_2(y)]$$
$$\vee\ C_0(x)C_0(y) \vee C_1(x)C_0(y) \vee C_0(x)C_1(y) \vee C_2(x)C_0(y).$$

For this function show (a) a Type 1 PLA and (b) a Type 2 PLA.

E10.2   Consider the Type 2 PLA for the 3-valued function $g(x, y)$ shown in figure 10.6. In this figure the decisive inputs $C_0(x)$, $C_1(x)$, $C_2(x)$ are disjoint, the decisive inputs $C_0(y)$, $C_1(y)$, $C_2(y)$ are disjoint, and the decisive outputs $b_1(g)$, $C_2(g)$ satisfy $g = e_1 b_1(g) \vee C_2(g)$. Give a Type 2 PLA for $g(x, y)$ which has the same decisive inputs, but has disjoint outputs $C_1(g)$, $C_2(g)$ with $g = e_1 C_1(g) \vee C_2(g)$.

E10.3   Consider the 4-valued positive function

$$h(x, y) = xy \vee D_2(x)D_3(y).$$

Show a Type 2 PLA for this function using monotonic decisive inputs $D_1(x)$, $D_2(x)$, $D_3(x)$; $D_1(y)$, $D_2(y)$, $D_3(y)$ and monotonic decisive outputs $D_1(h)$, $D_2(h)$, $D_3(h)$ with

$$h = e_1 D_1(h) \vee e_2 D_2(h) \vee D_3(h).$$

E10.4   Consider the LFSR $Da_5 = a_1 + a_3$ given for $n = 2$, $m = 5$ in Section 10.2. Starting with the state $a_1 = 1$, $a_2 = 0$, $a_3 = 0$, $a_4 = 0$, $a_5 = 0$, give the $2^5 - 1 = 31$ distinct states which ensue, before a return to the initial state.

E10.5 Show that the 5×5 binary matrix **M** corresponding to the LFSR given in **E10.4**

$$\mathbf{M} = \begin{bmatrix} 0 & 1 & 0 & 0 & 0 \\ 0 & 0 & 1 & 0 & 0 \\ 0 & 0 & 0 & 1 & 0 \\ 0 & 0 & 0 & 0 & 1 \\ 1 & 1 & 0 & 0 & 0 \end{bmatrix}$$

satisfies

$$\mathbf{M}^s \neq \begin{bmatrix} 1 & 0 & 0 & 0 & 0 \\ 0 & 1 & 0 & 0 & 0 \\ 0 & 0 & 1 & 0 & 0 \\ 0 & 0 & 0 & 1 & 0 \\ 0 & 0 & 0 & 0 & 1 \end{bmatrix} \quad \text{for } 1 \leq s < 31$$

and

$$\mathbf{M}^{31} = \begin{bmatrix} 1 & 0 & 0 & 0 & 0 \\ 0 & 1 & 0 & 0 & 0 \\ 0 & 0 & 1 & 0 & 0 \\ 0 & 0 & 0 & 1 & 0 \\ 0 & 0 & 0 & 0 & 1 \end{bmatrix}$$

E10.6 Consider the LFSR $Da_3 = (2a_1) + a_3$ given for $n = 3, m = 3$ in Section 10.2. Starting with the state $a_1 = 1$, $a_2 = 0$, $a_3 = 0$ give the $3^3 - 1 = 26$ distinct states which ensure, before a return to the initial state.

E10.7 (a) In **E10.4** modify the linear equation for Da_5 to a nonlinear equation such that the shift register generates a cycle of 32 distinct states. (b) In **E10.6** modify the linear equation for Da_3 to a nonlinear equation such that the shift register generates a cycle of 27 distinct states.

E10.8 Give the augmented PLA for the 3-valued function $q(x, y)$ of **E10.1**(b).

E10.9 Give a universal test set for augmented PLAS when $n = 3$ and apply this test set to the 3-valued function $q(x, y)$ of **E10.8**.

E10.10 In Section 10.5, the result of data compaction is shown for the binary combinational circuit of figure 10.17 with an s-a-1 fault at line 13. This uses the 4 flip–flop LFSR stimulator and the 3 flip–flop LFSR data compactor of figures 10.19 and 10.20. What would be the result of the data compaction if the fault at line 13 was an s-a-0 fault?

E10.11   In figure 10.17 suppose that there was no fault at line 13, but instead there was an s-a-1 fault at line 15. What would be the result of the data compaction in such an event?

E10.12   In figure 10.17 suppose that there was no fault at line 13, but instead there was an s-a-0 fault at line 15. What would be the result of the data compaction in such an event?

E10.13   With respect to the design and implementation of ternary LFSRs, state a possible advantage of using polynomials over the balanced ternary number instead of polynomials over the ternary number system.

Answers to the Even-numbered Exercises

Chapter 1

E1.2 (a) 15 tracks. (b) 9 tracks.

E1.4 The usual traffic light under normal operation consists of three *on–off* lights. If the top light is *on*, the other two lights are *off* and red shows at the top. If the middle light is *on*, the other 2 lights are *off* and yellow shows at the middle. If the bottom light is *on*, the other two lights are *off* and green shows at the bottom. Under normal traffic operation, the traffic light may be regarded as a binary-coded 3-valued device whose three values are red, yellow, and green,

Chapter 2

E2.2

X	$D_i N(X)$	$N(X)$	$D_{n-i}(X)$	$N(D_{n-1}(X))$
0	$n-1$	$n-1$	0	$n-1$
1	$n-1$	$n-2$	0	$n-1$
$\vdots$	$\vdots$	$\vdots$	$\vdots$	$\vdots$
$n-1-i$	$n-1$	i	0	$n-1$
$n-i$	0	$i-1$	$n-1$	0
$\vdots$	$\vdots$	$\vdots$	$\vdots$	$\vdots$
$n-2$	0	1	$n-1$	0
$n-1$	0	0	$n-1$	0

The column for $D_i N(X)$ at the left is identical with the column for $N(D_{n-1}(X))$ at the right.

E2.4

$X \& N(X)$	$N(X)$	X	Y	$N(Y)$	$Y \sqcup N(Y)$
0	$n-1$	0	0	$n-1$	$n-1$
1	$n-2$	1	1	$n-2$	$n-2$
2	$n-3$	2	2	$n-3$	$n-3$
$\vdots$	$\vdots$			$\vdots$	$\vdots$
2	2	$n-3$	$n-3$	2	$n-3$
1	1	$n-2$	$n-2$	1	$n-2$
0	0	$n-1$	$n-1$	0	$n-1$

When n is odd, each entry in the column for $X \& N(X)$ at the far left is $\leq (n-1)/2$ and each entry in the column for $Y \sqcup N(Y)$ at the far right is $\geq (n-1)/2$. When n is even, each entry in the column for $Y \sqcup N(Y)$ at the far right is $\geq n/2$ and each entry in the column for $X \& N(X)$ at the far left is $\leq ((n/2) - 1)$. Hence for any $n \geq 2$, $X \& N(X) \leq Y \sqcup N(Y)$.

E2.6

X	$E_1 \& C_{n-2}(X)$	$E_2 \& C_{n-3}(X)$	$\cdots$	$E_{n-2} \& C_1(X)$	$E_{n-1} \& C_0(X)$	$N(X)$
0	0	0		0	$n-1$	$n-1$
1	0	0		$n-2$	0	$n-2$
2	0	0		0	0	$n-3$
$\vdots$	$\vdots$	$\vdots$	$\cdots$	$\vdots$	$\vdots$	$\vdots$
$n-4$	0	0		0	0	3
$n-3$	0	2		0	0	2
$n-2$	1	0		0	0	1
$n-1$	0	0		0	0	0

X is shown in the column at the far left and $N(X)$ is shown in the column at the far right. It is clear that the disjunction of the remaining columns yields $N(X)$.

E2.8 $A \supset A$ by Theorem 2.4, substituting A for A_1
$(A \supset A) \supset (B \supset (A \supset A))$ by axiom (M2), substituting $A \supset A$ for A_1 and B for A_2 in axiom (M2)
$B \supset (A \supset A)$ by detachment.

E2.10   First, each of the n^2 entries in the table for $A_2 \supset A_1$ is $\geq$ each of the corresponding n^2 entries in the table for A_1, using two letters A_1, A_2. Thus $A_1 \supset (A_2 \supset A_1)$ is a tautology by Definition 2.5. Second, it can be shown that each of the n^3 entries for $A_1 \supset (A_2 \supset A_3)$ is $\leq$ each of the corresponding n^3 entries for $(A_1 \supset A_2) \supset (A_1 \supset A_3)$, using three letters A_1, A_2, A_3. Thus $(A_1 \supset (A_2 \supset A_3)) \supset ((A_1 \supset A_2) \supset (A_1 \supset A_3))$ is a tautology.

E2.12

	carries	-1	0	0
	augend	1	-1	-1
	addend	-1	-1	0
	sum	-1	1	-1

The leftmost nonzero digit of the sum is equal to -1, so the sum is negative.
The augend in decimal is $(1)(3^2) + (-1)(3^1) + (-1)(3^0) = 5$.
The addend in decimal is $(-1)(3^2) + (-1)(3^1) + (0)(3^0) = -12$.
The sum is $(-1)(3^2) + (1)(3^1) + (-1)(3^0) = -7$,

E2.14
(a) 21210,
(b) 101111.
(c) Each quaternary digit of the number corresponds with a binary pair given by the table below.

Quaternary	Binary pair
0	00
1	01
2	10
3	11

For example, using this table, quaternary 2301 is binary $(10)(11)(00)(01) = 10110001$. As a second example, binary 101111 may be written as $(10)(11)(11)$, which is quaternary 233 by this table. As a last example, given binary 110, to use the above table, pad with a 0 at the left: $110 = (01)(10)$, which is quaternary 12.

E2.16   From $(b - c) = q_1 n$ and $(d - e) = q_2 n$

$$(b - c) + (d - e) = q_1 n + q_2 n$$
$$(b + d) - (c + e) = (q_1 + q_2)n.$$

Hence

$$b + d \equiv c + e \,(\text{mod } n).$$

E2.18   From $ca \equiv cb \,(\text{mod } n)$

$$ca - cb = qn$$
$$c(a - b) = qn$$
$$c(a - b)/n = q.$$

Since n does not divide c, n must divide $(a - b)$ and $a \equiv b \,(\text{mod } n)$.

E2.20   Since $(-9) + (3) + (-5) + (1) + (-4) + 2 + (-2) + 3 = -11$ is a multiple of 11, $93\,514\,223$ is a multiple of 11 by **E2.19**.

Chapter 3

E3.2
(a)

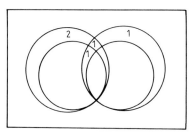

where X is at the left
and Y is at the right

(b) $E_1 C_1(Y) \sqcup C_1(X) C_0(Y)$.

E3.4

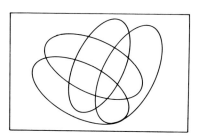

E3.6

	$C_0(Y)$	$C_1(Y)$	$C_2(Y)$
$C_0(X)$		$1^{\checkmark}$	
$C_1(X)$	2	$1^{\checkmark}$	
$C_2(X)$		$1^{\checkmark}$	

The first placement is that of the conjunctive-2-player with name $E_1 C_1(Y)$ shown on the K-map above. There are two different conjunctive-2-players which touch the remaining nonzero cell: $C_1(X)C_0(Y)$ and $C_1(X)N(Y)$. The first of these yields the answer of **E3.2**(b): $E_1 C_1(Y) \sqcup C_1(X) C_0(Y)$. The second of these yields a different answer: $E_1 C_1(Y) \sqcup C_1(X) N(Y)$. There are no redundant players in either of these answers.

E3.8

	$C_0(Y)$	$C_1(Y)$	$C_2(Y)$
$C_0(X)$	$1^\vee$	2	$1^\vee$
$C_1(X)$	2	2	2
$C_2(X)$	$1^\vee$	2	$1^\vee$

The conjunctive-1-player with name E_1 has the first placement, shown above. The two conjunctive-1-players $C_1(X)$, $C_1(Y)$ are placed next in either order. There are no redundant players, and the single answer is

$$E_1 \sqcup C_1(X) \sqcup C_1(Y).$$

E3.10 The conjunctive-2-player with name XY has the first placement, shown on the K-map below.

	$C_0(Y)$	$C_1(Y)$	$C_2(Y)$	$C_3(Y)$
$C_0(X)$	0	1	2	3
$C_1(X)$	1	$1^\vee$	$1^\vee$	$1^\vee$
$C_2(X)$	2	$1^\vee$	$2^\vee$	$2^\vee$
$C_3(X)$	3	$1^\vee$	$2^\vee$	$3^\vee$

The two conjunctive-2-players $XC_0(Y)$ and $C_0(X)Y$ are placed next in either order. There are no redundant players, and the single answer is

$$XY \sqcup XC_0(Y) \sqcup C_0(X)Y.$$

E3.12 No.

x, w do not have an lub
w, y do not have an lub
u, w do not have an lub.

E3.14

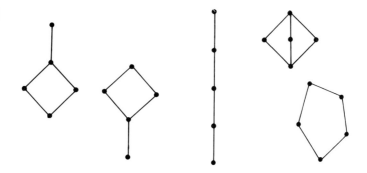

E3.16

$$x \wedge y \leq x \wedge (y \vee z)$$
$$x \wedge z \leq x \wedge (y \vee z)$$
$$(x \wedge y) \vee (x \wedge z) \leq x \wedge (y \vee z).$$

E3.18

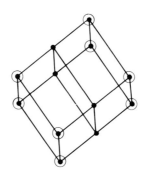

E3.20

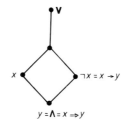

Chapter 4

E4.2 (a) To prove that $x \rightarrow y = \bar{x} \vee y$, first $x(\bar{x} \vee y) = x\bar{x} \vee xy = \Lambda \vee xy \leq y$ by distributivity, complementarity, and Λ-property; second, if $xw \leq y$, then $\bar{x} \vee xw \leq \bar{x} \vee y$. Since $\bar{x} \vee xw = (\bar{x} \vee x)(\bar{x} \vee w) = \bar{x} \vee w$ by distributivity, complementarity, and **V**-property, it follows that $w \leq \bar{x} \vee w \leq \bar{x} \vee y$.

Finally, $x \Rightarrow y = !(x \rightarrow y) = \bar{x} \vee y$, by Theorem 3.41(i).

(b) This follows from Theorem 3.28.

E4.4

(a) Since $D_j(x)$ is a complemented element,

$$C_{n-1}(D_j(x)) = D_j(x)$$

$$C_i(D_j(x)) = \mathbf{\Lambda} \qquad \text{for } 0 < i < n - 1$$

$$C_0(D_j(x)) = \overline{D_j(x)}$$

by Theorem 4.6.

(b) Since $C_i(x)$ is a complemented element, $D_j(C_i(x)) = C_i(x)$ by Theorem 4.6 and Definition 4.9.

E4.6

$$e_{n-2}x = \mathbf{\Lambda}$$

$$D_1(e_{n-2}x) = D_1(\mathbf{\Lambda})$$

$$D_1(e_{n-2})D_1(x) = D_1(\mathbf{\Lambda}) \qquad \text{by Theorem 4.20}$$

$$\mathbf{V} \wedge D_1(x) = \mathbf{\Lambda} \qquad \text{by Theorem 4.11}$$

$$D_1(x) = \mathbf{\Lambda} \qquad \text{by } \mathbf{V}\text{-property.}$$

Thus $x = \mathbf{\Lambda}$ by Theorem 4.13(i)–(ii).

E4.8

$$e_{i-1} \vee x = e_i$$

$$D_j(e_{i-1} \vee x) = D_j(e_i)$$

$$D_j(e_{i-1}) \vee D_j(x) = D_j(e_i) \qquad \text{by Theorem 4.14.}$$

For $j > i$ this becomes

$$\mathbf{\Lambda} \vee D_j(x) = \mathbf{\Lambda}$$

$$D_j(x) = \mathbf{\Lambda}$$

and for $j = i$ this becomes

$$\mathbf{\Lambda} \vee D_j(x) = \mathbf{V}$$

$$D_j(x) = \mathbf{V}$$

by Theorem 4.11 and $\mathbf{\Lambda}$-property. Hence $x = \bigvee_{j=1}^{i-1} e_j D_j(x) \vee e_i$ by Theorem 4.13(ii). Since $e_j D_j(x) \leq e_j \leq e_i$ for each j in the range $1 \leq j \leq i - 1$, $x = e_i$.

E4.10 $e_1 C_0(x) C_1(y) \vee C_0(x) C_0(y) \vee e_1 C_1(x) C_1(y) \vee C_1(x) C_2(y)$
$$\vee\; e_1 C_2(x) C_1(y) \vee C_2(x) C_0(y)$$

$$= C_0(x)[e_1 C_1(y) \vee C_0(y)]$$

$$\vee\; C_1(x)[e_1 C_1(y) \vee C_2(y)]$$

$$\vee\; C_2(x)[e_1 C_1(y) \vee C_0(y)]$$

$$= C_0(x) N(y) \vee C_1(x) y \vee C_2(x) N(y)$$

$$= [C_0(x) \vee C_2(x)] N(y) \vee C_1(x) y.$$

E4.12   Since $x \rightarrow y = (x \Rightarrow y) \vee y$ by Theorem 4.33

$$!(x \rightarrow y) = !((x \Rightarrow y) \vee y)$$

$$= !(x \Rightarrow y) \vee !y \quad \text{by Postulate } P4 \text{ (ii) and Corollary 4.30}$$

$$= (x \Rightarrow y) \vee !y \quad \text{by Theorem 3.41(i)}$$

$$= (x \Rightarrow y) \quad \text{by Theorem 3.52(iv).}$$

E4.14

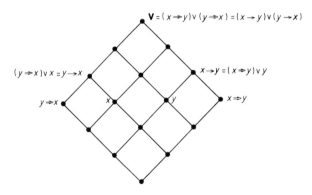

Chapter 5

E5.2   The answer is 2. One 24-element sub-Post algebra of order 6 is a direct product of 2 chains: a 6-element chain with a 4-element chain. The other 24-element sub-Post algebra of order 6 is a direct product of three chains: a 6-element chain with a 2-element chain with a 2-element chain.

E5.4 $x \wedge y = (0, 1, 0, 0, 0, 1, 2, 1, 3)$

$x \vee y = (1, 1, 0, 1, 2, 2, 2, 4, 4)$

$x \Rightarrow y = (1, 1, 1, 0, 0, 2, 2, 0, 4)$

$x \rightarrow y = (1, 1, 1, 0, 0, 2, 2, 1, 4).$

E5.6 $D_1(x) = (0, 1, 0, 1, 2, 2, 2, 4, 4)$

$D_2(x) = (0, 0, 0, 0, 2, 0, 2, 4, 4)$

$D_3(x) = (0, 0, 0, 0, 0, 0, 0, 4, 4)$

$D_4(x) = (0, 0, 0, 0, 0, 0, 0, 4, 0).$

E5.8

$$f_i = \bigvee_{k=1}^{n-1-i} e_k \overline{D_{n-1}(e_{k+i-1})} \qquad \text{for } 0 \le i < n-1$$

and

$$f_{n-1} = \wedge \qquad \text{by Theorem 5.17.}$$

Hence

$$f_i = \bigvee_{k=1}^{n-1-i} e_k \overline{\wedge}$$

for $0 \le i < n-1$ by Postulate $P5$(iii)

$$= \bigvee_{k=1}^{n-1-i} e_k \quad \text{for } 0 \le i < n-1$$

and

$$f_i = e_{n-1-i} \text{ for } 0 \le i \le n-1.$$

Next

$$N_0(x) = \bigvee_{j=1}^{n-1} \overline{D_j(x)} f_{j-1} \quad \text{by Theorem 5.17}$$

$$= \bigvee_{j=1}^{n-1} \overline{D_j(x)} e_{n-j}$$

$$= \bigvee_{i=1}^{n-1} \overline{D_{n-i}(x)} e_i = N(x) \quad \text{by Theorem 4.17.}$$

E5.10 $D_1(xy) = [\wedge C_0(x)C_0(y)][\wedge C_0(x)C_1(y)]$

$[\wedge C_0(x)C_2(y)][\wedge C_1(x)C_0y)]$

$[\vee C_1(x)C_1(y)][\vee C_1(x)C_2(y)]$

$[\wedge C_2(x)C_0(y)][\vee C_2(x)C_1(y)]$

$[\vee C_2(x)C_2(y)]$

$= C_1(x)C_1(y) \vee C_1(x)C_2(y)$

$\vee C_2(x)C_1(y) \vee C_2(x)C_2(y).$

E5.12

$$k_0(x) = \bigvee_{j=1}^{n-1} \overline{b_j(x)}$$

$$k_i(x) = b_i(x) \bigwedge_{j=i+1}^{n-1} \overline{b_j(x)} \quad \text{for } 0 < i < n-1$$

$$k_{n-1}(x) = b_{n-1}(x).$$

For the lines of proof, see Theorem 4.8(ii).

E5.14   First, any element x in A has a monotonic representation

$$x = \bigvee_{i=1}^{n-1} e_i d_i(x)$$

where $d_1(x) \geq d_2(x) \geq \cdots \geq d_{n-1}(x)$.

Let

$$y = \bigvee_{i=1}^{n-1} e_i c_i(x)$$

where $c_1(x) \geq c_2(x) \geq \cdots \geq c_{n-1}(x)$.

Second, an easy induction proof yields

$$y = \bigwedge_{i=1}^{n-1} (c_i(y) \vee e_{i-1}).$$

It can be proved that if c, d are complemented elements and $e \to f$ exists then $de \to (c \vee f)$ exists and is equal to

$$\bar{d} \vee c \vee (e \to f).$$

Thus $x \to y$ exists and is equal to

$$\bigwedge_{1 \leq i,j \leq n-1} [\bar{d}_i \vee e_j \vee (e_i \to e_j)]$$

for the proofs of Theorem 3.47(viii), (ix) apply.

E5.16

(a) It is given that $x_1 \leq x_2$, so

$$x_1(x_2 \twoheadrightarrow y) \leq x_2(x_2 \twoheadrightarrow y) \leq y.$$

Since $x_2 \twoheadrightarrow y$ is in the exocenter, $(x_2 \twoheadrightarrow y) \leq (x_1 \twoheadrightarrow y)$.

(b) First, $(w \rightarrow x)(w \rightarrow y)$ is in the exocenter because the exocenter is a sublattice. Second, $w(w \rightarrow x)(w \rightarrow y) = w(w \rightarrow x)w(w \rightarrow y) \leq xy$. Third, suppose that c is in the exocenter and c satisfies $wc \leq xy$. It follows that $wc \leq xy \leq x$ and $wc \leq xy \leq y$. Hence $c \leq (w \rightarrow x)$ and $c \leq (w \rightarrow y)$. Thus $c \leq (w \rightarrow x)(w \rightarrow y)$.

E5.18   First, $d_i(x) = (e_i \rightarrow x)$ and $d_{i+1}(x) = (e_{i+1} \rightarrow x)$. Since $e_i \leq e_{i+1}$, $d_{i+1}(x) \leq d_i(x)$ by **E5.16**(a).
　　Second, $d_i(xy) = d_i(x)d_i(y)$ by **E5.16**(b).

Chapter 6

E6.2   First

$$a \wedge (b \vee c) = a \otimes (b \oplus (b \otimes c) \oplus c)$$
$$= [a \otimes b] \oplus [a \otimes b \otimes c] \oplus [a \otimes c].$$

Second

$$(a \wedge b) \vee (a \wedge c) = [a \otimes b] \oplus [a^2 \otimes b \otimes c] \oplus [a \otimes c]$$
$$= [a \otimes b] \oplus [a \otimes b \otimes c] \oplus [a \otimes c].$$

E6.4 $a \oplus a = (a \wedge \bar{a}) \vee (\bar{a} \wedge a)$

$$= \wedge \vee \wedge$$
$$= \wedge.$$

E6.6   The even integers $\ldots, -6, -4, -2, 0, 2, 4, 6, \ldots$.

E6.8
(a) $q^{-1} = (1/30) - (1/15)i - (1/10)j - (2/15)k$
(b) If $q = q_0 + q_1 i + q_2 j + q_3 k$, then $q_0^2 + q_1^2 + q_2^2 + q_3^2 > 0$ and an easy computation shows that

$q^{-1} = (q_0/(q_0^2 + q_1^2 + q_2^2 + q_3^2))$
$\qquad - (q_1/(q_0^2 + q_1^2 + q_2^2 + q_3^2))i$
$\qquad - (q_2/(q_0^2 + q_1^2 + q_2^2 + q_3^2))j$
$\qquad - (q_3/(q_0^2 + q_1^2 + q_2^2 + q_3^2))k.$

(c) The quaternions $q = q_0 + q_1 i$ with $q_2 = q_3 = 0$ form a subsystem of the quaternions which is isomorphic with the field of complex numbers.

E6.10

a_i	b_i	BOR_i	DIF_i	BOR_{i+1}
0	0	0	0	0
0	0	1	1	1
0	1	0	1	1
0	1	1	0	1
1	0	0	1	0
1	0	1	0	0
1	1	0	0	0
1	1	1	1	1

E6.12

$$a \otimes e_1 = e_1 C_1(a) C_1(e_1) \vee e_1 C_2(a) C_2(e_1) \vee C_1(a) C_2(e_1)$$
$$\vee C_2(a) C_1(e_1)$$
$$= e_1 C_1(a) \vee \wedge \vee \wedge \vee C_2(a) \qquad \text{by Theorem 4.7}$$
$$= e_1 C_1(a) \vee C_2(a) \qquad \qquad \text{by } \wedge\text{-property}$$
$$= a \quad \text{by } P6 \text{ in subsection 4.1.2.}$$

There is a similar proof that $e_1 \otimes a = a$.

E6.14

$$a \vee a = a \oplus a \oplus (a^2 \otimes a) \oplus 2(a \otimes a) \oplus (a^2 \otimes a^2) \oplus (a \otimes a^2)$$
$$\text{by Theorem 6.19(ii)}$$
$$= a \oplus a \oplus a^3 \oplus 2a^2 \oplus a^4 \oplus a^3$$
$$= a \oplus a \oplus a \oplus 2a^2 \oplus a^2 \oplus a^3 = 0 \oplus 0 \oplus a = a \qquad \text{by Definition 6.17.}$$

E6.16   If the initial borrow BOR_0 is equal to 0, subsequent ternary borrows do not exceed 1. Hence entries for DIF_i and BOR_{i+1} at the nine rows in which $BOR_i = 2$ are don't-cares.

E6.18   If the initial carry c_0 is equal to 0, subsequent quaternary carries do not exceed 1. Hence entries for the sum S_i and carry c_{i+1} at the 32 rows in which $c_i = 2$ or $c_i = 3$ are don't-cares. However, if the initial carry c_0 is equal to 3, subsequent quaternary carries may exceed 1.

Chapter 7

E7.2   The pairs xy are shown in the ternary FSD below.

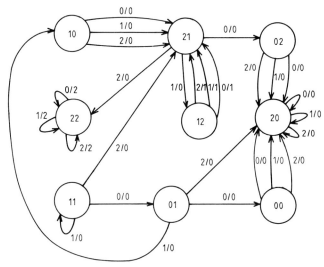

E7.4   The pairs xy are shown in the binary FSD below, for input z and output s. The corresponding finite state table is shown at the right.

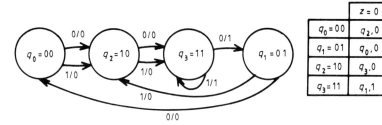

	$z = 0$	$z = 1$
$q_0 = 00$	$q_2, 0$	$q_2, 0$
$q_1 = 01$	$q_0, 0$	$q_2, 0$
$q_2 = 10$	$q_3, 0$	$q_3, 0$
$q_3 = 11$	$q_1, 1$	$q_1, 1$

E7.6

	$IN = 0$	$IN = 1$	$IN = 2$	$IN = 3$
q_0	$q_0, 3$	$q_1, 0$	$q_2, 1$	$q_0, 0$
q_1	$q_0, 0$	$q_1, 2$	$q_1, 1$	$q_2, 2$
q_2	$q_0, 3$	$q_2, 1$	$q_2, 3$	$q_2, 2$

E7.8

	$IN = 0$	$IN = 1$	$IN = 2$
q_0	$q_1, 0$	$q_3, 2$	$q_1, 0$
q_1	$q_2, 0$	$q_3, 2$	$q_2, 0$
q_2	$q_0, 0$	$q_3, 2$	$q_0, 0$
q_3	$q_4, 0$	$q_5, 2$	$q_4, 0$
q_4	$q_3, 0$	$q_6, 2$	$q_3, 0$
q_5	$q_5, 0$	$q_5, 0$	$q_5, 0$
q_6	$q_6, 0$	$q_6, 0$	$q_6, 0$

Step 1.

a		b				
q_5	q_6	q_0	q_1	q_2	q_3	q_4
a a a	**a a a**	**b b b**	**b b b**	**b b b**	**b a b**	**b a b**

Step 2.

a		b			c	
q_5	q_6	q_0	q_1	q_2	q_3	q_4
a a a	**a a a**	**b c b**	**b b b**	**b c b**	**c a c**	**c a c**

Step 3.

a		b		c		d
q_5	q_6	q_0	q_2	q_3	q_4	q_1
a a a	**a a a**	**d c d**	**b c b**	**c a c**	**c a c**	**b d b**

Step 4.

a		b	c		d	e
q_5	q_6	q_0	q_3	q_4	q_1	q_2
a a a	**a a a**	**d c d**	**c a c**	**c a c**	**e d e**	**b c b**

The minimum number of states is 5. In the FSD below, class **a** corresponds with state E, class **b** corresponds with state A, class **c** corresponds with state K, class **d** corresponds with state B, and class **e** corresponds with state J.

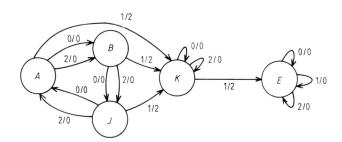

E7.10

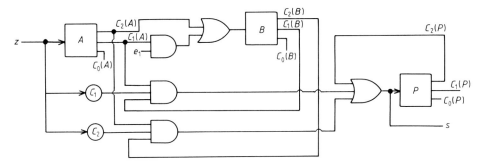

Initial conditions
$A = B = P = 0$

with

$$DA = z$$

$$DB = e_1 C_1(A) \vee C_2(A)$$
$$= A$$

$$DP = C_2(P) \vee s_0$$

where

$$s_0 = C_1(z)C_1(A)C_1(B) \vee C_2(z)C_2(A)C_2(B)$$

$$s = C_2(P) \vee s_0.$$

E7.12 $Dx = N(z)$

$$s = C_1(x)C_2(z) \vee C_0(x)C_1(z) \vee C_0(x)C_2(z).$$

The logic equation for s has the same cost as the logic equation for s in (37). The logic equation for Dx here requires one unary operation N, where the logic equation for Dx in (36) is simply $Dx = z$.

E7.14 The other four solutions are given below.

(1) $Dx = e_1 C_2(z) \vee C_0(z)$

$$s = C_2(z)C_0(x) \vee C_1(z)C_1(x) \vee C_2(z)C_1(x)$$

(2) $Dx = e_1 C_2(z) \vee C_1(z)$

$$s = C_2(z)C_2(x) \vee C_1(z)C_1(x) \vee C_2(z)C_1(x)$$

(3) $Dx = e_1 C_0(z) \vee C_1(z)$

   $= z \oplus e_1$

   $s = C_2(z)C_2(x) \vee C_1(z)C_0(x) \vee C_2(z)C_0(x)$

(4) $Dx = e_1 C_0(z) \vee C_2(z)$

   $s = C_2(z)C_0(x) \vee C_1(z)C_2(x) \vee C_2(z)C_2(x).$

While the four logic equations for s above have the same cost as the equations for s in (37) and in **E7.12**, the logic equations for Dx above have a higher cost than the cost of the equations for Dx in (36) or the equation for Dx in **E7.12**.

Chapter 8

E8.2

$(A \supset A) \supset (((A \& B) \supset A) \supset ((A \vee (A \& B)) \supset A))$ by Ax 10, substituting A for A_1, $A \& B$ for A_2, A for A_3
$A \supset A$ by Theorem 2.4, substituting A for A_1
$((A \& B) \supset A) \supset ((A \supset (A \& B)) \supset A))$ by detachment
$(A \& B) \supset A$ by Ax 5, substituting A for A_1, B for A_2
$(A \vee (A \& B)) \supset A$ by detachment.

E8.4

$((C \supset (A \supset B)) \supset ((C \supset A) \supset (C \supset B)))$

$\supset ((A \supset B) \supset ((C \supset (A \supset B))$

$\supset ((C \supset A) \supset (C \supset B))))$ by Ax 3

$(C \supset (A \supset B)) \supset ((C \supset A) \supset (C \supset B))$ by Ax 2

$(A \supset B) \supset ((C \supset (A \supset B)) \supset ((C \supset A) \supset (C \supset B)))$

by detachment

$(A \supset B) \supset ((C \supset (A \supset B)) \supset ((C \supset A) \supset (C \supset B)))$

$\supset (((A \supset B) \supset (C \supset (A \supset B))) \supset ((A \supset B)$

$\supset ((C \supset A) \supset (C \supset B))))$ by Ax 2

$((A \supset B) \supset (C \supset (A \supset B))) \supset ((A \supset B) \supset ((C \supset A) \supset (C \supset B)))$

by detachment

$(A \supset B) \supset (C \supset (A \supset B))$ by Ax 3

$((A \supset B) \supset ((C \supset A) \supset (C \supset B)))$ by detachment.

E8.6 This additional axiom is a rule of excluded middle. The resulting propositional calculus is the 2-valued propositional calculus.

E8.8

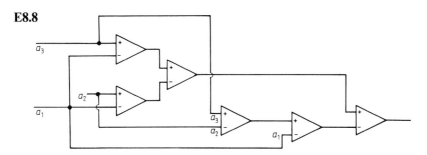

E8.10

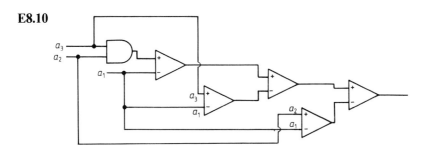

E8.12 Since $i > j$ and $e_0 \leq e_j$ for $j \geq 0$

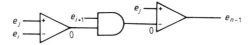

Chapter 9

E9.2 For $n = 4$, $m = 2$

$$C_1(xy) = f_{0200} \vee f_{0110} \vee f_{0101}.$$

E9.4 For $n = 3$, $m = 3$

$$g = e_1 C_1(g) \vee C_2(g)$$
$$= e_1(f_{210} \vee f_{012}) \vee (f_{201} \vee f_{111} \vee f_{102}).$$

E9.6 For $n = 6$, $m = 8$, Theorem 9.4 and its proof yields

$$f_{320102} = C_0(\tau_8)C_0(\tau_6) \vee C_1(\tau_5)C_1(\tau_4) \vee C_3(\tau_3)C_3(\tau_3) \vee C_5(\tau_2)C_5(\tau_1)$$
$$= C_0(\tau_6) \vee C_1(\tau_5)C_1(\tau_4) \vee C_3(\tau_3) \vee C_5(\tau_2).$$

E9.8 This follows from the second half of the proof for Theorem 9.6, using $m = 2$, $x_1 = x$, $x_2 = y$, $i_1 = j$, $i_2 = k$. Note that $1 \le j$, $k \le 2$ corresponds to the term $e_i D_j(x) D_k(y)$; $j = 0$ corresponds to the term $e_i D_k(y)$; $k = 0$ corresponds to the term $e_i D_j(x)$; and $j = k = 0$ corresponds to the term e_i.

E9.10 Replace each (i, j) with $(3 - i, 3 - j)$, yielding

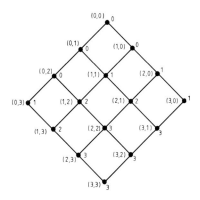

then redraw the above as the positive function below.

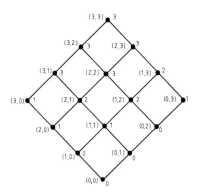

This positive function has the expression

$$e_1 C_2(x) \vee e_1 C_1(x) C_1(y) \vee e_1 C_3(y) \vee e_2 C_2(x) C_1(y) \vee e_2 C_1(x) C_2(y)$$
$$\vee\ C_3(x) C_1(y) \vee C_2(x) C_2(y) \qquad \text{by Theorem 9.6.}$$

Thus

$$F(x, y) = e_1 C_2(N(x)) \vee e_1 C_1(N(x)) C_1(N(y)) \vee e_1 C_3(N(y))$$
$$\vee\ e_2 C_2(N(x)) C_1(N(y)) \vee e_2 C_1(N(x)) C_2(N(y))$$
$$\vee\ C_3(N(x)) C_1(N(y)) \vee C_2(N(x)) C_2(N(y)) \qquad \text{by Definition 9.9.}$$

E9.12 There are six 2-valued symmetric functions using exactly three variables w, x, y which are positive functions or negative functions:

$$w \vee x \vee y, \; wx \vee wy \vee xy, \; wxy, \; \bar{w} \vee \bar{x} \vee \bar{y}, \; \bar{w}\bar{x} \vee \bar{w}\bar{y} \vee \bar{x}\bar{y}, \; \bar{w}\bar{x}\bar{y}.$$

E9.14
(1) $x\bar{y} \vee \bar{x}y$
(2) $xy \vee \bar{x}\bar{y}$.

E9.16 $W_1 = W_2 = 1$, $T_1 = 0.3$, $T_2 = 0.7$
using Definition 9.15(a).

E9.18 $x_1 N(x_2) \vee x_3 N(x_4)$.

Chapter 10

E10.2   Since

$$C_2(g) = C_1(x)C_1(y) \vee C_2(x)C_1(y) \vee C_2(y)$$

and

$$C_1(g) = C_0(x)C_1(y) \vee C_1(x)C_0(y) \vee C_2(x)C_0(y)$$

a Type 2 PLA for g is

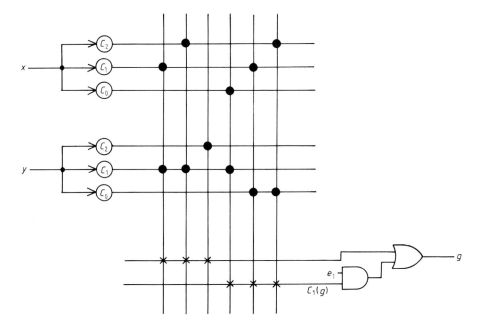

E10.4

a_1	a_2	a_3	a_4	a_5
1	0	0	0	0
0	0	0	0	1
0	0	0	1	0
0	0	1	0	0
0	1	0	0	1
1	0	0	1	0
0	0	1	0	1
0	1	0	1	1
1	0	1	1	0
0	1	1	0	0
1	1	0	0	1
1	0	0	1	1
0	0	1	1	1
0	1	1	1	1
1	1	1	1	1
1	1	1	1	0
1	1	1	0	0
1	1	0	0	0
1	0	0	0	1
0	0	0	1	1
0	0	1	1	0
0	1	1	0	1
1	1	0	1	1
1	0	1	1	1
0	1	1	1	0
1	1	1	0	1
1	1	0	1	0
1	0	1	0	1
0	1	0	1	0
1	0	1	0	0
0	1	0	0	0
1	0	0	0	0

E10.6

a_1	a_2	a_3
1	0	0
0	0	2
0	2	2
2	2	2
2	2	0
2	0	1
0	1	2
1	2	2

(*continued on next page*)

E10.6

a_1	a_2	a_3
2	2	1
2	1	2
1	2	0
2	0	2
0	2	0
2	0	0
0	0	1
0	1	1
1	1	1
1	1	0
1	0	2
0	2	1
2	1	1
1	1	2
1	2	1
2	1	0
1	0	1
0	1	0
1	0	0

E10.8

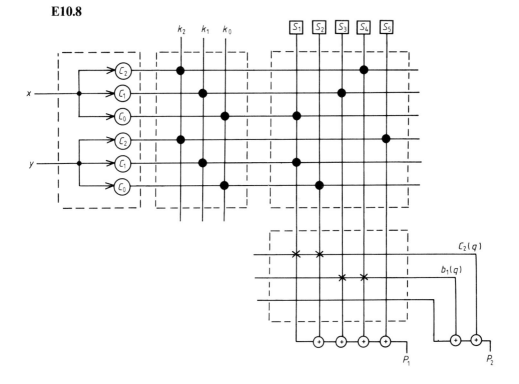

The simplifications used above for $C_2(q)$ and $b_1(q)$ may be obtained algebraically through the following

$$C_2(q) = C_0(x)C_0(y) \vee C_1(x)C_0(y) \vee C_2(x)C_0(y) \vee C_0(x)C_1(y)$$

$$= (C_0(x) \vee C_1(x) \vee C_2(x))C_0(y) \vee C_0(x)C_1(y) = C_0(y) \vee C_0(x)C_1(y)$$

$$C_1(q) = [C_1(x)C_1(y) \vee C_2(x)C_1(y) \vee C_1(x)C_2(y) \vee C_2(x)C_2(y)]$$

$$\vee (C_1(x)C_0(y) \vee C_2(x)C_0(y))$$

$$= C_1(x)[C_0(y) \vee C_1(y) \vee C_2(y)] \vee C_2(x)[C_0(y) \vee C_1(y) \vee C_2(y)]$$

$$= C_1(x) \vee C_2(x).$$

E10.10   The result is given below.

a_1	a_2	a_3	a_4	f with line 13 s-a-0		b_1	b_2	b_3
1	0	0	0	0	→	0	0	0
0	0	0	1	1	→	0	0	1
0	0	1	0	1	→	0	1	1
0	1	0	0	0	→	1	1	1
1	0	0	1	0	→	1	1	0
0	0	1	1	1	→	1	0	1
0	1	1	0	0	→	0	1	1
1	1	0	1	0	→	1	1	1
1	0	1	0	0	→	1	1	0
0	1	0	1	0	→	1	0	0
1	0	1	1	0	→	0	0	1
0	1	1	1	0	→	0	1	0
1	1	1	1	0	→	1	0	1
1	1	1	0	0	→	0	1	1
1	1	0	0	0	→	(1	1	1)

At the bottom line the circled 3-tuple 111 is unequal to the bottom line of figure 10.21. Hence an s-a-0 fault at line 13 is detected.

E10.12   The result is given below.

a_1	a_2	a_3	a_4	f with line 15 s-a-0		b_1	b_2	b_3
1	0	0	0	0	→	0	0	0
0	0	0	1	0	→	0	0	0
0	0	1	0	0	→	0	0	0
0	1	0	0	0	→	0	0	0
1	0	0	1	0	→	0	0	0
0	0	1	1	1	→	0	0	1
0	1	1	0	0	→	0	1	0
1	1	0	1	0	→	1	0	1
1	0	1	0	0	→	0	1	1
0	1	0	1	0	→	1	1	1
1	0	1	1	1	→	1	1	1
0	1	1	1	1	→	1	1	1
1	1	1	1	0	→	1	1	0
1	1	1	0	0	→	1	0	0
1	1	0	0	0	→	(0	0	1)

At the bottom line the circled 3-tuple is unequal to the 3-tuple at the bottom line of figure 10.21. Hence an s-a-0 fault at line 15 is detected.

References

Due to the frequency of its citation in the references given below, the Proceedings of the International Symposium on Multiple-valued Logic is abbreviated to *ISMVL*.

Again J 1960 SETUN' *Naucho-Tekh Obshchestva SSSR* **2**(3) (Mar. 1960) 25

Aibara T and Akagi M 1970 Generation of ternary threshold functions of up to 3 variables *Syst. Comput. Controls 1* **5** 4–12

Allen C M and Givone D D 1977 The Allen–Givone implementation oriented algebra *Computer science and multiple-valued logic* ed D C Rine (Amsterdam: North-Holland) 262–82

Anderson A R and Belnap Jr N D 1975 *Entailment, the logic of relevance and necessity* vol 1 (Princeton, NJ: Princeton University Press)

Anderson F W and Blair R L 1961 Representations of distributive lattices as lattices of functions *Math. Ann.* **143** 187–211

Andrew R 1986 An algorithm for eight-valued simulation and hazard detection in gate networks *ISMVL* **16** 273–80

Arrathoon R 1986 Optical multiple-valued logic and multiple-class discrimination, *ISMVL* **16** 146–7

Arrathoon R and Kozaitis S 1986 Shadow-casting for multiple-valued associative logic *Opt. Engng* **25** 29–37

Bahraini M and Epstein G 1987 Simplified disjunctive forms for 3-valued functions of one variable *Bull. Multiple-valued Logic* IEEE Comput. Soc. **8**(2) 8–9

—— 1988 Three-valued Karnaugh maps *ISMVL* **18** 178–85

Balbes R and Dwinger P 1974 *Distributive lattices* (Columbia, MO: Missouri University Press)

Bardell P H, McAnney W H and Savir J 1987 *Built-in test for VLSI: pseudorandom techniques* (New York: Wiley)

Bartee T C 1981 *Digital computer fundamentals* 5th edn (New York: McGraw-Hill)

Bechtel R 1976 On a constructive method for generating Venn diagrams for *n* variables *Proc. 2nd Bienn. Conf. Computing* (Indiana) 5–10

Birkhoff G 1934 Applications of lattice algebras *Proc. Cambridge Phil. Soc.* **30** 115–22

Birkhoff G and MacLane S 1965 *A survey of modern algebra* 3rd edn (New York: Macmillan)

Bochvar D A 1939 Ob odnom tréhznačnom iscislénii iégo priménénii k analizu paradoksov klassičéskogo rasširénnogo funkcional'nogo iscislénia, *Matématičéskij sbornik* **4** 287–308

Boole G 1847 *The mathematical analysis of logic. Being an essay towards a calculus of deductive reasoning* (Cambridge, England: Macmillan, Barclay and Macmillan) and (London: George Bell)

Bowen W 1986 The exocenter of a double Heyting algebra *Coll. Math.* **50** 173–85

Breuer M A and Epstein G 1973 The smallest many-valued logic for treatment of complemented and uncomplemented error signals *Conf. Record of Int. Symp. on Multiple-valued Logic* (1973) 29–37

Brouwer L E J 1908 De onbetrouwbaarheid der logische principes *Tijdschrift voor wijsbegeerte* **2** 152–8

Brusentsov N P 1960 The computer "SETUN" of Moscow State University *Conf. New Developments in Computational Mathematics and Computing Techniques* (Kiev) 226–34

Butler J T 1986 Efficient tests for diagnosability in three-valued models of local area networks embedded in a wide area network *ISMVL* **16** 100–3

—— (ed) 1991 *Multiple-valued logic in VLSI* (California: IEEE Computer Society)

Butler J T and Schueller K A 1991 Worst case number of terms in symmetric multiple-valued functions *ISMVL* **21** 94–101

Byrne L 1946 Two brief formulations of Boolean algebra *Bull. Amer. Math. Soc.* **52** 269–72

Caldwell S H 1958 *Switching circuits and logical design* (New York: Wiley)

Cat Ho Ng and Rasiowa H 1987 Semi-Post algebras *Studia Logica* **46**(2) 147–58

—— 1989 Plain semi-Post algebras of a poset-based generalization of Post algebra and their representability *Studia Logica* **48**(4) 509–30

Chang C C and Horn A 1961 Prime ideal characterization of generalized Post algebras *Proc. Symp. Pure Math.* Amer. Math. Soc. **2** 43–8

Chiang K W and Vranesic Z G 1982 Fault detection in ternary NMOS and CMOS circuits *ISMVL* **12** 129–38

Chrestenson H E 1955 A class of generalized Walsh functions *Pacific J. Math.* **5** 17–31

Church R 1935 Tables of irreducible polynomials for the first four prime moduli *Ann. Math.* **36**(1) 198–209

—— 1940 Enumeration by rank of the elements of the free distributive lattice with seven generators *Abstract 65T-447* Not. Amer. Math. Soc. **12** 724

—— 1965 Numerical analysis of certain free distributive structures *Duke Math J.* **6** 732–4

Dedekind R 1897 Über Zerlegungen von Zahlen durch ihre grössten gemeinsamen Teiler *Festschr. Tech. Hoch. Braunschweig* **II** 103–48

Diawuo K and Mouftah H T 1987 A three-valued CMOS arithmetic logic unit chip *ISMVL* **17** 215–20

Dueck G W and Miller D M 1990 RCM-MVL: a recursive concensus MVL minimization algorithm *ISMVL* **20** 136–43

Dunn J M and Epstein G (eds) 1977 *Modern uses of multiple-valued logic* episteme 2 (Dordrecht, Holland: Reidel)

Dwinger P 1968 Generalized Post algebras *Bull. Ac. Pol. Sci., Ser. Sci., Math., Astron. Phys.* **16** 559–63

Ehrenfest P 1910 Review of the Russian translation of L Couturat's 'L'algèbre de la logique' *Zh. Russ. Fiz-himices. Obsc.* section of *Physics* **42** Pt 2 382–7

Eichelberger E 1965 Hazard detection in combinatorial and sequential circuits *IBM J. Res. Dev.* **9** 90–9

Engineering Research Associates 1950 *High-speed computing devices* (New York: McGraw-Hill)

Epstein G 1958 Synthesis of electronic circuits for symmetric functions *IRE Trans. Elec. Comput.* **EC7**(1) 57–60

—— 1960 The lattice theory of Post algebras *Trans. Amer. Math. Soc.* **95** 300–17

—— 1973 An equational axiomatization for the disjoint system of Post algebras *IEEE Trans. Comput.* **C-22** 422–3

—— 1976 Decisive Venn diagrams *ISMVL* **6** 142–9

Epstein G, Feaster D and Rajamani S 1985 Enumeration of monotone increasing functions on some hypercubes of small order *Bull. Multiple-valued Logic* IEEE Comput. Soc. **6**(3) 18–19

Epstein G, Frieder G and Rine D C 1974 The development of multiple-valued logic as related to computer science *Computer* (Sept.) 20–32

Epstein G and Horn A 1974a *P*-algebras, an abstraction from Post algebras *Algebra Universalis* **4** 195–206

—— 1974b Chain-based lattices *Pacific J. Math.* **55** 65–84

—— 1976 Logics which are characterized by subresiduated lattices *Z. Math. Logik und Grundlagen D Math.* **22** 199–210

—— 1983 Core points in double Heyting algebras and dissectable lattices *Algebra Universalis* **16** 204–18

Epstein G, Lee J and Mandayam P O 1984 Some observations on *n*-valued disjointly separable functions *ISMVL* **14** 44–7

Epstein G and Liu Y W 1982 Positive multiple-valued switching functions—an extension of Dedekind's problem *ISMVL* **12** 248–52

Epstein G and Loka R R 1985a Block functions—a new class of sequency preserving *n*-valued orthogonal functions *ISMVL* **15** 38–44

—— 1985b Extensions of block functions *ISMVL* **15** 264–71

Epstein G, Miller D M and Muzio J C 1977 Some preliminary views on the general synthesis of electronic circuits for symmetric and partially symmetric functions *ISMVL* **7** 29–34

—— 1980 Selecting don't-care sets for symmetric many-valued functions: a pictorial approach using matrices *ISMVL* **10** 219–25

Epstein G and Mukaidono M 1987 Some properties of Kleene–Stone algebras *ISMVL* **17** 5–7

Epstein G and Rasiowa H 1990 Theory and uses of Post algebras of order $\omega + \omega^*$. Part I *ISMVL* **20** 42–7

—— 1991 Theory and uses of Post algebras of order $\omega + \omega^*$. Part II *ISMVL* **21** 248–54

Fleisher H and Maissel L I 1976 An introduction to array logic *IBM J. Res. Dev.* **19**(2) 98–109

Frege F L G 1879 *Begriffsschrift, eine der arithmetischen nachgebildete Formalsprache des reinen Denkens* (Halle: Nebert)

Frieder G, Fong A and Chao C Y 1973 A balanced ternary computer *Conf. Record of Int. Symp. on Multiple-valued Logic* (1973) 68–88

Fujiwara H 1985 *Logic testing and design for testability* (Cambridge, MA: MIT Press)

Golomb S W 1967 *Shift register sequences* (San Francisco, CA: Holden-Day)

Goto S 1985 The fifth generation computer systems and logic programming *ISMVL* **15** 2–7

Grätzer G 1971 *Lattice theory, first concepts and distributive lattices* (San Francisco, CA: Freeman)

Green D 1986 *Modern logic design* (*Electronic Systems Engineering Series*) (London: Addison-Wesley)

Grosch H J R 1952 Signed ternary arithmetic *Digital Computer Lab. Memo M-1496 at MIT* Cambridge, MA

Gulliver T A, Serra M and Bhargava V K 1988 Primitive polynomials with independent roots and their applications *Can. Conf. Electrical and Computer Engng* 818–22

Haberlin H and Muller H 1970 Arithmetische operationen mit binar codierten ternarzahlen *Mitteilungen AGEN* **11** 55–8

Hacking I 1963 What is strict implication? *J. Symbolic Logic* **28** 51–71

Halmos P R 1963 *Lecture on Boolean algebras, Mathematical Studies No 1* (Princeton, NJ: Van Nostrand)

Halpern I and Yoeli M 1968 Ternary arithmetic unit *Proc. IEEE* **115**(10) 1385

Hamacher H C and Vranesic Z G 1971 Multivalued versus binary high-speed multipliers *Conf. Record Symp. Multiple-valued Logic Design* (1971) 42–53

Hanson W H 1963 Ternary threshold logic *IEEE Trans. Elec. Comput.* **EC-12**(6) 191–7

Harrison M A 1965 *Introduction to switching and automata theory* (New York: McGraw-Hill)

Herstein I N 1975 *Topics in algebra* 2nd edn (New York: Wiley)

Hilbert D and Ackermann W 1959 *Grundzüge der Theoretischen Logik* 4th edn (Berlin: Springer)

Hill F J and Peterson G R 1981 *Introduction to switching theory and logical design* 3rd edn (New York: Wiley)

Hławiczka A and Badura D 1982 The method of recognition of critical hazards, critical races, essential hazards and D-trio *ISMVL* **12** 298–312

Hohn F E 1966 *Applied Boolean algebra; an elementary introduction* 2nd edn (New York: Macmillan)

Hong S J and Ostapko D L 1980 FITPLA: a programmable logic array for function independent testing *Proc. 10th Int. Symp. Fault-Tolerant Computing* 131–6

Hopcroft J E 1971 An n log n algorithm for minimizing states in a finite automaton, in *Theory of machines and computations* ed Z Kohavi and A Paz (New York: Academic) 189–96

Horn A 1962 The separation theorem of intuitionist propositional calculus *J. Symbolic Logic* **27** 391–99

Hortensius P D, Mcleod R D, Pries W, Miller D M and Card H C 1989 Cellular automata-based pseudorandom generators for built-in self-test *IEEE Trans. Computer-Aided Design* **8**(8) 842–59

Hsu L S, Teh H H, Chan S C and Loe K F 1990 Multi-valued neural logic networks *ISMVL* **20** 426–32

Huang K and Chen T 1985 Three-valued system diagnosis *ISMVL* **15** 356–60

Huffman D A 1954 The synthesis of sequential switching circuits *J. Franklin Inst.* **257** 161–90, 275–303

Hughes G E and Cresswell M J 1968 *An introduction to modal logic* (London: Methuen)

Huntington E V 1904 Sets of independent postulates for the algebra of logic *Trans. Amer. Math. Soc.* **5** 288–309

Huntsberger T L, Rangarajan C and Jayaramamurthy S N 1986 Representation of uncertainty in computer vision using fuzzy sets *IEEE Trans. Comput.* **C-35**(2), 145–56.

Hurst S L 1980 Fiber-optics, a multiple-valued interconnection means? *ISMVL* **10** 115–19

—— 1984 Multiple-valued logic: its status and its future *IEEE Trans. Comput.* **C-33**(12) 1160–79

—— 1986 A survey: developments in optoelectronics and its applicability to multiple-valued logic *ISMVL* **16** 179–88

Hurst S L, Miller D M and Muzio J C 1985 *Spectral techniques in digital logic* (London and New York: Academic)

Kabat W C and Wojcik A S 1981 On the design of 4-valued digital systems *IEEE Trans. Comput.* **C-30**(9) 666–71

Kameyama M and Higuchi T 1988 Prospects of multiple-valued bio-information processing systems *ISMVL* **18** 237–42

Kaplansky I 1947 Lattices of continuous functions *Bull. Amer. Math. Soc.* **53** 617–22

Karnaugh M 1953 The map method for synthesis of combinational logic circuits *Trans. AIEE* **72** Pt 1 593–8

Karpovsky M G (ed) 1985 Spectral techniques and fault detection *Notes and reports in Computer Science and Applied Mathematics* (Orlando, FL: Academic)

Katriňák T and Mitschke A 1972 Stonesche verbände der ordnung *n* und Postalgebren *Math. Ann.* **199** 13–30

Katter Jr O E and Razavi H M 1990 A new CMOS gate—the balanced gate—for detecting physical failures *ISMVL* **20** 25–31

Kawahito S, Kameyama M and Higuchi T 1986 VLSI-oriented bidirectional current-mode arithmetic circuits based on the radix-4 signed-digit number system *ISMVL* **16** 70–7

Kleene S C 1952 *Introduction to metamathematics* (Princeton, NJ: Van Nostrand)

—— 1956 Representation of events in nerve nets and finite automata *Automata Studies* Princeton, NJ 3–41

Knudsen M S 1982 A nine-valued logic simulator for digital N-MOS circuits *ISMVL* **12** 293–7

Knuth D E 1969 *Seminumerical algorithms* (*The art of computer programming vol 2*) (Reading, MA: Addison-Wesley)

Lalanne L L C 1840 *Comptes Rendus II* (Paris) 903–5

Leonetti R A and Butler J T 1985 A characterization of diagnosability in systems with four-valued test results *ISMVL* **15** 52–6

Lewin D 1974 *Logical design of switching circuits* 2nd edn (New York: Elsevier)

Lewis C I 1918 *A survey of symbolic logic* (Berkeley, CA: University of California)

Liebler M E and Roesser R P 1971 Multiple-real-valued Walsh functions *Conf. Record 1971 Symp. on the Theory and Applications of Multiple-valued Logic Design* 84–102

Ling H 1981 High-speed binary adder *IBM J. Res. Dev.* **25** 156–66

Łukasiewicz J 1920 O logice trójwartościowej *Ruch Filozoficzny* **5** 169–71

Maly W 1987 *Atlas of IC technologies: an introduction to VLSI processes* (Menlo Park, CA: Benjamin/Cummings)

Manzoul M A and Bommireddy A 1988 Quaternary logic for carry-lookahead binary addition *ISMVL* **18** 294–9

Manzoul M A, Moorthy S and Swartwout R E 1989 An improved *m*-valued carry look-ahead adder *ISMVL* **19** 280–2

Marsh R W 1957 *Table of irreducible polynomials over GF(2) through degree 19* (US Dept. of Commerce)

McAllester D 1980 A three-valued truth maintenance system *MIT Artificial Intelligence Lab. Memo* 473

McCluskey E J 1986 *Logic design principles with emphasis on testable semicustom circuits* (Englewood Cliffs, NJ: Prentice-Hall)

McCoy N H 1948 *Rings and ideals* (Menasha, WI: Math. Assoc. Amer.)

McCoy N H and Montgomery D 1937 A representation of generalized Boolean rings *Duke Math. J.* **3** 455–9

McCulloch W S and Pitts W 1943 A logical calculus of the ideas immanent in nervous activity *Bull. Math. Biophys.* **5** 115–33

Mealy G H 1955 A method for synthesizing sequential circuits *Bell Syst. Tech. J.* **34** 1045–79

Merrill R D 1964 Some properties of ternary threshold logic *IEEE Trans. Elec. Comput.* **EC-13** 632–5

Metze G 1955 An application of multi-valued logic systems to circuits *Proc. Symp. on Circuit Analysis* (Univ. Illinois) 11-1–11-14

Miller D M 1990 Integrated circuit testing *Encyclopedia of Physical Science and Technology, 1990 Yearbook* (New York: Academic) 377–88

Miller D M and Muzio J C 1979 On the minimization of many-valued functions *ISMVL* **9** 294–9

Mine H and Fujita S 1970 Testing and realization of three-valued threshold functions *J. IECE Japan* **52-C** 439–46

Mine H, Hasegawa T and Shimada R 1971 Four ternary arithmetic operations *Syst. Comput. Controls* **2** 46–54

Mirsalehi M M and Gaylord T K 1986 Content-addressable memory processing: multilevel coding, logical minimization, and an optical implementation *ISMVL* **16** 174–8

Moisil G C 1941 Notes sur les logiques non-Chrysippiennes *Ann. Sci. Univ. Jassy* **27** 86–98

Moore E F 1956 Gedanken-experiments on sequential machines *Automata Studies* ed C E Shannon and J McCarthy (Princeton, NJ: Princeton University Press) 129–53

Mor M 1976 On the three-valued simulation of digital systems *IEEE Trans. Comput.* **C-25** 1152–6

Moraga C 1977 A monograph on ternary threshold logic *Computer science and multiple-valued logic* ed D C Rine (Amsterdam: North-Holland) 355–94

—— 1984 Systolic systems and multiple-valued logic *ISMVL* **14** 98–108

—— 1987 A parallel algorithm for the computation of the Chrestenson power spectrum *ISMVL* **17** 237–42

—— 1989 Multiple-valued threshold logic *Optical computing, digital and symbolic* ed R Arrathoon (New York: Dekker) 161–84

Moraga C and Schulte-Ontrop R 1982 On some cardinality questions in multiple-valued extended threshold logic *ISMVL* **12** 253–9

Mouftah H T and Garba A I 1984 VLSI implementation of a 5-trit full adder *IEE Proc. Pt. G.* **131**(5) 214–20

Muroga S 1971 *Threshold logic and its applications* (New York: Wiley)

Muroga S, Tsuboi T and Baugh C R 1970 Enumeration of threshold functions of eight variables *IEEE Trans. Comput.* **C-19**(9) 818–25

Muzio J C 1990 *Concerning the maximum size of the terms in the realization of symmetric functions ISMVL* **20** 292–9

Muzio J C, Miller D M and Epstein G 1983 The simplification of multiple-valued symmetric functions *ISMVL* **13** 111–19

Muzio J C and Wesselkamper T C 1986 *Multiple-valued switching theory* (Bristol: Hilger)

Nakasima A and Hanzawa M 1938 The theory of equivalent transformation of simple partial paths in the relay circuit *Nippon Electric. Commun. Engng* **9** 32–9

Nomura H 1973 Characteristic vectors of multivalued logic functions and their application to the realization of multivalued threshold functions *Syst. Comput. Controls* **4** 18–24

Padmanabhan R 1969 Two identities for lattices *Proc. Amer. Math. Soc.* **20** 409–12

Pao Y H 1988 Neural nets as model for the study of multivalued logic *ISMVL* **18** 142

Peterson W W and Weldon Jr E J 1972 *Error-correcting codes* 2nd edn (Cambridge, MA: MIT Press)

Piesch H 1939 Begriff der Allgemeinen Schaltungstechnik *Archiv Elektrotechnik* **33** 672–86

Post E L 1921 Introduction to a general theory of elementary propositions *Amer. J. Math.* **43** 163–85

Programming Research Group 1954 *Preliminary report, specifications for the IBM mathematical FORmula TRANslating system, FORTRAN* (Applied Science Division, IBM)

Rasiowa H 1969 A theorem on the existence of prime filters in Post algebras and the completeness theorem for some many-valued predicate calculi *Bull. Acad. Pol. Sci., Sér. Sci., Math., Astron., Phys.* **17** 347–54

—— 1973 On generalized Post algebras of order ω^+ and ω^+-valued predicate calculi *Bull. Acad. Pol. Sci., Sér. Sci., Math., Astron., Phys.* **21** 209–19

—— 1974 *An algebraic approach to non-classical logics* (Amsterdam: North Holland)

Razavi H M and Bou-Ghazale S E 1987 Design of a fast CMOS ternary adder *ISMVL* **17** 20–4

Rescher N 1969 *Many-valued logic* (New York: McGraw-Hill)

Rich D A, Naiff K L C and Smalley K G 1985 A four-state ROM using multilevel process technology *ISMVL* **15** 236–40

Rine D C 1974 Conditional and Post algebra expressions *Discrete Math.* **10** 309–23

—— (ed) 1977 *Computer science and multiple-valued logic* 1st edn (Amsterdam: North-Holland)

—— 1987 A system design method from programming logic to multiple-valued logic *Int. J. Electron.* **63** 163–70

Rosenbloom P C 1942 Post algebras. I. Postulates and general theory *Amer. J. Math.* **64** 167–88

Rosser J B and Turquette A R 1952 *Many-valued logics* (Series in: Studies in logic and the foundations of mathematics) (Amsterdam: North-Holland)

Rousseau G 1969 Logical systems with finitely many truth-values *Bull. Acad. Pol. Sci., Sér. Sci., Math., Astron., Phys.* **17** 189–94

—— 1970 Post algebras and pseudo-Post algebras *Fund. Math.* **67** 133–45

Rudell R and Sangiovanni-Vincentelli A 1987 Multiple-valued minimization for PLA optimization *ISMVL* **17** 198–208

Sasao T 1986 On the optimal design of multiple-valued PLA's *ISMVL* **16** 214–23

—— 1988 Multiple-valued logic and optimization of programmable logic arrays *Computer* April 71–80

Saxena N R 1987 Effectiveness measures for data compression techniques under unequally likely errors *Developments in integrated circuit testing* ed D M Miller, (London: Academic) 257–78

Scott N R 1985 *Computer number systems and arithmetic* (Englewood Cliffs, NJ: Prentice-Hall)

Serra M 1986 Tables of irreducible and primitive polynomials for GF(3) *Univ. Victoria Tech. Report No. 13* (Dept. of Computer Science)

—— 1987 Applications of multi-valued logic to testing of binary and MVL circuits *Int. J. Electron.* **63** 197–214

Serra M, Miller D M and Muzio J C 1988 Linear cellular automata and LFSR's are isomorphic *3rd Tech. Workshop New Directions IC Testing* 195–205

Serra M and Muzio J C 1986 Multiple-valued linear feedback shift registers *ISMVL* **16** 94–9

Shannon C E 1938 A symbolic analysis of relay and switching circuits *Trans. AIEE* **57** 713–23

Shestakov V I 1941 Algébra dvuhpolúsnyh shém, postroénnyh isklúčitel'no iz dvuhpolúsnikov (Algébra A-shém) *Avtomatika i Téléméhanika* **2** 15–24 and *Žurnal Téhničéskoj Fiziki,* **11** 532–49

—— 1953 Modélirovanié opéracij isčisléniá prédložénij posrédstvom prostéjših čétyréhpolúsynh shém *Vyčislitel' naja matematika i vyčislitel' naja texnika* **1** 56–89

Sholander M 1951 Postulates for distributive lattices *Can. J. Math.* **3** 28–30

Sioson F M 1964 Equational bases of Boolean algebra *J. Symbolic Logic* **29** 115–24

Smith J E 1980 Measure of the effectiveness of fault signature analysis *IEEE Trans. Comput.* **C-29**(6) 510–14

Smith K C 1981 The prospects of multivalued logic: a technology and applications view *IEEE Trans. Comput.* **C-30** 619–34

Smith W R III 1977 Minimization of multivalued functions *Computer science and multiple-valued logic* ed D C Rine (Amsterdam: North-Holland) 221–61

Stone M H 1936 The theory of representations for Boolean algebras *Trans. Am. Math. Soc.* **40** 37–111

—— 1937 Topological representations of distributive lattices and Brouwerian logics *Časopis Pěst. Mat.* **67** 1–25

Tirumalai P and Butler J T 1988 Analysis of minimization algorithms for multiple-valued programmable logic arrays *ISMVL* **18** 226–36

Traczyk T 1963 Axioms and some properties of Post algebras *Coll. Math.* **10** 193–209

—— 1964 An equational definition of a class of Post algebras *Bull. Acad. Pol. Sci., Sér. Sci., Math., Astron., Phys.* **12** 147–9

—— 1967 On Post algebras with uncountable chain of constants. Algebras of homomorphisms *Bull. Acad. Pol. Sci., Sér. Sci., Math., Astron., Phys.* **16** 789–92

—— 1968 Prime ideals in generalized Post algebras *Bull. Acad. Pol. Sci., Sér. Sci., Math., Astron., Phys.* **16** 369–73

—— 1977 Post algebras through P_0 and P_1 lattices *Computer science and multiple-valued logic* ed D C Rine (Amsterdam: North-Holland) 115–36

van der Waerden B L 1953 *Modern algebra* vol I, translated from the second revised German edition (New York: Unger)

Varma D and Trachtenberg E A 1988 A fast algorithm for the optimal state assignment of large finite state machines *IEEE ICCAD-88*, Santa Clara, CA 152–9

Veitch E W 1952 A chart method for simplifying truth functions *Proc. ACM* 127–33

Venn J 1894 *Symbolic logic* (London: Macmillan)

Wade L I 1945 Post algebras and rings *Duke Math. J.* **12** 389–95

Wakui F and Tanaka M 1989 Comparison of binary full adder and quaternary signed-digit full adder using high-speed ECL *ISMVL* **19** 346–55

Walsh J L 1923 A closed set of normal orthogonal functions *Am. J. Math.* **45** 5–24

Ward M 1946 Note on the order of free distributive lattices Abstract 135 *Bull. Amer. Math. Soc.* **52** 423

Watanabe T, Matsumoto M, Enokida M and Hasegawa T 1990 A design of multiple-valued logic neuron *ISMVL* **20** 418–25

Wheaton L B and Current K W 1981 A quaternary threshold logic modulo-four multiplier circuit for residue number system nonrecursive digital filters *ISMVL* **11** 48–53

Wijngaarden A V (ed) 1969 Report on the algorithmic language ALGOL 68 *Numerische Mathematik* **14** 79–218

Williams T W, Daehn W, Gruetzner M and Starke C W 1986 Comparison of aliasing errors for primitive and non-primitive polynomials *Proc. 1986 IEEE Int. Test Conf.* 282–8

—— 1988 Bounds and analysis of aliasing errors in linear feedback shift registers *IEEE Trans. Computer-Aided Design* **7** 75–83

Winkel D and Prosser F 1980 *The art of digital design* (Englewood Cliffs, NJ: Prentice-Hall)

Wirth N 1971 The programming language PASCAL *Acta Informatica* **1**(1) 35–63

Yamamoto Y and Mukaidono M 1989 A P-ternary threshold element network—an application of ternary logic to a neural system treating ambiguity *ISMVL* **19** 137–43

Zarebski W 1982 A dual space characterization of P_1- and P_2-lattices of order ω^+ *Coll. Math.* **47** 165–71

Zhang G 1984 Two complete orthogonal sets of real multiple-valued functions *ISMVL* **14** 12–18

Zinov'ev A A 1963 Philosophical problems of many-valued logic rev. edn ed and transl G Küng and D D Comey (Dordrecht: Reidel)

Index